WOMEN BREAKING BOUNDARIES

Women Breaking Boundaries

A Grail Journey, 1940–1995

Janet Kalven

STATE UNIVERSITY OF NEW YORK PRESS

Published by
State University of New York Press, Albany

© 1999 State University of New York

All rights reserved

Printed in the United States of America

For information, address State University of New York Press,
State University Plaza, Albany, NY, 12246

Production by Cathleen Collins
Marketing by Anne Valentine

Library of Congress Cataloging in Publication Data

Kalven, Janet, 1913–
    Women breaking boundaries : a grail journey, 1940–1995 / Janet
Kalven.
        p.   cm.
    Includes bibliographical references and index.
    ISBN 0–7914–4331–0 (alk. paper). — ISBN 0–7914–4332–9 (pbk. :
alk. paper)
    1. Grail movement (Catholic)—History.   2. Women in the Catholic
Church—United States—History—20th century.   I. Title.
    BX809.G72K35   1999
    267'.442—dc21   99–10256
                                                                                              CIP

10 9 8 7 6 5 4 3 2 1

To my Grail sisters around the globe
Working to build a world
Where difference does not connote domination

Contents

Illustrations

Acknowledgments

In writing this book, I have relied almost entirely on primary sources: my own memories; my own collection of letters, notes, reports, memos, and articles; the materials in the United States Grail Archives, housed at Grailville; and the interviews I have conducted with Grail members and friends. It has been a long process, beginning in January of 1991, shortly after the celebration of the fiftieth anniversary of the Grail in the United States and ending in August of 1998. I was delighted to find in Annie Dillard's book, *The Writing Life*, her statement that "Writing a book full time takes between two and ten years," whether for the storyteller to fabricate a solid world or for the nonfiction writer to amass and assimilate her materials. I am well within her parameters and well acquainted with the processes of reviewing materials, uncovering new questions, writing, and rewriting as the shape of the story reveals itself.

Many people have helped and encouraged me along the way. First of all, I want to thank all the Grail members and friends whom I have interviewed for their generous sharing of their life experience (their names are listed in the bibliography). Many friends and colleagues, both in the Grail and outside it, have read and commented on major sections, among them Cay Charles, Mary Condren, Frances Kern Crotty, Rachel Donders, Alice Dougan, Monica Erler, Jamie Kalven, Marie Therese McDermit, Anne Mercier, Patricia Miller, Mary Louise Tully, and Lydwine van Kersbergen. Members of Mary Pierce Brosmer's Monday-night writing class, since September of 1993, have listened attentively and given valuable feedback as I shared sections of a work in progress. My special gratitude goes to the following who read and critiqued the next-to-last version of the entire manuscript: Donna Ambrogi, Judith Bechtel, Mary Pierce Brosmer, Mary Buckley, Dierkje Donders, Eva Fleischner, Ruth Gallant, Mary Jo Grote, Anne Hope, Mary Elizabeth Hunt, Mary Kane, Lyllis Ling, April McConeghey Goering, Dorothy Jane Rasenberger, Eileen Schaeffler,

Barbara Troxell, Dana Vannoy, Mariette Wickes, and Teresa Wilson. Finally, I want to acknowledge the unfailing support of Mary Elizabeth Hunt who has functioned as the midwife during this long birthing process and has always been ready with her warm hospitality, keen critical judgment, and words of encouragement.

Personal Prologue

I Discover the Grail

"Tell what is yours to tell," Margaret Atwood advises the writer. What is mine to tell is the story of a small group of women, who since 1940 in these United States have been struggling to empower women to change a patriarchal church and a sexist society. It is the story of the Grail movement in the United States, and because my own history is intimately interwoven with the Grail story, I begin with a personal prologue. Who am I as teller of the tale? How did I, a nice upper-middle-class Jewish girl from Hyde Park in Chicago come to throw in my lot with a group of radical Catholic women who wanted to convert the world?

I met the Grail just six months after Lydwine van Kersbergen and Joan Overboss arrived in New York on one of the last boats to leave Holland before Hitler's invasion, charged with the task of beginning the Grail movement in America.

It was a crisp, sunny day in October of 1940 when my good friend, Bob Heywood, invited me to drive out to Doddridge Farm outside Libertyville on Chicago's north shore to meet these extraordinary Grail women. Bob was a graduate student in English, recently arrived on campus from Notre Dame University where he was a disciple of famous Professor Frank O'Malley.[1] I was a recent convert to Catholicism, baptized in 1937, working as the teaching assistant in the Hutchins-Adler "Great Books" course at the University of Chicago, and eager for any opportunity to deepen my involvement with things Catholic. Both of us were very active as leaders in the Calvert Club, the Catholic student club at the University.

I had already heard about the Grail from no less a personage than the auxiliary bishop of Chicago, Bernard Sheil, who had come to speak at a Calvert Club meeting. He talked enthusiastically about these remarkable Dutch women who had done marvels in Holland. He was bringing them to

1

the Chicago Archdiocese where they would take care of four hundred orphans he was rescuing from war-torn Belgium.

I had had a little experience with the ebullient Irish bishop at the Calvert Club. In my estimation, he talked big but failed to deliver. The Calvert Club was a bit of an anomaly at Chicago, since Cardinal Mundelein had forbidden Catholics to attend the University, reportedly because a priest and a nun had lost their faith while studying there. Despite the Cardinal's edict, there were about five-hundred Catholics among the six-thousand graduate and undergraduate students. Professor Jerome Kerwin, one of the two Catholics on the faculty, acted as unofficial counselor to the Catholics and had helped to organize the Calvert Club. As acting head of the archdiocese (the Cardinal had died and a new ordinary had not yet been appointed), Bishop Sheil had made great promises to our little group—official recognition, a chaplain, perhaps a house, but certainly the furniture and equipment for an office. Nothing had been forthcoming. Listening to his glowing praise of "The Ladies of the Grail," I thought to myself, "Another one of the bishop's pipe dreams. I'll believe it when I see it."

Now, six months later, I was about to "see it" for the first time. As Bob drove through the impressive gateway and up the long drive, I saw a number of gaily painted frame buildings placed in a nicely landscaped setting: white with yellow trim, light blue with orange, buff with maroon, light green with dark. "The Grail likes color," Bob informed me. In a few minutes we were seated in a small reception room, across from Lydwine van Kersbergen and Joan Overboss. I saw a tall, stately woman in an attractive teal blue woolen dress, wearing a ring on the fourth finger of her left hand. I wanted to ask whether she took vows, but somehow knew that this was not the right question. With her were Joan Overboss, shorter but equally sturdy, with a humorous, impudent look about her, and Mary Louise Tully, a young American recently returned from a time of training with the Grail in Holland. The room was chilly, I kept my coat on, but soon forgot any discomfort, as I listened to the two Dutch women talk animatedly about what the Grail had done in Holland and what they hoped to do in America. They spoke of the Grail as a movement of thousands of young women. They showed us pictures of the mass dramas performed in the Olympic Stadium in Amsterdam with thousands of young women in brightly colored costumes, using music, dance, and drama to bring the message of God's love to the throngs in the stands. They mentioned casually that while in New York they had gone backstage at Radio City Music Hall to measure the stage and see if it would be suitable for a Grail performance. I was deeply impressed by their vitality and self-confidence. Here were women who could tackle anything!

Shortly thereafter, Bob and I invited Lydwine and Joan to speak at one of the Calvert Club weekly luncheons. They spoke of the Christian foundations of Western civilization, of the present crisis of secularism that had given birth to communism and fascism, and they called for a great movement of the laity to restore the Christian spirit to all aspects of life. Their historical sketch turned on their view, expressed with contagious conviction, that at each period of history the Holy Spirit raises up a form of Christian life especially adapted to the needs of the time: in the decadent Hellenistic culture, the desert fathers; at the fall of the Roman Empire, Benedictine monasticism; in the rising urban civilization of the thirteenth century, the mendicant orders; in the Reformation, the Jesuits; in the misery occasioned by early capitalism, the active religious orders; and in the contemporary crisis of secularism, the lay apostolate. I was captivated by this vision. In the next two years I was often invited to Doddridge Farm, invitations which I accepted eagerly. I heard such well-known speakers as publisher Frank Sheed on the Trinity, Catherine de Hueck of Friendship House on interracial justice, artist Ade Bethune on the relation of art and daily work.[2] I was also recruited to serve as a counselor in the summer camps of 1941 and 1942. Gradually the conviction grew in me that this was the way I was meant to spend my life. In October of 1942, I left my job at the University and my family (my mother was profoundly upset by my choice) and joined the little group at Doddridge.

What moved me to take this drastic step? I was serious about my spiritual life; I wanted to be a saint and I needed direction. I admired some of the nuns I had met, but I never felt the slightest attraction toward their way of life, even when they made overtures to me. The guidance Lydwine and Joan gave me was vastly superior to anything I received either from the priests or from the nuns at the retreat house I frequented—much more direct, realistic, and rewarding. I had the sense that they understood me and my potential. In my visits to Doddridge Farm and my participation in programs, I found a new depth of spiritual experience as well as a host of new skills. I found myself doing all sorts of things I had never done before—giving public lectures, baking bread, inviting important speakers, writing articles, working in the garden. Then there was the charisma of Lydwine and Joan, both attractive, challenging personalities. I enjoyed the sense of community at Doddridge, a sense of belonging and also of being part of something tremendously significant and world shaking.

Family: Growing up Jewish

Let me trace the influences that moved me to leave my Jewish family for the radical Catholicism of the Grail. I grew up in a world that was clearly and sharply divided between Jew and gentile. My grandparents were poor immigrants from Germany and Russia who had done well enough in Chicago to rise to a comfortable middle-class lifestyle. My father did even better. Leaving school in fifth grade to help support his family, by age twenty-five he was a full partner in a major wholesale dry goods company in the Chicago Loop.

On his dresser my father had a picture of his mother wearing a sheitl, the wig that marked an orthodox Jewish woman as married, so his family must have been orthodox. But in our family, my mother's German Jewish Reform tradition prevailed. The level of practice in our home was minimal. My parents belonged to Temple Sholom, attended services on the high holidays of Rosh Hashonah and Yom Kippur, spoke a little Yiddish when they did not want my brother and me to understand, and sent us to the temple Sunday school where at age thirteen we were confirmed—no bar mitzvah and only a dozen words of Hebrew learned by rote. My mother shopped at the kosher butcher's, but she also served ham and bacon, which she hid when my grandmother came to visit. "Keeping kosher" was for "kikes," eastern European Jews. We were definitely not "kikes," we were Americans. My parents belonged to a Jewish country club and a Jewish city club. We went to public schools. My mother was always hospitable to the friends my brother and I brought home, but they were immediately , though implicitly, classified as Jew or goy. "*Goyische*" was not a word of approbation in my mother's vocabulary. We were encouraged to seek our close friends among Jewish families, as much like our family as possible, that is, Jewish but not too Jewish. My mother was equally upset when I dated an orthodox Israeli boy and my brother dated a *schicksa*, a gentile girl.

My brother and I were bright children, avid readers who quickly turned into young intellectual snobs. By age ten or eleven, we had perceived that our family was higher on the financial and social scale than mother's brother, our Uncle Casper, that our temple was superior to the one our uncle and aunt belonged to, and that pretty much the same people belonged to our temple and to the two social clubs. We did not like any of it. The instruction at the Sunday school was far inferior to what we received at the public school. We thought the children we met at the clubs were stupid; we preferred our school friends. Nevertheless, we identified as Jewish. By some subliminal process—I don't remember anything ever being said explicitly— we knew that there had been pogroms in Russia, that there was still hostility to Jews in the world around us although we hardly ever experienced it personally. One summer on our annual vacation in Northern Michigan to relieve my brother's hay fever, I persuaded my mother to visit the hotel in Charlevoix that offered more attractions to teenagers than dull old Petoskey, where we stayed each summer. On the reception desk was a sign,

"The patronage of Hebrews is not solicited." I felt as if someone had slapped my face and I beat a hasty retreat.

College: "Great Books" at the University of Chicago

By the time my brother and I were ready for college in 1930—it was a foregone conclusion that we would attend the University of Chicago—we had given up on the Judaism of our parents. It seemed to us an inherited tradition that was breaking down in irrational ways—why eat ham and bacon but refuse to serve pork chops? We saw our parents' Jewishness as more a socio-economic identification than anything else. We identified as Jewish; we did not want to "pass" as gentiles; that seemed to us dishonest, but we complained a bit to each other about having to suffer discrimination for something that had no inherent meaning for ourselves. Our family name, "Kalven," does not carry a quick ethnic identification as say "Goldstein" or "Perlman" does. I think some careless clerk at Ellis Island must have misunderstood my paternal grandfather's surname. In any event, I received three rushing invitations from three of the gentile girls' clubs that took the place of sororities on the Chicago campus. There was no Jewish girls' club. I was terribly embarrassed by the invitations. I knew if I accepted and they realized I was Jewish, they would not want me. I did not know how to respond. In the end I did nothing, did not answer and did not go. The next year the same thing happened to my brother with the gentile fraternities.

The University thoughtfully provided entering freshmen with "big sisters" or "big brothers" of a similar ethnic and religious background to the newcomer to help interpret the complexities of campus life. My big sister, Jane Kesner, who became a close friend, solemnly informed me that it was better not to have a Jewish girls' club controlling Jewish social life. Jewish girls could date whom they pleased, although Jane advised against dating members of the third-ranking Jewish fraternity. The social scene was unambiguously hierarchical; being seen with members of a low-status group could damage one's own status.

The "Great Books" were the formative experience of my college years. Mortimer Adler, twenty-seven and newly arrived at the University, interviewed the applicants for the course. At first I thought this short, dark, rosy-cheeked young man was the office boy. A seventeen-year-old freshman, I was flattered by being one of twenty entering freshmen to be chosen for the first Great Books class to be offered at the University. It was thrilling to be in the two-hour weekly seminar led by Robert Hutchins, then the youngest and best-looking American university president, and Mortimer Adler, a brilliant dialectician with a reputation as an *enfant terrible*. We were provided with keys to our own Great Books room in the Classics building, furnished with a seminar table and a library of about fifteen hundred volumes for our exclusive use. I was too naive to realize how contrary to academic protocol these arrangements were. We met one evening a week for a two hour session, sitting around the table, with almost everyone smoking. Often Hutchins would bring one of his distinguished guests to observe the class—political commentator Walter Lippman, scholar Mark van Doren. The course ran for two years, discussing one great book a week, beginning with the *Iliad*, progressing through the Greeks, the Romans, the Bible, the medievals, the Renaissance, and the moderns, ending with *Das Capital*, Freud, and Maritain.

I was challenged and immensely stimulated by the Socratic method—Hutchins and Adler never told us anything—they simply asked questions and we had to defend our answers. For example, in the first year, we read a large section of the Old Testament. More than half a century later, my memory of that session is still vivid. It began with a deceptively simple question: "What is the title of this book?"

Someone replied, "Holy Scripture."

What does "holy" mean?

A Mormon boy in the class stated firmly, "It means that this book is revealed by God." Hutchins and Adler responded together, "That is what we believe." After an incredulous gasp from the class, we spent the next two hours trying to prove that this text could not possibly be the word of God. As each person advanced an argument, either Hutchins or Adler would take it apart and show that it did not hold up. A similar evening in that first year centered on Augustine's proof for the existence of God in his dialogue on the free will. Adler outlined the argument and then simply refuted our objections, one by one.

This class was by far the most exciting and involving of my college experiences. I would often be so keyed up by the end of a class session that I would keep my roommate up for hours, going over the main points of the discussion with her. At the end of the first two years, I was part of the group that asked to do it again, reading different books by the same authors and adding a few new ones. I had come into the class full of the ideas current in the contemporary culture: I believed in progress, I thought that religion (and especially Catholicism) was for the ignorant and superstitious, I thought that science was bringing us into a better world. While Hutchins and Adler never stated their own views, somehow their convictions rubbed off on me. I learned to question the received wisdom of the semanticists, psychologists, sociologists, and cultural relativists; to suspect the reductionism of the physical and biological sciences. And I acquired some intellectual skills: the ability to read a text on its own terms, define a concept and analyze an argument. Gradually, my mindset changed. I was disabused of the idea of history as an inevitable progress to modern times, learned to regard the middle ages as far from dark, thought of atheists as both ignorant and illogical, became acquainted with the perennial philosophy, and began to look for insight in the pages of Aristotle and Thomas Aquinas.

There was great intellectual ferment on the campus and even in the city, stirred by Hutchins's speeches on education and Adler's criticisms of the social sciences. The campus paper, *The Daily Maroon*, accused Hutchins of "A New Medievalism." Thomas Aquinas was one of the medievals we read in the Great Books class. I remember being in the elevator at Marshall Field's department store in downtown Chicago, with a volume of the English translation of Aquinas's *Summa Theologica* under my arm, when a stranger next to me commented, "My, you must go to the University of Chicago." Hutchins and Adler wanted to reform the university, putting more emphasis on the skills of critical thinking and less on professional training and "filling students' minds with rapidly aging facts." They argued that excessive specialization had made communication among the faculty almost impossible, and saw the Great Books program as a means of building a common intellectual tradition and frame of reference. As a step in this direction, Hutchins had promoted the four general survey courses—humanities, social sciences, physical sciences, biological sciences—required in the first two years of liberal education. In my senior year, the syllabi for these courses were published for the first time. I was invited to review the humanities syllabus for *The Daily Maroon*, and wrote a scathing review, criticizing the faculty for holding up the ideals of individualism and secularism and deploring their neglect of the perennial philosophy. My review was headlined "Humanities Course Misinterprets and Mistreats Philosophic Questions." I ended my piece with the judgment, "In short, the syllabus is sophistical, dogmatic, anti-intellectual, inaccurate, misleading, inconsistent, sentimental and slovenly . . . a handy compendium of commonplace errors." Hutchins remarked to me that I had supported all these judgments except the "slovenly." I was puzzled when a priest studying at the University congratulated me on my review.

Conversion

When I try to pinpoint what led me into the Catholic Church in April of 1937, I see a number of factors. First was the Great Books training, which certainly prepared the way for Catholicism by questioning the prevailing secular culture and by making the Catholic faith intellectually respectable. By the time I graduated, I respected the Church as a formative influence in Western civilization, as a source of great art and philosophy, as a moral and spiritual force. I could no longer dismiss Catholicism out of hand; it had become a defensible position. This change of attitude was a necessary but not a sufficient condition for conversion. A much more powerful and intimate witness was needed to enable me to act as contrary to my upbringing as I eventually did.

A second factor was my deep dissatisfaction with my own life. I felt like a rudderless boat—what was I supposed to do with my life? What was there that was worth doing? I was searching for meaning, for something worthy of my best efforts, and the possibilities the culture presented did not offer any role I could identify with. The Judaism of my parents had seemed empty to me already as a thirteen year old. My mother's expectation was that I would marry, preferably a nice doctor or lawyer, and raise a family. She needed me to validate her life choices. But I had been quite clear early on that I did not want a life like hers. However, I did internalize some of her ideas about marriage, especially that a suitable husband should be older, taller, smarter, stronger, and, if possible, richer than the prospective bride, who should, of course, devote herself to supporting her husband in his life projects. I wanted marriage and children, but I found the usual dates boring. The men I met whom I considered to be brighter than I were already married, and I think that somewhere in my unconscious there was resistance to a simply supportive role. However, I was not oriented to pursuing a career. My father was perfectly willing to pay my way through college, but, unlike my brother, I was not expected to emerge with a way to earn my living. In fact, my father, the good provider, was still insisting that no daughter of his had to go to work when my salary check was paying the rent on the family apartment. From my family's perspective, college was a way for me to pass the time until marriage and a likely place to meet a suitable spouse.

I graduated in 1934 in the depths of the Great Depression—there were no jobs. I eagerly accepted an invitation from Hutchins and Adler (supported by a tuition scholarship) to study for an MA in the new interdisciplinary program in the history of ideas. I enjoyed the course work, but I simply did not think of myself as a philosopher, one making an original contribution to thought. I could perhaps see myself as a teacher of philosophy, but by some subliminal process I already knew that being Jewish and female I had two strikes against me. Moreover, the campus was highly polarized into two camps: pro- and anti- Hutchins and Adler. Being closely identified with them, I did not think I would be welcome at the University of Chicago philosophy department. In the spring, I inherited a job from a friend as editor of the *Woodlawn Booster*, a miserable little community newspaper. After a year, I left the paper to do research and ghostwrite reports for a foundation executive, and in 1937, was invited back to the university as teaching assistant in the Great Books program.

I did not lack for intellectual stimulation in these years—I was always involved in some study group—but at the deepest level of my being I was restless and unhappy, looking for a purpose in life, trying to solve my problem by a strictly intellectual approach. The year I began graduate work, a new group appeared on the campus that opened a world of religious experience to me. To strengthen their efforts for educational reform, Hutchins and Adler had invited a number of new scholars to the campus: Richard McKeon to be Dean of the Humanities, and a group of younger men, graduate students and recent Ph.Ds, which included Herbert Schwartz, Herbert Ratner, Kenneth Simon, and Bill Gorman. Gorman was a "cradle Catholic," the other three were Jewish. They joined our coterie of Hutchins-Adler followers—there must have been twenty or twenty-five young women and men in various stages of their academic careers—who organized a number of extracurricular study groups, reading Aristotle, discussing theories of literary criticism, metaphysics, and ethics. This group embodied everything I admired: they were very bright, brilliant at argument, steeped in the perennial philosophy, and clearly making sacrifices in the pursuit of truth. Ratner and Simon were doing a critique of modern medicine; Herbert Schwartz was writing a poetics of music. Schwartz was a gifted and charismatic person, musician, poet, artist, philosopher, and something of a guru in our little group. He had a fantastic ability to look at you and read the inmost secrets of your soul. Gradually I learned that many of my new friends had either converted to Catholicism or were considering conversion. Nothing could have startled the university community more than to discover that in our group of sophisticated graduate students in a few years time about twenty men and women—Jews, Protestants, nonbelievers—had been baptized into the Roman Catholic Church. In fact, one wit described the Chicago campus as a Baptist university where Jews teach Catholic doctrine to pagans and Protestants. A joke was current in Hyde Park, the university neighborhood, that we could soon expect the end of the world, since the conversion of the Jews appeared to be proceeding apace.

At this point in my life, several factors contributed to move me closer to conversion: encounters with spiritual realities and practices I had not met before; intense intellectual activity—reading contemporary Catholic thinkers, endless theological discussions; the concern of my close friends, many of whom had become converts. My friends invited me to Catholic gatherings: Mass in the dark, impressive interior of St. Thomas Apostle Church near the university, Holy Week services at the Cathedral (I remember marveling at the power of a church that could get stout old American men to process down the aisle in outlandish medieval garb). They took me to visit the Dominican House of Studies in River Forest. I was intrigued and awed by the chapel full of men in white robes, chanting the psalms. These people were live representatives of an organization that dated back to the thirteenth century. I had been reading St. Thomas Aquinas for years without ever asking what "saint" meant. Now I began to get an idea of sanctity, holiness. Two of my close women friends were baptized—Alice Zucker and Peggy Stern. I met Sarah Benedicta O'Neill, a retired schoolteacher who had started the St. Benet Catholic Lending Library out of her personal resources. She introduced me to works of the European Catholic revival—Gilbert Chesterton, Hilaire Belloc, Vincent McNabb, E. I. Watkin, Christopher Dawson, Eric Gill, George Bernanos, Francois Mauriac, Paul Claudel, Jacques Maritain, along with *Commonweal* and *Orate Fratres*, progressive Catholic magazines. Hutchins and Adler admired Maritain, had added his book, *Freedom in the Modern World*, to the Great Books list and had brought him to campus several times as a lecturer. I remember Maritain's first appearance, speaking on religion and culture, to a packed audience in Mandel Hall, the largest auditorium on campus. At the time, he spoke no English and was reading from a text translated into phonetic symbols. It was quite unintelligible, but nevertheless he was an impressive figure, gentle and unassuming, with a sensitive, spiritual countenance.

Some of my friends invited me to join a group that was studying medieval Latin, meeting weekly at St. Thomas Apostle church, under the leadership of Father Timothy Sparks, a Dominican priest from the House of Studies in River Forest. He chose the treatise on the Incarnation from the *Summa Theologica* as a text from which to expound the fine points of Latin grammar. I was impressed when at the first session he donned the white Dominican habit over his black clerical suit to be properly garbed for teaching. After the sessions, during the winter and spring of 1937, we would go for coffee and pursue our discussions. As I look back, I remember that whole year as one long, continuous conversation on the relation of faith and reason, the elements of the "good life," the meaning of original sin, whether human beings could attain virtue without the intervention of divine grace, whether there were any rational grounds for choosing between religions. Much later in life I learned that I am a high "T" on the Meyers-Briggs personality profile, that is, a thinker, one who relies heavily on reason and logic. I certainly took a relentlessly intellectual approach in my personal quest for meaning, reading voraciously, writing out arguments pro and con, discussing issues far into the night. Somehow, all the philosophical ideas I had garnered from Aristotle and Aquinas did not suffice to help me chart my course. The modern Catholic writers were some help since they applied the traditional insights to my contemporary world but were not enough to move me toward a decision. I was looking for something more personal and experiential, some tangible evidence of the action of grace.

The baptisms in my circle of friends constituted a witness and a challenge. We spoke often about living what you believed and were critical of Hutchins and Adler on that score. I wanted desperately to bring my life into line with my intellectual convictions. It was Herbert Schwartz who made the connections inescapably concrete for me. "If you think the Catholic Church might have answers to your questions," he told me, "why don't you find out more about what the Church demands? Go take instruction at the parish. It doesn't commit you to anything, but at least you will have accurate information." At his urging, I began instruction with a naive young priest, Father Flannery, who was quite overwhelmed by the influx of university people and who artlessly shared with me his class notes from the seminary. In another memorable conversation, Herbert Schwartz challenged me directly: "If you are convinced that God exists, why don't you pray?" That same night, feeling awkward and uncertain, I got down on my knees in a patch of moonlight in my bedroom and began to pray. One of the priests gave me a rosary—blue glass beads and a little metal crucifix—along with a booklet of meditations based on Gospel texts. I began to read "spiritual" books, books about the life of grace and how to live it. I readily took to mental prayer, stopping in church on my way home from work. I began to feel a presence in these prayer times and a sense of peace and joy. The Church promised clarity and certainty. Sanctity began to appear to me as a goal to which I could give my whole self.

All these activities were an occasion of great distress for my mother. She had a kind of sixth sense about my activities—she always knew if I had stopped in church or had a session with Father Flannery, even though I kept within my usual daily schedule. Her two worst fears were eventually realized: her daughter became a Catholic and her son married a *schicksa*. At her insistence, my brother and I went to see the rabbi of the largest Reform Temple in Hyde Park. We spent several hours with the rabbi and his wife, countering their arguments with our own. In frustration the rabbi's wife finally burst out, "Don't you know any normal people?" The more my mother protested and stormed, the more I stayed away from home.

At the same time, I was moved by the signs of grace that I saw around me. I was impressed by the simple goodness of the two priests. Father Flannery made no pretense of being an intellectual—he was available, he listened, he offered what he could. Father Sparks, who was a professor of theology, had none of the egotism I had observed in many of the men at the university. He simply radiated inner peace, kindness, and patience. I saw changes in many of my friends—a new simplicity and self-acceptance in Alice, a new optimism in Peggy. I wanted the clarity and certainty the Church promised, I wanted the healing and strengthening of the life of grace, I wanted the deepening of the sense of community I felt with my

Catholic friends. Finally, I made my decision during a retreat at the House of Studies. My baptism, attended by a group from the university, was held in the baptistry of St. Thomas the Apostle Church with its metal grillwork and elaborate baptismal font. Afterward, Professor Jerome Kerwin had invited the group to his apartment for a party in my honor. Dom Virgil Michel, a Benedictine priest from St. John's Abbey and a leader in the liturgical movement, was at my baptism and at the party. I remember moments of panic—what had I done? Did I really have the gift of faith or did I only imagine it? It was Father Virgil who saw my distress, took me aside and reassured me. Afterward, in his extensive correspondence with Mortimer Adler, he always added a few words to me.

The Calvert Club: Lay Leadership on the Campus

Immediately after my baptism, I plunged into Catholic life with all the enthusiasm of a new convert. I thought I had discovered a whole world of people who shared my vision and values, and in my first years as a Catholic I was not disappointed. My experiences were almost all positive. Somehow I was mercifully preserved from finding out what many of the people in the pews actually thought.

The weekend after my baptism, at Jerry Kerwin's invitation, I began to take an active role in the Calvert Club. Other religious groups had chaplains and even houses on campus, but the Cardinal had refused to assign a priest, insisting that Catholics had no business in such a godless university. Jerry Kerwin carried on a one-man apostolate, counseling individuals, drawing groups of students together for study and for religious services in an environment where religious faith was often either ignored, ridiculed, or dismissed as irrational.

With the influx of new converts, we soon had a lively program in place for the Calvert Club, with weekends at Childerly, a country place owned by the Club, featuring such stars from the Notre Dame campus as philosophers Yves Simon and Leo R. Ward, political scientist Waldemar Gurian, literature scholar Frank O'Malley, rural life advocate Willis Nutting; weekly luncheon meetings in Hutchinson Commons with talks by John Cogley and Jim O'Gara from the local Catholic Worker house, people from Friendship House, Ed Marciniak, and other lay leaders; regular dialogue masses in the chapel of St. Thomas church; even a liturgical drama on Advent themes presented in the University's Bond Chapel. We startled the campus by organizing a banquet in Ida Noyes Hall on March 7 to celebrate the feast of St. Thomas Aquinas with prayer and song as well as speeches. To move from intellectual discussions of Thomism to a religious celebration was a new departure.

I had some negative experiences in the three years between my baptism and my discovery of the Grail, but I tended to dismiss them as aberrations. For instance, Mary Alice Duddy, whom I had met through the Calvert Club, invited me to join the YCS (Young Christian Students) group in the parish. A dozen or so young women, a few from the University, others working in clerical jobs or at the telephone company (at the time considered a fine place for Catholic girls—clean, safe, well-supervised) were meeting regularly and trying to apply Christian principles to their surroundings. It was a struggle—we were all in different situations. Our judgments, supposedly based on study of the Gospels, seemed to me superficial, and we had great difficulty in coming up with any appropriate actions.

Mary Alice, who later became a Grail member, also introduced me to the Catholic Worker house, where John Cogley and Jim O'Gara conducted weekly evening discussions on Maritain's *Freedom in the Modern World*, while devoting their days to begging food for the bread line and their nights to offering shelter to the homeless. The stark white walls were decorated with large-scale reproductions of Ade Bethune's depictions of the works of mercy. We drank coffee out of cracked cups. John made it clear to us that after the discussion the homeless men would bed down on the floor of the room in which we were sitting. I could see that this work was a heroic way of living out the Gospel message, but it seemed more than I could manage. Mary Alice also took me to Martin de Porres House in a Black, inner-city neighborhood. It was a small building that had been willed to the Dominicans in River Forest by a devout Catholic. One of the priests had started a program of after-school activities for the neighborhood children.[3]

I remember attending a big national meeting of the CYO, the Catholic Youth Organization, founded by Bishop Sheil. I did not find the program at all congenial—it seemed to me to have very little Catholic about it, simply adding a few prayers to a recreation program one could find anywhere. Shortly after this disappointing experience, I attended the Liturgical Week.

I must have heard about the first national Liturgical Week from Sarah O'Neill, who was a great enthusiast for the liturgy. It was a heady experience for the several hundred priests and laypeople gathered in the basement of Holy Name Cathedral under the aegis of its pastor, Msgr. Morrison. This was 1940; standard daily practice was a low Mass, swift and silent, muttered by a priest with his back to the congregation, while an altar boy garbled the Latin responses, and the faithful in the pews said their rosaries. Moreover, since the Masses were usually being said for the dead, the practice was to say the requiem, called the "black" Mass since it required black vestments. Most bishops and priests regarded lay participation in the liturgy with considerable suspicion. A few years later, when the Grail was seeking entry into the New York Archdiocese, I was explaining to one of Cardinal

Spellman's twelve auxiliary bishops the kind of activities we planned to carry on at a New York Grail Center. I mentioned that on Sundays we often gathered a group of young people to say vespers in English. "Vespers for the laity," the bishop responded, "that's very dangerous." Liturgists were widely regarded as cranks, yet here we were, hundreds of us, joining in a *Missa Recitata*, a Mass in which the entire congregation spoke the responses aloud, and listening to distinguished scholars expound the theology of the Mystical Body. The hall was filled with energy and excitment. This was the Catholicism that attracted me.

As I look back on this period of my life—from 1937, when I was baptized, to 1942, when I joined the Grail—I see that my desire to live my new-found faith as fully as possible led me step by step to the Grail. I loved the life I experienced at Doddridge Farm during Grail weekends and in the summers of 1941 and 1942—participating in the liturgy, learning to meditate, helping to plan programs and celebrations, giving talks, inviting important speakers, writing articles and reports about the activities. I felt myself growing in every dimension of my being. Finally, in October of 1942, after long, thoughtful discussions with Lydwine and Joan, I made my decision, quit my job, and was accepted into the group at Doddridge preparing for a lifetime commitment in celibacy as the core group of the Grail.

Change in the Church: Growth of the Lay Apostolate

My first task after I joined the Grail was an extensive speaking tour with Joan Overboss, a rich experience which gave me a realistic overview of the Catholic Church in the United States, both the new movements which were stirring everywhere and the conservative, ghettoized, clericalized Church that was the norm.

In the fall of 1942 and the winter of 1943, we traveled first to the major Catholic centers in the northeast, then as far west as the Dakotas. As laywomen promoting the lay apostolate, Joan and I met with a mixture of distrust (on the part of the official Church, the bishops and pastors) and enthusiastic welcome (on the part of small groups who had been touched by the new movements). It was not easy to get invitations to speak. First of all, we had to have explicit permission from the bishop in order to enter his diocese. Often, this required a bit of political strategizing—finding which priest had the bishop's ear and would be willing to reassure him that the Pope was in favor of the lay apostolate. The prevailing mentality was conservative, super loyal to Rome, still attempting to live down the condemnation of "Americanism" in Pope Leo XIII's 1899 encyclical. Most priests were not at all interested in new ideas that might prove dangerous or in experiments that wandered from the tried-and-true paths of routine Catholic practice.

The idea that mere laywomen might be seriously aspiring to holiness and might have their own ideas about liturgy and theology was rejected out of hand.

As we moved across the country, Joan and I met with people involved in all the new movements. In the words of theologian Romano Guardini, "The Church was coming to life in the souls of men [sic]." Everywhere we went there were little groups—a few young priests, a married couple, a nun or a lay teacher in a Catholic school—who had caught a glimpse of a different kind of Church, an organism pulsing with the life of the Holy Spirit, rather than a hierarchical structure bound by a restrictive code of canon law. Usually these pioneers were looked at askance by their colleagues. A nun who had started lively Catholic Action groups with the girls in her high school was transferred to another school; a young priest who attempted to introduce African-Americans into the parish was reprimanded. Often Joan and I found ourselves in someone's back room—in a private home or a struggling Catholic bookstore—meeting with five or six people, some of whom had to conceal from their superiors exactly what meeting they were going to. We felt so much like conspirators that we entitled our summer program for 1945 "The Christian Conspiracy."

It was not until I began to write this chapter and looked up the founding dates of the movements that had attracted me that I realized that most of these movements were almost as new to the Church in the United States as I was. *Commonweal* was founded in 1924 by a group of east coast intellectuals (nine laymen, four priests), as a weekly journal commenting on current events, public policy, and the arts from a Christian point of view. *Orate Fratres*, a monthly journal promoting the liturgical movement, was begun in 1926 by Virgil Michel, OSB, a pioneer in both the liturgical renewal and in the movements for Christian social action. In 1933, Dorothy Day, a former communist turned Catholic and Peter Maurin, a Basque peasant and disciple of the French personalist philosopher, Emmanuel Mounier, founded *The Catholic Worker*. The first issue of the paper appeared on May Day, 1933, to be followed soon after by the Houses of Hospitality that spread across the country. That same year, Frank Sheed, an Australian lawyer with training in theology, and his wife, Maisie Ward of an aristocratic English Catholic family, moved their innovative publishing house from London to New York and began making the works of the European Catholic revival available to Americans.

In 1938 Baroness Catherine de Hueck, a Russian émigré, who had started interracial work in Toronto, opened Friendship House in New York. Ade Bethune, a young artist, born in Belgium and studying art in New York, was drawn into *The Catholic Worker* orbit and soon was illustrating the paper with her vigorous interpretations of the corporal and spiritual works of mercy. Dedicated to fostering strong contemporary expressions in religious art, Ade helped to found the Catholic Art Association. Helene Iswolsky, an aristocratic Russian émigré who converted from the Russian Orthodox to the Roman Catholic Church, founded The Third Hour, an influential ecumenical group that met regularly in New York in the 1930s and 1940s, a time when the Catholic Church frowned upon any contact with other religions.

On another front, Luigi Ligutti began the National Catholic Rural Life Movement, which had a strong impact on Catholic couples. In the 1940s and again in the 1960s, the "back to the land" movement drew young Catholics to experiment with communities of homesteaders in Minnesota; in Michigan; in Loveland, Ohio; in Nyack, New York; in South Bend, Indiana.

In Europe, Pius XI, faced with the advance of communism, especially among the working classes, had called for a lay apostolate based on the notion of "like to like," workers to workers, students to students, farmers to farmers. A Belgian priest, Canon Joseph Cardijn, had begun organizing young men in the factories and the mines, using a method he described as "see" (i.e., observe your milieu), "judge" (in the light of the Gospels), and "act" (in union with others in your small group) to Christianize the environment. This method soon became the basis of the Jocist movement (for Jeunesse Ouvrière Chrétienne) in Europe. It became influential in the United States, especially among the priests, through the work of an Australian writer, Paul McGuire, who, together with an English priest, John Fitzsimons, produced a book *Restoring All Things: A Guide to Catholic Action*, published by Sheed and Ward in 1938. In that same year, I remember hearing McGuire give a rousing talk in Chicago, focused on the message that the laity were called to participate in the apostolate of the hierarchy. In McGuire's wake, and with the strong support of Monsignor Reynold Hillenbrand, rector of Mundelein Seminary in Chicago, groups of "specialized Catholic Action," Young Christian Workers (YCW), Young Christian Students (YCS) and later Christian Family Movement (CFM) were organized.[4]

The various movements were in touch with each other and were usually mutually supportive though sometimes there was competition between YCW/YCS and the Grail over recruitment of new members. All the groups were small, we needed allies, and we also recognized in each other the same ideas, attitudes, and values. We were not on the defensive; rather we were inspired by the Catholic Revival, convinced that the reintegration of Western Civilization depended the restoration of its Christian foundations and we were eager to help with that task.

Forming a Realistic Picture of the Catholic World

On my tour with Joan, I began to get a more realistic picture of my fellow Catholics and of the Church as institution. I think the first time I looked at the Church sociologically was with Msgr. Luigi Ligutti of the National Catholic Rural Life Movement. Born in Italy but educated for the priesthood in the United States, as a rural pastor in Granger, Iowa, he had succeeded in getting federal funds to provide five-acre homesteads for fifty unemployed miners and their families. When Joan and I visited him, he sat us down before a map of the United States and explained that faced with the nineteenth-century flood of immigrants from Ireland, Germany, Italy, and Poland, the bishops had tried to keep the Catholics in the cities where it was easier for one priest to minister to a large congregation. Ligutti thought this policy was mistaken, that in the long run it was more conducive to healthy family life and to the growth of the Church to encourage families to settle on the family farm. He pointed out three places in the United States where German Catholics had successfully organized large-scale rural settlements, complete with parish priest, namely: Stearns County, Minnesota; the area around Wichita, Kansas; and Mercer County, Ohio. These were areas with solid Catholic families, where even in the 1940s one still might find a Corpus Christi procession on the feast day going through the streets of small towns with names like St. Henry and St. Rose. Joan and I immediately saw the implications for the Grail. Since the Church in the United States was urban and concentrated east of the Mississippi River and north of the Ohio, our strategy was to focus on the big cities of the northeast—Brooklyn, New York City, Philadelphia, Pittsburgh, Chicago, plus these three Catholic rural areas and Catholic Louisiana. When we had drawn and trained enough capable leaders from these teeming Catholic populations, we could move into other regions. Mercer County was never very responsive to Grail outreach efforts, but many young women came to Grailville from Kansas. They were country girls, with hosts of practical skills, coming from large families—ten, fourteen, eighteen children. While those from the big cities found the farm attractive and vied with each other to work in the cow barn, the Kansas women wanted nothing to do with the farm, and gravitated to the Christian culture programs. But I am getting ahead of my story.

Very soon in my Catholic life I had discovered the juridical face of the Church. Catholics were hedged around with countless laws of the Church, spelled out in minute detail. For instance, in order to receive Holy Communion, one had to be fasting from the previous midnight. However, my Catholic friends told me with glee that if your city was on daylight savings time, you could eat and drink until 1 A.M., keeping your fast on standard time. There was also a legalistic concern over keeping the Eucharistic fast—if you inadvertently swallowed a little water while brushing your teeth, could you still go to communion? The question of fish on Friday posed similar problems—what if you were in a situation where nothing but meat was available? I knew vaguely that Catholics were forbidden to participate in non-Catholic religious ceremonies. Thus, when I was invited to the wedding of a Jewish friend, I checked with my confessor. He confirmed that for a Catholic to attend a non-Catholic service could be "a cause of scandal," but in my case he was willing to grant a dispensation. Then there was the *Index of Forbidden Books*. Of course, in my Great Books days, I had read a great many books on the *Index*. I now learned that if, for my writing or teaching, I wanted to use Descartes or Voltaire, I was supposed to get special permission from the Chancery Office. When Joan Overboss and I were on tour, we did not dare mention the fact that we were staying at the YWCA (a safe and inexpensive place for two women traveling alone). Good Catholics did not even swim at the Y!

I accepted these restrictions without difficulty. In our university circle, we had often discussed the need for an institution, something beyond the whims and fancies of the individual to guide our Christian life. I knew that it was not enough to have a private religion, to practice the love of God in my heart—the dangers of self-deception were too great. At that point in my life, I wanted the guidance of objective standards enforced by an institutional structure.

Following the strategy suggested by Msgr. Ligutti's sociological analysis, Joan and I began our tour with the major Catholic centers in the northeast, and then after Christmas went as far west as the Dakotas. This tour immersed me in the world of the institutional Church. Almost everywhere we went, the Church was well organized, with an impressive array of institutions—parishes, schools, colleges, hospitals, charitable institutions, Holy Name Society for the men, Altar and Rosary for the women, Sodality for the girls, CYO for the boys, a seemingly endless variety of religious orders for men and for women. It was a self-contained world with a Catholic organization for every need—spiritual, intellectual, social, or charitable. There were even Catholic organizations to parallel secular ones—a Catholic Press Association alongside the National Press Club, the Catholic Daughters alongside the Daughters of the American Revolution. The vast organizational structure focused on keeping Catholics together in an environment that would not challenge their faith but would protect them from secular influences and provide them with "ready answers" for criticisms they might meet in an unbelieving world. Catholics lived for the most part in Catholic ghettoes. They were urged to send their children to Catholic schools, camps, social clubs, so they would meet and marry Catholics and avoid the dangers of "mixed marriages." The emphasis, so far as I could see, was on "keeping the faith," rather than taking responsibility to announce the "Good

Tidings" to the world. I learned that the United States had been mission territory until 1909 and that Maryknoll, the first American mission-sending society, was not founded until 1911. The Catholics Joan and I were meeting were secure, even smug, in their confidence that the Church had the truth. They gloried in their rapidly increasing numbers and in the big public displays of Catholic strength like the Holy Name parades and the Eucharistic Congresses.

I saw signs, too, particularly in the colleges we visited, of the lack of a vigorous intellectual life. I was used to the University of Chicago, where the people I knew had a strong interest in reading books, attending lectures, going to concerts, theaters, art exhibits, discussing cultural and political issues. There seemed to me to be a much stronger interest in life-long learning among my secular friends than among the Catholic faculty and students I was meeting. The latter seemed to rest content with the truths they had acquired from their textbooks. I remembered two remarks of Mortimer Adler, who was very popular on the Catholic lecture circuit and had a wide acquaintance among the Catholic colleges and universities. He complained that his Dominican friends tended to look to what St. Thomas had said on a given question, rather than trusting that they themselves had assimilated the basic Thomistic principles and could think for themselves in that light. And after a meeting of the Catholic Philosophical Association, he remarked that the American Philosophical Association had all the questions and the Catholics had all the answers. For my part, as I went around lecturing on secularism and the lay apostolate in the colleges, I was distressed by the values the students appeared to hold—their dreams seemed centered on the comfortable marriage, the house in the suburbs with the latest automatic washer in the basement and a good car in the garage. I developed a talk full of pointed examples of the materialism of Catholic College girls. It did not make me popular, but it did get a reaction from the audience!

As to spiritual life, there seemed to me to be both a good deal of formalism and a rather sentimental piety, concentrated on "special devotions" rather than on the liturgy. On our lecture tour, Joan and I often stayed in convents. There were strict rules about which parts of the convent "seculars" could be allowed to visit. There was a rigid daily schedule. Often there was a long list of prescribed prayers to be said after Mass, rattled off quickly and routinely. Some communities said the Little Office of the Blessed Virgin, which did not vary with the feasts and seasons but was the same every day. I gathered that in many cases these forms of prayer had been prescribed when communities of women were largely illiterate and therefore needed to memorize their prayers. There were lots of large, highly colored statues of various saints and a host of special devotional practices—novenas, the nine First Fridays, nocturnal adoration, Forty Hours, many of them directed toward obtaining "favors" for the petitioner. I remember one morning being served breakfast by a novice, who informed us proudly that she was about to go for her fifteen minutes of meditation—mental prayer, she explained kindly, quite sure that we as laywomen knew nothing about such a spiritual practice. I had been introduced to mental prayer before my baptism, and at Doddridge Farm had received further training in methods of meditation. In the Grail courses we recommended half an hour as the minimum time needed to center down effectively; we ourselves reserved a full hour each day for meditation. Often my priest friends would leave a social evening with the excuse, "Have to say my office." It seemed an obligation and a burden (especially since it was said in Latin) rather than a source of spiritual refreshment. I remember a priest friend who was a member of a religious community sharing his amusement at the novices in his community. "We have a chapter of faults," he explained, "and they regularly confess to worldliness because they can't think of anything else." I was shocked—at Doddridge if we confessed faults, they were real and specific. We did not dream of simply going through a formality.

Conclusion

The Church I joined was the church of the new movements. I found them so appealing and energizing that the negative experiences of Catholic life had little impact on me. Even after I acquired a more realistic picture of American Catholicism on my tour with Joan, I was not dismayed. I came back from the tour wishing that Lydwine van Kersbergen could be made a bishop, and quite sure that what we were doing was alive and would grow.

Looking back at the new movements, I now see that much of the vitality and creativity that I found so attractive was coming from below, from people who had little or no standing in the official church. In fact, although I did not realize it at the time, when officialdom took over, the vitality tended to diminish.

Finally, I see that the Grail arrived on these shores at a propitious moment, when vital new movements were stirring in a conservative, juridical, urbanized, clericalized, ghettoized Church. Had the Grail arrived ten or even five years earlier, I think it would have been almost impossible for the movement to find a foothold. In the context of the new movements, the Grail did find a foothold and and was able to grow. It is alive today, when many of the other movements—among them, Friendship House, the YCW, the YCS, the Third Hour, even Sheed and Ward as an independent publishing house—no longer exist.

Introduction

Women Breaking Boundaries

Twendeni wote, Twendeni wote
Tubadilishe dunia-a-a-a.
Kwa amani, twendeni wote
Kwa amani, twendeni wote
Tubadilishe dunia-a-a-a.

(Let us all go, let us all go
To change the world.
In peace, let us all go
In peace, let us all go
To change the world.)

(Swahili song from Tanzania)

The procession dances toward the altar, led by two women from Papua New Guinea wearing grass skirts. Behind them two Tanzanians in colorful kangas, several Mexicans in embroidered blouses, and a long line of women—white, black, and brown—move to the rhythm of the drums. We continue with a Spanish song, then one in English, then back to Ki-Swahili.

I am in the middle of the procession as we wind around the altar and then take our seats in the Oratory at Grailville.[1] The time is July, 1993, and the occasion is the International General Assembly of the Grail Movement, a gathering of fifty-some women from twenty countries "to address in a spirit of urgency three interrelated themes: Building Justice and Solidarity, Facing Cultural Changes, Contributing to the Survival of the Planet."[2] I marvel that the movement, which began in the Netherlands in 1921 with a handful of young women who as "umarried Roman Catholic laywomen"

21

wanted to help "spread the Kingdom of God over the whole world,"[3] now exists in twenty countries on all six continents, from Canada to Australia, from Germany to Uganda.

The story of the Grail in the United States is just one part of a much wider and longer history of the Grail around the world. I do not attempt to sketch that wider history, but confine this narrative to the North American scene.

I want to tell this story because it is a good story and good stories deserve to be told. It is even, I dare to say, a heroic story, a story of a small, determined band of women working against impossible odds. It is a case study of a group adapting creatively to enormous changes. It is an example of women with a global vision, breaking boundaries of race, class, nation and creating bonds of solidarity around the world. It is a hopeful story of what human beings are capable of, the hidden creativity, the multiple potentialities that can be tapped in apparently ordinary folks.

Moreover, it is a significant chapter in women's history and in the history of American Catholicism. It is only in the last quarter century that we have begun to realize that "all history as we now know it is merely prehistory, that is, history written by men about men's experience."[4] Feminist scholars are hard at work on "herstory," writing women into the records of the human past. However, the story of women in the churches is still lagging behind the general herstory. Much work needs to be done to tell the story of women as religious agents, makers of religious history. I want to add my piece to this picture.

Why am I telling the story? Because I was there—I met the Grail pioneers, Lydwine van Kersbergen and Joan Overboss—in October of 1940, just a few months after their arrival in the United States and became a permanent member of the movement in 1942. I was directly involved in many of the major developments and much of the policy making of the last fifty-five years. In short, I can tell the story from the inside, achievements and failures, insights and mistakes.

Every history relies on a conceptual framework to define subject and methods, to guide selection of events and interpretations. I propose to tell the story from a feminist perspective, a context crucial to understanding a women's group struggling for autonomy in a patriarchal church and a sexist society.[5] It is a feminist analysis that enables me to define the society as sexist and the Catholic Church as patriarchal. In the light of that analysis, I cast the Grail story in terms of a struggle to empower women to become self-defined and self-directing human beings. My story then becomes one of identifying the seeds of autonomy in the original vision and tracing the gradual development of feminist actions and a feminist consciousness in the movement.

In feminist analysis I find both a critique of "objectivity" and support for passionate scholarship. In the light of recent feminist epistemologies,[6] I would claim that caring and closeness give a knowledge that cannot be had by distancing and detachment. In either case, at a distance or close up, I would insist that one's vision is clearer and more accurate in proportion to the self-awareness of the viewer. It is the unconscious assumptions and biases that distort the account, more than the passion or dispassion.

Feminist analysis has also empowered me in writing this book to combine memoir and history, the passionate "I" of the eyewitness with a variety of other sources: the extensive materials in the Grail archives; my personal files of letters, memos, notes, reports, and articles; and interviews with eighty-four Grail members and associates, many of whom I consulted more than once between 1991 and 1997. I interweave my own memories, perceptions, feelings, and opinions with the other documentation, endeavoring to label my interpretations as such. This combination of genres raises a problem of language that many writers have noted. Thus, bell hooks writes, "Language is also a place of struggle. . . . This language that enabled me to finish graduate school, to write a dissertation, to talk at a job interview, carries the scent of oppression."[7] I choose not to use the language of the dissertation but to write for the most part in the first person, either singular or plural, in a style that tries to capture feeling as well as fact and enlivens analysis with the telling anecdote.

Women Breaking Boundaries—the Grail in the United States has worked on the cutting edge of many issues—for the laity, for women, for liturgy, for Christian culture, for overseas service, for modern catechetics, for ecumenism, for alternative education, for community development in the inner cities and overseas, for feminist theology, for sustainable agriculture, for global consciousness. We sought to empower women, to encourage them to realize their full potential. The experience of empowerment, discovering strengths I did not know I possessed, attracted me to the Grail. It has attracted other women and kept us involved. Empowerment necessarily involves breaking out of the boundaries that constrain our lives. Our faith in the power of women together to make a difference has made us innovators, pushing the envelope. In our first quarter century, we broke through boundaries to move into fields that a patriarchal church reserved to the professional religious, priests and nuns. As I look back on that first quarter century I see us claiming religious agency for women, for laywomen. We would not have used this language, but we certainly acted it out. We laid claim to the pursuit of holiness, to setting the goals and methods of our apostolate, to giving spiritual direction to women, to creating liturgies, to creating culture, to serving as missionaries overseas, to devising innovative approaches in education, to engaging in ecumenical dialogue. We were explicit about aiming to be saints and apostles. However, we did not speak of ourselves as liturgists or spiritual directors, although we certainly functioned as such.

Being innovators, as soon as the new idea was taken up by other groups, we have most often moved on, concentrating our energies on a fresh frontier. To some this has looked like inconstancy, superficiality, but I think it is a consequence of the Grail's pioneering spirit, a willingness to be open to the "signs of the times," a willingness to adapt to changing conditions and to adopt new ways.

In the first quarter century, our energies focused especially on making a difference in the Church—restoring the liturgy, activating the laity, creating a Christian culture, educating Catholics to their social responsibility locally and globally. We wanted to share these riches with non-Catholics, and our principal means of acting was to bring others into the life of the centers we had established. In some sense, we were trying to bring the world into the Church. Since 1965, we have focused much of our energies on the struggle for justice in the world, finding the holy in the midst of the struggle. Along with the image of the overflowing cup we have placed the image of women weaving a network of connections through which new life can flow.

Another characteristic emphasis that runs through the history is the Grail's genius for making abstract principles concrete and practical. Nothing *pro forma*, no patience with simply going through the motions, no empty forms in liturgy or in life. Prune the vine, act out the Easter Gospel, dance the psalm, express joy of spirit in bright colors and lively songs, translate love of neighbor into community living and concrete sharing.

I divide the story into four parts.

Part I, Planting the Seeds, deals with the European origins, the germinal ideas and their first adaptation to the American scene. Both in Europe and in the United States, it is the story of how a small group of women starting with no money but with great ideas and determination managed to survive and grow despite a patriarchal environment. We began with a boundless faith in the ability of women working together to create change and with a vision of a world in which justice and peace would reign, imaged perhaps in the peaceable kingdom of Isaiah or the apocalyptic vision of the Kingship of Christ. That we were vague about the details did not diminish our conviction, enthusiasm, and certainty. Had we heard Margaret Mead's words about a small group of thoughtful, committed citizens being the only thing that ever changes the world we would have agreed wholeheartedly.

In Part II, Fast Women in a Slow Church, I trace the development of a movement of young women (we thought anyone over twenty-five was probably too set in her ways for the risks of Grail life). We were young women in a hurry, pressured by a sense of urgency, in a Church that views issues in terms of centuries or even in the light of eternity. By 1963, the movement had established thirteen centers across North America; included a hundred women who had made a lifetime dedication in the Grail and thousands more who had participated in Grail programs and identified with the movement; had placed a hundred Americans in overseas service in Latin America, Africa, and Asia; and was working creatively in a wide variety of fields— everything from contemporary Christian art to ecumenism to teaching English as a second language for Chicano immigrants to serving as journalists at Vatican II.

In Part III, Winds of Change, I analyze the breakup of this model under the impact of Vatican II and various other intellectual and socioeconomic trends, the emergence of creative new initiatives and projects, the development of new guidelines and structures, and the trauma of adapting to drastic changes.

In Part IV, Coming of Age, I survey the changes in each area of our major concerns—education, empowerment of women, social justice, overseas service, living faith. I see the reconceptualizations and the changes in practice as transformations of the original Grail vision, transformations that are in basic continuity with that vision and contain seeds of hope for the future.

An epilogue looks at people, problems, and promise as we enter the new millennium.

Part I
Planting the Seeds, 1940–1951

1

Grail Beginnings

The Germinal Ideas and the Pioneers

> *Have acquired beautiful site with several*
> *buildings near Chicago. Will you arrange*
> *to start work at earliest convenience?*

This telegram from Bishop Bernard Sheil of Chicago arrived at the Tiltenberg, International Grail Training Center near Amsterdam, on December 30, 1939. To send a team to the United States had been part of the Grail plan for a long time. Professor Jacques van Ginneken had founded the group in 1921 as "a society of unmarried Roman Catholic lay-women . . . at the disposal of the Church to help with the spreading of the Kingdom of God over the whole world."[1] He had often spoken to the enthusiastic young members of the society about the three forces struggling to win the modern world—America, Russia, and Christianity. Clearly, the Grail,[2] with its goal of world conversion, needed to be at the heart of the action, that is, in America.

A team of five had been carefully chosen to start the Grail in America: Joan Overboss, fresh from Germany where Hitler had just suppressed the Grail movement; Lydia Mulders, an artist; Ans Coebergh van den Braak, a youth leader; Mary Louise Tully, a young American in Holland for training to become the first United States Grail member; and as leader-in-charge, Lydwine van Kersbergen, PhD, recently returned from establishing the Grail in Australia. When the Bishop's cable arrived, they intensified their preparations—collecting materials to take with them, following special courses that might prove useful, completing tasks or turning them over to others. Margaret van Gilse, the International President of the Grail, was uneasy as war appeared to be looming closer and closer. She insisted that Lydwine and Joan set out without waiting for the others.

On March 30, 1940, Lydwine van Kersbergen and Joan Overboss boarded the boat train in The Hague, the first step on their journey to

America. A group of Grail members was on the platform to see them off. In the excitement of their departure, the two travelers did not notice that Margaret van Gilse had been called aside to receive a cablegram from Archbishop Gilroy in Australia, informing her that Judith Bouwman, the leader of the Grail in Australia, had been killed in an automobile accident. Another woman might have delayed the departure, considered sending Lydwine back to Australia to take charge of the young, inexperienced team there. But Margaret did not say a word to anyone until after the train had pulled out. When Lydwine and Joan arrived in New York, they found Margaret's letter waiting for them with the news of the loss of one of the movement's most dynamic and creative leaders.

A few initial contacts had already been made in the United States, but they must have seemed very few to the two newcomers. In the whole of the United States with its 22,000,000 Catholics, they were acquainted with just five people: James Coffey, a young priest of the Brooklyn diocese, who, while studying at Louvain, had visited Holland and fallen in love with the Grail. He was now the newest assistant in a large Irish Catholic parish in Brooklyn. John and Anina Tully, parents of Mary Louise, who were at their home in La Grange, Illinois, trying frantically to get news of their daughter who was still at the Grail Center in occupied Holland. Helen Mann, wife of an international banker, whom Joan had worked with in Berlin and who was now living in Manhattan. And Bishop Bernard J. Sheil, auxiliary bishop of Chicago, who had been sent to Europe in 1938 by Cardinal Mundelein to survey European youth movements and had been well received at the main Grail center. He had seen one of the mass dramas with several thousand young women expressing their convictions through color and movement, singing and choral speaking. The bishop was duly impressed and urged the Grail to come to the United States. The next year Lydwine and Alberta Lucker, a German Grail leader, had come to the States as delegates to a Congress of *Pax Romana*, the international organization of Catholic university students. Lydwine took the opportunity to go to Chicago, visit with the Tully family, and see Cardinal Mundelein. "We talked about the lay apostolate," she told me, "and he said that he had always wanted it in his diocese. He invited the Grail to come to Chicago at our convenience. I should have asked for a written statement but I did not think of that at the time."[3]

During the *Pax Romana* Congress word came that Hitler had invaded Austria. The Congress broke up as the European delegates hastened to return to their own countries. On May 10, 1940, Hitler's armies crossed into Holland, Rotterdam was bombed, the Queen and the Dutch government went into exile. Events had proved the soundness of Margaret van Gilse's intuition: Lydwine and Joan had left Holland on one of the last boats to sail from Rotterdam before the German invasion. The two newcomers in New York were cut off from their home base.

There they were, staying in the hostel run by the Sisters of Jesus and Mary on Fourteenth Street in Manhattan: two Dutch women, one of whom, Joan, did not yet speak English. Their seed money of Dutch guilders had been rendered worthless by the invasion; their patron, George Cardinal Mundelein, had died before their arrival; in the inter-regnum until a new archbishop would be appointed, Bishop Sheil had no authority to act. He kept them waiting three weeks before he came to New York to talk with them. He did not offer any financial aid. Instead he urged them first to stay on in New York and "get to feel the swing of the city."

It was not an auspicious beginning. It seemed particularly chilling to Lydwine van Kersbergen, who, when she had arrived in Australia to begin the Grail "Down Under," had been received by an impressive delegation of Australian and New Zealand bishops eager to welcome the Grail team and to offer housing and funds to help them get started.

Who were these two women? With what were they armed? What gave them the courage to get into their car—a gift from the Tully family—and drive to Chicago? Two things: the vision of the founder, Jacques van Ginneken, and their own experience of how these ideas worked out in practice.

Jacques van Ginneken

Van Ginneken was a Dutch Jesuit, born in 1877 in a small town, Oudenbosch, in the South of Holland, to a prosperous family (his father owned a brewery). There were French and Celtic influences in his background, which perhaps accounted for his exuberant, charismatic personality. He was a brilliant scholar, who earned a doctorate in philology at the secular University of Leiden and was the only Jesuit to be elected to the prestigious Royal Academy of Science. He read widely in many fields and pioneered in bringing other disciplines—psychology, ethnology, biology—to bear on philology. He was a man of amazing intuitions—he foresaw planes speeding through the stratosphere, and in one of his conferences he even remarked that one day men would go to the moon.[4]

He was a popular and persuasive lecturer; in fact, so popular were his Saturday lectures in the Great Hall of the university that some of his colleagues, annoyed at his ability to draw large crowds, instituted a ruling that only formally enrolled graduate students be allowed to attend. He had strong opinions and strong convictions, which he was always ready to translate into action. His studies in psychology issued in experiments in psychological testing and attempts to use the tests in job counseling. At the time, Dutch Catholics were just emerging into public life after centuries of post-Reformation oppression. They tended to keep to themselves in a fortress mentality, very much on the defensive in relations with non-Catholics. Van Ginneken's impatience with this "fear Catholicism" led to his organizing with Gerard Brom the Committee for the Conversion of the Netherlands and to his popular retreats for non-Catholics.

He "lived Catholicism in a Netherlands style, which united the exuberance of the South with the decisiveness of the North," Gerard Brom wrote of him. At heart he was "an ambassador of Christ,"[5] a priest dedicated to the apostolate and haunted by the question, "Why has the world not been converted?" Surely God's grace is always present; the failure must be on the part of our response, on the lack of leadership willing to risk everything in the one great work. He wanted Catholics who would take the initiative, who would be willing to embrace and use all modern means and who would risk everything to bring the Gospel into the contemporary world. Pursuing this idea, he founded in rapid succession four lay communities, each intended to work actively with a specific population: the Ladies of Bethany in 1919; the Knights of St. Willibrord; and in 1921 the Crusaders of St. John and the Women of Nazareth. The Ladies of Bethany were to work among the dechristianized young people in the big cities; they disappointed him by forsaking their lay status to become a canonical religious community. The Crusaders of St. John were to work with boys to help them learn a trade after leaving school; they eventually became a secular institute. The Knights of St. Willibrord were for "the drawing-room apostolate" among the well-to-do elites; and the Women of Nazareth were originally to work with girls after they left school, a goal that soon was broadened to take on worldwide dimensions. He began speaking of this worldwide movement of young women and the great things they would accomplish. A listener asked, "How many members do you have?" Undaunted, the ever-optimistic van Ginneken replied, "None yet."

Four ideas were particularly dear to his heart and soon captured the imagination and fueled the energies of the first Women of Nazareth: namely, the elbow of time, the three forces struggling to unify the world, the contribution women could make in this struggle, and the practice of the Cross as the key to spiritual energies.

His analysis of world history led him to the conviction that Western civilization was in crisis. The old order was breaking down. He compared it to a huge domed church crumbling into ruin. But the crisis was also an opportunity, for in such "an elbow of time," there is a fluidity that makes major changes possible. He foresaw a relatively short period, perhaps fifty to seventy-five years, in which the world would tremble in the balance, able to be turned in a new direction by a group with vision and determination. "Rejoice that we are living now," he told the young women gathered at the

Tiltenberg, the training house outside Amsterdam, in 1932, "because we have the chance to give the world a push."[6]

Moreover, in this time of feverish unification of the world by modern transportation and communications, he saw three forces struggling for control: Russia with her communism, America with her capitalism, and Christianity. He was not under any illusion about the strength of Christianity. "Catholicism would not even be mentioned in any ordinary objective history,"[7] he remarks. But there is a new factor on the world scene, the rising force of feminism. He explained that

> economic and technical conditions have been the cause of a new matrilineal culture which is now coming into existence, now—to put it in a more correct way—a civilization with a more feminine orientation is about to materialize. The cause of all this is the invention of machinery. Machinery does two things: in the first place, it brings the woman out of the home into the factory where she earns money, a good deal of money, sometimes even more than a man. And, on the other hand, it takes a great deal of the housekeeping out of her hands.[8] Housekeeping has fallen to pieces, and in another generation, it will have gone completely, except for the upbringing of the children. And that asks only a few years after which the Montessori school takes over.[9]

The lecture elaborates in detail how the old domestic crafts—providing fuel, light, and water; gardening, cooking, canning, and preserving food; spinning, weaving, sewing, knitting, laundry—have all moved to the factory. As a result of these trends, he envisaged a rising matriarchy, holding the balance, able to turn the world in a new direction:[10]

> If only we could stop considering the man as the only force in public life. . . . Feminism is working in that direction. . . . Oh, if that feminism would succeed . . . if indeed that becomes true, we will have mobilized that half of humanity which up till now did not count, and this half will make its choice of party and will become itself a great party, a great force. . . . Feminism is a terrific rising force and if it will go at the speed which ethnology proves, it may well happen that we return to our former matriarchal culture . . . then woman will get the greatest chance to let the conversion of the world succeed.[11]

And here precisely is the task for the Grail. To organize these young women and make use of their gifts and talents for "the conversion of the world." On the one hand, he is quite pragmatic:

> The world has (I shall make a rough guess) some ten million
> women too many, who have no longer enough to do, and we shall
> organize these women and we shall convert the world with them.[12]

These women, lacking a purpose in life, finding time heavy on their hands,
he saw as ripe for a movement to give meaning to their lives. On the other
hand, beyond the pragmatism, he also had a boundless faith in the potential
of women, a potential that he maintained had never been tapped either in
society or in the church. "You have been given all kinds of deep and wonderful talents which up till now have not been exploited in the Catholic
Church," he told the young women. His faith was grounded both in his personal experience—his father died when he was a small child; he was raised
by a family of capable women—and in his studies of history and anthropology, including Bachofen's *Das Mutterrecht*. Women can change the world
because they have already done so. He reinforced this conviction by his
broad sketch of women's contributions throughout history, beginning with
women's discovery of the seed, of spinning and weaving, of pottery and
fixed dwelling places, and coming down through the Bible, the medieval
queens and abbesses, the missionary nuns, to the twentieth century.

His notion of conversion of the world was not as triumphalist as it
sounds to contemporary ears. While his retreats for non-Catholics did result
in bringing people into the Catholic Church, his ideas of the apostolate
focused rather on permeating both public and private life with Christian
values. His notions tended more toward transformation than toward imposition of an orthodoxy.

> And what is your task? To counterbalance in the world all mascu-
> line hardness, all the angles of the masculine character, all cruelty,
> all the results of alcoholism and prostitution and sin and capital-
> ism, which are ultra-masculine, and to Christianize that with a
> womanly charity. What else is that than the conversion of the
> world?[13]

How was the Grail to organize the millions of young women and
through them create a stream, a veritable torrent, of love and self-sacrifice
to change the world? His method was a radical one: by living an intense
Christian spirit *in the world*. The leaven must be in the dough. The Women
of Nazareth must achieve the widest possible contact with the world of
young women, in the factories and the universities, in workshops and
offices, in the department stores and the banks, in the radio and film studios. They must learn to radiate the joy of their faith, not shut up behind
convent walls, but in the midst of contemporary society, as laywomen, not
set apart by dress or enclosure, vows or special rules and customs. It was a
point of pride with the group that he was speaking of the importance of the

lay apostolate already in 1921, a year before Pope Pius XI wrote his encyclical on the topic. In naming the group Women of Nazareth (WoN), he intended to stress their lay character, for he observed that no organized group in the Church had attempted to live the life which Mary had lived in Nazareth, a laywoman carrying out her tasks in her family and community.

Moreover, the WoN were to make use of all that modern science and technology had to offer. He had no patience with the siege mentality of nineteenth- and early-twentieth-century Catholicism, on the defensive against liberalism, democracy, and technology and occupied in constructing Catholic institutions as safe havens from the world. On the contrary, he urged the WoN to utilize all modern means in their work, mentioning particularly automobiles, airplanes, radio, film, cabarets, theaters, stadiums. They should establish their own film studios, design and build their own airplanes, emblazon the Grail symbol in neon lights over the doors of the Grail houses.

They were also to make full use of their womanly beauty and charm. He complains that the Church has not recognized this aspect of women's gifts:

> If she wanted to do good, (the Church) has shut her up in great cloisters behind thick walls; and has thought that every woman who walked along the street in a nice dress was a permanent danger to good morals and to all decent piety. It's of tremendous importance for the Grail movement that you should appear in the streets as well-dressed women. You must be women from all classes and attractive women. If we want to win the world and you are not charming, we can not use you.[14]

He looked to the early church as an example of the lay apostolate, when the faith was spread throughout the Mediterranean world by the slave women in the households, the soldiers on the Roman roads, the noble ladies in the palaces. To keep this idea alive, many of the first WoN took names from the New Testament: Lydia, Persis, Damaris, Syntiche, Thecla.

But how to assure that in the midst of the world with all its preoccupations, distractions, and temptations, the WoN would not only be able to hold to their quite different values but to bring the witness of a radiant, irresistible Christian spirit? He fell back on the only means he knew—the traditional spirituality of the counsels set forth in a document modeled in large measure after the Jesuits. He explains:

> You are actually religious at heart, but you remain lay people for the sake of the other lay people, in order to influence them and safeguard them.[15] You are the quasi-religious nucleus of the lay apostolate. That does not mean that you should be only half reli-

gious, but it means that you form one big organization with the lay people. . . . You should bring more and bigger sacrifices than the religious, but you should not come inside the framework of ecclesiastical canon law which always prescribes a religious habit that would only be a hindrance to you. If the WoN should become a religious order, a partition would automatically arise between you and the Grail and the Grail would become like a Third Order. The new thing is that the laity form a hierarchy—the Round Table (the council of the chief Grail leaders), the leader of a city, the leader of a house, and so on . . . like the army.[16]

The concept of a quasi-religious nucleus of the lay apostolate was a bold idea, attempting to unite opposite poles—religious and lay, "strictest spirituality and freest worldliness,"[17] WoN and the Grail, a highly trained elite and a mass movement of young women. But is it really lay, or are the nucleus members nuns in disguise? "Lay" in Catholic terminology has two distinct meanings: (1) the laity are those who are not ordained, that is, not clerics or priests; and (2) the laity are those who are not religious, that is, not bound by vow to the evangelical counsels of poverty, chastity, and obedience. Since the institutional Catholic Church insists that women cannot be ordained, all women are lay in the first sense. However, the religious orders create a second distinction, that between religious and secular. In setting up the WoN and the Grail, Father van Ginneken spoke of a return to the early church, before it was clericalized, when all the women were "completely apostle and completely lay." His concept was an attempt to break down the wall between religious and secular, the wall that reserved holiness to the professionally religious, that is, nuns and priests. The Grail and its "quasi-religious nucleus" claimed the fullness of Christian life for the laity, specifically for lay women. An early Grail slogan proclaimed the lay apostolate as an "all saints movement." Moreover, another slogan, "Women should lead women," claimed the full responsibilities of leadership for women—taking the initiative, setting goals, choosing means—under the guidance of the bishop, to be sure, but definitely not subject to the parish priest. Father van Ginneken is careful to explain that the WoN and the Grail form one big organization under lay leadership, not like the Franciscan Third Order where the priest moderator makes all the decisions.

In working out the structures and spirituality for the movement, Father van Ginneken drew on traditional forms. Structurally, the WoN as the nucleus of the lay apostolate were to lead the movement, infusing the spirit out of their lengthy spiritual formation, and fulfilling the major functional roles. They were also to safeguard the international unity of the movement. The WoN was organized in a pyramid structure, with the international president at the top of the chain of command. She appointed the national presidents who in turn appointed leaders of centers, teams, and other projects. There was always someone clearly in charge of even the smallest project. A novitiate of three to five years prepared the WoN for an oath of obedience, a promise of poverty, and a private vow of virginity for as long as they remained members. These pledges could be dissolved by the international president, but the intention was that the individual dedicate herself to Christ in the WoN for her lifetime. This structure, with its emphasis on an oath rather than a vow of obedience, was carefully calibrated to maintain the lay status of the WoN and to establish them as a mere *pia unio*, pious union, outside the jurisdiction of the Sacred Congregation for Religious. To the often asked question, "Do you take vows?" we members could always reply in good conscience with a definite "No, only our baptismal vows."

Spiritually, the WoN were to be as dedicated, as willing to sacrifice— or even more willing to sacrifice—than the members of the most austere religious order. At the same time, they were to be free to wear fashionable clothes, to make use of all modern technology, to take any job, to travel and work alone. Initially these polarities were expressed in dress: in the training house members wore a quasi-religious habit, a white robe and veil with a blue sash; in the work, they wore attractive modern outfits. Father van Ginneken was at pains to explain that they should never think of their in-house costume as their real costume, nor their modern dress as a disguise. Both forms of dress were equally theirs.[18]

For the training of the WoN, he drew on the traditional monastic model with an additional emphasis on "an extremism of religion,"[19] "without compromise."[20] Training centered on the total surrender of self to God through a life of joyful self-denial and mortification lived under strict obedience to the duly constituted authorities. Obedience was understood in the Ignatian sense of conforming not only one's outward action but also one's mind and will to the directives of the leader. Moreover, nothing was to be done out of routine or *pro forma*. Rather WoN were urged to use initiative and ingenuity in discovering new ways of prayer and mortification. Father van Ginneken admired the spirit of sacrifice and devotion to a cause which he saw in communism, in fascism, even in the capitalists' dedication to the pursuit of profit, and he frequently urged the WoN to practice an extremism of love, self-sacrifice, and devotion to the cause of world conversion even greater than that of their secular counterparts. "We will have to exceed our opponents in their heroism of hate with the radiantly happy heroism of love," he exhorted his listeners.[21]

Was the original foundation really lay? The answer is clearly "yes" in terms of canon law. The oath put us outside the sphere of the Sacred Congregation for Religious with all its regulations. But I would contend that this was more than a legalistic device; it was a deeply held value. Our self-understanding was emphatically lay, although it has taken many decades to work out the implications of the term. I find it evidence of a lay consciousness that the in-house costume was soon abandoned. A magazine article featuring a picture of Dutch members in their "habit" was an embarrassment to us in the early days in the United States. From my present vantage point, I see that the tradition we inherited was both dualistic (spirit/matter, church/world, soul/body) and hierarchical. I see our history as a struggle to work our way out of both dualism and hierarchy, a struggle to develop a lay spirituality, an evolution growing out of insights and values in the original vision.

Both Lydwine van Kersbergen and Joan Overboss were deeply imbued with Jacques van Ginneken's vision and had taken part in the demanding training for "the quasi-religious nucleus of the lay apostolate," but they interpreted the vision differently according to their very different personalities and their quite different experiences in the burgeoning movement in Europe.

Lydwine van Kersbergen

Lydwine was born Geertruida Catharina Hendrika Maria van Kersbergen[22] on May 6, 1905, in The Hague, the sixth of seven children, five boys and two girls. The family were prosperous and devout Catholics. Her father and brothers ran a highly successful horticultural business, breeding new varieties, providing flowers for the major churches and hotels, supervising acres of greenhouses and growing things. "My father loved his family and his plants," she told me. "In winter, he and my brothers would get up in the middle of the night to make sure the heating for the plants was all right. When I was growing up, I did not like trees or flowers; I felt my father considered them more important than anything else." Her mother was a major influence in her life. She was a deeply religious woman, who went to daily Mass no matter what the weather and spent her Sundays in works of charity. As a child, Lydwine accompanied her mother, bringing gifts to orphanages, old age homes, the poor. "I did not like these visits at all," she remembers. "The poverty, the miserable surroundings, the smells, but my mother insisted."[23] Her mother had control of the family purse and responded generously to the appeals from her many friends among the priests and religious. Lydwine and her younger sister had a happy childhood—their big garden with its swings was a focal point for the neighborhood children.

One of the priest visitors, impressed by her intelligence, advised her mother, "This child should go to the gymnasium," the secondary school that prepared students for the university. At that time it was not at all usual for girls to undertake such serious intellectual work. Lydwine was the first girl in her primary school class to go to the gymnasium and the tenth woman to earn a doctorate at the newly established Catholic University of Nijmegen.

A naive nineteen-year-old, after six years in the gymnasium, she entered the university and chose to study under Dr. Jacques van Ginneken, philologist and professor of Dutch language and literature, despite the fact that she had been warned against his unconventional ideas by some of her mother's good Catholic friends. She was immediately impressed by the breadth of his vision and the brilliance of his lectures. In public, he spoke of world history and the current crisis in Europe; in private conferences, he divulged his dream of a woman's movement that could change the world. By 1926 he had attracted five of his students—Lydwine, Mia van der Kallen, Liesbeth Allard, Louisa Veldhuis, Yvonne Bosch van Drakestein— to join the little group of Women of Nazareth that he had founded in 1921. Their fellow students referred to their exodus from the university as "The Rape of the Sabine Women."

Lydwine's mother, disappointed that her daughter did not become a nun but nevertheless supportive of her choice of this risky new venture in the lay apostolate, demanded that van Ginneken promise that Lydwine would have opportunity to complete her studies. He kept his promise. In between her duties as president of the Grail, first in Holland, then in England, she earned her doctorate in 1936 with a dissertation in linguistics, translating and commenting on a medieval Dutch version of the life of Christ, *Het Luikse Diatessaron.*

An enthusiastic disciple, fascinated by the ideas of her mentor, she nevertheless held her ground with him. In their first encounter, he startled her by demanding, "What dialect do you speak?" "No dialect. I speak the universal Dutch language." "No," he insisted, "you speak the dialect of The Hague." Again, he assigned as her work for a seminar an important current work on the red-light district in Amsterdam, that is, the novel, *De Jordaan* by J. Querida. An indignant Lydwine returned after one week announcing that she did not want to read about prostitutes. He was furious but agreed and assigned the *Diatesseron* instead, which eventually became the subject of her dissertation.

The group of university students, recruited for van Ginneken's new worldwide venture, began a period of serious spiritual formation at "De Voorde," a country house near The Hague. They also assisted in van Ginneken's retreats for non-Catholics, but their major goal, the idea that inspired their commitment, was to start a university for women in the Dutch East Indies, based on the Javanese culture, with the study of Sanskrit and

Javanese instead of Latin, the arts and culture of India instead of the European classics. However, Bishop Callier of Haarlem, who had approved their plans, died and his successor had other ideas. The new bishop wanted the little group to work with Catholic girls and young women of the diocese of Haarlem. He laid down an ultimatum: either to accept the work he offered them or to disband. One by one, dressed in their best outfits and summoning all their tact and powers of persuasion, they went to plead with the bishop, explaining their missionary calling and the value of their approach to the Indonesian culture, but the bishop was unmoved. Finally, they spent an entire night in prayer. Jacques van Ginneken had just obtained his driver's license, and was immensely proud of it, though he was not a good driver and had already knocked down the gate of the estate and run over the flower bed. In keeping with his heroic approach to Christian living, he tore up his license, vowing never to drive again, if only God would change the bishop's mind. The bishop remained firm. With heavy hearts the group accepted the decision as God's will. With his characteristic optimism, van Ginneken soon saw possibilities in the new mandate: "Are they asking you to educate the young women of the working class? Well, I have an idea! We must turn our girls' education into a movement for the conversion of the world."[24]

Thus in 1928 the Grail as a youth movement was begun, and Lydwine at the age of twenty-three was launched into a career as president of a swiftly burgeoning, colorful, assertive movement of young women. For this movement Father van Ginneken chose the name Grail, which translates easily into most European languages, and carries the overtones of a heroic quest after a high and far-off ideal. "De Voorde" was transformed into the first Grail Center, with nine others soon to follow in the major cities of Holland.

As president, Lydwine had the experience of organizing hundreds and later thousands of young women, training leaders, setting up houses, producing the mass dramas with three thousand, seven thousand, ten thousand participants. Mia was the artist who had choreographed the movements for the three thousand in *The Royal Road of the Cross*, but on the day of the performance in Amsterdam's Olympic stadium, Margaret van Gilse realized that Mia, exhausted by the rehearsals, did not have the energy to direct the three thousand women on the field. She gave Lydwine the task of standing at the podium and directing the thousands, while Mia prayed. Lydwine, fit and fresh, made up for any lack of practice by the energy of her direction. That combination of spiritual demands and practical judgment was typically Grail.

To Lydwine also fell the experience of dealing with bishops and priests who were often not at all sympathetic to a woman's movement that claimed a large measure of autonomy. Bishop Aengenent had proclaimed the Grail to be the only youth movement for girls and young women in his diocese of Haarlem, but he was not always at hand when a crisis arose. Thus, he invited Lydwine to be on the diocesan youth council together with a number of the priests and prominent laymen, but when a priest proposed a rule that council members be at least twenty-five years old (thus excluding Lydwine who was only twenty-four), he did not object. And he left to Lydwine and Mia van der Kallen the difficult task of explaining to three hundred irritated priest moderators what was meant by the Grail slogan: "Women should lead women." Lydwine had experience, too, in defending the autonomy of the fledgling movement against priest leaders of other movements who were only too eager to absorb the Grail as part of their organizations. Her stands did not make her popular with the clergy. "It was good that I left for England," she reflected, "because I had become an impossible person here in clerical Holland."

In 1932 Lydwine was posted to England, again as President of the Grail, to work with Baroness Yvonne Bosch van Drakestein, who had already set up a Grail Center at Sloane Street in London and was attracting young members of the aristocracy to the lay apostolate. Again the Grail turned to mass dramas, among other activities, producing both the medieval miracle play, *Everyman*, and Francis Thompson's poem, *The Hound of Heaven*, in the Albert Hall in London. "We had three Grail Centers," Lydwine recalled, "one for the aristocracy, one for the students, one for the working girls. I think it was the first time in England that the aristocracy, the students, and the working classes all joined together in a project." In the midst of all the activity as head and spokesperson for the Grail, she completed her studies and was awarded the doctorate in 1936, just before she set sail for Australia, head of a team of five, charged to start the Grail in that huge, thinly populated land. After two years of strenuous work to establish the Grail in Australia, Lydwine was recalled to Europe to begin preparations for starting the Grail in the United States.

Joan Overboss

Joan Overboss was not the first choice to accompany Lydwine to America. The original intention had been that Dr. Alberta Lucker, one of the first German Grail members, should be part of the team, since she already had experience in England and had visited the United States with Lydwine in 1938. However, the outbreak of the war changed the plans. Joan Overboss was quite different from Lydwine in temperament and talents. Van Ginneken believed that a strong team required different, indeed opposite, temperaments and talents. The strength of the team depended not only on

the variety of gifts but also on the spiritual discipline, the patience and for-
bearance, required for generous cooperation between persons who were not
naturally attracted to one another. "Joan and I were never great friends,"
Lydwine remarked to me, "but we respected each other and we knew we
had to work together. We succeeded, partly because of our different viewpoints and ways of dealing with our task."[25] In a letter to Eileen Schaeffler,
she summed up Joan's role. "Joan and I started the Grail in America
together—it was a 50/50 deal. She had tremendous creativity and original-
ity, extraordinary generosity, a fantastic sense of humor, which, together
with her optimism, enabled us to overcome all difficulties. Without Joan,
the Grail would never have become what it is now in America."[26]

Joan was born Marietta Overboss to a middle-class family for whom
the idea of a university education for a daughter would not have occurred as
a possibility. Only a well-to-do elite considered sending a girl to university.
Joan's parents provided her with a good education at the Hogere Burger
School, the first Catholic secondary school for girls in Amsterdam. "We had
an excellent training," one of her schoolmates remembers, "five years of
thorough study of four languages, Dutch, German, French, and English;
economics, government, history, geography, biology, bookkeeping, drawing, embroidery. Afterwards, at eighteen or nineteen, most of us went on to
take a secretarial course, or to study physical education or nursing or social
work to prepare for a job." Her schoolmate remembers Joan as a strong,
vivid personality, good at sports and games, full of initiative and often taking the lead.[27]

By her own account,[28] Joan was teaching catechism to youngsters in
Amsterdam and was dissatisfied with the results, when she was approached
by a Grail leader ("someone with whom I am now working," she explained
in a talk at Doddridge Farm in 1942—presumably Lydwine): "I came to ask
if you are interested in the conversion of the world. If you are interested,
come next Sunday because we are having an important meeting. We will see
what you are and if you are worthy to be taken in." She was challenged by
the Grail vision and ideals and soon plunged into the work, starting small
groups among working girls in Amsterdam, capturing their interest through
sports, music, drama. The method was to begin with the current interest of
the girls and then draw them, step by step, into the idea of their task in the
conversion of the world. After a few years of this work, there were thousands of young women ready to participate in the mass dramas of *The
Royal Road of the Cross* and the *Pentecost Play*. The texts, setting forth the
basic Christian messages of the cross and the commandments of love, were
memorized, but more important, they were lived out in daily life in the
months of preparation. One of Joan's tasks for the first mass drama, *The
Royal Road of the Cross*, was to mark on the field of the Olympic Stadium

the white lines that indicated where each participant was to stand, a task that took her from sunset to dawn the following morning to complete.

The mass dramas and the dramatic appearance of the three-hundred-member Grail delegation at the Eucharistic Congress in Dublin impressed many of the bishops and invitations poured in, asking the Grail to start work in England, in Germany, in Australia. Joan was chosen, along with Ruth Bernard, to join Mia van der Kallen in starting the Grail in Berlin in June of 1932, at a time when Hitler was preparing to take power. Hitler took over the government in January of 1933, and in that same month the Grail performed *The Rorate Play* in the Sportspalast in Berlin with twelve hundred young women. The Christian youth groups were not yet forbidden but they were harassed by the Gestapo. Three hundred young Dutch women had come to help with *The Rorate Play* and were marching through Berlin to the cathedral when they were stopped by the police. Joan, who was leading the group, immediately started singing a popular song, "Wir lassen uns nicht halten," "We won't let ourselves be stopped"; the police laughed, applauded, and let the group through.[29]

From 1932 to 1939, Joan worked in Germany under increasingly difficult conditions as the girls' section of the Nazi movement took over the education of the young women. With her wit, charm, and courage, she managed for a long time to get permissions from the Nazi officials to continue Grail courses and activities. Finally, in August of 1939, the Grail was ordered to disband. Margaret van Gilse sent Lydwine to Germany to meet Joan and help her close down the Grail Centers. The Gestapo were already searching one of the three Grail houses in Berlin. The two women went quickly to the other two houses to collect and burn all important papers. It was crucial not to let any membership lists fall into Nazi hands. Then with heavy hearts, they got into their car and drove back to Holland, stopping from time to time to read Pope Pius XII's encyclical on Naziism, *Mit brennender Sorge*.

Joan was a daring and creative person, with a strong feeling for new ways of thinking and acting. She was a risk taker, a radical with a revolutionary spirit and the courage to follow her intuitions. A passionate person, she brought intensity and absorption to whatever she undertook. With her warmth and humor she could enliven any group she entered. She was an excellent storyteller who could recount the most ordinary event in a way to enchant her listeners. She did not have a particularly good voice, but she was a most effective song leader, able to catch up a group in her own zest and enjoyment of singing.

Lydwine and Joan made a good team to start the Grail in the United States. They were both young—Lydwine was thirty-five, Joan thirty-one—and brimming with vitality and enthusiasm. Lydwine was tall, almost six feet, a stately, dignified figure. Joan was medium height, rather stocky, with a jaunty and humorous air. Lydwine came from The Hague, which was a staid, sober, dignified official government city; Joan was from Amsterdam— a lively, irreverent, humorous, earthy city. The difference between the two cities, rather like that between Philadelphia and Brooklyn, was reflected in their temperaments and upbringing. Lydwine, with her strong liberal arts background, was an impressive speaker, able to inspire her listeners with a vision that demanded dedication. Joan's approach was more informal—she was usually ready with a witty comment.

While Lydwine and Joan were in full agreement on the task of women in the conversion of the world and on the importance of a solid spiritual formation for the lay apostolate, their views tended to diverge increasingly as they entered more deeply into American Catholic life. Lydwine's experience in Holland, England, and Australia had made her adept at dealing with the bishops, reassuring them about the soundness of the lay apostolate; she tended to think in terms of working within established guidelines and within the existing Grail structures. Joan, out of her experience in Germany, had worked in opposition to government structures and both temperamentally and experientially was inclined to question authority, whether in the state or the church or the Grail. In the first years at Doddridge and Grailville, I did not detect these differences of approach. Our two leaders seemed to me to be absolutely united and in full agreement on all issues. I marveled at the way Lydwine could glance at Joan across the room and Joan would know immediately what Lydwine had in mind and would proceed to carry it out. However, once Joan started in Detroit, their underlying differences became quite pronounced and were a source of tensions and conflicts that we did not have the means to resolve.

Reflecting on the first years in the United States, Lydwine remarked: "It was good that Joan and I were cut off from Holland during the war. Otherwise, I would have been going to Holland often to discuss things, and more Dutch women would have come. But, as it was, we had no contact for four or five years and had immediately to rely on the Americans."[30] Thus, the Grail quickly took root in the lives of American young women and it was soon possible to rebut charges that Grail innovations were "European."

Mary Louise Tully

The third member of the team, Mary Louise Tully, "the first American," was still in Holland when Lydwine and Joan arrived in Chicago in May, 1940. The two Dutch women were invited to stay with the Tully family, since Doddridge Farm, "the beautiful site" of the bishop's telegram, was by no means ready for occupancy. John Tully, Mary Louise's father, was an

Irish Catholic, Notre Dame graduate, close friend of Archbishop O'Hara. He was a successful businessman, a banker, and a founder of the Thomas More Association, which promoted Catholic books. Her mother, Anina Melcher, a convert and former schoolteacher, was active as a leader in her community. After Mary Louise graduated from the College of St. Teresa, in Winona, Minnesota, her parents took their three daughters on a European tour. Mary Louise, who had read about the Grail in *Commonweal* and *Ave Maria*, was eager to meet this new group. Through Frank Sheed, John Tully secured an invitation to tea with Baroness Yvonne Bosch van Drakestein at the Grail Center in London. The Baroness, in turn, gave the Tullys an introduction to the Grail in Holland. From her early teens, Mary Louise had wanted to help convert America. "I didn't think in terms of domination, but in terms that it would be good for people, give them joy and love. I wanted to give my life to God, but not as a nun. I thought nuns were too much removed from ordinary people."[31] She was impressed with the people she met, with the articles in the English *Grail Magazine*, with the vitality of the plays, most especially with the fact that these young women were proudly and confidently witnessing to their faith in a public way.

In September of 1938, Mary Louise returned to England as a Grail guest and soon made the decision to become a trainee. She was on retreat in Holland when England entered World War II, so she stayed on in neutral Holland. The formation program continued despite the approach of the war. "I was ripe for that lifestyle at that moment," she recalled.[32] "I am grateful for that time of almost total silence, centered on the Eucharist. It does something to you—like living in a different country." She was in Amsterdam in May of 1940 to see the Nazis occupy the city "with beardless youths on motorcycles." She helped other Grail members destroy Grail records, tearing them into bits and flushing them down the toilets. Soon it was clear that if she stayed on in Holland, she would be a danger to the other Grail members. As a U.S. citizen, she was free to leave, but it was difficult to find transportation. Every day she went to the American Express Office, carrying her suitcase and hoping to be able to buy a bus or train ticket. Finally, she was able to join forces with a Jewish family and by a devious route make her way across southern France to Spain and then to Lisbon where she boarded a freighter to New York. When she arrived in New York, she had just enough money for bus fare to Chicago.

Early Days at Doddridge Farm

The summer months were not an easy time for Lydwine and Joan. The Tullys were terribly worried about the fate of their daughter. Every night, after listening to the war news on the radio, they would quiz their guests:

Figure 1. Joan Overboss, Lydwine van Kersbergen, and Mary Louise Tully in a planning session at Doddridge Farm, Libertyville, Illinois, September 1940.

"How far is the Tiltenberg from Rotterdam?" as they tried to calculate whether the day's bombing had come close to their child.

Then, too, there were difficulties in their situation at Doddridge Farm. The property had been standing vacant for quite some time and was in poor condition—leaky roofs, broken windows, plumbing out of order, mice nesting in the mattresses, and squirrels scampering in the rooms. The committee charged with overseeing the renovations did not plan efficiently; money was wasted; some repairs were badly done. The group of teenagers from a home for underprivileged boys, sent by the Bishop to help with the clean-up and the landscaping, were unruly, poorly supervised, and often destroyed more than they repaired. When Mary Louise returned at the end of August, she found Lydwine and Joan dividing their time between her family home and Doddridge Farm, as they worked to get the buildings furnished and to make them habitable.

A second American, Mary Catherine Leahy, arrived at Doddridge that first summer. Recently graduated from Bishop McDonnell High School in Brooklyn, she had heard about the Grail from Father James Coffey. "I have a girl for you," he had told Lydwine when he met her in New York, and promptly arranged an interview for Mary Catherine. The Leahy family were recovering from the depression. Catherine had a job as a waitress in a department store, which allowed her a one-week vacation. She responded eagerly to Lydwine's invitation to visit at Doddridge Farm, and after her arrival, took Lydwine's advice: "My child, you cannot decide anything in a week." She immediately gave up her job and stayed on for the summer.[33]

By the end of August, 1940, there were four women residing at Doddridge Farm, two Dutch, two American. They were conscious that they were pioneering, on the cutting edge. They were women in a hurry, impelled by a sense of urgency, based on van Ginneken's idea about "the elbow of time." In 1932 he had estimated the window of opportunity for significant change at fifty years; in 1940 Lydwine had crossed out fifty and penciled in seventy-five. Either way, time was short and they needed to move fast. However, they were deeply convinced that an effective lay movement required serious, in-depth formation of lay leaders and were committed to take the necessary time for that. They knew that they were introducing a new element into American Catholicism—attractive young women who were serious about living a committed Christian life and were not nuns. They went about their work confidently, steadfastly refusing to be slotted into existing categories, patiently correcting misconceptions that were rein-forced by an article in *Time* magazine about "nuns in mufti."[34] "Mufti" literally means not in uniform, or in this case, not in a religious habit. The reporter who coined the phrase, impressed by the red flowered dress Mary Louise was wearing, evidently thought we were nuns in disguise. In fact, there are nuns in mufti in the Catholic Church, women who are fully quali-fied vowed religious, but who live in the parental home, hold a job, and wear ordinary dress to facilitate their contacts with others. They maintain secrecy about their religious commitment. That was emphatically not the Grail idea. We were laywomen, striving to demonstrate that holiness was for everyone. Our effectiveness depended on the principle of "like to like." We wanted our very being to say to the young women we met, "See, we are lay like you, we are striving to lead a full Christian life in the world and you can do this too." The article haunted us for years—every reporter writing on the Grail and doing any research quickly found it in the *Guide to Periodical Literature.*

Four women in a hurry to change the world—what were their hopes and plans?

2

Doddridge Farm

Novitiate for the Laity, 1940–1943

"We want to make Doddridge Farm a novitiate for the laity," Lydwine Van Kersbergen explained to me as we were sitting under a tree near the Round Table, the reception building, one June day in 1941. She went on to enlarge on the importance of a thorough, solid spiritual formation if the laity were to take seriously their role as leaders in the apostolate.

At that moment she was recruiting me as a counselor in the summer camp for underprivileged children which the Grail was undertaking at the request of Bishop Sheil—and Doddridge was an ideal place for a summer camp. The property was not a real farm, but an estate of a hundred or so acres of wooded land near Libertyville on Chicago's North Shore. Built by the Episcopal Diocese as a summer camp for children, it had eventually been taken over by the Catholic Archdiocese. It was laid out as a little village, with the chapel at one end, the dining hall in the middle, the assembly hall and swimming pool at the other end, the dormitories in between, all nicely landscaped and connected by winding paths. Volunteers, under Grail direction, had painted the buildings in bright colors, yellow, blue, green. All the colors of the rainbow adorned the rafters in the Assembly Hall.

I had already taken part in the first Grail course in the United States, Holy Week of 1941, which was a revelation to me of the depth and riches of Catholic life. As a recent convert, baptized in 1937 and searching for a way to live my faith more fully, I was deeply impressed by the experience of community—prayer and work, fasting and feasting, study and song, in a group of forty young women. We participated actively in the Mass, reciting or singing the responses, and in paraliturgies, that is, unofficial forms of prayer, inspired by the themes of the sacred triduum (the three days before Easter). I was particularly struck by the time on Good Friday when we gathered around a large wooden cross on the grounds and said our own spontaneous prayers for all sorts and conditions of people. My task was to pray for the Jews. My voice

49

shook as I spoke my prayer—this was a new experience for me, to share my inmost thoughts and feelings in a large group, quite different from voicing my opinion in a discussion or giving a lecture. At Mass, we sang after communion, a radical departure from the usual individualistic "time alone with Jesus." The Grail spirituality was communal; the Mystical Body meant that the life of grace was a shared life; the Grail called for sharing the intimacy of prayer and the joy of communion. This was living the liturgy, being the Mystical Body, active at the altar, actively reaching out to the whole world. The elation of this experience stayed with me for weeks afterward.

The summer camps were not a work which the Grail would have chosen. In her letters and reports to Bishop Sheil Lydwine stressed a number of short- and long-term goals:

1. to get acquainted with America and American Catholics through traveling and lecturing, meeting priests, religious, and lay leaders;
2. to build up, gradually and slowly, a novitiate for "free workers,"[1] American young women who would give their whole lives to the apostolate (she stressed the need for a three-year program of strict spiritual discipline, in privacy and solitude, apart from all apostolic activities);
3. to train other leaders who would work as apostles in their own surroundings and to create a spirit of cooperation among the different groups (she disavowed any intention of starting a special Grail movement, at least not until there would be a well-trained group of Americans to take the lead); and
4. to start an agricultural college for women.

This last point was a new departure for the Grail, a result of Lydwine's meeting with Msgr. Luigi Ligutti, founder of the Catholic Rural Life Conference. She had been deeply impressed by his arguments in favor of the farm or at least the homestead as the ideal environment in which to raise a family. She was also of the opinion that American young women lacked vitality—too much dieting. She saw the farm with its good food and outdoor work as a way to improve their health. Then, too, the farm had economic advantages—raising our own food could save on the food bills.

In the report, she also listed a number of other possibilities as part of a ten-year plan: a school for women aviators; an apostolate among the Negroes; a department of Catholic culture; a film department; a publications center; work among non-Catholics; work with women in the factories; work among educated women in the missions; a marriage preparation apostolate for women by women.[2] A school for women aviators was in line with Father van Ginneken's idea of embracing modern technology. Moreover, Lydwine and Joan thought that flying would attract the right sort of young women—courageous, capable, risk-taking types. As soon as Mary Louise Tully could be spared from Doddridge, she was sent to a flying school, completed the training and received her pilot's license in November of 1943. However, she never made use of her skill, although she remained briefly at the school as a ground instructor.

Lydwine continually emphasized the need to start slowly, to build on a solid foundation of spiritually trained people, and to avoid premature publicity. While Bishop Sheil never explicitly disagreed with these goals, often he simply ignored them. The first task he assigned to the Grail was to prepare for the arrival at Doddridge Farm of five hundred refugee children from war-torn Europe. When no refugee children were forthcoming, he changed the task to summer camps for children from the inner city. The Bishop was evidently not a long-range planner. A memo dated June 9, 1941, of a meeting between the Bishop, the Ladies of the Grail, and the CYO staff reports a discussion on whether to have the camp, how to raise the $5,000 needed for a minimum budget, and how to get competent staff since there was no budget for staff salaries. The decision—to start the camp on July 7—allowed exactly twenty-seven days for preparations. The Bishop volunteered to be personally responsible for the $5,000 budget (his staff were insistent that none of the other CYO budgets could be drawn on for the camp!); the Grail agreed to provide competent staff at no salary.[3]

I was one of the forty-five volunteers who staffed the camp—drawn from the colleges, the parishes, and the Catholic Action groups where Lydwine, Joan, and Mary Louise had been speaking during the year. I soon became aware that there were at least three levels of activity going on simultaneously at Doddridge Farm: the camp program for the children; the apostolic training for the counselors; and the novitiate for the small group preparing to become Ladies of the Grail.

Lydwine's personal slogan was "*In omnibus rebus respice finem,*" roughly translated as "always keep your eye on the ball" or "never lose sight of your goal." Her two primary goals were to establish the novitiate and to train other lay leaders; she and Joan worked out an ingenious plan to make the burdensome task of the children's camps serve both these ends. First, they created a special atmosphere by naming the buildings, the tasks, and the program sessions according to the Grail legend. Thus, the reception building became the Round Table; the dormitories were Galahad, Percival, Gawaine and Gareth; the leaders in the dormitories, Pages in the service of the King; leaders in the activities, Jesters. Cleaning was "Slaying the Dragon"; the activities program was dubbed "In Quest of Adventure" and took groups in turn to the following areas: Camelot, the playing field; the Swan, the swimming pool; the Magic Grove, the handicraft center; the Promised Land, the garden. After supper, the "Ladies of Sir Galahad" were invited to the "Witching Hour," storytelling for the youngest campers before "Diminuendo" and the

"Perfect End," undressing and going to bed. Counselors and children entered into the game with zest.

The program for all three groups was integrated around the special theme chosen for each day and explicitly related to the lay apostolate and the liturgy of the day. Thus, the first camp had as theme "The Virtues of an Apostle," and began with two days on the idea of the Mystical Body and what it requires of Christians as a cooperative community. As part of the training for the counselors, there were regular evening sessions in which the theme of the next day was discussed, both in its application to their own lives and in terms they could use with the children. For instance, the theme of the Mystical Body was interpreted as "Family Day" and carried out practically by counselors and campers together undertaking all the necessary work of the camp as members of one family helping each other. Often the counselors had the benefit of talks by leaders in the liturgical movement—Msgr Reynold Hillenbrand, rector of the seminary; Gerald Ellard, SJ., author of numerous influential books on the liturgy; Godfrey Diekmann, OSB, editor of *Orate Fratres*, the leading liturgical journal—who were taking part in a liturgical summer school for priests at nearby Mundelein Seminary. Part of my task was to make the arrangements for these special events.

Each morning, everyone participated in a *Missa Recitata*, a Mass with the congregation making all the responses. I had special sessions with the children to teach them the Latin responses and explain their meaning. At the Mass, the Epistle and the Gospel of the day were read in English. These practices were an innovation, regarded with suspicion by some priests. At the meals, there were readings and explanations related to the theme of the day. After evening prayers everyone was asked to keep the "Great Silence" until breakfast the next morning, a practice that incidentally afforded a measure of privacy in the crowded dormitories. Each counselor had her own personal program, which included a book for spiritual reading, a half hour for private mental prayer, and a time for manual work in addition to her task in the camp program.

The work with the children was often not easy. We had a camp rule that you finished whatever was on your plate. Many of the children were not used to that level of discipline. I have a vivid memory of Mary Alice Duddy sitting in the dining hall with her twenty-four young charges after everyone else had gone on to the morning's activities, insisting that no one was to leave the table until everyone had eaten all her porridge. Among the campers, there were eighteen African-American children, five Chinese, seventeen non-Catholics. One day there was a racial incident, one child called another "nigger." The leader in that group took the time before night prayers to explain in detail to the children just how unchristian and unloving such conduct was. "In the end," she told me afterward, "they were all weeping, and that line in the *Salve*

Regina (a favorite hymn to the Virgin Mary) about 'this vale of tears' took on new meaning for me."

Another important feature of the program was the Christian use of leisure time—how to use our leisure in ways consistent with our values. The camp had the usual talent nights when the campers volunteered to entertain each other. The Grail leaders and the counselors were often shocked by the songs, dances, and jokes the children chose, as well as by the comic books and pulp magazines they brought with them. "The stories with which they seemed most familiar," the report notes, "dealt with murder, seduction and sudden death."[4] We made strenuous efforts to find folk songs, singing games, folk dances, and folk stories to replace these elements of popular culture. Joan Overboss was a gifted leader in this field and could teach songs in a way to fascinate a group. The experience made clear the need for a Christian culture and led to later Grail work in expressing Christian values through the arts.

This level of integrated Christian living was quite alien to the CYO staff, a priest and a religious brother, who were in charge of the twenty boys from a Catholic institution. The boys were supposed to be taking care of the landscaping. The staff were quite hostile to the Grail program and regarded many of the Grail practices with suspicion as "European" and not suited to the United States.

In the midst of the program for the children and the introduction to the apostolate for the counselors, the five young women who had been accepted for the novitiate went on with their training. Initially, the diocese had placed a farmhouse, separate from the camp, at their disposal, but unfortunately this building had burned down. Undaunted, Lydwine and Joan continued the training in the midst of the camp. Even though it was not possible to provide physical solitude, psychological solitude was possible. I remember how impressed I was at seeing these young women going about their work in silence in the kitchen, setting the tables, serving the meals, washing up, working in the garden. One afternoon I stopped Josephine Drabek as she was pushing her wheelbarrow to the kitchen to ask her a question. She simply smiled at me, put her finger to her lips, and went on her way.

The pattern of the summer camp exemplified van Ginneken's idea of working with a nucleus and a periphery as a series of concentric circles. The intensity of spirit of the core group radiated outward simply through attitude and example without a word being spoken. In their turn the counselors could immediately put their new ideas and attitudes to work in dealing with the children. With all its difficulties and shortcomings, the camp nevertheless became a Christian community with a perceptible vitality and joyfulness. The report on the summer concludes:

> The incorporation into a real Christian community is a very effective means of training young women to be apostles. The fundamental values, the basic attitudes are transformed and supernaturalized

simply by the example and fervor of the group. The experience of this summer camp made it evident that much more can be accomplished in training American young women for the apostolate by concentrating the training in unbroken periods rather than spreading it over several weeks or months. A weekend spent in living the supernatural life in a group, free from distractions and interruptions, is much more effective than the same amount of time spread out over a series of weekly meetings.[5]

Once the summer camps were concluded, the small group at Doddridge continued a three-pronged program: the novitiate; a traveling team, making contacts and speaking at schools and parishes; and the reception of various Catholic groups coming to Doddridge for a day or a weekend. There was a Grail course at Christmas 1941, and a two-week program, *The Vineyard*, in June of 1942, before the second series of summer camps, which again brought four hundred children from Chicago to Doddridge. *The Vineyard* dealt with the Mystical Body and the lay priesthood as the foundations for the lay apostolate, with Father Benedict Ehmann, well-known liturgical leader, speaking on the social character of the church; Vincent McAloon, a young layman, treating the need for radical Christianity; Monsignor Hillenbrand, giving his moving discourse on the Mass and the Cross, and my friend, graduate student Bob Heywood, drawing on the ideas of Professor Frank O'Malley to present an eloquent talk on the sacramentality of life. The two weeks were rounded out by Catholic Worker artist Ade Bethune on sacramentality and the dignity of manual labor. In September, after the children's camps were over, there was another two-week program for young women, a Rural Life School, with Professor Willis Nutting of Notre Dame, philosopher Mortimer Adler of the University of Chicago, and Emerson Hynes of the "back-to-the-land " group in Minnesota as speakers.

By October of 1942, I had given up my job at the University of Chicago, teaching Great Books with Mortimer Adler and Robert Hutchins, and decided to join the core group at Doddridge, giving my life to full-time work in the Grail. My first task was to barnstorm the country with Joan Overboss, speaking to any groups that would have us in Pittsburg, Philadelphia, New York, Columbus, Springfield, Peoria, and Green Bay before Christmas and going as far west as the Dakotas after Christmas. Our message was simple and direct, namely, that holiness was not just for priests and nuns, that we were all called to be saints and to play a part as laywomen and men in the spreading of the Good Tidings. Our talks usually evoked decisive responses: young women were either strongly attracted or wanted no part of the lay apostolate; very few remained neutral. After a talk, we would meet with small groups, make suggestions for what they could do in their own environment, and urge some of them to come to Doddridge for training.

We had continually to defend our lay status, not helped at all by that "nuns in mufti" article in *Time* magazine. One of the Grail practices was to wear bright colors as an expression of the joy of Christian life. For the lecture tour, I had acquired a kelly green wool suit with a red-and-yellow-flowered blouse. There was a collection of donated clothing at Doddridge from which Joan had to make up a travel outfit, since money was in very short supply. The best she could do was a blue-and-yellow plaid coat and a red-and-green plaid dress; the two plaids clashed unbearably, but everywhere we went she was asked, "Is that your uniform?" The concept of lay apostles, that is, laywomen living an intense Christian life in the world, was a difficult one for people to grasp. They wanted to slot us into their existing set of categories while we wanted to disrupt those categories. However, this mentality made it easy for us to create an impression as speakers—all we had to do was to appear on the platform in our bright outfits and talk about the apostolate as an "all saints movement." The newspaper reports reflect the fascination of the press with this novelty—women, not in habits, talking enthusiastically about living for God.

At the beginning of Lent in 1943, Joan and I returned to Doddridge. After the hectic activity of the road, I was plunged into the strict discipline of the training. Living at Doddridge in a Chicago winter with its blizzards and subzero temperatures was already an experience of austerity. The buildings had been built for summer, no foundations, the wind whistled up through the floorboards. We had space heaters that burned oil and had to be filled by hand from five-gallon cans, but they were totally inadequate for their task of heating the dormitory. If I moved more than five yards from the heater, I might as well have been outside. Mary Louise Tully remembers, "I wore my gloves in the house all winter long." As sacristan I remember putting hot water in the cruet for Mass, hoping that it would not freeze before the priest needed to pour a few drops into the chalice. Mundelein Seminary furnished a priest for our daily Mass in the chilly chapel. Mary Louise had the task of driving the fifteen miles to pick up the priest, a task that often involved shoveling the snow from the garage driveway in the early hours of the morning.

The training was built on the traditional Catholic spirituality of the pursuit of perfection, using as texts the Bible, the *Imitation of Christ*, and *The Practice of Perfection and Christian Virtues* by Rodriguez (a sixteenth-century Jesuit), and employing the traditional means of prayer, fasting, watching, physical penance, almsgiving. However, the Grail gave the traditional approach a special character through two particular emphases: careful adaptation to the needs of each individual; and the consistent refusal to allow anything to be done *pro forma*, that is, routinely. One of van Ginneken's insights was that almost all spiritual books had been written by men for men and were therefore poorly adapted to the needs of women, whose faults were quite different from those of men. In this respect he anticipated some aspects of the work of feminist theologians in the 1970s, for instance, Valerie Saiving's analysis of the difference in men's and women's sins. Above all he insisted that a meaningful asceticism should address the dominant faults of the individual; she should be challenged to use her initiative in devising mortifications to fit her individual needs and to develop her individual gifts and talents. We did not yet think in terms of a lay spirituality—we followed a spiritual discipline more severe than that of many religious communities—but we were certainly experiential.

Not for the Grail the recitation of prescribed vocal prayers that so easily become a formal routine. Prayer should be encounter with the living God in the liturgy of the Church and in personal meditation. To keep participation in the liturgy alive, the training stressed the active role of the Christian in the Mass through reciting or singing the responses, offertory and communion processions, and personal intentions voiced at the appropriate time. Time was spent in studying the liturgical texts and working out their practical application in our daily lives. We were encouraged to memorize the psalms and liturgical hymns, to steep our minds in the sacred texts. Almost everyone memorized certain Latin hymns—*Salve Regina, Veni Sancte Spiritus, Veni Creator Spiritus*—and a few people memorized an English version of all one hundred and fifty psalms. There was a group meditation every morning, with the leader reading from a text, pausing after every few sentences to discuss its meaning and practical application. The focus was always on how do we live what we believe. More contemporary writers were used along with Rodriguez: Cardinal Newman, Abbot Columba Marmion, popular retreat leader Edward Leen, Abbot Vonier. And each person was given a meditation book for her own use, chosen to suit her educational background and particular interests, and was encouraged to become better acquainted with the Bible—the Hebrew scriptures as well as the Gospels and Epistles. Other means were also used to help people learn to meditate. I remember Mary Louise one day inviting me to meditate by putting myself in the place of Isaac as Abraham prepared to sacrifice his son. She tied my wrists and ankles, a method that certainly stimulated my imagination to enter into Isaac's experience. Often an individual would be given a day or a half-day of prayer in a quiet spot in the woods. To concretize the idea of surrender to the will of God, another member of the group would be charged with directing this kind of retreat, bringing the individual a text on which to meditate, a meal of bread and water, a pleasant surprise of a ripe peach or a bar of chocolate.

Meaningful asceticism requires self-knowledge and self-knowledge requires *feedback*, to use a term current in group dynamics. The Grail novitiate provided a number of channels for feedback. First of all, each individual had a mentor who helped her to work out her personal program; following the traditional spiritual wisdom about avoiding self-will, no one was to undertake any special penance without permission from her mentor or from the leader in charge of the group. At each season of the church year, the group would meet and decide on some practices that everyone would follow—for instance, extra times of silence, or a basic fasting menu for Lent. Throughout the year, there was a strong norm against wasting food; one was always supposed to finish everything on her plate, including sometimes unfortunate experiments by an inexperienced cook. Initially some of the old monastic forms of penance were used, but soon these were quietly abandoned in favor of mortifications arising naturally in the course of the daily work. In the barn and gardens, kitchen and studio, office and publications center, there was ample opportunity to test one's limits.

Then, there was the giving of tasks. A group of women, living and working together, a good part of the time in silence, are excellent observers of the mote in the other's eye. When the community was gathered at meals or prayer, one could ask permission to give a task to another or propose a task for oneself, for example: "Ellen, I notice that when you are keeping silence, you do a lot of looking around and gesturing. I'd like to give you the task to keep your eyes down for the next two days to help you keep recollected." Or, "May I have permission to rise at midnight and pray for an hour for the traveling team?" All tasks had to be approved by the leader presiding, who used her mature judgment in granting or amending them. As part of the Mystical Body, sharing the life of grace with each other, we were conscious that both our gifts and our faults affected the community. Hence, there was a practice of confession of faults, when the community gathered at a meal time or prayer time. For instance, if two people had had an angry disagreement over the work, one or both might confess this fault at the next opportunity, ask forgiveness of each other, and ask the leader for an additional task. We tried hard to practice the scriptural injunction, "Let not the sun go down upon your wrath." We were not above sometimes conspiring with each other to line up so many tasks before the meal that the leader was kept busy dispensing judgment while the soup got cold.

There was also the possibility to draw on the insights of the whole group by asking for feedback from the group as such. In this case, after a period of silent prayer, each member of the community told the individual how she perceived her strengths and weaknesses in a process which we called "spiritual alms." I had come from a group of graduate students at the University of Chicago in which we regularly gave each other straight feedback, usually one-on-one, and often accompanied by pointed recommendations for personal improvement. I was delighted to discover similar practices in the Grail and considered them a great improvement on the forms I was used to, precisely because they were placed in a religious context, seeking the guidance of the Holy Spirit and striving to be informed by love rather than less worthy motives. For the most part, we intuitively followed the rules for constructive feedback that I later learned in group dynamics classes: feedback should be specific, about recent and modifiable behavior, nonjudgmental, given one point at a time, when the recipient is ready for it. For myself, and I think for most of the others in our training group, these practices were liberating, promoting personal growth in self-knowledge and self-acceptance and strengthening the bonds of community. On the whole, there was a tremendous release of energy, spontaneity, and creativity because we felt free to be ourselves in a community that accepted and supported us.

Although we spent a good deal of our time in silence, we came to know each other intimately through the spiritual sharing which was a powerful means of bridging both class and educational differences. The ideal that permeated the training was the value of total self-giving, expressed concretely in obedience to the entire chain of command in small things as well as large. Obedience, cheerfully and generously given, made it possible to marshal the energies of individuals effectively around a program or project. Often we all pitched in together, Lydwine and Joan included, to get a particular job done, whether it was canning an unexpected gift of bushels of ripe tomatoes or organizing a big mailing. I experienced this kind of common work as a powerful means of building group unity. Under the impetus of assigned tasks, many individuals developed capacities and talents that otherwise might well have remained dormant. Personally, it was through Grail tasks that I learned to speak effectively in public, organize a group, write brochures and articles, put together a prayer hour, work as the member of a team, and make requests of famous people without shyness. Of course, much depended on the maturity, discernment and wisdom of the leaders. As the numbers grew and less experienced young women were placed in charge, mistakes were made: some tasks were inappropriate, even damaging to the recipient. Sometimes demands were placed on individuals which created resentments and other psychological problems, but on the whole I think that the giving of tasks did promote personal growth.

What Barbara Ellen Wald wrote after her first year at Doddridge, I think expressed the feelings of the rest of us:

> This has been the most exciting year of my life! I have spent my first year with the Grail. If you had told me last June that I was a "minimum" Christian suffering from spiritual anemia, I would have protested vigorously! . . . The confined cramped little 'alley' of my individual spiritual life has suddenly miraculously expanded and I find myself marching joyously in the ranks of the Church Militant on the vast avenue towards heaven! Through this short time at the Grail, I have learned a little of what it means to live the life of the Church and to live it wholeheartedly . . . a truly valuable adventure—and best of all, the beginning of a new life for me on an entirely different level.[6]

3

Women in Search of Autonomy

The Move to Grailville, 1943–1944

In the spring of 1943, the difficulties with the Archdiocese of Chicago came to a head. The number in the novitiate had increased to nine. Mary Louise had been dispatched to Louisiana to try to interest a group of young African-American women in the apostolate. Those of us at home base were busy preparing for an expanded summer program, five courses of two or three weeks plus four two-week periods of leadership training in the summer camps for the children from Chicago. We had printed and distributed ten thousand colorful flyers to all the contacts the traveling team had made in their scores of lectures across the country, and registrations for the courses were coming in.

Our preparations for the summer were integrated into our Lenten program of prayer and penance. Mary Louise, back at Doddridge for a Lenten retreat, had prepared a group meditation in dramatic form based on the Book of Job. We went in procession from place to place—the cross on the hill, the vegetable garden, the porch of one of the cottages—stopping at each site for a brief episode to be enacted to inspire our prayer. For a major scene in the drama, Mary Louise had chosen as a setting our new compost heap, built in the approved organic form of a truncated pyramid with sloping sides. Lydwine as Job, dressed in a burlap robe, sat on the compost pile and lamented her losses. We completed our meditation in peace; the next morning at breakfast, Lydwine told us that her laments were truly heartfelt, for the archbishop had ruled that we were to leave Doddridge Farm by the beginning of June.

It was an unexpected blow, although tensions with the diocese had been present from the beginning. Cardinal Mundelein had died before any of the practicalities could be settled. Bishop Sheil as an auxiliary had limited authority to make decisions. He and Lydwine van Kersbergen were temperamentally and culturally poles apart. Lydwine was a university graduate who had earned her PhD in philology; the Bishop was an athlete, who would have become a professional baseball player had he not decided to enter the seminary. Lydwine, the dignified Dutch woman, was usually referred to by the rest of us as "the Doctor." Bishop Sheil, the rough-and-ready Irish-American, greeted her with a boisterous, "Hi, Doc!" to which she gamely replied, "Hi, Bish," though "Your Lordship" or at least "Your Excellency" would have come more readily to her lips. Lydwine emphasized a Christian culture as a key element in building an apostolate among young women; the Bishop as the founder of the CYO and its Golden Gloves boxing tournaments was at home with street gangs and prize fighters. The Grail wanted to start slowly and quietly to build a well-trained group of American leaders before launching big public programs. The Bishop wanted large-scale activities immediately and insisted that any publicity was a good thing. The Grail was interested in turning the education of girls and young women into a movement for the conversion of the world. The CYO had as its aim recreation, education, and social service for underprivileged boys and girls. "Bishop Sheil wanted social work in Chicago," Lydwine explained. "To get a job in Chicago and earn a few dollars, what's the use? How do you influence people if you work eight hours a day at a job nobody wants?"[1] The Grail wanted to train lay apostles, leaders who would influence their surroundings with the Gospel message. The CYO staff, at least those who worked at Doddridge Farm, were satisfied with the routine observance of ordinary "good Catholics": Mass on Sunday, confession once a month, a hasty "Our Father" to begin classes in a Catholic school. They accepted the division between religion and the rest of life characteristic of a secular society and were not responsive to the Grail idea of building a Christian culture.

Doddridge Farm belonged to the Catholic Archdiocese, a point which Archbishop Stritch stressed in his criticism of the brochure announcing the summer course, *The Vineyard*, in June of 1942. "It is hardly true," he wrote, "that Bishop Sheil placed at your disposal the Doddridge Farm. The Bishop very kindly arranged for you presently to use the Doddridge Farm which is a property of THE CATHOLIC BISHOP OF CHICAGO." [sic][2] Bishop Sheil's cable of invitation was dated December 30, 1939. Cardinal Mundelein had died October 2, 1939. Samuel Stritch was appointed archbishop of Chicago on December 27, 1939. In his conversations with Lydwine, Archbishop Stritch insisted that the Grail was in his diocese illegally.[3] Evidently Bishop Sheil had sent the invitation without Archbishop Stritch's knowledge, perhaps following an earlier directive of Cardinal Mundelein.

The position of the Grail was ambiguous at best, more than guests, since they were charged with preparing to receive hundreds of children, but less than directors, since they did not have control of the physical environment. When Lydwine and Joan first arrived, the place, which had been vacant for a long time, was dirty and dilapidated. One of the first issues between the Grail and the Bishop had to do with the repairs. The committee in charge of the renovations, in the opinion of Lydwine and Joan, mismanaged the project, did not keep track of tools and supplies, let the carpenter erect a new building on an unsuitable site, and insisted that the painters work on Sunday. Grail protests were overruled by the Bishop, who exhorted the Grail to be more friendly to the repair committee. The groups of boys from diocesan institutions whom the Bishop sent out to help with the work were another problem, more of a hindrance than a help.[4]

After the place was renovated and the camps had begun, the Bishop continued to send a group of twenty boys from "Our Lady of the Missions," to do the landscaping. The problems with the boys escalated: they went joy-riding in the cars of the Grail's visitors; they took gasoline from the farm tanks and one lad, trying to start a fire in the bath house with gasoline, caused an explosion which resulted in severe burns for himself; they misused tools and machinery, damaging the farm truck and wrecking a new mowing machine after using it for a few weeks. Instead of being reprimanded, they were treated to movies and ice cream.

When protests to Bishop Sheil proved of no avail, Lydwine finally wrote a carefully phrased report to Archbishop Stritch.[5] In addition to the lack of supervision of the boys, she listed the following difficulties in trying to work with Bishop Sheil and the CYO: the use of Doddridge Farm as a year-around recreation center for young people, leaving little space for the Grail training programs; the presence of a caretaker whom Lydwine considered untrustworthy both with the farm supplies (he tried to sell tools from the farm in Libertyville) and with the young women; Sunday work by the volunteers; insistence on publicity and open house for reporters; disagreements about appropriate dress for the campers and counselors; undermining of the Grail's authority over the camp program—the CYO staff at the camp encouraged both children and counselors to ignore the Grail rules, telling them that the Grail was too strict and too pious with regard to dress, smoking, and drinking; difficulties arising from mixed groups. This last point was of particular concern, since the physical layout of Doddridge with its twenty-two separate buildings and acres of grounds and woods made supervision difficult. Although the Archbishop had ordered that the boys and girls should be kept strictly separate, the brothers in charge of the boys allowed them to hang around the dormitories and take the older girls for walks in the woods. When one of the junior counselors stayed out in the woods with a boy until after midnight, Lydwine sent her home the next day. Bishop Sheil disagreed with this decision, telling Lydwine that she did not understand American young people.

Underlying the general incompatibility between the Grail and the CYO was still another difficulty; the fact that Lydwine had turned to Archbishop Stritch for help broke the relationship with Bishop Sheil. In the spring of 1943, Bishop Sheil announced that Doddridge would be used by the government for recreation for the armed forces; then, that it would be turned into a boys' camp for the summer of 1943, regardless of the Grail's plans. Archbishop Stritch's solution was to insist that the Grail find its own place. He wrote:

> The use of Doddrige Farm solely by you involves a commitment on my part which is not possible. . . . After much deliberation, I have reached the conclusion that the only sound solution of your problem is in your establishing yourselves on a property for your sole use. . . . This may involve some immediate difficulties, even the omission of your Summer School this year, but if it is done, you will begin to place your work on a solid footing. It is the condition on which I agree to undertake the direction and supervision of it.[6]

We accepted the Archbishop's decision as the will of God, but there was no way we were going to give up our plans for the summer program. We immediately began to cast around for another place. Since Mary Alice Duddy, Mary Anne Kimbell, and I had all been active members of the Calvert Club, the Catholic student club at the University of Chicago, we at once thought of Childerley, a country estate near Wheeling, Illinois, belonging to that group. The property was a gift to the Calvert Club by Frances Crane Lilly, daughter of the Crane plumbing family and wife of the dean of biological sciences at the University. Frances Lilly, a devout Episcopalian with a devotion to St. Francis of Assisi, had enriched the property with a replica of Francis's Portiuncula, a lovely little red brick chapel, with a walled garden joining it to a small library. There were two large, rambling frame houses, formerly summer homes for the Crane family, and a small cottage with the legend over the door, "*O beata solitudo, sola beatitudo*" (O blessed solitude, sole blessedness). Across the road was the Villa Addolorata, a nursing home for elderly women, run by the Servite Sisters. It had been built originally, also by the Crane family, for the widows and children of Crane employees and included a large classroom building, a number of cottages attractively arranged around a central green, a swimming pool, and a barn with fields beyond. We quickly made arrangements with the Calvert Club for the use of Childerley for the summer, and with the Servite Sisters for the rental of one of the cottages and for the use of the barn for our livestock.

The move from Doddridge to Childerley was a project in itself. The country was at war; labor and equipment were in short supply; the only truck we were able to rent was a small dump truck, whose owner was willing to make it available after his day's work was done. We had a great deal of equipment to move—all the furnishings at Doddridge that we had obtained as gifts from various women's groups; all the farm equipment that we had thriftily purchased at auctions; the animals—a cow, a calf, a sow, eight little pigs, fifty chickens; all the office equipment, program materials, files, desks, typewriters; and the personal belongings of twelve women. We were paying the truck owner by the load, so we were careful to pile his truck with the maximum possible before undertaking the fifteen-mile trip to Childerley. As a result, it was near midnight when the truck would pull into the barn at Villa Addolorata with its noisy load, clanking or grunting as the case might be, and disturbing the sleep of the Villa's elderly guests.

Lydwine wrote immediately to both bishops about the Grail plans for the summer courses. Archbishop Stritch in his reply[7] reiterates his conviction that his decision "is the best for your interests and the interests of religion. It places your work on a stable foundation." While he was pleased to hear that the summer courses would go forward, he warns: "This arrangement is purely temporary and does not indicate your affiliating your work with the Calvert Club. When we are able to set up your work according to our plans, it will be without any sort of affiliation other than with ecclesiastical authority." To Bishop Sheil Lydwine wrote that she had been unable to obtain an appointment with him but that she would like to come to an understanding regarding financial arrangements, since the Grail for three years without remuneration had taken over the maintenance of Doddridge Farm (formerly provided by three men on salary) and had built a $1,500 barn as well as making other permanent improvements to the buildings. So far as I know, the bishop never answered this letter.

On June 12, the 1943 summer program began at Childerley, with a three-week course, *The Valiant Woman*, on the crisis of our time and the tremendous task God had given to young women to use their talents and energies in a spirit of sacrifice to steer the world in a Godward direction. "We will discover the special qualities that young women have and can use in bringing peace and order to the world . . . in homes, colleges, offices, war organizations, wherever we are," the brochure announced. There was a course on liturgy and Gregorian chant; one on Christian culture; and two on agriculture, one a general introduction to the theme of women and the land, the second, a more specialized training in the skills necessary for rural living.[8] Some three hundred young women came through Childerley that summer. They were all young—between eighteen and twenty-five—and unmarried, either studying in high school or college, or working in offices or stores or at the phone company. They came from all the places where the traveling team had given talks. Often they were sent by the parish priest, or else the school or the Catholic Action group would help to raise scholarship and travel funds. For speakers, we drew on Catholic experts: Dom Ermin Vitry, leader in liturgical music, for Gregorian chant; Monsignor Ligutti and Emerson Hynes on rural life; Monsignor Hillenbrand on the Mass; Father Michael Mathis of Notre Dame University on the psalms and rural life. Lydwine gave a major presentation on the task of woman; Joan and I spoke at some length on the lay apostolate, on Christian culture, on woman and the land. Those who had been in the training at Doddridge headed the work projects—baking bread and altar breads; making butter, cheese, wine, and cider; canning fruits and vegetables; weaving. The trainees also gave short talks, based directly on their own experience of the integrated Christian life and the dignity of manual work. The work projects were an important part of the program, giving the participants an introduction to practical skills and a taste of the satisfactions of making things with their own hands.

Every course was meant to be an experience of integrated Christian living, with the Mass as "the absolutely central and most beautiful part of each day."[9] There was either a recited or a sung Mass, complete with offertory and communion processions, in the chapel every morning. Often there was more than one Mass, since newly ordained priests came especially for the rare experience of offering Mass with a congregation that participated actively. One morning we joked that the Mass was in the "Brooklyn Rite," since the priest, the altar boy, and the reader who rendered the epistle and gospel in English all had pronounced Brooklyn accents. The spirit of the morning's liturgy was carried through the day in group recitation of vespers and compline (parts of the official prayer of the Church for which we had made mimeographed copies in English), in private prayer, in lectures and discussions, manual work, feasting, and planning for the future.

We did not have uninterrupted use of Childerley, for the Calvert Club had already scheduled several weekends for other groups. Joan Overboss, as part of her original approach to life, had a gift for turning an embarrassment into a benefit. During the course on the liturgy, she simply announced that we were going to have an exodus experience, packing up and moving across the road. Everyone accepted this move as part of the planned program and fell to with good will, sweeping out the barn and preparing it for the lectures. Our chief speaker, distinguished Father Benedict Ehmann, took up a broom and joined in the sweeping before giving us his cosmic vision of Christ. During the course on Christian culture, we participants, inspired by tales of the mass dramas produced by the Grail in Holland, wrote and presented an original drama on the theme of the struggle between the children of light and the children of darkness. At the climax of the play, the leader of the children of light was to be crucified, in keeping with the Gospel theme that Christ's victory over death and sin came through the cross. Joan had the local carpenter erect a six-foot wooden cross at one end of the green which was surrounded by the cottages of the Villa Addolorata. All afternoon she rehearsed the speaking and singing choruses on the green, a proceeding that interfered with the naps of the elderly cottage occupants. At 5 P.M. the drama was presented; as the company moved back across the road to supper, Joan gave a task to the young woman who played the leader of the children of light, namely, to continue to stay on the cross and pray during the meal for all the participants in the drama, the audience as well as the actors, that we might all become children of light. There were ribbons to hold her hands in place and a little shelf on which to stand, but from a distance, and in the twilight, the crucifixion scene was quite realistic and frightened the ladies in the cottages, who complained to the nuns. I think that this incident definitely destroyed whatever bond existed between the Grail and the Servite Sisters.

Woman and the land was an important theme in the summer program. Lydwine and Joan had been much impressed with Monsignor Luigi Ligutti and his program for the Catholic Rural Life Conference. At one of the national meetings of the NCRLC, after listening patiently for several hours to talks on agriculture as a way of life and the family farm as an ideal environment for the Christian family, Lydwine had risen to her feet to ask why no one had said anything about the role of women on the land. She pointed out that no renewal of life on the land would be possible without the support of the women. Ligutti promptly made her a vice-president of the NCRLC. For her part, Lydwine saw the advantages of a farm as a training center, away from the distractions of city life. Moreover, the farm, with its abundance of fresh foods and outdoor work, was an ideal setting for improving the health of American girls. Then, too, rural life helped to turn people toward God, contributing to our understanding of scripture, and enabling us to grasp the profound harmony between the natural cycle and the liturgical cycle. Repeatedly in her reports to both Bishop Sheil and Archbishop Stritch, she outlined plans for an agricultural school for young women. On the one hand, she wanted courses for city women to introduce them to the dignity of manual work and to some practical skills. On the other hand, she wanted courses for rural women on the beauty and importance of a Christian culture, on the advantages of the farm for fostering such a culture, and on the family farm as a natural school in which to educate children in initiative and responsibility. The bishops were not responsive, but the young women who attended the rural life courses were enthusiastic.

The Search for a Permanent Home

The summer ended successfully, and the search for a suitable permanent place began. Lydwine sent us out two by two, to go to Mass in the surrounding towns and then inquire of the pastor whether there were any farms for sale in his parish. We found that if we stopped at a farmhouse to ask whether it was for sale, nine times out of ten the response would be, "No, this place is not for sale. You want Jones's place over there." Every night the searchers came back elated with their discoveries, only to have a second visit reveal some fatal flaw—no dependable water supply or poor soil, buildings too few or too small.

To our dismay, we learned that we could not stay on either at Childerley or at the Villa Addolorata beyond the end of October. Our search intensified—it was tantalizing, the ideal place was always just beyond our grasp. We did not want to disband, each one going home to her family. On October 29, Lydwine and Joan had been to the guest house of the Society of the Divine Word (usually called the SVDs) at Techny, Illinois, to ask if they could put up sixteen women for a week or two, until we found a place of our own. They were turned down. Deeply discouraged, they were driving back to Childerley when they passed the motherhouse of the Sisters of the Holy Ghost, the female counterpart of the SVDs. On impulse, remembering that these sisters had a convent in Holland, they knocked at the door. Both the sister superior and the mother provincial were in residence. They responded immediately, in a spirit of great faith and generosity. They simply said that they did not know what was happening to their sisters under the Nazi occupation, but that they thought the Lord had sent us to their door, and they would do for us what they hoped others might be doing for their group in Holland. On November l, fourteen of us moved into the convent at Techny, where the sisters made us welcome, putting at our disposal a dormitory, a dining room, a work room, and private rooms for Lydwine and Joan. Two people, Josephine Drabek and Gabrielle Miner, stayed on in one small cottage at the Villa to look after the animals.

With exquisite tact, on our second or third day in the convent, the superior, Sister Othmara, came to ask where we would like our Advent wreath. That was her way of letting us know that she knew we were going to be with them for more than a week or two and that she was pleased to have us. I was in charge of the training group, while Lydwine and Joan were combing the area, looking for a suitable farm. We followed the nuns' schedule, rising for meditation and early Mass, taking our turn with them in keeping their all-night vigil before the Blessed Sacrament every Thursday night. I will never forget that dormitory with its curtained cubicles, where we were awakened every morning by a loud 4 A.M. rising bell. I could not see my peers, but I could hear fourteen pairs of feet hit the cold, cold floor. I led group meditations based on a book by Bede Jarrett, OP, with the appropriate title, *Here We Have No Abiding City*. It must have been agonizing for Lydwine and Joan, but the rest of us were in high spirits, perfectly confident that the Lord was guiding us in this great adventure and would sooner or later lead us to the perfect place. The sisters were wonderfully hospitable and generous, but we did find some points of convent etiquette rather irksome. Their practice of silence was perfect; one never heard a footstep in the halls or a door opening or closing. However hard we tried, we were noisy by contrast. Moreover, to encourage practice of the presence of God, their founder had given them a quarter-hour prayer. Wherever you were— in the halls, in the chapel, in the library— when the clock struck the quarter-hour, the senior sister present would intone a short versicle and those present would respond. I found this extremely distracting, especially since the clocks were not synchronized and one could get caught twice in the same quarter hour.

But hardest of all was the absence of manual work. The workroom was a former classroom. Barbara Wald and I had plenty of urgent work to do, because we handled the correspondence and were preparing the lectures from the summer courses for publication. But for the others, there was only busy work and that sedentary—filing, mending, sewing. We were used to vigorous activity, cooking for large groups, baking, weeding, hoeing, milking, churning. In the convent, we could not even wash the dishes, since the scullery like the kitchen was in the cloister. We were served ample and delicious meals three times a day and could clear and set the tables but that was all. We could not clean the public areas, because each postulant or novice had her assigned area to clean. I have never lived in such a clean and orderly place—if one opened a cupboard, everything was in neatly labeled boxes with the contents corresponding absolutely to the label. There was not a dust mote to be seen anywhere. I remember taking our group out to hike along the roads just to have an outlet for our abundant physical energies.

Hospitably, the sisters worried about the two at Childerley and insisted on inviting them to Sunday dinner. They also graciously received our guests. In mid-December, we received word from three young women who had been at the rural life course in September. Lydwine had encouraged them to go home with another participant, a farm woman from

Arkansas, to get further experience in the necessary skills. The three, Mary Buckley, Irene Naughton, and Mildred Iriberry, were returning to their homes in New York for Christmas and wanted to stop off with the Grail on the way. The sisters rose to the occasion and housed and fed our guests with their usual generous hospitality.

While we were at Techny, Monsignor Ligutti sent a letter to Lydwine, advising her to see Archbishop McNicholas of Cincinnati, who was a supporter of the NCRLC and had a farm that he wanted to put to good use. Lydwine phoned for an appointment, and taking Mary Alice Duddy with her, set out for Cincinnati. McNicholas kept the two women all day, firing questions at them. Satisfied with their answers, he ended the interview by assuring them that they had "the green light." "What do you need?" he asked. "A place to hold our Christmas course," Lydwine replied, "and your real estate agent to help us find a permanent home." We celebrated Christmas with the sisters at Techny and set out the next day for Cincinnati.

Archbishop McNicholas had arranged for us to have the use of Emory Hall at Our Lady of Cincinnati College for our Christmas course. It was a wonderful old mansion, with a white marble atrium, boasting a white marble fountain at its center, and a white marble ballroom next door. Dom Ermin Vitry, OSB, a monk of the liturgical abbey of Maredsous in Belgium, editor of *Caecelia*, the journal of liturgical music, a great expert on the liturgy and the chant, was our speaker. He found all that white marble a bit chilly, and aided and abetted by young Father Getty from Pittsburgh, he proceeded to add some color. Father Getty procured poster paints and decorated all the windows with liturgical symbols. Red velvet drapes from other parts of the building were brought into the ballroom to add color and warmth. Every day Dom Vitry had another idea for transforming the place. I have a vivid memory of Fathers Vitry and Getty on the balcony of the atrium, draping wide red satin ribbon diagonally from one corner of the balcony to the opposite corner, so that the two ribbons crossed precisely over the head of the cherub on the fountain. The course was a joyous celebration of the Christmas mystery, the three comings of Christ—in history at Bethlehem, in mystery in the Eucharist, in majesty at the end of time. I remember a prayer hour on New Year's Eve, which ended with the group outside on a hilltop overlooking the city and singing a *Gloria in excelsis Deo* as a prayer for justice and peace to come to a world at war.

The course ended on January 1, 1944. That morning the Sisters of Mercy came trooping back into Emory Hall, astonished and not too well pleased with the changes the Grail had made in their building. Lydwine was on the phone to Archbishop McNicholas, asking for a place to house sixteen people while we looked for a farm. McNicholas immediately obliged by arranging for the Grail to stay temporarily at Crusade Castle, the Cincinnati headquarters of the National Catholic Students Mission Crusade, directed by Monsignor Edward Freking. The Castle, which had been an inn in the 1790s, had accommodations for retreatants on its top floor, a rectory on the second floor and on the ground floor, offices for the Crusade that organized high school and college students to support the Catholic missions. It was definitely a men's place, a strong contrast to the neat and tidy convent. Lydwine immediately organized her group: Josephine Drabek was sent to the agricultural school at Farmingdale, Long Island; I was sent back to Villa Addolorata with Catherine Leahy, to look after our belongings and to finish editing the lectures from the summer courses. A few people joined in the search for a farm; the others were assigned to house cleaning. Monsignor Freking commented, "Those girls cleaned my house as if it was some new kind of indoor sport." The search for the perfect place began anew, this time with the support of a bishop who was actively interested and who lent his real estate agent to aid the project.

A Place of Our Own

Our requirements were daunting: we needed a place in which we could immediately house at least fifty people, with space for large and small meeting rooms, all this to be on a real farm, and within walking distance of a railroad station. This latter qualification was important because war time gas rationing had forced a cut back on transportation by automobile. We soon learned that the water table in Ohio was dangerously low, a fact that added one more qualification to the list, namely, that the farm should be supplied with city water. The agent had taken Lydwine to see a place on the outskirts of Loveland, a property later purchased by Daniel and Mary Kane, when they moved to Loveland to join in the lay apostolate with the Grail. Lydwine had dismissed it as too small, only forty acres and one modest house. As they turned toward Cincinnati, they drove past the farm that eventually became Grailville. Lydwine glimpsed all the large buildings. "That's the kind of place we need," she said to the agent. He immediately looked up the owner, Thomas Wood, head of a well-known Cincinnati insurance agency. Mr. Wood had bought the place in the 1920s, but had never been able to persuade his wife to move so far from the city. He ran it with a tenant farmer, kept a few race horses in one of the barns, and even had a race track laid out along the boundaries of the largest field. Our offer took him by surprise—he had not intended to sell—but he agreed.

The Grail had already been established as a nonprofit corporation in the State of Ohio, on February 1, 1944. The charter of incorporation reads:

The objects and purposes of the corporation are to conduct a school or schools; to maintain and carry on educational institutions, or institutions of learning; to promote social activity, and foster the religious and cultural development of women and girls; to establish an agricultural training center or centers for young women; to teach the application of Christian principles to everyday life; to promote Christian morals and benevolence; and in general, for all educational and charitable activities in connection with the foregoing. [10]

The offer by the Grail is dated March 8, 1944. However, there were a number of complications, arising out of Mr. Wood's contract with his tenant farmer, which had to be negotiated, so it was not until April 21, 1944, that the agreement was duly signed by both parties. The Grail had purchased a farm of a hundred and eighty-three acres together with a half interest in all livestock and crops thereon for the sum of $49,250.[11] The Grail made a downpayment of $22,000, which Mary Louise Tully had obtained from her father as her inheritance. The balance was in the form of a loan from the Archdiocese of Cincinnati. Lydwine had a good eye for real estate and over a period of years acquired four adjoining parcels, making the total acreage three hundred and eighty acres, and adding a number of buildings.

The Grail had moved into Crusade Castle at the beginning of January, and the novitiate training went on no matter where the group was living. However, as the weeks of searching lengthened into a month and then continued into a second month, pressures began to build to cease being guests, no matter how welcome, and to move into a place of our own, even if it fell short of the ideal. The Archbishop had offered a farm at Foster, Ohio, which Lydwine had refused as too small. Finally, she reconsidered and accepted the offer. The place consisted of ten acres on a steep hillside, overlooking the Little Miami River. We promptly dubbed it "Super Flumina," "Above the Waters," and prepared to move in. Unfortunately, both houses on the property had been taken over by squatters. Somehow arrangements were made for the Grail to occupy half of one house, with the squatters still in the other half. The setup was primitive—no plumbing, no central heating, cisterns for the water supply, an outhouse, and one fireplace for both heating and cooking, since the kitchen was on the squatter's side of the house. Moreover, all the Grail furniture and equipment was still in the cottage at Villa Addolorata, where Catherine and I were standing guard. Communication with Cincinnati was very difficult—there was only one telephone at the Villa, in the office of the superior, who made it clear that the phone was to be used only in emergencies. We received a telegram, "Send mattresses." Puzzled but obedient, we found that if we rolled the thin mattresses of the double-decker beds and bound them tightly with brown paper and string, they could be sent through the mails. A second directive ordered us to ship everything to the Grail at Foster, Ohio. We had long since butchered all the livestock and put the meat in a frozen food locker. We sold the fence posts, barbed wire, and other farm equipment. The agent of the moving company was dubious when he saw the little five room cottage at the Villa, but when he came inside and realized that it was crammed solid from cellar to attic with furniture and cartons, he made arrangements for an eighteen-wheel truck to take the job.

I arrived at Foster in March to find the group keeping a strict Lent and working hard to make the place habitable. The former occupants had simply tossed cans, jars and other rubbish out the windows. We filled many truckloads with debris to be taken to the village dump. Lydwine had a new outhouse built, on the Australian model, using buckets which were then emptied every day onto a compost pile. The pile produced excellent compost, but we were careful never to use it on root crops. Anxious to show that rural living could be made attractive, Lydwine wanted the inside of the outhouse painted white and furnished with proper enameled toilet seats. Dorothy Day was spending Lent with the Grail, sharing in the group meditations in the mornings and joining in the manual work in the afternoons. I remember Dorothy, sitting on the floor of the outhouse and wielding a paintbrush, an operation which Lydwine termed "gilding the lily," since she usually referred to the outhouses as "lilies of the field."

We studied scripture and the history of the liturgy, meditated on the rich texts of the Lenten Masses, memorized prayers in both Latin and English. Breakfast and the noon meal were in silence, but often we sang the whole of the *Veni Sancte Spiritus* or the *Veni Creator Spiritus* in Latin as a grace before meals. The squatters were still on the other side of the house. The combination of the silent meals and the long hymns in a strange language was too much for them, and they quickly moved out.

Even before all the paperwork on the sale was completed, a small group had moved on to Grailville to begin preparing the buildings for the summer courses. The main house, a three-story Victorian mansion of thirteen rooms plus a complete finished basement, had not been occupied for years. Built before central heating, it had four fireplaces on the first floor, each with a rococo mantel, beautifully carved and decorated with gilding, mirrors, and tiles. These did not suit the Grail's standard of simplicity, so when I first saw the house, all four mantels had been laid out on the floor, somehow suggesting coffins. The cartons Catherine and I had shipped from Childerley were piled around the room. A crew of eager workers had been using steamers to remove the layers of wallpaper from the walls and then had been knocking out the rotten plaster, creating a layer of plaster dust over everything. It was March and very cold; it was wartime and heating oil was rationed—we had no heat. Altogether it was a dismal scene. Lydwine had reported to Archbishop McNicholas about the wonderful place we had found. He liked to pay surprise visits, walked in unannounced, and clearly showed that he thought we had saddled ourselves with a hopeless place. But he took pity on us and sent his chauffeur out the next day with a care package, a big basket packed full of groceries. Later, when we had the place in shape, he continued the surprise visits and tended to credit us as miracle workers. I once overheard him showing his guests around and stating confidently that "the girls" had even dehorned the bull. He invented the name "Grailville," commenting that the arrangement of the buildings around the semicircular drive was like a little village.

Gradually most of the group moved from Super Flumina to Grailville to help with the preparations. We stripped the varnish from the beautiful oak, walnut, and cherry woodwork in the main house, painted walls, set up double-decker beds in all the bedrooms and in the horse barn and the loft of the carriage house. There were not enough dressers to go around, so we improvised, begging orange crates from the local grocery and turning them into into shelves, washstands, and filing cabinets. Because of the war, it was difficult to get labor and materials, but we managed to find a one-eyed carpenter and an elderly plumber to put extra bathrooms in the main house and to add an extension for a kitchen.

The summer was a busy one, with a three-week course at Frontenac, Minnesota in June, followed by a week in Rugby, North Dakota, and then the Grand Opening of Grailville on July 17, 1944. We had invited several hundred guests. Lydwine, always punctilious about not keeping a bishop waiting, had asked the guests to come at 2 o'clock and Archbishop McNicholas to come at 3 for an official blessing of this new center of the lay apostolate. The bishop's secretary got lost looking for Grailville, with the result that the episcopal car was an hour late, and we had a nervous time keeping our guests entertained until the blessing could begin. I had spent several days translating all the prayers from Latin to English. We had prepared a lengthy ceremony—everyone wanted her workplace or residence blessed. Although a small man, McNicholas was an impressive figure in mitre and cope, crozier in hand and pectoral cross gleaming on his breast, as he led the procession from place to place, keeping a respectful distance as he waved the aspergillum to sprinkle holy water on the bee hives in the orchard, marching grandly down the central feed aisle in the barn, sprinkling everyone of the thirty cows, who obliged with moos and the plop of cow pats hitting the manure gutter.

Figure 2. An aerial view of Grailville in 1983, showing the Victorian House, the modern dining room, and the raised beds in the organic garden.

Archbishop McNicholas was always pleased to give his support to the Grail both publicly and privately. In the brochure announcing one of our summer programs, he wrote:

> I wish to extend my paternal blessing to the Grail schools of apostolate for 1946, and to give my cordial approval to the work of Catholic Action which the Grail is undertaking among young women. The necessity for a restoration of the dignity of Christian womanhood cannot be emphasized strongly enough in the modern world. The Grail is doing a significant work in preparing young women for their role in the universal lay apostolate of the church under the direction of the Hierarchy, and I am happy to give full encouragement to their program.[12]

At long last the pioneer group of Grail women had found a place to call home, under the protection of a bishop who understood and appreciated their work.

4

Grailville—A Countercultural Oasis

Making the Grail More Lay

It was November 1, 1944, the official birthday of the Grail, commemorating the date of the establishment of the first small group in Holland. We were exactly two weeks into our first long-term residential program at Grailville, known as the Year's School of Apostolate. Joan had summoned those of us who had been in the training at Doddridge to a meeting in the Council Room, the front room on the second floor of the Victorian mansion that was our main residence. The night before we trainees had given a surprise party for Lydwine and Joan to mark the day, which we had regularly celebrated at Doddridge. Joan scolded us soundly, telling us in no uncertain terms that we should not be separating ourselves from the rest of the group. This session was the only explicit mention of a profound shift in emphasis away from the novitiate for the laity toward simply the training of leaders for the lay apostolate. Nothing more was said about this shift which collapsed into one overriding aim the two distinct goals which had been repeatedly outlined in Lydwine's reports to Bishop Sheil, namely, the novitiate for "free workers," the Women of Nazareth, free from marriage, committed to total availability for the needs of the apostolate, and the training of leaders for the general lay apostolate. Joan quietly got rid of all the things that symbolized the existence of the Women of Nazareth as a separate group. The brown robes which we had worn for meditation at Doddridge appeared in the costume department at Grailville. There was no longer a special room, like the one in the Quest at Doddridge, with the six-foot yellow cross at one end, and the low U-shaped table around which we knelt for meditation. Nothing was said about the possibility for a lifetime dedication in the Grail. Holiness was for everybody; therefore, serious spiritual training ("novitiate" was the best word we had to indicate our seriousness) should be open to everyone.

I felt confused by this change, but somehow the charisma was so strong that we all simply accepted these changes without question. However, I remember a joke that was current among those of us who had spent three or four years at Grailville and still were identified as students. The local Presbyterian church announced a sermon title on its outside bulletin board, "Students Forever." We repeated it among ourselves, "Students forever, that's us." I know that I thought we were protecting the lay apostolate (which, in my opinion, the bishops did not understand very well) and the Grail by being able to say that we did not take vows and had not made any liftetime commitment. I believe that Joan, out of her experience, had come to the conclusion that the existence of a separate group within the movement created a barrier. Lydwine had experienced the jealousies that could arise between movements in the Church and was content to go quietly for some years and not aim immediately and explicitly at building a Grail movement in the United States. Lydwine and Joan occasionally referred to themselves as "Grail workers," or "free workers in the lay apostolate," but there was no definition of Grail membership. Women who had spent a year or more at Grailville tended to keep contact, but did not think that they could speak of themselves as Grail members. Those who wrote about the work spoke either of students at Grailville or of "Grail girls." I was completely caught up in the Grail vision of the role of women in "the conversion of the world." Everything I was doing—handling correspondence, writing apostolic programs, lecturing, planning and conducting workshops, advising young women to come for the Year's School—seemed to me to be directly serving our great goal. I was happy because I felt I was spending my energies—the work was often exhausting—for what I cared most about.

As part of her move to make the U.S. Grail more lay—a move that I suspect proceeded more from intuition than from any explicit analysis— Joan took the lead in encouraging young married couples to settle around Grailville and join in Grail activities. Mary McGarry and Daniel Kane from Philadelphia had purchased a forty-acre farm adjoining Grailville in October, 1944, and moved in the following January, immediately after their wedding. These first homesteaders were followed in quick succession by Catherine and James Shea, Mary and William Schickel, Miriam and Vincent Hill, Grace and James Rogan, Patricia and Bernard Hutzel. With the exception of Bernard Hutzel, a local farmer, all the others were city people—from Philadelphia, St. Louis, Chicago, St. Paul. The wives had all participated in Grail training. The couples saw themselves as beginning a family apostolate inspired by the Grail and the National Catholic Rural Life Conference. In the 1940s they came regularly to Sunday breakfast; Lydwine, Joan, and the rest of us on the Grailville staff worked hard to provide spiritual and intellectual nourishment at those breakfasts. The Kanes, Bill Schickel, and Jim Shea helped to staff courses both at Grailville and in other parts of the country. The Kanes also worked with groups of couples in Cincinnati. The couples formed an organization, Land and Home Associates, which stated its purpose as:

> As a group we are called to a life of wholeness, to a Christian community life, rooted in the primary things and aimed at the highest development of the material, physical, intellectual, spiritual and supernatural talents of the individuals and families in the group and of the group as a whole. . . . The community life . . . will require of its members a pledge of mutual help to the attainment of these goals. . . . We believe in the productive family homestead as the chief source of provision for the needs of the family . . . the families will need to advance in the knowledge and skills of the home arts and crafts and of husbandry and agriculture.[1]

Married women had always been welcome at Grail courses in the United States, a departure from the practice of the Grail youth movement of the 1930s in Holland. There, once a girl married, she could no longer be a member of the movement. Some married women had taken part in the short courses at Doddridge Farm. From the beginning at Grailville, the most serious times of training were open to women of various vocations— the engaged, the undecided, the married, as well as those preparing for a lifetime dedication in celibacy as lay apostles. Although we no longer spoke of the Vrouwen van Nazareth or the Ladies of the Grail, nor of lifetime dedication, and although Joan wanted one group with one training, in practice we did distinguish two levels of training: an introductory level at Grailville and a more advanced level at Super Flumina, but we no longer spoke of a "novitiate." In the Catholic vocabulary, "novitiate" means an intensive training for prospective members of a religious community to start them on a serious pursuit of holiness, a kind of training generally only available to professional Catholics, that is, nuns and priests. The condition for entry into a novitiate was the willingness to commit to lifelong celibacy and obedience. As we in the Grail understood the lay apostolate, the core message was that holiness was for everyone. Therefore, we wanted to offer all women—married, single, celibate—the opportunity for a "novitiate," that is, a time of serious spiritual formation. What did "the most serious times of training" consist of? An in-depth study and practice of methods of meditation and prayer, a rigorous asceticism, a conscious striving to meet the demands of love in the daily interactions of community living, a study of classic spiritual texts.

In the general training for leaders at Grailville, Lydwine and Joan proceeded to develop further the pattern of integrated Christian living already begun at Doddridge Farm. The emphasis was on integration as the means of countering the pervasive secularism at the root of the crises of contemporary civilization. My main task in 1946 was to put together the *Program of Action*, a study-action guide published by Grailville, which applied the analyses of leading Christian thinkers—Hilaire Belloc, Gilbert Chesterton, Nicholas Berdyaev, Jacques Maritain, Emmanuel Mounier, Christopher Dawson, Eric Gill—to the lives of young women. In the introduction, I explained:

> Secularism, the heresy of modern times, is the separation of religion from every aspect of public and social life, confining all questions of God's existence and man's [*sic*] obligations to Him to the privacy of the individual conscience. This division of life into two compartments begins by paralyzing Christian influence on the social order and inevitably results in the complete denial of spiritual reality in all phases of life, private as well as public. . . . Our generation stands at a turning point of history and must make the decisive choice: either the reign of the powers of darkness or a new social order founded and centered upon the principles of Christ.[2]

In support of this view, I quoted Nicholas Berdyaev, *The End of Our Time:*

> The old world, or rather "modern times," have come to their end and are in decomposition. A new and unknown world is coming to birth. The crisis of culture means that where religion is concerned, it cannot maintain a humanist neutrality but must inevitably become either an atheist and anti-Christian civilization or else a sacred culture, animated by the Church, a transformed Christian life.[3]

A Countercultural Oasis

That transformed Christian life was what Grailville attempted to embody. To that end the broad acres of the Grailville farm were an effective means, an ideal site on which to build a countercultural oasis. The physical distance from Loveland—over a mile to the nearest store but less than a mile to the train station— and the lack of transport (there was only one automobile and it was reserved for special missions) made frequent trips to town quite difficult. To avoid the distractions and seductions of contemporary popular culture, radio and newspapers were banned; television was not yet in use. A good deal of austerity was built into daily life simply by the physical layout of the place. The only indoor plumbing was in the main house. Other accommodations were of the simplest—cisterns; outside privies; washstands improvised from orange crates for pitcher, basin and slop pail; double-decker beds; space heaters; lots of hard manual work in the fields, barns, gardens, kitchen, bakery. Merely keeping to the daily schedule offered many opportunities for self-denial to young women who were used to such comforts of city life as central heating and hot and cold running water. The simplicity was a challenge. I felt I was proving my hardihood, like a pioneer woman.

There were impassioned arguments, especially with the Catholic Action groups—the Young Christian Workers and the Young Christian Students—on whether formation for the lay apostolate should take place "in the environment" or "out of the environment." The YCW and YCS wanted to train people where they were, in their schools or jobs, in their homes, immersed in the popular culture of the cities. The Grail wanted them to leave home for a shorter or longer period of training. We were convinced that formation outside of the usual environment was the only way that people brought up in our fragmented modern culture could grasp a vision of integrated Christian life. Christianity, Grail courses insisted, is a way of life, not a matter of Mass on Sunday and living like everyone else the rest of the week. Everything a Christian does all day long should be imbued with the vision and values of the faith. Having experienced an integrated life in the supportive community at Grailville, the individual would see her back home environment with new eyes and would be prepared both to critique it and to start changing it.

A pamphlet published in 1948 spells out six pillars of Grailville, principles that shaped the program:

1. A Christian Vision of Life, transforming and unifying all the activities of the day in the praise of God, centering the day in the Mass, and living in the rhythm of the liturgical year.
2. The Family as the Organic Unit of Society, basic to both the natural and the supernatural order. In the total group and in the small living units, life was organized on a family pattern of mutual giving and receiving, in which each one took on a specific responsibility to contribute to the common life and was enriched by the communal experience.
3. The Nature and Task of Woman. The program focused on woman's spiritual mission and its practical consequences for her role in the social order, with an emphasis on developing the specific womanly qualities of loving self-surrender, generous self-giving, and motherly care for others.
4 Intellectual Formation was directed toward a sure grasp of Christian principles and values and was carried on through lec-

Figure 3. Participants and staff of the Year's School singing the Sunday High Mass in St. Columban's parish church, 1945.

tures and discussions led by outstanding Christian thinkers as well as by study of "great books both classic and contemporary."

5. A Philosophy of Work emphasized the dignity of manual as well as intellectual work. Work—and especially the necessary work of every day—was seen as cocreation with God; as "love made visible"; as a means of personal growth, physically, mentally, and spiritually; as an image of spiritual realities and the root of a genuine culture.

6. Development of a Christian Culture, as the outward expression of our beliefs and values, and a necessary condition for a spiritual renewal. Culture was understood as spirit translated into matter, values lived out in daily work and relationships. Hence it included all the routines of every day, clothing and household decor, work well done and hospitality generously offered to a guest as well as literature and the arts.[4]

Sometimes "agriculture as a way of life" was included as one of the principles, sometimes, as in this listing, it was omitted, because for many of those who read or wrote about Grailville the novelty of women running a farm tended to obscure our apostolic purpose. Of course, in the actual experience at Grailville in the 1940s and 1950s, the farm was a major aspect of life. In affirming the value of agriculture as more than a business, as a way of life, an ideal environment for the family, a way to develop healthy personalities and to deepen spiritual insights, Lydwine had been much influenced by the Catholic Rural Life Conference. In embracing the philosophy of work, she was influenced by reading the works of Eric Gill and by William Schickel, a young artist who had married a "Grail girl" and settled near Grailville.

The farm had high prestige on our cultural oasis. We city women vied for a chance to work in the cow barn. I spent a winter on the barn crew and loved every minute of it. I remember rising in the dark, dressing quickly and walking across to the barn under the stars. On the door to the silo in elegant calligraphy was the text, "All ye beast and cattle, bless the Lord." We gathered to sing a hymn and recite a psalm. Then in silence, we proceeded to the routine: mucking out the manure gutters, currying our cows, washing the udders, milking while the crew leader fed grain and silage, carrying buckets of warm, foamy milk to the milk house where it was divided between cans for our kitchen and cans for the Cincinnati market. It was satisfying work with a clearly visible result, peaceful and free from the pressures of organizing a program or giving a talk. It put me deeply in touch with the rhythms of the seasons. I learned the winter constellations, became conscious of the slow changes in the night sky, and rejoiced when I could finally see the sun rise over my cow's rump as I milked. That meant that spring was on the way.

Van Ginneken disagreed emphatically with both emphases—on rural life and on manual work. "Why did you buy a farm?" he wrote to Lydwine. "Revolutions start in the cities and you bury yourself on a farm![5] "I tore up the letter," Lydwine told me. "I was very upset about it, but I knew I had done the right thing." In another letter, van Ginneken wrote, "I don't agree with the emphasis on practical womanliness. Let them be unhandy in the practical for a while. Be sure that the spirit comes first."[6] Lydwine went on, "It was for me a revelation that to milk a cow or cook a meal was as important as making a picture. I learned that from Gill and others on the philosophy of work. I had never been good at work, and at thirty-four, I was too old to learn, but I saw its importance. I wanted a place where we could be free and could have a community life." After the experience in the Chicago Archdiocese, Lydwine saw clearly the need for the Grail to own property and not to be economically dependent on any bishop.

We had been eager to buy Grailville because it had so many buildings that could readily be adapted to Grail use. Over the years, we gradually moved the animals out of the barns and moved ourselves in. The first step was simply to name the buildings. Not for us such dull designations as barn and cottage. Instead, we drew on the liturgy for inspiration: *Hodie*, the Latin for "today," the first word of the antiphons for major feasts, became the name of the big horse barn; its field stone basement (a cool spot in summer) became *Laetare*, rejoice, from the entrance song for mid-Lent Sunday; the two cottages became *Modicum* (a little while) and *Benedicite* (bless ye the Lord); the smaller horse barn, which had space on the ground floor for the tractor and farm truck, was called the *Caravansery*, the place where caravans stop, in honor of the Christmas story. We also ventured into Greek, naming the house for the farm crew *Pneuma*, for the spirit that renews the face of the earth; the farm across the road, added to the original Grailville acres in 1945, *Parousia*, for the final coming of Christ; and the 1947 addition to the old carriage house, *Metanoia*, for the change of heart that the Year's School aimed to bring about. One could hardly give even a quick tour of Grailville without getting involved in some explanations of the liturgy. The first summer at Grailville, we took over Laetare as a lecture hall, moving the heifers into the pasture, sweeping it out and giving it a coat of whitewash. However, some of the stalls upstairs were still in use for the horses; I remember sitting in Laetare, listening to a lecture, and watching wisps of straw drift down through the cracks in the ceiling. Some of us became quite expert at putting up insulation and dry wall, painting, refinishing floors. As we added adjoining properties to the original hundred and eighty acres, our puzzled neighbors, watching us transform barns into living quarters and meeting rooms, asked: "Is that what you are—a group that goes around putting old buildings into shape?" After repeated dealings with architects, contractors, and building inspectors, Mary Margaret Schlink, Veronica Forbes, Catherine Leahy, and Elise Gorges acquired sufficient know-how to function as general contractors on subsequent remodeling jobs.

Life on Grailville's "cultural oasis" quickly built a strong vibrant community with its own culture, a culture that ran counter to the America of the 1940s in almost every respect. The backbone of the community was the Year's School of Apostolate, starting each October and continuing through the following September, to give the experience of the complete cycle of both the natural and the liturgical year. In a group of sixty to sixty-five women, approximately twenty-five would be new students, with the rest divided between second-year students and staff. Short courses—weekends to two or three weeks—at Thanksgiving, Christmas, Holy Week, and during the summer brought several hundred additional young women to Grailville, some of whom returned for the year.

The Family Pattern

In my opinion, the factors that contributed most strongly to building the community were the family pattern, the subsistence economy, and the liturgical life, all three elements interwoven and expressed in the group culture. First, the family pattern. Even in the 1940s (and still more today) the prevailing patterns in United States society tended to pull the average young woman in different directions. She went to school with one group of people, met others in an after school job, had a social life with a third group, perhaps related to a church. While she might still be living with her family, family meals were becoming a rarity. Thus, for many of the participants in the Grail courses, it was a new experience to live, work, study, pray, and play with the same group of people. The sixty-five women in the Year's School were divided into smaller "families" of eight or ten in each living unit, but the total group participated in the Mass together, said vespers each evening, took part in an hour of lecture/discussion/meditation most mornings, and sat down to meals three times a day in the central room of the main house, now called the "House of Joy." The meals were quite formal; punctuality was a strong norm—one did not come late or leave early. The table was carefully set and we took turns acting as servers. The leader, acting as presider, waited until everyone was present before saying—or singing—grace, usually echoing a theme from the liturgy of the day. Many of the meals were in silence, broken by a reading or discussion, or by reports on events in the group or in the world at large. The meals were second only to the Mass as a source of unity and were meant to nourish mind and spirit as well as body.

The daily routines gave a sense of stability and serenity to life, a satisfying sense that everything one did was ultimately worthwhile. Let me describe a day in Lent, the most austere time of the year. I remember being awakened at 6 A.M. by a cheerful voice, announcing *"Benedicamus Domino"* (Bless the Lord). The proper response was *"Deo gratias"* (Thanks be to God), spoken while one leaped out of bed, knelt, and offered the day to God. Once a heavy sleeper responded, *"Domine non sum dignus"* (Lord, I am not worthy) and turned over for five minutes more. I dressed quickly—often ice had formed in my water pitcher—and joined my group to recite lauds from the *Short Breviary.* My mind would be full of the imagery of the hymns and psalms as I went about my morning chore— feeding and currying one of the sway-backed old horses that we used to cultivate the gardens. At 7:30 we lined up for the walk to Mass, a silent, peaceful procession through the fields, across the brook and up the hill to the parish church. I sang the Mass with gusto, managing to stay on pitch by standing next to a strong soprano. At breakfast—a thick slice of whole wheat bread and a cup of coffee liberally laced with whole milk—the silence was broken by Joan reading from Abbé Michonneau's book on the worker priests, followed by a spirited discussion of how the text could apply to ourselves. Then off to my task, coping with the voluminous correspondence from priests and young women wanting information on the Grail. At 11:00 A.M. the entire group met for what we called "meditation"—Lydwine reading from a spiritual book, for example, a sermon by Cardinal Newman, again with discussion and applications. Half an hour for private prayer, on our knees on the hardwood floor—we all developed callouses on our knees—then dinner, a substantial meal, with a reading from the Bible. After dinner, more letter writing for me until 5:30, when we met as a group for vespers. Supper was bread and cheese with milk or tea and conversation, often interspersed with reports on the activities of the various work groups. After supper, I could join a group learning new folk dances or rehearse a play reading or read on my own, looking for a text suitable to share at Sunday breakfast. Compline was said *en famille* at 9 P.M. By 9:30 the eighteen of us who shared double-decker beds in the Caravansery were ready for lights out, and a final text from the greeter.

During the first years at Grailville, Lydwine or Joan would give out the tasks for the day at the end of breakfast. Later stable groups, called "guilds," were established for each major area: kitchen, bakery, canning, laundry, schola (the singers who mastered the more difficult chants), sewing and weaving, administration, writing, visual arts, reception, and, of course, the farm. When Ralph Borsodi, founder of the School of Living at Suffern, New York, visited, he was particularly delighted with the breakfast list of tasks, since it made explicit the many roles that self-sufficient homesteaders needed to fulfill.

The underlying principle of family living, as Grailville understood and practiced it, was "from each according to her ability and to each according to her needs." Everyone had a task, everyone made some contribution to the common life and the common apostolic goal. Everyone knew what everyone else was doing; individuals were encouraged to report on their activities at the meals; the leaders took pains to give public recognition to work well done, whether it was digging the post holes to fence in the front pasture or setting a favorite text to music. Tasks were done with great generosity, thoroughness and finish, in keeping with a Dutch saying that was translated as "putting a gold fringe around it." The idea was to do every task, and especially the more distasteful ones, to perfection, and if possible with a flair, an original touch, something above and beyond the call of duty. We were not working for some anonymous public but for people we knew and cared about. Tasks were usually assigned with due regard both for the individual's talents and to further her education. The responsibility for contributing to the community served as a spur, encouraging individuals to develop hitherto unsuspected capacities. Life was both austere and luxurious: the simple meals were carefully prepared and delicious; the home-baked whole wheat bread was nourishing and tasty; we had whole milk, sweet butter, really fresh eggs and fruits and vegetables. The furnishings were sparse. In the first few years, we borrowed tables for the dining room from the parish and folding chairs from the local undertaker. During the annual parish festival, when we had to return the tables, we simply picnicked on the floor. But always careful attention was paid to "atmosphere," to appropriate decorations for the table, to a picture or text or hanging on the wall to delight the eye and stimulate the mind. The housekeeping kept to a very high standard of cleanliness and order.

Developing a Self-sufficient Economy

I think of Grailville in the 1940s and 1950s as a kind of precommune commune, a community on the land, striving for self-sufficiency and succeeding to a remarkable degree. We were almost all city women—from Amsterdam, The Hague, Chicago, Brooklyn, Philadelphia, Los Angeles, Detroit—but we learned fast with the help of the county agent, a resident farm manager, and supportive neighbors. During our homeless period, Josephine Drabek had had the benefit of seven months of study at the agricultural institute in Farmingdale, New York, and for the rest, we studied agricultural text books and government pamphlets. After a few years, to the amazement of the local farmers, a team of three women took over the management of the entire three-hundred-eighty acre operation: thirty dairy cows, milked by hand morning and evening; the breeding schedule and the raising of the young stock; a herd of fifty white-faced Hereford beef cattle; five hundred chickens for eggs and meat; running and repairing the tractors, corn planter, mower, disc, hay baler; cropping a hundred acres on a three-year rotation of hay, corn and wheat; putting up two-hundred-fifty tons of silage each fall; experimenting with milk goats; cultivating acres of vegetable gardens and an orchard.

I estimate that we were perhaps 85 percent self-sufficient in food for a community that numbered about sixty-five during the year and increased to over a hundred during the summer. We bought very little—coffee, salt, sugar, flour (until we got our own electric stone mill), and a few foods we could not raise ourselves. I remember that for the weekly garbage collection we usually had only one ten-gallon can, and that partly empty. We canned some ten thousand quarts of fruits and vegetables each year; grew sorghum and made molasses; extracted honey from the bee hives in the orchard; experimented with herb teas (quite successfully) and with a coffee substitute made of roasted wheat (dreadful!). While Bernard Hutzel was farm manager, butchering became a special occasion for which the community gathered around the big hackberry tree behind the Metanoia building. Bernard was an elegant butcher—quickly and deftly he would dispatch a steer and two hogs. We caught the blood in buckets and proceeded to master the mysteries of making blood pudding, head cheese, and sausage as well as curing the hams and bacon. The rest of the meat was stored at the local frozen food locker. After Bernard left, we let the food locker handle the butchering. The cow hides were tanned and used as floor coverings— handsome and durable. We attempted the tanning once, found it a malodorous and messy process, and after that sent the hides to a professional in Cincinnati. We tried our hand at country crafts—making butter and cheese, keeping a flock of sheep for the wool, spinning, weaving, candlemaking. We found the ideas of Chesterton, Gill, and the other English distributists congenial, welcomed their criticisms of capitalism, and identified with the "green revolution."

Many hands make light work; on the whole, I think that this was true for early Grailville. We had the luxury of abundant and willing labor. When there was an emergency—for instance, if rain threatened the hay crop, or if the publications department needed help collating a pamphlet— the team could call on the entire community to come to the rescue. If a given individual needed a rest, it was usually possible to find an alternate to take her place. The pattern of the day did not encourage workaholics—the usual work day, except for the farm crew, was about six and a half hours, including an hour of household chores each morning and five-and-a-half hours of work in the guilds. Everyone went to daily Mass in the parish church, had an hour and a half for spiritual reading and meditation, and took part in three rather leisurely meals. Each area had a leader who was responsible for times of study in her group as well as for on-the-job training. Strenuous efforts were made to bridge the gap between intellectual and manual work. There were frequent discussions of a philosophy of work, work as the human vocation. The program drew on the writings of Eric Gill and Ananda Coomaraswamy for the definition of art as "the right making of what needs to be made," a definition which embraces the useful as well as the fine arts and lays the foundation for honoring both. There was always opportunity for creative work in the visual arts and crafts, in music, dance, writing, and drama, all in the context of contributing to the life of the community. The leaders were at pains to take part in the manual work. Of course, the gap between fine and useful, intellectual and manual, was not always bridged successfully; sometimes there were resentments between the "grunts" behind the scenes and the "stars" in the limelight, but on the whole, Grailville deserved the description given by one Loveland pastor: "The place where you find the Ph.D. with the M.O.P."

Living the Liturgy

Of course, the ultimate bonding factor was the liturgy. We were entranced by the harmony between the rhythms of nature and the liturgical cycle. Lauds, vespers and compline from the *Short Breviary* gave shape to the day, endowing sunrise and sunset, light and darkness, with sacred meanings. The staff worked hard to help all those in the program to actually experience the Mass as the central reality of each day—studying the texts ahead of time; participating actively through speech, song and processions; keeping the great silence (from after compline at night until after grace at breakfast next morning); applying the message of the day concretely in daily activities. Jackie Disalvo, who spent a year at Grailville in 1962–1963 as part of her program at Antioch College, remembers her experience of the spiritual energy of the group: "It was most intense at communion and after Mass, remaining in the silent presence of the Holy, a palpable feeling."[7] The Gregorian melodies—we all participated in singing practice several times a week—tended to linger in one's consciousness as a kind of background music, particularly during manual work. The celebration of Sunday as the "day of the Lord," "the eighth day," a foretaste of heaven, set the rhythm of the week. All work stopped at noon on Saturday. There was time for physical preparations—a bath and shampoo, getting Sunday clothes ready. Then in the late afternoon a leisurely Mass preparation, studying the texts and working out their practical applications. In the evening, a form of matins, with lessons chosen from contemporary writers. After Mass, Sunday breakfast was an elaborate affair, "a high holy sit-down" in Elaine Jones's words, lifting up and celebrating all the work and relationships of the community. There was a three-course meal, punctuated by two readings (one on a serious spiritual theme, one in a lighter vein) and a full program of songs—plain chant, polyphony, folk songs, sing-alongs—led by the schola. In the evenings there was often folk-dancing on the tennis court, with guests from Loveland joining in. The Grailville interpretation of integrated Christian living was in many respects a rural and monastic pattern and it had its difficulties when the Grail expanded into the cities, but it was a deeply satisfying pattern, especially for us city women. For us, life on the land gave new meaning to scripture and liturgy.

Figure 4. Kay Farmer, Eva Fleischner, and Mary Jane Twohy making whole wheat bread, rolls and cookies in the Grailville bakery, 1953.

The liturgical year set the rhythm of the Grailville year—the times of fasting and feasting, the themes of meditation and study, the style of interior decoration. We delighted in Lent as "Holy Spring," saw the work in the fields and gardens as an image of the spiritual work we were doing in ourselves to prepare for the new life at Easter. We related Advent longing for the light of Christ to the winter solstice. During the Christmas holidays, we did dramatic readings of T. S. Eliot's *Murder in the Cathedral* and Paul Claudel's *Tidings Brought to Mary.* We celebrated Rogation Days and Ember Days in relation to the planting of farm crops and the Assumption and Thanksgiving as harvest festivals. Table decorations, leaflets of meal prayers, the food, the wall hangings, all the interior environment reflected the liturgical season. We saw all this as part of building a Christian culture. Jackie Disalvo sums it up: "[Grailville was] a high achievement of what you want human life to be: community as a way of fulfilling and enriching individual life, unique in that spirituality became the heart of an alternative communal life style. Grailville was an integration of spirituality, work and culture. People were not trapped into narrow roles. Professionalism, special skills, were integrated and used to enhance the performance and achievement of the community. The experts were teachers, communicating the skills to the group. Living and working in the same place, no separation between the domestic and the economic—all the work was in our home, a female space. Real work of economic support, an extended subsistence economy, but sophisticated—art as a part of it as in primitive societies. In a shared psychological experience, the group spiritual energy takes over, people get lifted out of their own limited consciousness."[8]

In the spirit of the Catholic revival, we succeeded in reviving precapitalist values in a capitalistic society. Grailville gave people an experience of work as producing use-values, not commodities for exchange. Whether it was Eva Fleischner in the bakery proving that delicious pastry could be made with whole wheat flour, or Trina Paulus in the art studio designing meal prayers, or Mary Dougherty in the laundry ironing our white blouses, we were working for individuals whom we knew and cared about. When I was recovering from major surgery, I had full-time care by a registered nurse who was participating in the Year's School. There were no servants, we were serving each other as comembers of a Christian community. Living for the most part outside the market economy, we enjoyed the luxury of labor given without stint which made for an extraordinary quality of life. At the same time, the community life and the apostolic goal were intimately interwoven—we were living a life that we wanted to share as widely as possible.

5

Grailville—A Center of the Lay Apostolate

Grailville was not only a school on a cultural oasis; it was also a center of the lay apostolate. The emphasis on building up the internal life of the community was balanced by an equal concern for reaching out to influence the rest of the world. After all, we had come together for the sake of building the Kingdom of God in the whole world! A dominant motif was the overflowing cup: whatever members produced to enhance the life of the group—ideas, music, artwork, organically grown food—was also meant to be shared with a wider circle. Grailville functioned as a magnet, drawing to itself all kinds of people interested in the new currents stirring in the Catholic church. It was conceived as an oasis, a place of refreshment and renewal, most certainly *not* a permanent refuge from a Godless world. Or rather, it was conceived as a center, pulsating with energy and radiating influences in all directions, spreading ideas, promoting individual and group actions to a series of ever-widening concentric circles. Even these images are perhaps too mild to capture the spirit of the early days. Father van Ginneken spoke of a "fiery nucleus," recalling Jesus' words, "I have come to cast fire on the earth and what will I but that it be kindled." We saw ourselves as kindling such fires wherever we went, in everyone we encountered, and we wanted to do this as fast as possible, urged on by his idea of "the elbow of time," feeling an acute need to act before the window of opportunity closed and the world settled again into rigidity.

Apostolate: Intentional and Methodical

We went about kindling our fires in an intentional and methodical way, according to a basic method outlined in Father van Ginneken's lectures. "The first requirement of a nucleus is to have the power to generate life," he told the group at the Tiltenberg. "The nucleus has to be the utmost. . . . A good candle burns up 100 percent. Tell the girls with examples what to do, how to render ten services to others. . . . Thus you gradually form a nucleus. If you have twelve girls whom you have treated this way, you can start a group. After six months, send them two by two to start other groups, and so on."¹ Each one committing herself wholeheartedly to God and trained for generous, loving service should become the center of a new group and thus the apostolate would spread. It did not work quite this easily; it took more than six months to prepare most young women to take leadership. Moreover, as we were soon to discover, the fire of a radical Christian spirit could repel as well as attract. But our intention and our hope was that each trainee would become the center of a new group, the core of a new "fiery nucleus." In addition, Grailville as a whole did function as a kind of large nucleus to which new people continually came for shorter or longer periods of training and from which individuals and teams were sent out to carry the message of the apostolate to new areas. Almost always there were one or two teams on the road, speaking in schools, colleges, parishes, public forums, and sometimes giving short courses in Connecticut or Louisiana or Minnesota or other distant places.

Paradoxically, our approach to recruitment was both inclusive (there was a place for everyone in the apostolate) and selective (not everyone had the capacity for leadership). On our lecture tours, we usually threw out a strong challenge. I remember describing most Catholic college girls as "pagans with a liturgical veneer," giving examples in support of my thesis. It felt like dropping cold water on a hot stove—my audience positively sizzled as each example hit home. We always contrived to follow up the public lecture with a smaller meeting for those who were excited and attracted by the presentation, getting names and addresses and seeking to recruit them for Grail courses. In almost every city there was a small group already interested who would sponsor the Grail visit, set up the lectures, keep in touch with the girls who responded and help them through the often formidable obstacles in the way of their making it to Grailville.

In the short courses at the weekends and during the summers, we had a system of "guardian angels," staff and junior staff, each of whom was assigned to help one or two newcomers and ease their entry into the customs and lifestyle of the community. The process was quite selective. The staff met regularly during the courses to discuss the course participants and decide which ones were ready for further training. Part of the angels' task was to encourage those we thought had potential for leadership to return for the Year's School. At the end of each Year's School some trainees would be recruited as junior staff at Grailville, some would return to their homes to try to start a group, and others would be asked to join teams undertaking various apostolic works around the country. Priests who had sent young women to the courses often requested that a team return—to staff a Catholic student center on a secular campus, to work with high schoolers, to take leadership in a family apostolate or to join a group of family service workers. Occasionally, a team of two or three would take jobs in a factory to make contact with women there. There was a continual flow back and forth, people coming from work in the field for a time of renewal and further training, new trainees seeking a place to try their wings.

Like a magnet, Grailville itself functioned as a point of contact with "new people." Our concept of apostolate stressed hospitality to everyone who came our way. We welcomed carloads of visitors in the spirit of the traditional motto, *Venit hospes, venit Christus* (when a visitor comes, Christ comes). In the summers, a staff of four were busy all day long—and often had to comandeer additional aides—receiving those who arrived: nuns and priests, an occasional bishop, casual inquirers, organized groups from schools, parishes and clubs, parents and teachers of students in the programs. Grailville was known as a "liturgical hot spot"; many priests came our way for the experience of offering Mass with a responsive congregation. In the summer, there were often six Masses[2] in a morning, with a harried choir director trying to recruit a congregation for each one. Invited guests, and those who came for more than an afternoon's tour, were usually incorporated into the life of the group and might find themselves joining in a work project or speaking at a meal. Often during the summers volunteers came to work on the farm for a few weeks—seminarians, laymen, young priests. Bill Birmingham, an editor of the scholarly quarterly *Cross Currents*, writes of his first experience at Grailville:

> Welcome! The spirit of welcome that pervaded Grailville struck me most forcibly the first time I arrived there to speak at a conference. . . . I was in nominal charge of four of our chaos-bent children. The welcome we received was unconditional and was, I soon enough realized, extended to every stranger who came to Grailville's doors.[3]

While we cultivated a world vision, we did not neglect needs close to home and endeavored to render service wherever possible in the Loveland and Cincinnati areas. The Grailville group sang the Mass in the parish every morning, sang at funerals and weddings without pay, sang the Christmas and Easter liturgies. We sold milk on the Cincinnati market and whole wheat bread and pastries in Loveland. The greater Cincinnati community was regularly invited to lectures, to evenings of folk singing and folk dancing on the tennis court, to meet guests from overseas. Guests were always welcome to roam Grailville's fields and woods or browse in the art and bookstore. The bookstore had been established early in Grailville's existence to make available works representative of the Catholic revival and to exhibit the works of local artists. We identified talents in the local area—a folk singer, several musicians, an herbalist—and invited them to share their gifts with our group. We often lent a helping hand to families in the local community, helping to take care of the sick and the newborn, collecting and distributing food and clothing for the poor, assisting with the cleanup after the waters of the Little Miami River flooded homes.

From the very beginning, publications were a part of our apostolate. A steady stream of brochures, articles, booklets, and books emanated from Grailville to be joined in the 1950s by recordings and works of contemporary religious art. Lectures given at Grail courses were published as booklets. Many of the publications were intended as study-action guides for groups of young women or for families. Two of the earliest examples—*Let Us Baptize Thanksgiving* and *Advent Ember Days*—were intended "to make the feasts of the liturgical year and the Christian feasts of the civil year celebrations which will bring the people closer to God."[4] To that end, along with background material on the feast, each booklet contained practical suggestions for the home, school, parish, and apostolic group. At the time, there was very little material on the liturgy available for the people in the pews. The Grail bulletins took materials from the volumes of Gueranger's *Liturgical Year* and the issues of *Orate Fratres*[5] and adapted them for popular use. A 1950 program for beginning groups, *Love the Chief Instrument*, includes detailed directions for beginning and leading a group, scripture study on the two commandments of love, questionnaires to stir reflection on one's talents and faults, and suggestions for personal and group actions. The focus was on how to use one's talents for others, with the discussion of intellectual, social, and practical talents intended to build self-esteem and self-confidence. Other publications popularized the idea of Christian witness, a philosophy of work, a world vision, along with a whole series on seasons of the liturgical year.

The Fiery Style: Empowerment and Reaction

We were acutely conscious of being pioneers as laywomen in the apostolate, on the cutting edge, ahead of the rest of the church. In a word, we were pushy, fast women in the basic sense of being in a hurry to translate all the great new ideas into action in what might be termed a "fiery style." Our sublime self-confidence was based not only on the certitudes of our Catholic faith but also on the sense that we were called to an historic mission, rescuing Western civilization from collapse by reanimating it with a Christian spirit. Our sense of urgency joined to the Grail gift for the concrete and experiential was an explosive combination that led to some flamboyant actions. For instance, in 1944, we gave a course at Frontenac,

Figure 5. Participants in the Grail course at Frontenac, Minnesota, with the banner that stopped traffic on U.S. I-61, June 1944.

Minnesota, on the qualities of an apostle. One of the qualities was courage and lack of concern for what others might think. The task assigned to the team who were to practice this virtue was formidable. The planning team had prepared a banner about forty feet long and a foot and a half wide, inscribed in block letters with a text from Leon Bloy, "The only tragedy in life is not to be one of the saints." The task was to take the banner down to U.S. Highway 61 and stop traffic with it. I still meet people who remember that incident.

We spoke the language of leadership rather than empowerment, but in effect we were empowering young women, giving them a sense of their own importance and imbuing them with self-confidence. They returned to home base able to organize groups, introduce new ideas, persevere in the face of setbacks. However, empowerment is a heady brew. Once people learn to take the initiative, they will do unexpected and perhaps unwise things. Our trainees were young and enthusiastic. Captivated by the vision of their historic task, they sometimes applied their new insights in rather ill-advised ways. One college sophomore, after her first Grail course, returned to her campus to gather a group whose apostolic action was to write on all the blackboards, "Because you are lukewarm, neither hot nor cold, I will vomit you out of my mouth."[6] A woman, who had already earned her MA before coming to Grailville in 1951, remembers being irritated by a very young housemother, who "would lecture me on topics such

as art, music, theology, about which she thought she was very knowledge-
able after one year at Grailville."[7] One year at Grailville could and often
did produce self-confidence, but it did not guarantee the attainment of
mature judgment!

Grail insistence on a radical Christianity, our integrated lifestyle, and
our assertive methods often produced a real division of spirits both at
home as well as on tour. Strong actions can produce reactions. People we
encountered seldom remained neutral—they either loved our spirit or
hated it. At Grailville, in our zeal for the integrated Christian life, we
worked out practical norms of behavior for every aspect of daily life—
food, clothing, work—and we tended to absolutize these norms. Thus, we
saw food as meant first of all for health. Our application: natural foods—
whole wheat bread and cereals, raw sugar, sea salt, organically grown
fruits and vegetables, and, of course, no junk food. We promoted a
Christian ideal of womanhood, women were not meant to be sex objects,
hence modest dress: colorful and attractive clothes but high necklines, calf-
length skirts, cotton stockings, and no makeup, no slacks or sleeveless
blouses, however hot and humid the weather. These departures from "normal" American lifestyles were sometimes quite threatening to course participants. One woman who is now a dedicated social worker wrote of her
experience as a teenager in a 1947 Grailville course, "Our principal
required us to spend a week at Grailville. When we talk about it now, we
agree that our primary emotion was 'scared.' Here was a strange world
dominated by women, not men, women who were comfortable with that
fact. . . . We were impressed but still scared by their differentness. . . . One
afternoon several of us ran away to Loveland to have a hamburger and a
Coke. It felt like reentering our own world. The Grail women blew my
mind with their ideas. I know now that that is a necessary first step. . . .
Those early experiences were a high point in high school, a significant
experience, even though we fought it as a group while it went on."[8]

While our service in the local community won us many friends, we
also met with some hostility, especially in the Loveland Parish, St.
Columban. It was a small rural parish: one priest offering two Masses on
Sunday; four nuns in the convent, one serving as housekeeper and the other
three teaching the eight grades of the elementary school. Both our numbers
and our level of religious practice proved overwhelming for the parish,
despite the best efforts of the pastor and Lydwine to solve problems as they
arose. We insisted that as laypeople we wanted to go to the parish like
everyone else. We were training lay apostles who were being prepared to
give active cooperation in parish life. We did not want a private chapel, set
apart from the local community. We were also aware that a chapel might
well involve a chaplain, something we wanted to avoid at all costs. Father

van Ginneken had warned us never to become "the hands and feet of the priest." Many of our practices struck the parishioners as different, even "extreme." We came to church early laden with missal, *Liber Usualis* (a thick black book containing the Gregorian chants for the feasts and seasons), and a meditation book. We stayed for a full fifteen minutes of silent prayer after Mass. We sat in the front pews (most Catholics preferred the rear of the church). We wore mid-calf skirts and head scarves rather than current fashions. All sixty-five of us went to confession every week. We asked the pastor for a key to the church so we could use it for private prayer before the Blessed Sacrament. We sang the Sunday high Mass, going up and down the aisles passing out song sheets to encourage congregational participation. When we sang wedding or funeral Masses, we went to communion during the Mass, contrary to the local custom.

A small group resented the Grail presence, complaining that "Grailville is taking over our church, crowding us out, creating a financial burden for the parish."[9] With the pastor, we worked out solutions: a third Mass on Sundays, communion before Mass for funerals and weddings, confession on Thursdays. The rumblings of discontent would die down and then be revived by a small group of disaffected people. In the spring of 1951, a newcomer to the parish took the lead in organizing a formal petition to the chancery office, asking that the Grail be removed to its own chapel. I heard about the petition through the grapevine. Lydwine was in the East; I was in charge. Veronica Forbes, a cheeky Detroiter who was part of the Grailville farm crew, phoned the organizer, playing the role of a potential signer, and got the latest word on the petitioner's plan. I remember leading the group up the hill to the church every morning in fear and trembling, not knowing what kind of opposition we might meet on the church steps. Some of our friends fired off letters to the chancery in our defense.

Archbishop Alter was our great friend and supporter. Like Archbishop McNicholas, he sometimes dropped in at Grailville for an impromptu visit and a relaxed chat. Eventually, as missives from Loveland reached the chancery, the Archbishop sent his chancellor to meet with Lydwine, myself and a group of five men who claimed to represent the aggrieved parishioners. It was a tense meeting—the men even objected to my note-taking as they recited their complaints. They rejected every possible solution suggested by the chancellor. Faced with this hostility, Lydwine sorrowfully wrote to Archbishop Alter, asking permission to withdraw from the parish.[10] Finally, on July 29, 1951, Archbishop Alter himself came to the parish to celebrate Mass and give his solution to the problems. He stated that most of the complaints were based on misunderstandings or misinterpretations of facts, including our rebuttal verbatim as part of his talk. He explained that Grailville did not have the means to build a chapel, that he as bishop did not have a priest to spare as chaplain, that Grailville as an institution should contribute $2,000 a year to the support of the parish, and that "the members of Grailville are laypeople and as such have the right to receive the benefits of any services available at the local parish." He added that "It is a work approved by the Church, and it should be a privilege and an honor to give assistance to this program."[11] Privately, he assured Lydwine that he would supply the $2,000 for Grailville's annual contribution to the parish funds. Via the grapevine, I heard that some parishioners were offended that the Archbishop every June celebrated Mass at Grailville to open the summer program, but had never visited the parish. This visit perhaps soothed some injured feelings; it certainly was a strong public vindication of the Grail and of our desire for a full liturgical life in the local parish.[12]

In our innocence, we did not realize that our desire to share the riches of the faith as we were experiencing it might appear as arrogance or imposition to others. Gradually we learned that Newton's third law—every action has an equal and opposite reaction—might apply to the apostolate, perhaps not in terms of an equal reaction but certainly an opposite one. In time, we modified our approach and found ways to invite without demanding.

How did the Grail fare in the American Catholic church, that patriarchal, juridical, clerical institution? The reactions of the priests were quite similar to those of the laity. Some, especially the older men, were suspicious of these new-fangled ideas; others were strongly attracted and became fast friends and supporters. For the clerical mentality the Grail precept that women should lead women presented two major difficulties: the idea of initiatives coming from the laity and the idea of leadership by women. For the Grail, a lay apostolate meant lay leadership—under the bishop, to be sure—but largely autonomous. In a church where the lay role had been defined for centuries as "pray, pay and obey," and where priests were accustomed to think of themselves as the sole source of initiatives, it demanded a real change of mind and heart to accept the priest's role as advisory and supportive but not controlling. In a patriarchal institution, deeply imbued with sexism and misogyny, the idea that women might be well-grounded in theology, able to teach adult men as well as children, and able to take the lead in important projects was quite foreign.

Nonetheless, younger priests and seminarians were often deeply touched by their contacts with the Grail and became warm allies. Raymond Lucker, Bishop of New Ulm, Minnesota, which he describes as the least important diocese in the United States, writes of his experience at Grailville in the early 1950s, "It was a real shot in the arm to participate in the liturgy with a faith-filled, enthusiastic, joyful and participatory group and to enter into discussions with internationally known speakers. The members of Grailville began to open for me the call to equality and mutuality that women were bringing to our attention. . . . I have counted it as a special blessing in my life that the members of the Grail touched me in a time when I was just beginning to be aware of the renewal of the Church brought about by the action of the Spirit in our lives."[13] Another priest, Joseph Wittbrod, who later became a Trappist monk, recalls "those days of 1951–52 when we celebrated such 'dangerous' practices as the altar facing the community, the offertory and communion processions, etc. . . . As my liturgy students at Glenmary commented at the end of the school year 'there were three things we learned in liturgy this year: Grailville-Grailville-GRAILVILLE.' "[14] And Peter Sullivan, SJ, described his visit in June of 1945 as "I met Grail in action. And action is an anemic word, I can assure you. It was like touching a live wire and living to tell the story. . . . The Grail is startlingly, provocatively Christian, and hence revolutionary."[15]

Issues with a Patriarchal Institution

As I read through the files of correspondence with officials of the Cincinnati archdiocese, I am struck both by the degree of tight and centralized control Catholic Church officials maintained over teaching and worship and by the way we managed to retain considerable autonomy. Anything having to do with teaching about religion required explicit permission from the bishop. An early publication, the first draft of the pamphlet, *Advent Ember Days*, was circulated to our closest associates in a modest edition of five-hundred mimeographed copies for a try-out with a view to later revisions. The chancery judged it to be "of general circulation" and therefore ruled that it must be submitted to the archdiocesan censor for approval, which was promptly granted. After that experience, we routinely submitted every publication for an *imprimatur*, a formal certification in the name of the bishop that the work had not swerved from orthodoxy and therefore could be printed. The chancellors seemed to regard our works primarily as a nuisance and an undue burden on the censors. The following comment is typical: "Apparently Grailville is still at work and causing labor for the censor!"[16] The censors, whose task was simply to decide whether there was anything against faith or morals in our writings, often could not resist criticizing the content. The censor for *Feast Day Melodies*, a booklet of short songs with English texts set to Gregorian style melodies, was also the seminary professor of music. Along with permission to publish, he offered this comment: "Had the composers taken the time to discuss the matter with competent musicians not of their own group, particularly with men schooled in the chant or in adapting melody to free verse, they might have profited much and saved themselves criticism."[17] The chancery also kept a close watch on speakers at Grailville. Initially, in May 1944, Lydwine had submitted a list of possible speakers. This sufficed until 1950, when the bishop sent a memorandum outlining canon law on the need for his written permission for any preaching, lecturing, or conducting of spiritual exercises within his diocese. From then on, we sent lists of speakers for each course, along with the standard request for faculties for priest visitors from other dioceses to say Mass and hear confessions. I do not remember that there was ever any problem with our invitees. Even after Vatican II had brought about some relaxation of the rules, the archbishop wrote a letter of inquiry (prompted by a letter from a local Catholic) about Dorothy Day speaking at Grailville. "While I have always admired greatly the spirit of Dorothy Day, I certainly do not share her sentiments or consider her judgment in practical situations a reliable one."[18] Prophetic voices do make the institution uncomfortable!

We simply accepted the church regulations governing the *Index of Forbidden Books*. As late as 1959, Dr. Eleanor Walker of the Grailville staff felt obliged to obtain permission from the chancery to read *The Second Sex* by Simone de Beauvoir for a study she was doing on women. The chancellor in granting the permission adds that she is not to allow others access to the book and notes that "books that are obscene in character are absolutely prohibited."[19]

The strictest controls of all were exercised over the liturgy and the spiritual direction of individuals. In 1954, we sought an imprimatur for a booklet entitled *Promised in Christ*, which contained a prayer hour for a bride-to-be and a ceremony for a solemn engagement. This really upset the diocesan censor. In an unsigned memo to the chancellor, he wrote: "THIS SHOULD *NOT* be approved . . . a group of girls at Grailville have no authority etc. to write a Ritual for church services and what is more, one that has canonical effects of which they know nil . . . call it a suggested betrothal procedure and NOT rite of betrothal."[20] (Capital letters in the original.) We made the change from "ceremony" to procedure, the booklet was published and was widely used. In 1963, we wanted to adopt the suggestion of the liturgical experts and receive communion standing instead of kneeling. This request produced a long letter from the archbishop's secretary, explaining that while there were historical and theoretical reasons in support of this practice, and while there was nothing in the rubrics as to the posture of the the layman [sic], nevertheless such a novel practice could not be introduced without the authority of the local bishop.[21]

Figure 6. The solemn engagement of Dolores Kramer and Tom Bruggeman in St. Vincent Ferrer Church, Cincinnati, with pastor Charles Blum presiding, April 1958.

Perhaps the most sensitive issue was the matter of spiritual direction. Priests were trained to think of giving spiritual direction as a role belonging exclusively to themselves, in virtue of their study of theology. The traditions of Catholic spirituality are very clear on the principle that those who are serious about growing in holiness need direction, but who is best able to guide young women and help them to gain a realistic picture of their strengths and weaknesses? We were convinced that living with a group of young women, we could know them much better than a priest who heard them only in confession or saw them from time to time for a brief pastoral conversation. Therefore, we thought that we were in a better position to give guidance in both small and large decisions. I think on the whole this was true, although sometimes we overstepped and yielded to the temptation to play God, for instance insisting that coming to the Year's School was clearly the will of God for a given individual. Generally, I believe, we gave good advice, helping young women to gain a realistic sense of their potentialities and encouraging them not to be constrained by conventional expectations. I think of one shy, awkward young woman who was challenged to make a serious commitment as an artist and became a distinguished silversmith. I think of a number who became serious scholars and writers. For the majority, I think it is fair to say that they have not settled for conventional lives and have made outstanding contributions to their families, professions, and communities.

As Joan and I traveled around the country, we observed some disquieting aspects in the relationships between a number of the priests and the young women with whom they were working. We were disturbed by the degree of dependence on the priest, both for the work and for decisions in their personal lives, which we noticed in some of the young women. It seemed to us that many of these girls had developed crushes on the good-looking young priests and were confusing romantic longings for male approval with a desire for holiness. I am not talking about sexual abuse on the part of the priests, but simply about their lack of awareness of adolescent psychology and their fostering of an unhealthy kind of dependency. Some priests were happy to cooperate with Grail leaders in guiding young women. Some others saw a need for "judicious priestly direction." As one priest wrote in a letter to Archbishop Alter, "We cannot forget that they are a group of women being led by women, with a great deal of female emotions and instincts guiding them. . . . [W]hat is lacking is unified direction by a competent spiritual director and theologian."[22] In these comments written in 1957, I hear an echo of the comments of the Jesuit superior in the sixteenth century about Mary Ward and her Ladies of Loretto: "They are but women. . . . If women were to undertake that [i.e., a rule like that of the Jesuits] it will lead to the most profound corruption and it will never yield good results."[23] The assumption that women are inferior, incapable of the reasoned judgment and emotional control of men, is very long-lived.

I find it amazing that, faced with this cautious juridical mentality, we were able to establish ourselves as a lay group and carry out our programs and projects pretty much as we wished. The juridical mentality, playing it safe, abiding by the rules, is admirably suited to maintaining the status quo. The problem is common to all institutions—maintaining the organization takes priority over its mission—and the church is by far the oldest institution in the West. In our zeal for the mission, we were intent on making changes—by definition that meant acting in new ways, ignoring the rules or breaking or at least bending them. How did we manage to do so much pioneering, and under female leadership to boot? I think we owed this freedom in part to the support of Archbishop McNicholas and to his willingness to take a risk, a rare characteristic in a bishop; in part to the support of Archbishop Alter; in part to Lydwine's abililty to reassure bishops and priests of the soundness of the Grail. We kept close contact with the bishop, always informing him well in advance of any new initiative and asking his blessing rather than his permission. We exercised our womanly charm and tact—remembering the bishop on his feast day and the anniversary of his ordination, sending baskets of homemade delicacies at Christmas and Easter. Finally, we used our practical common sense in deciding when it was necessary to ask permission and when simply to go ahead and act.

In brief, in the 1940s and 1950s in the midst of a clerical and patriarchal church, Grailville functioned as a center of the lay apostolate, a vibrant Christian community, a seed bed for new ideas, a home base for enthusiastic young teams, a meeting ground where scholar and activist, priests and laity, artist and student, social worker and secretary, celibates, singles, and married could exchange insights and experience in an atmosphere of common concern for a resurgence of Christian values.

Part II
Fast Women
in a Slow Church,
1951–1964

6

Deepening the Roots

Establishing the Grail Nucleus, 1951

In the 1950s, the decade of careful preparation of Grail leaders paid off in a burst of growth. The movement expanded in all dimensions: increased numbers, new places, and new fields of work, with a speed that almost satisfied our desires as fast women for bringing about change. The expansion began with the policies of the new international president, Rachel Donders, who paid her first visit to the United States in the fall of 1951. She set in motion three courses of action that shaped the movement for the ensuing decade. First, on October 9, 1951, she formally established the nucleus of the Grail in the United States by presiding at the dedication of twelve Americans. Second, she strongly reinforced a policy of expansion to city centers. And third, she urged us to develop a program for sending young Americans to serve overseas. All these steps were rooted in the Grail vision and had been in preparation for a number of years.

"The Time Is Ripe": Formalizing Grail Membership

Grail vocabulary and Grail membership presented difficulties from the first days in the United States. Lydwine and Joan had come to these shores as *Vrouwen van Nazareth*, "Women of Nazareth," or, in the translation adopted in England, "Ladies of the Grail." Mary Louise Tully, after her return to Chicago and the completion of her three-year training period, had also been formally accepted as a member of the Ladies of the Grail, but in a wholly private ceremony. This name, which had worked well in England, struck a false note in America. After receiving mail addressed to "Dear Venerable Ladies," Lydwine quickly dropped the phrase. The Grail certainly did not want to be "venerable"; at Doddridge Farm young women over twenty-five were turned away as too old and set in their ways! During the war years, as discussed in chapters 4 and 5, the United States Grail continued to stress its lay character. Questions of formal commitment, membership, and formal structures were shelved, or rather, were not even raised. What to call the women involved in Grailville? Lydwine and Joan spoke of themselves as Grail Workers, Grail Staff, or "free workers in the lay apostolate," but did not apply these terms to the rest of us. The general public referred to us as "Grail girls."

Immediately after the war, in August of 1945, the Grail leaders from the Netherlands, England, Scotland, Germany, Australia, and the United States met with Father van Ginneken and Margaret van Gilse, who at that time was called the Mother General, at Eastcote, a house of the English Grail near London. At this meeting, it was evident that, during the war years, quite different directions had developed in different countries. On the one hand, particularly in England and Scotland, there was an emphasis on building up the Ladies of the Grail as a separate, strongly organized group, able to take apostolic initiatives under a centralized leadership. On the other hand, in the United States, the emphasis was on building up the general lay apostolate, without the Grail name or special Grail membership structures. Those at the meeting in England agreed that both approaches had their strengths and their dangers. As Rachel Donders writes in *The History of the International Grail*:

> In the first approach, there was the danger of institutionalization, self-importance, and in the end, the stifling of life; in the second, there was the possibility of a gradual disappearance into vagueness and anonymity. Wisely, it was decided at this juncture not to force anything, but to leave the possibilities open. Margaret van Gilse would go to the USA to see for herself. Her judgment would be decisive in the end.[1]

In November of 1945, Margaret van Gilse arrived at Grailville. At her first meal with the whole group, Joan, in keeping with the policy of promoting Grailville as a center of the general lay apostolate, introduced her simply as Miss van Gilse from Belgium, who had done a great deal for the lay apostolate in Europe. Margaret quietly took part in the Grailville program, following the same schedule as the newest recruit, and even working on landscaping under Josephine Drabek's direction. I remember her sitting quietly in our discussions, mending her underwear and never saying a word. Two other Dutch women, Lydia Mulders and Ans Coebergh van den Braak, who had been part of the original team for the United States, also arrived in the fall of 1945 and took their places in the group without being identified as Ladies of the Grail. Many years later, Ans told me how strange she had felt in the Grailville group, not being identified as a member of the core group and not knowing who, if any, of the Americans was committed to a lifetime dedication.

In June of 1946, Margaret had private conversations with those of us who had been functioning as staff for several years, trying to find out how we saw our situation. She invited me on a walk through the woods and asked me, "What do you think Lydwine and Joan are doing here?" I felt confused: I felt somewhat disloyal to Lydwine in having this private conversation, but on the other hand I knew that Margaret outranked her and had a right to question me. I launched into an explanation of the lay apostolate, how the bishops did not yet understand it, how we did not want to be seen as "nuns in mufti" and were happy to say we had not taken any vows. "Who do you think I am?" she asked next. I think she had never forgiven Joan for that anonymous introduction. I had read *The Call of the King*, the book which the Australian Grail had published on the life and death of Judith Bouwman, with its letter from "Mother Margaret," so I answered, "You're Mother Margaret." She heaved a sigh of relief.

To the Grail in Europe, Margaret wrote in praise of the extraordinary spirit at Grailville. Rachel sums up these letters: "She found the spirit there to be of a radicalism and generosity she had seldom seen before. Without any structural safeguarding or 'security,' there was a self-giving, an availability, a spirit of prayer and sacrifice exemplary for all. She was not sure how long Grailville would be able to maintain this high level, but still she did not think it was the moment to intervene or force a change."[2] Before she returned to Europe, she gave Lydwine and Joan a week-long retreat under her direction. Her only requirement for both Lydwine and Joan was that each should have a "sixth year," a kind of sabbatical. As part of his plan for maintaining the spirit, Father van Ginneken wanted regular times of contemplation—a day a week, a weekend a month, a week each year, and a full year after five years of active work. The person should be free from all responsibilities, with ample time to pray, to read, to reflect, to deepen her self-knowledge, develop her prayer life, and renew her spirit. Lydwine spent her year at Super Flumina, the small farm ten miles from Grailville, in a quiet rhythm of prayer and manual work. When she returned to Grailville in the fall of 1947, she recommended that Joan take her sixth year in Holland, where mature leaders would be available to guide her time of renewal.

When Cardinal Griffin in London was informed of the differences in the Grail internationally, he seemed wary of the direction taken in the United States and insisted that the English Grail should function as a separate entity under his direction and under the leadership of Yvonne Bosch van Drakestein. This separation of the English Grail from the international group was an unexpected and painful blow. In Father van Ginneken's vision, the Women of Nazareth had a threefold task: to maintain a spirit of radical Christianity, to carry the functional roles in the movement, and to safeguard the unity, both nationally and internationally. All of the Dutch Women of Nazareth at work in England (except Yvonne) and several of the English women chose to remain with the international Grail. I remember that Lydwine called a group of us together—I think it was in 1949—to share the news that the English Grail had broken away from the international movement. It was a solemn and painful moment, doubly painful because their publications had been a special source of inspiration for us. I felt betrayed. This breach in international unity was surely in Rachel Donders' mind as she set out for the United States, as was her concern that without some formal structure the Grail might simply disappear. "I pushed my trip," Rachel Donders told me. "The main thing is to come together again. The time is ripe. We must have Women of Nazareth here in the United States. Even if it is only one person, we have to establish the principle. I felt I had to save the Grail internationally."[3]

Joan Overboss strongly disagreed; she distrusted institutional structures and sharply defined rules of membership. She felt that setting up the WoN through a formal commitment to celibacy, obedience, and poverty would create barriers that would interfere with the apostolic work. Rachel spent much time and effort trying to persuade Joan that time was ripe for a minimum of formalization. In my perception, Joan gave way reluctantly, agreeing to change the name of her Detroit center from "Chattuck House" to "The Gateway" to "The Gateway Grail Center" and eventually encouraging some of her staff to embrace a nucleus vocation. However, after her return to Europe in 1955, she continued her criticisms of the nucleus structure. As designated leader, Rachel had the authority to make the decision. She proceeded with the dedication of twelve American women on October 9, 1951, at a Mass celebrated in the main hall at Grailville by Father Nicholas Maestrini, an Italian missionary priest who had been instrumental in bringing the Grail to his Catholic Center in Hong Kong. A great friend and loyal supporter of the Grail, he happened to be visiting at the time. The women, all of whom had had many years of training and service in the Grail, were Anna Agre, Mary Buckley, Josephine Drabek, Mary Alice Duddy, Thea von Eroes, Judith Hines, Mary Anne Kimbell, Catherine Leahy, Barbara Ellen Wald, Francine Wickes, Mariette Wickes, and myself. We had each written out the official dedication formula on parchment in our own hand. Before the communion, each one read aloud from her paper, voicing her desire to give herself to God as an instrument for the conversion of the world, swearing "an oath of absolute obedience to the International President of the Grail," and promising to live in apostolic poverty and in virginal chastity[4] "for so long as Thou dost allow me to remain a member of the dedicated nucleus of the Grail."[5] I was elated—I think we all were. We had made the grade, we belonged.

The dedication took place in semisecrecy—we were walking a fine line between nuns and laywomen and were still concerned about avoiding the "nuns in mufti" label. As I remember it, the new people in the Year's School were sent off on a picnic to Super Flumina while the new nucleus members and those almost ready for dedication participated in the Mass and the celebration afterward. However, the spirit was so high that the joy in the atmosphere communicated itself to the picnickers on their return from their outing. They knew something special had happened and they felt left out. The dynamic of the inner circle and the outer circle had been set in motion, creating problems for the future.

The twelve were new members, but what were they members of? Rachel and Lydwine had consciously worked out a new terminology more in keeping with a lay movement. Not Women of Nazareth or Ladies of the Grail but members of the Grail nucleus. Titles were changed accordingly from Mother General or Mother Superior to International President; from leader-in-charge to National President; from the Tiltenberg as Motherhouse to The International Grail Center; from "promise of the evangelical counsels" to "total dedication to Christ." Bishop Huibers in Haarlem approved of these changes, saying that his brother bishops already referred to him as "the bishop of the Grail." When Rachel communicated the changes to other bishops and to Grail members around the world, they were well received.

Before Rachel Donders returned to Holland, there was a second dedication ceremony, January 13, 1952, for eight more Americans.[6] Inspired by these experiences of total commitment, the group responded enthusiastically to Rachel's directive, voiced as a gentle suggestion, that we might conspire together, without undue pressure, of course, to see how many nucleus members we could attract. We soon settled into a definite program of recruitment. We already had a general selection process in place, drawing from our wide contacts those who were ready for a short course, and from the short courses choosing those who were ready for the year at Grailville and urging them to attend. Now, from the Year's School we selected those who were ready to hear about the nucleus for a Lenten retreat at Super Flumina, the small farm ten miles from Grailville. Rachel returned to the States every year, gave a Lenten course at Super Flumina, based on the writings of Father van Ginneken, and presided at a dedication ceremony in which the new nucleus members swore the oath of obedience and took on the obligations of virginity and poverty as the expression of their dedication to Christ and their desire to be used for the lay apostolate. The ceremony always took place at Mass. The celebrants were priests who were close friends of the Grail—Father James Coffey, Monsignor Ligutti, Father

*Figure 7. The second group to make a lifetime dedication in the nucleus of the U.S.
Grail, January 13, 1952. Front row: Lorraine Machan, Rachel Donders (International President), Jeanne Plante (Director of Grailville), Lydwine van Kersbergen
(President of the Grail in the USA), Helen Kelly. Back row: Mary Helena Fong,
Deborah Schak, Martha Orso, Mary Brigid Niland, Veronica Forbes. Shortly after
this picture was taken, Lorraine Machan and Helen Kelly left the United States to
join a Grail team in South Africa.*

George Fogarty. By 1961, the nucleus in North America (at this time, the
Canadians simply joined in with the group in the United States) had grown
to a hundred members. The nucleus recruitment process further intensified
the inner circle/outer circle dynamic. Those who were not invited to a Super
Flumina retreat puzzled over what was going on "over there," and sometimes felt excluded or even rejected as not quite making the grade. We tried
to counter these feelings by experimenting with a general Grail membership,
formalized in a commitment ceremony in which the person pledged herself
to lead a full Christian life in the Grail movement, without promising
celibacy.

A program of nucleus formation was developed which included, ide-
ally, a year at Grailville, a second year as junior staff at Grailville, an experience in a city center, and a time of prayer and penance at Super Flumina.

There was a good deal of international exchange during the nucleus training. Some Americans spent time at The Tiltenberg, the international training center in Holland; some young women from other countries had their training at Grailville and made their dedication at Grailville. There was considerable emphasis on the importance of virginity as a form of total dedication, and a policy of "protecting the vocations" of those who seemed called to virginity by keeping them in situations in which contact with young men was reduced to a minimum. These practices sowed the seeds of difficulties which cropped up later. But for the time being, we faced the tasks of starting city centers and sending teams overseas with a sizable pool of committed young women eager to serve wherever they were needed.

7

"Get Six City Centers"

Expansion Coast to Coast, 1951–1964

" **G**et six city centers" was Rachel Donders' parting message before she returned to Holland in January of 1952. She advised the new nucleus members to look for locations where they could integrate themselves into a parish community, establish "a house with a heart," and begin to influence the immediate surroundings.

Brooklyn

A center had already been started in Brooklyn, due in large measure to the influence of Father James Coffey and the urgings of Mary Buckley. Father Coffey, who had met the Grail when he was a student at the University of Louvain in Belgium, had since become a professor at the major seminary of the Brooklyn diocese. Under his tutelage, generations of seminarians and priests learned about the lay apostolate, visited Grailville during the summers, helped to organize Grail courses in the New York area, and, as they became parish priests, shared their enthusiasm for the lay apostolate with the young women in their parishes. A group of young women had formed in the summer of 1945, some of whom had been to Grail courses and some who were connected with the Young Christian Workers. For a time they met together in the name of Catholic Action. Later, with the help of the priests, who made monthly cash contributions, those who identified with the Grail rented a store front in St. Augustine's parish and dubbed it "Monica House," in honor of Saint Augustine's long-suffering mother. Mary Buckley, who had been touring the country with two Grailville students from Hong Kong, returned to Grailville in the spring of 1948, convinced that Grailville needed to send someone to give full-time service, a definite Grail identity, and greater stability to this fledgling group. She was appointed to the task in the spring of 1948.

Figure 8. A play reading at the Brooklyn Grail Center of Christopher Frye's verse drama, "The Lady's Not For Burning," 1949.

Soon the Brooklyn Center was in full swing with evening supper meetings for regular groups of college and working girls, talks in the schools and the parishes, and a popular Sunday afternoon program on modern Christian writers for young men and women. "We did play readings from T. S. Eliot and Paul Claudel," Mary Buckley recalls, "and a lot of marriages came out of that group."[1] The staff literally embraced poverty in a Franciscan style. The rent for the store front and the modest apartment where the staff lived was paid by the monthly contributions from a circle of priests and other friends; the staff begged food from the local markets; some of the priests brought care packages of food; sometimes there was no money at all in the house, sometimes a little cash came in from programs, but always there were willing volunteers to help with special projects. The priests were very generous, ready to lend a car and raise scholarship funds to send young women to Grailville. They also reassured anxious parents, worried about the strange movement their daughters were involved in. "In the beginning, I didn't have enough money to install a telephone," Mary Buckley remembers.[2] After a time, the team gained somewhat more financial stability and moved to larger quarters.

I arrived in October of 1953 to head the Brooklyn staff, replacing Mary Buckley who had left to become Dean of Women at the new Pius XII University in Basutoland. At the time, we rented the upper two floors of a Brooklyn brownstone, just off Flatbush Avenue, from an elderly widow who lived in the basement. At first I found it very difficult to adjust to city life after my years on the Grailville farm. I was quite exhausted just by making the subway trip from Brooklyn to the New York Center on Riverside Drive to consult with the Grail team there. It seemed to me that there was gritty, oily dirt everywhere—on the forsythia bush struggling to survive in our minuscule backyard, on the floors and windowsills of our crowded apartment, on my white slip when I undressed at night after a day of contacting people in the city. We cleaned faithfully every morning, but by noon I could write my name in the dust that had accumulated on any flat surface. I remember escaping to the Brooklyn Botanic Gardens nearby for a breath of fresh air and a sight of green things growing. Gradually, I became accustomed to the noise and dirt of the city and found that I was energized by the work.

Our living room was also our meeting room for regular sessions with groups of students and working girls, employed for the most part in office work. We no longer had the store front for large group meetings, so we immediately launched a rather ambitious interparish program, "You in Particular," using parish facilities. We invited groupings of three parishes to join together to put on a series of evenings for young women aimed at broadening their horizons as to their life choices. From these contacts we recruited young women for the ongoing groups and for programs at Grailville. We also coordinated arrangements for an annual one-week summer program, finding suitable locations outside the city and working in cooperation with staff from Grailville.

In the 1950s, any organized activity that wanted to use the name "Catholic" had to have the permission of the local bishop. Archbishop Molloy of Brooklyn was something of a recluse, meeting only with his priests, not with the laity. Father Coffey arranged for any necessary permissions for Grail activity in the diocese. Shortly after I arrived, the bishop suddenly endowed the Grail with two brownstones and a grant of $10,000 toward renovation costs. I remember the unaccustomed luxury of having two whole houses at our disposal, after our cramped apartment quarters. In the space of a few years, we turned the two houses into one, bought another smaller house down the block, and carried out a successful fund-raising campaign to pay for the extensive renovations. With the expanded quarters, came an expanded staff and a greatly expanded program. Now we had our own attractive meeting room which easily seated more than a hundred for regular Sunday evening lectures on the lay apostolate for the general public. In addition to the regular city center program of small group meetings, there were many special projects. We had room enough to offer the Paschal Meal on Holy Thursday to a hundred people, who were impressed by this presentation of the Last Supper in its historic context as a Jewish Seder. We housed the rehearsals for an Advent drama in 1955, which was then performed with a cast of a hundred in theaters in Brooklyn, Manhattan, and Philadelphia. We put on an international festival, and in 1956, we established the Overseas Institute to prepare young women for work in Africa and Latin America. I was in charge of the household that carried on all these activities. We were some thirty young women living together in the enlarged center, eight working full-time as Grail staff, ten in the Institute program, others going to school or working in their professions and helping with apostolic programs on evenings and weekends.

The City Center Pattern

The Brooklyn Center grew out of a local initiative to which Grailville responded. The other city centers were begun as a result of conscious planning by the Grail staff and usually focused initially on a specific need. Between 1949 and 1961, Grail city centers were established in Detroit; Cincinnati; Philadelphia; New York City; Toronto; Queens; Lafayette, Louisiana; and San Jose, California. While each center had its own special emphasis, they also shared many common patterns. The physical location consisted of a roomy house or apartment, large enough to accommodate ten to twenty-five residents, with a meeting room that could seat fifty or sixty, and the possibility, at least occasionally, to serve a meal to that number. In Cincinnati, Detroit, Philadelphia, Lafayette, and San Jose, the Grail acquired ownership of the property; otherwise, the facilities were rented. The New York Center occupied a ten-room apartment on Riverside Drive that could sleep a dozen people. The Cincinnati Center had two gracious old family homes in the university neighborhood. Usually, there were five or six full-time staff who were either members of the Grail nucleus or graduates of the Grailville Year's School. The other residents were young women interested in the lay apostolate, who were either holding down regular jobs or studying at a college or vocational school. The residents paid room and board, and this income together with program fees and donations sufficed to finance the house at a very modest level, since the staff all worked on subsistence.

The residents shared a community life, which was intended as an opportunity for both personal spiritual development and apostolic work. Usually, the group would attend daily Mass together, meet again for vespers before supper, enjoy a common meal, attend planning meetings or apostolic events several nights a week, and end the day with compline. Often a center would include an art and book store, which might be as small as a display case in the meeting room or as large as the Detroit store on a busy shopping street. All the centers celebrated the feasts and seasons of the liturgical year with various constituencies—students in the high schools and colleges, groups in the local parish, circles of married women. Usually, they had one or more small groups following one of the apostolic programs put out by Grailville. While residence was for women only, around each center were circles of families, friends (men as well as women), local priests, who joined in lectures, discussions, and celebrations of the feasts and seasons of the liturgical year. Whatever the specific focus of a particular center, the scope was always intergenerational, interracial, and international, opening many opportunities for community, celebration, and service to all who wished to join in.

Detroit

The Detroit Center was begun at the initiative of Joan Overboss, who succeeded in creating a unique experiment in urban community development in a low income, interracial neighborhood. After her time of renewal and study in Holland, she returned in the fall of 1949 with full support from Rachel Donders to try her noninstitutional approach. She proposed to start anonymously in Detroit, that is, as a private citizen of the Church rather than a representative of the Grail, working in a factory and drawing together a small group of potential leaders. This approach had been successful in the early days of the movement in Holland, but Lydwine doubted its effectiveness in America. "How can Joan expect to be anonymous when she has already spent six years as a Grail leader meeting Catholics all over this country?" was her tart comment. Nevertheless, she also supported Joan's right to try out her own plan of apostolate, and during the difficult early days in Detroit sent her frequent care packages of food and clothing. Joan worked in a restaurant, a laundry, and finally in the Dodge plant, discovering that her coworkers were mostly older women, often divorced, embittered by their life experience, "not good Grail material." She took a few courses at the local universities, finding there young women—and men—who were responsive to the idea of the lay apostolate. In 1951 she was joined by Petra Coyle, a graduate of the Grailville Year's School, who had accepted a job in Detroit. Soon the two had formed a group of young women—drawn from the high schools, colleges, and workplaces—and had begun a program of prayer and discussions in their small apartment. The activities quickly outgrew the apartment. They found a storefront with an apartment above it in an inner city parish, St. Leo's, conveniently located

Figure 9. Mary Kay Donohue, with pastor Walter Schoenherr and members of St. Leo's Parish in Detroit, setting up a neighborhood food co-op, circa 1955.

near the church, the university, and public transportation. On Pentecost 1952, the Center, named the Gateway "in honor of Our Lady, the gateway to heaven,"³ opened its doors. The following year, the Center expanded to the adjoining store front and apartment.

The Gateway described itself as "an experiment in cooperative living, geared to the needs of the community,"⁴ with an outreach far beyond the parish. In her account of the history of the center, Joan expands on the concept of cooperative living: "Our very first task is *to be*, no matter what needs to be done. Christ as the center of our own personal lives and of the life of our family, trying to be as whole, personally and communally, as we can . . . a life of docility to the inspirations of the Holy Ghost. . . . We want to cooperate among ourselves and then to cooperate with others around us in ever widening circles that the oneness of the Mystical Body may become visible."[5]

This vision of cooperative living was concretized first of all in the daily life of the resident community—in the buying, cooking, cleaning, studying, singing, artwork, prayer, hospitality. Then it expanded to a social awareness of the needs in Detroit and a focused effort to involve young women "in these ideas of personal and social revolution." The Gateway quickly developed a buying co-op and a credit union; a family service program; a personalized social service program in the neighborhood, based on home visits; a Christian culture program which included lectures, discussions, play readings, music, dance, original dramas, along with a crafts workshop; a liturgical program in the parish, fostering active participation by the parishioners. The store front included a shop selling "a wild variety of things, but linked together by the fact that they have quality, each in their own way." Most of the things for sale were made by the staff and their wider circles: whole wheat flour, cereals and bread; hand weaving and sewing; cards, jewelry, and other art objects; books. The work in the parish was soon incorporated in a book, *The Church Year in a City Parish*, complete with practical instructions as well as the actual materials used in the celebrations at St. Leo's. The drama group soon produced *The Rainbow*, a dance drama on the theme of bringing diverse races into unity. A more ambitious effort, *New Born Again*, was created by Elaine Jones, the first African-American nucleus member. She combined Negro spirituals, folk verse and original text in a moving presentation of the story of creation and redemption, enacted by Clarence Rivers, the first African-American priest of the Cincinnati diocese, and a chorus of young women from the Gateway. The play was performed a number of times in Detroit, Cincinnati, and other cities.

A report from 1955 spells out the structure of the Gateway in terms of concentric circles: first, the resident staff of fifteen, including several nucleus members, other Grail members explicitly committed for a year at a time to service in the center, and women working as teachers, nurses, social workers, secretaries, and so on, and contributing their incomes for the support of the center; second, the forty team members, students, business and professional women, cooperating closely with the staff in carrying out programs at the Gateway or in their own surroundings; third, the expansion, some four hundred young women who had just begun to participate in some phase of the Gateway and might later be drawn into team membership; fourth, the circle of friends, men and women, who took part in the public lectures, cultural programs and liturgical celebrations and who encouraged and assisted whenever possible. This group included a number of married couples.[6] Not mentioned in this report but constituting a vital part of the "circle of friends" were the many priests who celebrated the Mass, gave talks, sent young women to the programs, and generally offered advice and support.

In the summer of 1955 Joan was called back to Europe, intending to return in about six months. However, she was soon caught up in events in Holland. The tension which had surfaced in the postwar meeting in England in 1945 between the English model of Ladies of the Grail carrying on various works and the United States model of a flexible, free-flowing movement was alive in Europe. The postwar Dutch Grail had organized itself much as the English had—a celibate group carrying on specific works: a nurses' training school, a training for family service, the lay mission school at Ubbergen. Intense discussions were going on about the identity and future directions for the Grail. Joan gathered a small group who agreed with her anti-institution, anti-authority stance and were groping for a way to articulate a different vision—more decentralized and democratic. Not many in the European Grail understood her. Given the classical Ignatian spirituality in which we had all been trained, which emphasized obedience not only in action but also in will and thought, we were not well equipped to discuss profound differences of vision and policy. There was no forum in which to clarify ideas and negotiate differences. Disagreements were not valued as expressing diversities which could enrich the whole but rather were seen as threats to unity. When I saw Joan in Holland in December of 1957, I had the distinct impression that she was seen as a threat and had been marginalized. She was certainly exhausted by the struggle. Shortly thereafter, she opted for study. With support from the Grail, she undertook work in the social sciences at an institute in Tilburg, Holland, and earned her licentiate. She never returned to the United States but became a cofounder of Sedos, a documentation and training center in Rome, which oriented members of missionary orders to cross-cultural issues. She died suddenly in Rome in 1969. In her fifteen years in the United States she had had a profound influence on the American Grail with her emphasis on the liturgy and the communal dimensions of worship, her vision of the laity, her desire to work with married couples, her efforts to close the distance between celibate and married, her longing for a flexible, organic movement, her call to live recklessly and joyfully. She was a person ahead of her time and played a significant part in the shaping of the United States Grail.

After Joan's departure Mariette Wickes took over as leader in charge, followed by Audrey Sorrento and her teammates, Wynni Kelly and Cay Charles. The elan of the early days was followed by a period of consolidation. The rents for the two store fronts and the two apartments were outrageously high; the diocese advised against buying the property, considering it too unsound structurally. The group began to look for another location, seeking a changing neighborhood where they hoped to facilitate racial integration. In the fall of 1958, with a loan from one of the married couples, the group, now called simply the Detroit Grail Center, purchased a sizable single family house on Webb Avenue, a neighborhood where African-American families were beginning to move in. Shortly thereafter, they rented a storefront on the east side of Detroit for an enlarged art and book store and a point of contact with the suburbs.

The programs which the Grail had initiated in St. Leo's parish continued under local leadership. In the new center on Webb Avenue, the residential community of twelve young women was consciously interracial and international, including residents from Trinidad, South Africa, and Korea as well as African-Americans. The various programs of spiritual and intellectual development undertook to bring African-Americans and whites together for lectures, discussions, cultural events, and liturgical celebrations. The art and book shop served as a focal point for the Christian culture programs, with lectures, music programs, and exhibits. The interracial events included a training that prepared women to give religious instruction to high schoolers, a Service Careers team for young women who wanted their work to be more than "just a job," and an outreach program for international students.

Cincinnati

Family Service was the initial focus of the Cincinnati Center, which took its inspiration from a program in Holland that aimed to give young women a level of professional training comparable to that for social work or nursing, but focused on work in the home. The need was clear—the birth of a baby or the illness of a family member often created severe stress for families living far from helpful relatives or friends. Mary Brigid Niland, after several years as a social worker in Cincinnati, was deputed to start a Grail Family Service Center in the city. In September of 1951, she rented a small apartment with two young women from Brooklyn, Grace McGinnis and Celia Dotto, who had had some Grail training. They called the Center Gabriel House, partly because they were located in Annunciation Parish, partly because they were inspired by the idea of the Visitation, Mary's journey to come to the aid of her cousin Elizabeth in her pregnancy.[7]

Word of the service spread rapidly by word of mouth and soon the team was booked for months in advance. The service was never advertised, and in the first two years through an oversight it was not even listed in the phone book, but in that period four hundred and fifty requests were received, two hundred of which were filled. "We were resources and teachers for the families," Grace recalls, "not servants. We arranged the baptisms, brought the culture. I had good experiences in the families and made life-long friends."[8] While many family service workers developed friendships with the families they served, some others reported that they were treated as servants and felt ill-used. After a year in the apartment, the team moved to a roomy house on Hosea Avenue, with a group of twelve young women, six of them on the family service team, and later took over a second house next door. The Grail strove to present family service as a new career, a form of personalized social service, a worthy profession and apostolate, a genuine contribution to the building of Christian families and an excellent preparation for the worker's own marriage. The family service worker was expected to bring a Christian culture into the home as well as to render practical help with child care or tending the sick. The Center trained and placed young women in families, gave courses in Christian family living to students in the Catholic high schools, and made vigorous efforts to recruit young women to this new career. However, recruitment was always difficult. Grace McGinnis, reflecting on her experience on the team, commented that the American Grail did not take family service seriously enough. "It was an alternative way of delivering service that could have had an influence; everybody should have gone through it instead of it being an afterthought for the non-leaders."[9] Perhaps if the leaders and potential leaders had spent some time in family service, they could have raised the prestige of the work in the eyes of possible recruits. Perhaps the second-rate status accorded to women's work in the family by the general culture was too firmly rooted to be challenged by a handful of young women.

Certainly the family service workers made a lasting impact on many families. Anne Harmon, mother of eleven children, has fond memories of the young women who came to her rescue in her last four pregnancies. "They became lifelong friends. My children (her youngest was born in 1960) still sing the songs the girls taught them. That young woman who helped me with my eighth child was not stronger or more skilled in household arts than I, but she brought to it a real devotion. She went to daily Mass, she prayed—a marvelous example. She played with the children, helped them with their homework, taught them songs and games. These girls brought music, liturgy, prayer—all things I never had any exposure to before Gabriel House and Grailville. After my first phone call, Mary Anne invited me to the mothers' group. A new world opened up to me, gatherings with kindred spirits at Gabriel house, the bookstore, the lectures at Grailville."[10] The program easily expanded into a family apostolate, groups for mothers, cooperation with the Xavier University family life conference.

Figure 10. Janet Kalven and Mary Anne Kimbell welcoming Archbishop Alter to Gabriel House, the Cincinnati Grail Center, 1954.

Like the other centers, Gabriel House conducted small group meetings on apostolic themes for high school and college women, shared feast day celebrations with a wide circle, developed an outreach program to international students in the local colleges, worked closely with Seven Hills Neighborhood Houses in inner city Cincinnati. One program Mary Anne

Kimbell was particularly proud of was the workshops for women in the municipal housing projects in which Grailville students joined. "We developed friendships across the lines of race, class and age," she recalls.[11]

Another Gabriel House project with a strong interracial and cross-cultural emphasis was the Saturday morning play schools for the children in the municipal housing projects, led by teenagers from the Catholic high schools whom the Grail had trained. "We had a core group of middle- and upper-middle-class teenagers from the Catholic girls' high schools, to whom we gave a serious training," Carolyn Gratton recalls.[12] The purpose was to bring these privileged young people into contact with the real poverty and deprivation in the African-American and Appalachian neighborhoods in the inner city. There were summer camps for the high schoolers, with courses in child development as well as in storytelling, games, and crafts, all presented in the context of Christian responsibility for one's neighbor. During the year, the teams met regularly to plan the activities for each Saturday and to beg the supplies. "We did home visiting with these girls, and sometimes took them to the 'hollers' in Kentucky to acquaint them with the Appalachian culture," Carolyn remembered. "It made them aware of the culture of poverty, and it built self-confidence as they succeeded in handling the groups of children."[13]

New York

We were well aware of Catholic demographics in the United States—that, with the exception of Louisiana and California, the Catholic population was concentrated mainly in the big cities north of the Ohio River and east of the Mississippi. In following Rachel's directive to establish city centers, it seemed an obvious strategy to move into New York City and Philadelphia. In the Catholic world, New York City and Brooklyn are separate dioceses. Approval in Brooklyn did not carry any weight in Manhattan.

Preliminary work had been done in both Philadelphia and New York by small teams, surveying the scene and assessing the possibilities for Grail work. In New York, Abigail McCarthy, wife of Democratic Congressman Eugene McCarthy of Minnesota, helped the Grail to secure the use of an apartment on Fifty-fifth Street, just off Fifth Avenue; in Philadelphia, Anna McGarry, a pioneer in interracial work in the city, offered hospitality to Grail people exploring possibilities in that city. In 1952, while Lydwine van Kersbergen joined Margaret van Gilse in a year-long tour of Africa, looking for suitable locations to establish Grail mission teams, Barbara Wald and I began an energetic campaign to secure official permission to establish Grail Centers in these two key archdioceses. We wrote formal proposals to the bishops, appealed to Archbishop Alter for assistance (Please, Your Grace, could you put in a good word for us with the Cardinal?). The team of Barbara Wald, youthful and charming, and Mary Brigid Niland, reassuringly mature, met with diocesan consultors and were quizzed on their theology and methods. In September, 1952, Archbishop O'Hara gave official permission for the Grail to open a house in Philadelphia, and in December of the same year, Cardinal Spellman gave limited approval, for three years, to the Grail for an international student center in the New York Archdiocese.

International student work was another case of Grail pioneering, "fast women" moving into a field where Protestants had long been at work while Catholics were quite unaware of the problems and opportunities presented by the thousands of students from other countries in our midst. Our approach, stressing the need for Catholic work in this field, appealed to the Raskob Foundation, an organization dedicated to supporting Roman Catholic activities worldwide; they responded to our proposal in October 1952 with a grant of $39,000, to be paid over a three-year period. Early in 1953, under the leadership of Dolores Brien, recently returned from a period of formation at the Tiltenberg, the international Grail training center in Holland, a group moved into a large apartment on Riverside Drive, conveniently located near Columbia University and in the lively, liturgically oriented parish of Corpus Christi. Immediately the team, which included Florence Henderson and Marie Mohr, began publicizing the case for working with international students and setting up services to meet their needs. The numbers of international students were burgeoning, from 34,000 in 1954 to 60,000 in 1960; there were 10,000 in the New York area alone; about a third were Catholic, the fruit of strenuous missionary efforts in their home countries. By the mere fact of their education abroad, they were destined to form an elite and to play a part in shaping the future international policies in their own countries. It was therefore of the first importance that the Catholics among them be prepared for lay leadership and that all of them have a positive experience in the United States.

Reports from the Center analyzed the influences playing on these students: an unfamiliar environment, diet, language, customs, all of which could lead to confusion and exhaustion; racial discrimination which could embitter the individual; nationalism, which colored their judgments and paved the way for communist influence; immaturity (most were undergraduates) and lack of adequate academic preparation; materialism, surrender to the glamour and luxuries of American life. For the Catholics, there was a lack of contact with Catholic life in this country, an exposure

Figure 11. Eugene McCarthy, Democratic congressman from Minnesota, discussing politics with a group at the Grail International Student Center in Manhattan in 1959. In the 1968 election, he ran for the Democratic nomination for president but lost to Hubert Humphrey. Many Grail members across the country worked as volunteers in his campaign, which helped to consolidate opposition to the war in Vietnam.

to secularism (most attended secular institutions) and often a consequent loss of faith; and a strong and welcoming contact with Protestant agencies, who had actively conducted foreign student programs since 1914. The report noted that the number of women students from Asia, Africa, and Latin America was increasing rapidly; that the position of women in their societies was changing rapidly; and that they had special needs for clarifying their new roles, needs that as yet neither the academy nor the community agencies were addressing.

The Center quickly set up a threefold program of direct services, Christian formation, and specific training for the lay apostolate. The services included: meeting students at the port of entry; helping them to get settled, to make travel and housing arrangements, to find part-time and summer jobs, to solve various problems of adjustment; offering English conversation classes; arranging home hospitality with American families; setting up cultural exchange programs; organizing orientation tours of the city and of institutions directly related to the students' fields of study; providing some in-depth understanding of American life through lectures, discussions, seminars. The direct services were often quite demanding;

students and sometimes their advisers often turned to the Center in crisis situations, and at least once a staff member was called on to escort an emotionally disturbed young woman back to her home across the Pacific. For the Catholics there were acquaintance with American Catholic movements; opportunities for spiritual deepening through liturgical celebrations, retreats, conferences, and religious dramas. There were seminars on the lay apostolate, and for the women, opportunities for more intensive training in residential programs at Grailville, and for a few, the possibility of living at the Center in an international community.

From the beginning the international student work was conceived in terms of a world vision, grounded in the theology of the Mystical Body of Christ. Grail member Nicoletta Crosti from Italy, studying at Bryn Mawr, explained the perspective during a Pentecost ceremony:

> We, young people of Europe, of Asia, of Africa, of North America and of Latin America—we come to say that the flame of the Spirit burns brightly today as in the days of the first Pentecost. Ours is the generation which has rediscovered the Mystical Body of Christ. The life of the Church is our life; we are the Church. We take on, as Catholic lay people, a responsibility for the development of the world we live in.[14]

For the Grail as a women's movement, a world vision implied a two-way street: welcoming international students to the United States and awakening a world vision in young Americans that could lead some to serve in other countries as lay missionaries. The New York Center shared its experience and materials with the rest of the U.S. Grail. Soon international student programs were flourishing in Cincinnati; Detroit; Brooklyn; Philadelphia; and Lafayette, Louisiana.

The New York Center also did considerable research, surveying Catholic foreign students in the United States to ascertain their attitudes. The Center cooperated extensively with both the secular and the Catholic organizations in the field: the Greater New York Council for Foreign Students, the Institute for International Education, the Committee on Friendly Relations Among Foreign Students—all of which referred the Catholic students to the Grail Center; and with the Catholic Mission Secretariat, the Catholic Students Mission Crusade, the Columbia University Newman Club. Cooperation went more smoothly with the secular than with the Catholic groups. In the latter case there were questions of duplication of efforts, confusing the newcomers with too many groups claiming their allegiance.

Another facet of the Center's work was a long-term commitment as representative of UFER to the United Nations in New York. Union Fraternelle entre les Races et les Peuples (Fraternal Union of Races and

Nations) (UFER) is an association of lay-mission-sending organizations that has status as a nongovernmental organization at the Economic and Social Council of the United Nations (ECOSOC) in New York and at the United Nations Scientific and Cultural Organization (UNESCO) in Paris. One staff person from the Center was detailed to be a UFER presence among the Catholic nongovernmental organizations (NGOs) and a Catholic presence in the bewildering world of the UN in New York.

Philadelphia

The Philadelphia Center began with a diversified city center program in 1954, gradually developing emphases on ecumenism, Christian culture, and a world vision for the laity. Permission to start a Grail Center in Philadelphia had been granted in September of 1952. I remember that Barbara Wald and I felt somewhat uneasy that we were not able to produce a team, a house, and a burst of activities in short order. The ground had been prepared in Philadelphia, ever since Joan and I had lectured in the colleges there in 1942. There had been other lecture tours, an occasional weekend course, various contacts with the high schools and colleges, some women from Philadelphia at Grailville. Ivy Alves, a Grailville graduate from Jamaica, and Gabrielle Miner, a nucleus member, spent time during 1952-1953 working in the African-American community while living with Anna McGarry, a pioneer in interracial work. Mariette Wickes had been finishing her BA at Temple University and getting to know the city. At last, after Lydwine returned from her tour of Africa in 1953, the final decision was made to purchase a twenty-room house on a corner lot on Chester Avenue, fifteen minutes from downtown and close to the University of Pennsylvania campus.

Formerly run as an old-age home by a group of nuns, it was quite well arranged for a residential center. In the spring of 1954, an orgy of renovating went on, with invitations to all comers to join in removing varnish, sanding floors, plastering, painting, and repairing. The staff and residents moved in while the renovations were going on and immediately began several programs: an open house on Saturday nights for Mass preparation, Sunday breakfasts after Mass devoted to discussions on woman's apostolate, an evening a week for a choir and another on family service. An art and book store was soon set up in a large room on the first floor. The initial concept was of an all-purpose city center, built on the familiar structure of concentric circles, with a three-month residential training for young employed women as the centerpiece. Many stayed on an additional three to six months. From this center, activities radiated out in many directions. In 1967 to celebrate fifteen years of the Grail in Philadelphia, the following summary was prepared: one hundred and twenty-five young women trained in the residential program, twenty-five-hundred others in short courses; forty teenage team members helping to organize training days and weekends for their peers; family service to six hundred families; three-thousand international students contacted in a well-organized foreign student program; community development projects in three parishes, helping to draw parishioners into active participation in liturgy and celebrations, organizing mothers' groups, working with teenagers, aiding development of a neighborhood association; adult education for thousands through lectures, discussion groups, art exhibits, musical programs, and drama programs.[15]

In conservative, Irish Catholic Philadelphia, the Grail was often swimming upstream. Exhibits of contemporary religious art, a rather sophisticated "film forum," a series of programs on ecumenism—all these were pioneering efforts. A report on the foreign student program observes that "Philadelphians are barely involved in the international scene and the Catholic responsibility in the Church overseas."[16] Recruitment was often difficult: a major effort in 1960-1961 to interest high school and college students in a summer project in Louisiana and/or a two-year commitment with a Grail team in Brazil produced fifteen applicants for Louisiana, all of whom dropped out before the project actually began.[17] A report on the service careers program notes that unless the staff phoned the twelve group members before each meeting, attendance was apt to fall to just three young women.[18]

However, some programs were a brilliant success. In the fall of 1955, the three eastern centers—Brooklyn, New York, and Philadelphia—collaborated to produce an original liturgical drama with audience participation on the Advent theme of longing for the coming of the Savior. Under the title, *Desired of the Nations*, the drama integrated biblical and liturgical themes; the theological insights and world vision of the French theologian, Jean Danielou; international students; choral speaking, plain chant, folk song, modern dance; and concern for the emptiness and lack of meaning in modern life. Willy nilly, I found myself in the brand new role of producer, with Cay Charles, formerly a high school drama teacher, as director, and a script that was still being written (by Anne Mulkeen) long after rehearsals had begun. We had a cast of a hundred scattered in three cities and including temperamental dancers from Juilliard. What lifted the performance out of the genre of pious tableaux—the promise to Abraham, the prophecies of Isaias, John the Baptist, the Annunciation, the Nativity—were the dancers and the modern chorus. I shall never forget John the Baptist, danced by a sinewy, hairy male in a leopard skin, a Juilliard student who was willing to contribute his services gratis for the opportunity to hold center stage. The modern chorus was a group of players seated in the audience, who at the appropriate moment rose in protest: "If Christ has come, where is the blessing we have been promised?" In answer, a chorus representing the people of the present time came on the stage to speak Danielou's idea, that by making Christ known to all the nations of the world, we could hasten His coming. The drama climaxed with speakers from various countries of the five continents, each in national dress, speaking in their own tongues their hopes for the conversion of the nations. It was performed in the three cities to large and enthusiastic audiences.

Louisiana

Louisiana offered opportunities for both student and interracial apostolates. From the beginning Lydwine realized the importance of the race issue. Louisiana was an obvious place to begin, since it had the largest percentage of Catholic African-Americans in the United States. As soon as Mary Louise could be spared from Doddridge Farm, she was sent to New Orleans, where she stayed with an African-American young woman, spoke at the colleges and the seminary, organized short courses, and formed some small groups.

In 1950 Monsignor Irving DeBlanc, chaplain at Southwestern Louisiana Institute, a secular university, urged the Grail to send a team to the Catholic Student Center to coordinate activities for the Catholic students on the campus. Florence Henderson and Patricia Bell arrived on the campus in time to organize a celebration for the mid-Lent Sunday. The work soon developed beyond the campus: a report in 1960 lists three main lines of activity: (1) coordinating programs at the Catholic Student Center and supervising a student residence for young women; (2) conducting lay leadership training throughout the diocese for high school, college, and working women; (3) carrying on a community development program in several African-American parishes. After surveying the needs in these parishes, the team inaugurated a program of basic adult education to overcome illiteracy, helped the people to set up a credit union, and organized the educational program for a consumers' co-op involving people from twenty small towns in the region. At the same time, the Grail sponsored summer fieldwork programs for young women from northern schools and colleges, who devoted three weeks to conducting adult basic education in the African-American parishes, along with religious education classes and play schools for the children and teenagers. By 1963, the Grail counted thirty team members, African-American as well as white, in Louisiana; four teaching at the diocesan high school for African-American teenagers; five others teaching elementary school; two studying at Xavier, the

Figure 12. Summer fieldwork in Louisiana. 1950s.

African-American University in New Orleans; one staffing the Catholic Information Center in New Orleans and another at Catholic Charities.[19]

Racism was, of course, a major issue, and an explosive one, even for the most radical of the priests and bishops. The Grail wanted integrated programs, but given the climate of opinion, it was necessary to proceed carefully. Elizabeth McGee, who worked in Lafayette until 1959, remembers that Friendship House ran into legal difficulties because they had set up a house where African-Americans and whites lived together. At that time racially integrated housing was against the law in Louisiana. She recalls being invited to a confidential meeting with the Dean of Women at the university in which the Dean advised the Grail not to attempt an integrated residence.[20] In a 1955 report on a Grail weekend to Archbishop Rummel of New Orleans, who was known as "a nigger lover," Father Elmo Romagosa, one of the priest sponsors of the weekend, noted that "there is no evidence of any unfavorable criticism because of the integration."[21] Father Norman Francis, an African-American priest, was emphatic in his advice that any work in the South not on an integrated basis would alienate the African-Americans, regardless of the "prudent" reasons for organizing on an all-white basis.[22] Initially, the Grail formed separate study groups for African-American and white young women, bringing them together for special events—the final meeting of a series, a day of Christian living or a weekend. Some time after the 1954 Supreme Court decision on school integration, Southwestern Louisiana Institute in Lafayette was integrated peacefully. In 1962 Archbishop Rummel ordered the integration of all Catholic schools in New Orleans. In 1959, when the Grail had presented a plan to set up an integrated residence for college students, the bishop in Lafayette was startled, but agreed to consider it, provided that it be done, "quietly and on an informal basis." Evidently he eventually agreed, since in the 1960s the Grail's own residence was integrated. In 1963, the Grail organized a panel to visit all the African American high schools in the area to present "The Challenges and Problems of a Newly Integrated University," to help prepare the students for the campus.[23] The summer fieldwork experiences broadened the horizons of young northern whites by exposing them to the realities of poverty in the south and to the complexities of racism among good, churchgoing Catholics. One report on the fieldwork notes that by witnessing to love and equality and treading lightly in the beginning of the three-week period, the team were able to end their stay with integrated celebrations of first communion and baptism.

San Jose

California responded quickly and enthusiastically to the Grail with a center in the Hispanic community and a focus on Latin America. The first contacts had been made in 1958 by Elizabeth Reid and Eileen Schaeffler, who were struck by "tremendous potentialities and the depth of spirit seen in priests and laity alike."[24] In Eileen's opinion, the area had "a providential call to a deeper relationship with Latin America." Contact was continued through the Junipero Serra Shop, a Catholic art and book store, founded by Ethel Souza, where several Grail members worked for a time. Early in 1961, Archbishop Mitty gave permission for the Grail to establish a center in the San Francisco diocese. However, the decision was made to start in the San Jose diocese instead. "We were offered every possible good in San Francisco," Eileen explained, "but San Jose was the place where we were awaited."[25] The Center was established in record time. In April of 1961 two acres of land in San Jose were given to the Grail through the good offices of Father Donald McDonnell, a diocesan priest. There was a question of who should take title to the property. The diocese wanted to set up a California corporation with a board of three priests and three Grail members, since diocesan officials had had bad experiences with lay groups mismanaging property and running up debts for which the bishop was then held responsible. Grail policy was to hold title to all property in the name of the Ohio corporation, which simply needed to obtain permission to operate in California. This arrangement allayed the fears of the diocesan officials as to mismanagment and and lack of stability; it also spared the Grail the problem of clerical control.[26]

In true California style, Eileen Schaeffler and Barbara Wald visited a used-house lot, arranged for two small buildings to be moved to the Grail site, and found an architect to supervise fitting them together. The Tully family provided the modest funds needed to cover the cost of the housing. The parish community of Our Lady of Guadalupe Church gave generous support to the new venture. By July Irene Naughton was conducting play schools for four-hundred children at the property, and in October the Grail opened a four-month training for overseas service in Latin America under the direction of Peg Linnehan and Katherine Price. Sixteen young women enrolled in the first group. The training included an introduction to the lay apostolate and to missionary spirituality, Latin American area studies, and the community development approach; plus the practicalities—first aid, catechetics, language study and fieldwork in the Hispanic community. Participants were involved full time from 6:30 A.M. until 10 P.M.[27] Placements were arranged in cooperation with the Papal Volunteer Program (PAVLA). In April of 1962 twelve trainees left for Brazil; others were placed in community development projects in the United States or went on for further professional training. For a number of years, the San Jose center offered the four-month program twice a year, beginning in February and October, and also organized a three-week summer fieldwork program in Baja California and in their immediate local area.

A strong team, including Peg Linnehan, Katherine Price, Veronica Forbes, Licha Kraemer, Betty Rose, Ruth Vargas, and Carol Nosko, contributed their talents to the programs. The Center's staff members were heavily involved in ecumenism, in Church renewal projects, in Christians for Socialism. At the same time, one of the staff was completing two sets of catechetical materials for two different age groups, and another staff member was facilitating a married women's group.

By 1967, the emphasis had shifted; the decision was made not to continue the residential program, but simply to share a life with women resident at the Center and working locally in their professions. Several of the residents taught courses in English as a second language for the Spanish-speaking. The Center continued to offer opportunities for cross-cultural exchanges with Mexico.

Toronto

The Toronto Center grew from initial contacts by the staff in Detroit and from a lively parish group, begun by a friend of Carolyn Gratton's. As a result of these efforts, a number of Canadians had come to Grailville for shorter or longer periods and a few had served overseas in Africa and Brazil. From the beginning, the Toronto group was characterized by the involvement of the members in their jobs and professions. They held their meetings in each other's homes or in the Newman Club and it was not until 1960 that they felt the need of a full-time coordinator for the stability and growth of the movement. Dorothy Jane Rasenberger moved to Toronto and with five members of the core team set up an apartment that soon became the Grail Center in Toronto. They focused their work around liturgical celebrations and Grail study materials on "person, community, world," building community and a team spirit among themselves. The team organized seminars and lectures for adult Catholics at the Catholic Information Center; they trained a group of working girls to give religious instruction to children in the public schools; they set up a store to sell art work from Grailville together with catechetical materials; and they did some outreach to other parts of Canada, especially through arranging tours for Elizabeth Reid, an Australian Grail member with extensive experience in overseas service. They gave talks on the liturgy and the lay apostolate, contributed to the newly developing ecumenical forums, and served on the Toronto Diocesan Liturgical Commission.

A Time of Expansion: New Numbers, New Fields of Work

By 1963 the Grail counted one-hundred nucleus members in North America (at this point Canadians belonged to the "American" Grail; later they became a separate national Grail entity). More than two-hundred women were living in twelve Grail centers, spanning the continent, from New York to California and from Toronto to Louisiana. In 1962, a new center had started in Queens, New York, devoted mainly to religious education, and a thirteenth center was in the process of being established on a fifty-acre estate overlooking the Hudson River in Cornwall-on-Hudson, New York. In addition, there were outposts: the Inter-American Center, a few blocks from the main New York apartment, focusing on work with the Latin Americans; the Detroit bookstore, serving a suburban clientele; a Grail book and art store in midtown Manhattan. There were also teams and small groups in Chicago; in Wilmington, Delaware; in New Orleans; and in far away Nova Scotia, where several Grail members were pursuing studies in cooperatives and credit unions at St. Francis Xavier University in Antigonish. In addition, there were spin-offs, special projects undertaken by one or another of the centers: "Catholic Europe Lives," a six-week tour of apostolic centers in Europe, organized by Anne Mulkeen for fifteen American women in the summer of 1953; the staffing of a new parish school in Lawton, Oklahoma, undertaken in 1960 to offer lay teachers an opportunity to integrate the new approaches in religious education into the curriculum.

To coordinate and supply resources to the mushrooming activities of the movement, the National Committee set up five councils:

Family and Community, which was concerned with marriage preparation, family service, youth leadership programs, and community development in low-income urban areas;

World Community, which had the three facets: educating the Catholic public to their international responsibilities, international student work, and the recruiting and training of Americans for service overseas;

Service Careers, occupied with "womanly work," vocational guidance of young women, and a search for ways in which women could use their gifts to influence modern institutions;

Christian Culture, concerned with expressing Christian values in a contemporary style in daily living as well as in music, visual arts, writing, and drama;

Religious Education, which formed catechists in scripture, liturgy, and religious psychology, experimented with new methods, and produced materials that reflected the new approaches in this field.

The publications produced during these years (1951–1963) reflect both the variety of fields in which the Grail was working and the skill and sophistication of the work. While we continued to produce mimeographed study action guides for apostolic groups—*Love the Chief Instrument, Are You Ready, The Christian Witness, Toward a World Vision*, we upgraded our publications program with a series of well-designed printed booklets, illustrated with photographs of contemporary families. Among these were *New Life for New Year's Eve, Promised in Christ* on the solemn engagement, *The Church Blesses Motherhood* on the churching of women after childbirth. *The Paschal Meal* offered an "arrangement of the Last Supper as a historical drama," to be used either in the family or as a community celebration. It was a popular event during Holy Week at Grailville and in the city centers, and was reprinted in Spanish by the Christian Family Movement in Mexico. *The Twelve Days of Christmas*, published in hard cover by the Liturgical Press, offered ideas for the family and the community for each day from Christmas to Epiphany. In Cincinnati, it became a civic celebration, with a special event for each of the twelve days, including a live crib scene in Lytle Park, and a procession of the Magi, complete with camels from the zoo, on Epiphany. The book was accompanied by an inge-

Figure 13. Dancers in the Detroit performance of "New Born Again," an original musical drama by Grail member Elaine Jones, based on Negro spirituals.

nious *Twelve Days of Christmas Kit*, the work of artist Jeanne Heiberg. The kit included an Advent tower, Jesse tree symbols, and a crib set, printed on heavy cardboard, for the family to punch out and assemble. Several publications developed basic principles of the movement: on woman's mission in the world, Lydwine van Kersbergen's *Woman, Some Aspects of Her Role*; and on the theme of world vision, Elizabeth Reid's

I Belong Where I'm Needed; H. van Straelen's lectures on Asia,*Through Eastern Eyes*; Dolores Brien's *The Laity and the International Scene.* Numerous articles on the Grail either by Grail members or others appeared in Catholic publications: *America, Commonweal, Catholic World, Today, Ave Maria, Catholic Mind, Lamp, Integrity, Land and Home, Catholic Worker, Torch, Sign, Jubilee,* and *Liturgical Arts.*

In support of the practical suggestions for living with the Church, Grailville made available music and artwork, created originally for the residential community. There were four recordings, all professionally produced: music for Advent and Christmas, for Lent and Easter, and two collections of folk music from around the world. *Feast Day Melodies* and *Songs of the Covenant*, both published by the World Library of Sacred Music, offered liturgical texts in English, adapted to Gregorian melodies by members of the Grailville music center. The art center experimented with reproductions of Trina Paulus' sculptures, "Fiat," and "Holy Family." Offered at affordable prices, these contemporary expressions of Christian themes soon found their way into many homes, and marked the beginning of an extensive art production program, offering sculpture, silk screen prints, and metal work on religious themes. As the Christian Culture Council took shape at a national level, it stimulated art festivals at Grailville, in Philadelphia, in New York. In 1958, The Holiday of Arts on the theme of the Incarnation and the Arts featured a juried exhibit of forty-six works by contemporary artists, held in December in New York, in January in Boston, together with lectures, discussions, poetry readings, and a concert. The Culture Council also sponsored dramatic productions in the different centers. *New Born Again* was produced in Detroit, Louisiana, Philadelphia, New York and Brooklyn; *The Cosmic Tree* in Louisiana, St. Paul, and Nova Scotia.

In regular meetings, the five councils discussed questions of outreach, methods and techniques of the apostolate, the interracial apostolate, a long range public relations plan for the movement, and cooperation with related movements, among other topics. Several meetings listed conferences at which the Grail needed to be represented—everything from Catholic Intellectuals and the Liturgical Conference to Music Education and the Catholic Students Mission Crusade.

8

Laywomen to the Missions, 1950–1964

The third area of expansion for Grail work in the 1950s was in the field of overseas service. Laywomen to the missions—here was another cutting edge issue for Grail pioneering. Picture an auditorium filled with several hundred priests, nuns and religious brothers, gathered for the annual meeting of the Catholic mission-sending societies of the United States. The time is December of 1952. In that sea of black-clad figures there were only two spots of color, Marie Therese McDermit in a green tweed suit and myself in a teal blue dress, representing the Grailville Mission School. When Marie Therese announced to the assembly that she was leaving the following month, January 1953, for Uganda, she sent shock waves through her audience. Lay missionaries represented a radical new idea for Catholics, although Protestants had been sending laypeople to the missions for many years. After Marie Therese's talk, several elderly priests came to give her well-meant advice, clearly indicating by their patronizing attitudes that they did not think the laity, especially laywomen, had either the physical or the spiritual stamina that mission life demands. I was a bit irritated by the condescension but totally convinced that we would prove them wrong, as indeed we did.

The Lay Mission Idea

The very idea of sending any American Catholics to the missions was relatively new in 1950. The United States itself had been mission country, the beneficiary of missionaries from the established Catholic churches in Europe until the beginning of the twentieth century. Maryknoll, the first American mission-sending society, was not founded until 1911. The annual meeting of the U.S. mission-sending groups was a recent innovation by the United States bishops' Mission Secretariat. As Grail we were pioneering on two fronts—demanding a role for laywomen in the apostolate at home, and even more daring, insisting that laywomen could play a role in building the church in distant non-Christian lands.

The lay mission idea had been part of the Grail vision from the very beginning. In 1920 Jacques van Ginneken wrote, "Would it not be possible for the missions to draw lay people from Europe and America? Or bolder still, could not groups of lay people be sent into mission countries for which they are specifically trained? I see in our own time an apostolic laity going forward en masse to the mission fields."[1] At the time, he was regarded as a visionary dreaming an impossible dream. Nevertheless, he gave his new lay group the threefold goal: (1) to work in mission lands to train indigenous lay leaders, especially among the educated women; (2) to work among Catholic young women in the so-called Christian countries to prepare them for leadership in Christian social reconstruction; and (3) to work with non-Catholics.

He shared his dream with the first small band of Women of Nazareth. In a talk to the new Mission School at Grailville in 1950, Lydwine reminisced about the early days in Holland, when the group sat around the globe and divided up the world. "We had no rest until we got into all countries. Each one of us was allowed to choose a country. Everybody laughed at us, but now it is becoming a reality."[2] The young women who in 1926 divided up the globe by 1951 were realizing their dreams: Margaret van Gilse had arrived in Africa, Liesbeth Allard was established at the Indonesian Cultural Institute in Java, Louisa Veldhuis on the faculty of the new Grail Mission School in Holland, and Lydwine in the United States.

Toward a World Vision

In the Catholic schools, the mission emphasis tended to focus on statistics of baptisms—grade school children were urged to save their pennies to help baptize pagan babies. The missionary orders generally established humanitarian works—schools, hospitals—as a first step toward drawing people into Church membership. In the Grail, we organized our work around the concept of a world vision, uniting the task at home with the work overseas in terms of the responsibility of every Christian for the whole Church. As members of the Mystical Body of Christ, we insisted, we are all called to share in the universal mission of the Church, to bring Christ to all peoples and to all aspects of human life. We were convinced that the extraordinary role of leaving home and country could only succeed if it was grounded in a Christian community whose concerns encompassed the globe. Moreover, our goal was to build a movement among the local women; we were not primarily interested in building institutions but took over schools and hospitals in order to have a point of entry for a long-term program of empowerment for local women.

Figure 14. Lydwine van Kersbergen visiting Archbishop Kiwanuka (the shorter of the two priests), the first African bishop of modern times, in Masaka, Uganda, to arrange for the placement of a Grail team, 1952.

The concept of a world vision was expressed through a whole range of Grail programs: lectures, exhibits, international festivals and courses, all aimed at educating the general public to a world vision; the study of other cultures and their riches; hospitality to the international students and visitors in our midst; acquaintance with and participation in the UN agencies; and finally, recruiting and training volunteers for overseas service.

From Grailville's beginning there had been international students at Grailville, from the Philippines, then from China and Japan. Their presence had an immediate impact on us Americans, enlarging our horizons. I remember Kwok Kwoon, the first Chinese student at Grailville, explaining that she had a hard time remembering our names "because you all look so much alike." That remark gave me my first glimmering of a cross-cultural understanding. A young woman from Louisiana wrote of her experience at Grailville in 1953: "To live with these girls from all over the world who are preparing seriously for work in such vital and yet varied fields is a very broadening experience. . . . The spark is contagious and soon you find yourself thinking about and praying for Indonesia and Africa as you pray for members of your own immediate family."[3]

The Grail mission-sending program developed step by step. In 1946 Mary Louise Tully was sent to China in response to an urgent request from Father Nicholas Maestrini and Bishop Valtorta of Hong Kong. The American President oceanliner that brought this lone Catholic laywoman across the Pacific also carried nine-hundred Protestant missionaries. The next year Veronica Forbes went from Grailville to Hong Kong to join Mary Louise. In 1950 Grailville formally established a mission training program and an Oriental Institute, the latter meant especially for Asian young women studying in the States.

In the summer of 1952, Lydwine joined Margaret van Gilse in a 12,000-mile safari, by car, from Capetown to Uganda and the Belgian Congo and back, visiting eighty mission stations to find suitable placements for teams of lay missionaries. They met with a very cool response. Most of the mission bishops they visited were not at all interested in a lay apostolate. Those that were thought it was premature. One bishop explained, "You are twenty-five years too early for the lay apostolate in Africa. The position of women is still a position of slavery." Nothing daunted, Lydwine and Margaret replied that they felt they must start now "to get a footing in Africa because in five years time no white person could get in any more."[4] Impelled by their sense of urgency, in 1953 they took the risk of placing the first Americans: Marie Therese McDermit and Lorraine Machan at Rubaga Hospital in Kampala, and Professor Mary Buckley and student Mary Emma Kuhn at Pius XII University in Basutoland. In 1954, Alice McCarthy and Josephine Drabek arrived in the Masaka Diocese in Uganda to help start the first Catholic secondary school for girls in that diocese. In the 1950s, two young married couples—the wives had had Grail training and inspired their husbands with the idea of a lay apostolate overseas—set out for Africa. Joe and Alexa Kane went to Basutoland, where Joe taught at Pius XII University; James and Grace Rogan and their two children went to Durban, where James served as a nurse in the hospital for non-Europeans. Again, this was something the Protestants had been doing for years, but it was quite an innovation for Catholics. In 1956, as mentioned above, I opened the Grail Overseas Training Center in Brooklyn and in 1961, a west coast center was set up in San Jose, California, with a focus on Latin America. Each new development served also as an occasion to stir the minds and hearts of American Catholics with a world vision through articles in newspapers and magazines and special events with an international flavor.

A major figure in educating Catholics to a world vision and recruiting young women for work overseas was an Australian Grail member, Elizabeth Reid, who arrived in the United States in 1956, to take over from the New York Center the task of serving as the UFER[5] representative at the United Nations in New York

She plunged wholeheartedly into the Grail's world vision campaigns, barnstorming the country on lecture tours, participating in mission exhibits, writing articles and a book, *I Belong Where I'm Needed*.[6] She was

Figure 15. Elizabeth Reid, an Australian Grail member, who spent many years in the United States educating Americans on their responsibilities in the world scene. She served as the UFER representative to the United Nations Economic and Social Council in New York. Here she is pictured at the UN with Dr. Louis Longarzo of International Catholic Charities.

a dynamic speaker, drawing on her rich and varied experience in the Far East. A professional journalist and photographer, she had spent eight years in the Catholic Center in Hong Kong, where she had edited the Catholic paper, worked as a public relations officer for Catholic Relief Services, dispensed relief in person and through her column in the paper, received refugees after China fell to the communists in 1948. She had also started a Grail training house with a group of young Chinese women. She had watched the bamboo curtain fall in the Far East, traveling as a UN correspondent in Korea, Vietnam, Taiwan (then called Formosa), Japan and the Philippines. While based in the States, she carried on a shuttle apostolate— making short term forays to West Africa to help a Grail team start in Ghana, going to East Africa to serve on the staff at a social training center in Tanzania and to visit Grail Centers in Uganda. Finally, she settled in New Delhi, India, where she headed Action for Food Production (AFPRO), and developed a Grail mobile team of Indian women to do basic education with women in the villages.

I remember a festival of nations that we organized in Brooklyn in 1956, shortly after Elizabeth's arrival. We had obtained the use of the auditorium of the minor seminary, Cathedral College, which meant that our audience included the seminarians and the seminary faculty as well as our usual circle of members and friends. It was another occasion for shock waves, as exotic in staid, provincial Brooklyn as finding a herd of giraffes on Flatbush Avenue. We combined Elizabeth's rousing talk with an experience of other cultures through a program of entertainment. There were more than a dozen acts furnished by international students from the Manhattan Grail Center, who had also set up booths to display cultural artifacts and to serve native foods from twenty countries. I remember exquisite barefooted Filipenas doing the bamboo dance, a sober Japanese baritone in a gray kimono rendering a solemn chant, and the *piece de resistance*—eight Arabs in burnoose beating the drums for a belly dancer. Cathedral College had never seen anything like it!

The Overseas Institute program, begun in September of 1957, was fifteen months long, the first eight months in Brooklyn, the remainder at Grailville. The prerequisite for entry was competence in some professional or semiprofessional field—nursing, medicine, teaching, social work, office work, medical technology, or pharmacology. In handling the applications for the program, I soon discovered that the idea of working overseas attracted a good many unhappy and even emotionally disturbed people, those who were misfits at home and hoped to do better elsewhere. Our training program was lengthy and demanding. First place in the training was given to a solid spiritual formation, based on the liturgy, private prayer, and asceticism. While I was in charge at the Overseas Institute, the program was quite strenuous. Our day began with the 6:30 A.M. Mass in the parish, followed by breakfast, with a reading to give a spiritual thought for the day. Then the students went off to their jobs—a lay missioner must be prepared to earn her living—to return in time for vespers before supper. Three evenings a week there were formal classes, led by priests from the Mission Institute at Fordham University. They developed the theology of the missions, taught mission history in relation to the colonial expansion of Europe, discussed mission methods, and focused most strongly on the principle of adaptation and the need to develop cross-cultural understandings and attitudes. On weekends, the students took part in the various apostolic programs conducted by the Brooklyn Center, getting some experience in working with young women of different ethnic and educational backgrounds. We also introduced them to the United Nations and its various agencies. After the months in Brooklyn, they spent the summer at Grailville, where they had the opportunity to learn practical skills in gardening, foods and nutrition, first aid, and hygiene. They also took part in fieldwork projects in Appalachia. A few years later, as noted above, the San Jose Center began a four-month training for work in Latin America, which included fieldwork in the local Hispanic community and in Baja California.

A Change of Consciousness

As I read through the files on Grail lay mission work, I find a shift in vocabulary that reflects a profound change of consciousness both in the Grail and in the larger society. The very word *missionary* calls up notions of superiority—traditionally missionaries saw themselves as having important truths to impart to the ignorant heathen, whom they visualized as "sitting in darkness and the shadow of death." They were givers rather than receivers, going to do good to the other according to their own definition of good. As the colonized peoples have gained a voice and emerged into nationhood, the vocabulary to name the nonindustrialized world has moved from "underdeveloped" to "developing" nations and then to "Third World," all namings which carry overtones of inferiority. The Grail team in Kenya proposed that we speak of "the two-thirds world," since the nonindustrialized countries contain two-thirds of the world's population. As the idea of community development took hold, Grail members dropped the "lay mission" vocabulary in favor of "overseas service" and then in the 1980s and 1990s spoke simply of international exchange. As Emilia Charbonneau, an American from Detroit who has worked in South Africa since 1957, explained to me, "I don't describe myself as a lay missionary except occasionally when I have to explain myself to people in the USA. I'm part of an international team and an international movement."[7] Even though in the Grail we understood from the beginning that we wanted to adapt to the indigenous cultures and build a movement among the women, it took a long time to work out all the implications of these concepts and to translate them into the attitudes and practices of daily life.

In the training program, we were pretty clear about the effects of colonialism in Asia, Africa and Latin America. The missionaries came with the colonizers, their journeys and salaries paid by the colonizers; they imposed a liturgy in a western language—Latin—and brought with them many European customs, styles of architecture, and norms of behavior. In the journal of her African tour, Lydwine was repeatedly amazed at the way the missionaries in their compounds had set up a little Holland or a little Italy in the midst of the African bush, complete with a church, rectory, convent, and school, and daily menu in the style of their home country. Little wonder then that the Church appeared as a foreign importation or that moved by the rising tide of nationalism, some of the new nations expelled the missionaries.

Figure 16. Marie Therese McDermit with patients at Rubaga Hospital, Kampala, Uganda, 1953.

The first Americans to go overseas were clear about the concept of cultural adaptation, if somewhat naive about the difficulties of working it out in practice. In 1950, when Mary Louise Tully wrote about her experiences in Hong Kong, she insisted, "I would not want to leave you with the impression that we come to a pagan country and find the poor, ignorant, unenlightened heathen sitting in rows of darkness waiting for the light to shine. They may learn from us, but we also learn from them."[8] And Mary Buckley, writing from Pius XII University in Basutoland in 1953, stresses "the profound respect that the preservation of all that is true and good in the African culture demands of us; respect which must be united with a constant effort of study and thought if we are to help truly to integrate in this evolving Christianity all that is of the essence of the church in our Christian heritage in the West."[9]

By 1963, Grail members had begun to elaborate a statement of the "subsidiary role of foreign laypeople" in the light of ten years' experience in the field.[10] Alice McCarthy, a schoolteacher from Brooklyn, who worked in the Grail secondary school for girls in Uganda and also in the Grail training center at Mubende, analyzed four main tasks: (1) to give witness of a full Christian life led by ordinary lay people; (2) to supply professional and technical skills needed in the country; (3) to train local lay leaders; (4) to help local laity to revise cultural patterns in the light of Christian values and build a Christian society. Kay Walsh, writing at about the same time, out of her experience of five years in Brazil and two years directing a Grail program for Latin American students in New York, was even more emphatic on the auxiliary role of foreign laity: "Our contribution is limited and auxiliary . . . we cannot 'save' the situation with our North American solutions." Moreover, she recommends that we should work in Brazilian structures and not set up "good works" of our own choosing.[11] Fulfilling this role requires persons of great maturity, open and able to listen, searching persons who will take the time and energy to study the culture of the other and to enter into dialogue. The keynote is exchange—one must feel ignorance of the other culture as a privation—no superiority, no condescension, but the beginnings of a true multiculturalism. As the vision statement of the 1979 International General Assembly put it, "We envisage a society in which relationships of domination and submission are replaced by relations of mutuality in all spheres and structures, private and public, economic and political, religious and cultural."[12]

It is easy enough to speak about rising above ethnocentrism, but it requires a constant effort of self-awareness to detect the deep-rooted assumptions of cultural superiority that betray us in our language, attitudes, and behavior. The same Mission School brochure from Ubbergen that reprinted Mary Louise Tully's article about learning from the other includes letters from the Dutch nurses sent to Borneo deploring "native superstitions" and ignorance of hygiene: "They really can't help it that they don't know any better."[13] Lydwine and Joan at Grailville, despite their genuine openness to American ways, enforced Dutch standards of housekeeping; they also arranged for all Grailville to celebrate the Feast of St. Nicholas (a major public event in Amsterdam) but in the early years had no patience with the group's desire to celebrate St. Patrick's Day! The Americans on international Grail teams often complained that while they had expected to adapt to African ways, they were not prepared to adapt to the Europeans in language, in food, and in attitudes about the deference due to authority.

Grail people overseas generally rose to the challenge of adapting to the local lifestyle, eschewing Western amenities and special treatment. Mary Louise Tully chose to live in a hostel for Chinese women students. Mary

Buckley and Mary Emma Kuhn lived in the dormitory for women students in Basutoland. Mary Alice Duddy chose to live in the midst of a favela on a hillside in the state of Rio. When Frances Scott and Elizabeth Nabakoza came together to start the Grail secondary school in Uganda, they shared the staff quarters. Elizabeth was deeply touched to learn that Frances expected to share and share alike and "did not keep her dishes separate." She had been in situations where Africans were expected to live in segregated quarters. That one incident drew her to the Grail.

By 1963 more than a hundred Americans were serving on Grail teams in Africa, Asia, and Latin America. They were intent on building one international movement, not setting up separate communities for the indigenous women. When Lydwine on her African tour discussed with the African priests the possibility of starting a community of American and African women together, "they were simply delighted. They called the separate congregations for white and Black sisters 'unchristian.' "[14] The policy of separate congregations for the Africans had been established by Rome in the early years of missionary work in Africa. The rationale was that the missionary orders had their headquarters outside the country and often transferred their members from one country to another. The young churches needed stable local groups to serve their own people and should therefore be organized locally. After some years, the policy was changed and the missionary orders began to admit Africans as members. The Grail teams in Africa often received help and guidance from the missionary groups. The White Sisters were especially helpful on matters of learning the language and culture and on questions of how to approach the local people.

As Grail teams gained experience, they went deeply into the community development approach, influenced by the work of Brazilian educator, Paulo Freire. Women in hurry, pushy women, by 1963 we had pushed our way into some twenty countries on the six continents of the globe.

Part III
Winds of Change,
1964–1975

9

Tumultuous Changes and
Creative Responses

The 1960s were a time of ferment, of tumultuous change in U.S. society, in the Catholic Church worldwide, and in the Grail. The civil rights movement shook the country and stimulated the women's movement, the student movement, the welfare rights movement, the antiwar movement. The new movements gave birth to a host of new organizations and groups—the Southern Christian Leadership Conference (SCLC), the Student Non-violent Coordinating Committee (SNCC), the Congress for Racial Equality (CORE), Students for a Democratic Society (SDS), National Organization for Women (NOW), Women's Liberation Movement (WLM). In Rome, Pope John XXIII announced an *aggiornamento* for the Catholic Church, a modernization of the oldest institution in Western civilization, and called for an ecumenical council to begin the process. He presided at its opening session on October 11, 1962.

The changes in one sector sparked changes in another. The civil rights movement, with its analysis of discrimination and oppression, awakened a response among students everywhere. "Our students identify with the Blacks," a Jesuit seminary professor remarked to me. And he added ruefully, "I belong to the last generation to be kicked by those above me and the first generation to be kicked by those below me." A popular book appeared with the title, *Student as Nigger*, and students in schools and colleges staged sit-ins and other protests, demanding a voice in educational decision-making. Just as the abolition movement of the nineteenth century stirred women's awareness of their own oppression and led to the suffrage movement, so the civil rights struggle roused women in the 1960s to an awareness of sexual discrimination and led to the "second wave," a vigorous feminist movement.

153

In turn, the Women's Liberation Movement, with its consciousness-raising groups and its refusal of hierarchy, had a profound impact on women in the churches. Women delegates at the 1969 assembly of the National Council of Churches staged a protest demonstration against their subordinate position in the churches.[1] In no uncertain terms, they affirmed their support for the women's liberation movement and demanded full participation for women in the building of a new church and a new society. The enrollment of women in the seminary programs leading to ordination tripled in a few brief years. Olivia Barrett, a sister of Mercy and president of her community's college, St. Xavier in Chicago, summed it up to me as we were organizing a conference for college students and administrators in 1968: "I'm coping with change in every aspect of my life," she said, "in my city, in the college, in the Church and in my religious community."

In every sector—public life, church life, Grail life—ideas which had been germinating for a long time suddenly blossomed. Or, to change the metaphor, forces which had been gathering strength underground suddenly surfaced, bursting through old forms, challenging traditional attitudes and demanding new structures. The changes, when they came, seemed all-encompassing, involving both the most intimate sense of self and personal relationships and large areas of public law. They produced bitter polarizations over everything from vernacular liturgies in the Catholic Church to open housing in the North and voter registration in the South. They brought about both creative new initiatives and a sense of loss and diminishment. In the Catholic Church the changes were dramatic as priests turned to face their congregations across simple table altars and spoke the prayers in English. Nuns shed their habits and appeared in ordinary clothes. Outside the sanctuary priests, nuns and laypeople by the thousands threw themselves into the struggles for social justice and undertook creative new forms of work.

At the same time, the changes were traumatic as thousands of individuals reevaluated their commitments in the light of new insights. Thousands of priests, including one American bishop and many leading theologians and scholars, left the priesthood. Thousands of nuns left their religious communities. Vocations to the priesthood and religious life fell off sharply, while many of those in charge of training candidates deplored the caliber and the rigidity of character of those who were entering. The concern for justice was also applied within the Church as individuals took the initiative to organize groups "from below," that is, without consulting the authorities. Thus, the nuns formed two groups: National Coalition of American Nuns (NCAN), and National Association of Women Religious (NAWR), later changed to National Association of Religious Women so as to admit laywomen; and priests' councils began to proliferate in dioceses across the country, eventually forming a national organization. A group of laymen and women founded *The National Catholic Reporter,* an independent Catholic news weekly, a decisive departure from the bland diocesan press. The Grail, as one of the vanguard movements that had helped to prepare the way for Vatican II, was caught up in the turmoil. The 1960s, for the Grail, was a period of bold new initiatives, creativity and pioneering, and at the same time a period of stressful changes as individuals, having reevaluated their commitments, decided to leave the Grail nucleus, and the city centers were phased out.

Creative Initiatives

Underlying the Grail initiatives were new currents of thought that were circulating in society and in the Church in the late 1950s and early 1960s—personalism, existentialism, new approaches to scripture and catechetics, ecumenism, developmental psychology, nondirective therapy, and feminism. A number of Grail members attended the summer schools of the liturgy at the University of Notre Dame where they became acquainted with such European theologians as Josef Goldbrunner, Josef Jungmann, Johannes Hofinger, Louis Bouyer, and Christine Mohrmann. Goldbrunner gave several weekend courses at Grailville, as did Boniface Luykx and Marcel van Kaster, stressing the personalist approach to spirituality and catechetics.

In spiritual formation, the Grail emphasis shifted from a spirituality of obedience, focused on self-surrender and sacrifice, to an ideal of authenticity, the need to discover oneself, to be true to oneself, to live from within rather than allowing oneself to be determined from without. In 1959, a set of materials "On Being a Person," was developed, drawing on insights from the works of Goldbrunner, Martin Buber, Eric Fromm, Gabriel Marcel, and Rollo May, and using scenes from Arthur Miller's *Death of a Salesman,* T. S. Eliot's *The Cocktail Party,* and Lorraine Hansberry's *Raisin in the Sun,* as concrete illustrations of the search for the authentic self amid pressures toward conformity. These ideas resonated strongly with the married women in the Grail. With the help of Jeanne Plante and Cay Charles, groups of married women formed in a number of cities to explore ideas of personal growth toward Christian maturity. From 1961–1964 they published a national newsletter.

In this same period, there was a new concern with the psychological health of the person as the basis for spiritual life and growth, which led to a critique of an asceticism that relied too heavily on obedience and on the sheer force of will to conform behavior to an external ideal. In the 1950s, under the influence of Bishop Fulton Sheen, we had distrusted psychotherapy as

Figure 17. Dr. Josef Goldbrunner, a leader in contemporary religious education, demonstrating his methods with a group of children on the Grailville lawn, 1963.

basically hostile to Christianity. However, one of my responsibilities then as a leader-in-charge was to be alert for signs of stress in my team members. Our remedy was simple—relieve the person of responsibilities, send her to Grailville or to the small farm at Foster for a time of rest and manual work. It was not until the 1960s, having become acquainted with humanistic psychology, that we began to refer individuals for professional counselling and therapy. In the light of a new understanding of the dynamics of personal growth, we became much more aware of the dangers of asking too much of an individual, and focused Grail training on the authentic response of the free person as the basis for responsible action.

The new approaches soon were embodied in an extensive religious education program. One of the strengths of the Grail from its earliest days at Doddridge Farm has been the ability to take ideas and make them concrete. In the new catechetics, we brought together liturgy, theology, psychology, music, and the arts in a program that emphasized the *kerygma*, the "Good News" of the Gospel, and the importance of human experience in the development of the life of faith. *Holiness Is Wholeness*, the title of one of Dr. Goldbrunner's books, became the guiding principle of the Grail teams that worked out lesson plans, translating fundamental Christian themes in an experiential way. The Youth Leadership Program, begun in Brooklyn and Detroit, and later carried on in most of the other Grail centers, trained young college and working women to lead religious education sessions for teenagers in the public schools. The programs were quite extensive—in Brooklyn some ninety leaders reached fifteen-hundred high school girls. As a variant on this program, religious vacation schools were conducted during the summer months by Grail teams in Louisiana and San Jose.

The Grail Council on Religious Education was set up in 1959 to coordinate the rapidly growing catechetical work. The Council almost immediately began publishing a modest bulletin in mimeographed form. Eva Fleischner, the editor, gathered resources on the new approaches, provided bibliographies, made translations from the French and German, and added news notes, practical suggestions, and materials for catechists. Originally intended simply for Grail members, the bulletin soon acquired subscribers nationwide. A high point of the Grail catechetical work was a two-week institute at Grailville, "Catechetical Crossroads," August 4–18, 1963. It brought together more than a hundred participants—bishops, priests, nuns, laity, teachers, Confraternity of Christian Doctrine directors, administrators—with such leaders in the field as Marcel van Kaster of *Lumen Vitae*, Gerard Sloyan of Catholic University, Bernard Cooke of Marquette University, Josef Goldbrunner, and Alfonse Nebreda, SJ. One participant commented that this program "launched the catechetical movement in the United States."[2]

Ecumenism was another current which had been stirring in the Grail long before Vatican II. Jacques van Ginneken had given his retreats for non-Catholics and had included outreach to non-Catholic Christians as one of the goals of the Grail, albeit more in the spirit of converting them to the true church than recognizing the value of their traditions. Through Msgr. Ligutti and the Catholic Rural Life Movement, Grailville from its earliest days had enjoyed friendly relations with the Quaker Rural Life Association. In the 1940s, I remember going with a team from Grailville to speak at Quaker and Brethren Churches in Indiana and Ohio. If the Brethren liked what one said, they voiced their approval with a loud, "Amen, sister, amen," a bit startling but nevertheless encouraging to a nervous speaker. Msgr. Ligutti himself conducted a weekend at Grailville for Protestant ministers and their wives. George Tavard, author of many books on ecumenism, was a frequent visitor and brought his ecumenical perspective to Grail programs. In the early 1960s, Jim Leslie and Barbara Troxell, chaplains at Ohio Weslyan University, brought groups of their students for ecumenical weekends at Grailville, as did Nancy Richardson from the YWCA at Oberlin College. Our contacts with the YWCA led to the participation of Protestants in Semester at Grailville. The Grail teams in the New York area cooperated closely with other religious groups in the international student work and formed lasting friendships with many of the women on the national staffs of the mainline Protestant churches. The San Jose Center was involved in "the escalation of ecumenism" that led to the establishment of the Graduate Theological Union, a consortium of Catholic and Protestant theological Schools in the Bay area. These contacts were to lead in 1969 to Protestant membership in the Grail.

Ecumenism was a congenial cutting edge issue for the Grail. In 1961, the Philadelphia Center pioneered in developing the first formal ecumenical group in that city, a group of Protestant clergy and Catholic laity, since Catholic priests were still forbidden to engage in ecumenical dialogue. Other Grail Centers across the country also initiated ecumenical discussion groups. The Grail was invited to participate in ecumenical conferences sponsored by various Protestant groups, and in 1964 was asked to send someone to join the staff of Packard Manse, a Protestant center of reconciliation in Boston. Donna Myers, joined first by Peg Linnehan and then by Anne Mulkeen, was the first Catholic to serve on this Baptist and Anglican staff. In January of 1964, Mary Brigid Niland and I coordinated a memorable weekend at the Grail Center, Cornwall-on-Hudson, in which ten Catholic women met ten Protestants from the Interchurch Center, 475 Riverside Drive, New York (known locally as "the God Box"), where many of the mainline churches had their headquarters. The dialogue that weekend was open, trusting and intimate, as we shared our desires and hopes for unity. I remember the pain I felt at the our Sunday morning Mass when we could not invite the Protestants to share communion with us. In 1969 by a decision of the United States Grail General Assembly, we admitted Protestant women to full membership in the Grail.

From 1961 to 1966 Donna Myers edited *Ecumenical Notes*, begun like the *Religious Education Bulletin* to help Grail members keep abreast of developments in a new field. It, too, soon attracted more non-Grail than Grail subscribers. Both bulletins provided a much needed service in burgeoning new fields; once other publications took up the task of supplying articles, translations, bibliographies and field notes, the Grail editors announced that their work had served its purpose and ceased publication. This process of launching a new project and then letting it go once the idea had caught on has often been characteristic of the Grail. To some it may appear as a lack of continuity, but to Grail members it is an expression of a missionary spirit that seeks to work itself out of a job as quickly as possible and then to move on to a new field.

Figure 18. Jeanne Heiberg, making a silkscreen print in the Grailville art barn for her popular series, The Good News in Pictures, *published by the Liturgical Press, 1962.*

The Grail initiatives in the field of Christian culture continued to expand during the 1960s. The art production program, begun in the late 1950s, was inspired by the desire to bring "good" religious art to people at affordable prices. We were critical of the weak and sentimental images we saw everywhere. For us, "good religious art" involved using contemporary forms to express a radical Christian spirit, thus demonstrating that faith was alive in the twentieth century as well as in the thirteenth. Our first project, part of a campaign "to put Christ back into Christmas," consisted of six contemporary Christmas cards, ten thousand of each design, sold retail in packages of six. Everyone at Grailville was involved in the packaging and mailing. We never did cards again, but turned to sculpture, prints, metal work, books, and records, adding new items every year. By the mid-1960s the catalogue contained sixty-five items and was mailed to 60,000 addresses. Sculptures by Trina Paulus—the Holy Family, Adsum, the Christmas creche—were very popular. Jeanne Heiberg did a series of vigorous silk screen prints on the liturgical year, intended for the home, and a set of bold, colorful renderings of biblical scenes, *The Good News in Pictures,* published by the Liturgical Press, and used extensively in the new catechetics. Occasionally, the catalogue provoked violent reactions. I remember one catalogue being returned to us with the word "communists" scrawled across the photo of an austere modern crucifix. In the sphere of the theater arts, Elaine Jones's original poetic drama, *New Born Again*, was made into a prize-winning film by Maclovia Rodriguez, a Grail member and a professional film maker. Maclovia also made several original films, *Change* (1966), a reflection on the tumltuous 1960s, and *Once Upon a Telephone Pole*, a delightful exploration of the reactions of local children to an environmental sculpture on the Grailville grounds created and built by artist Robert Wilson in the summer of 1968.

Music had always been a major element in life at Grailville. The Music Center under Eleanor Walker had a staff that not only directed the congregational singing but also formed a schola or special choir for the more difficult works, taught conducting, did research to locate new material, and composed new music, setting texts in English to melodies in the style of plain chant. They made four recordings, published by professional companies and recorded at Grailville by expert engineers. The recordings were community efforts, involving all eighty women resident at Grailville— thirty-five singing, the rest of us bringing them hot soup, keeping the stove going in the chilly barn with the good acoustics, cutting off a branch rubbing against the roof, keeping delivery trucks from entering the driveway, while the singers worked through two gruelling ten-hour days to satisfy the high standards of perfectionist choir director Angela Miller.

Acting on the new insights into the oneness of God's action in Church and world, in the late 1960s individual Grail members began to move into work in non-Grail structures, seeking to be fully involved in the struggle for justice in the world and seeing these activities as expressions of their Grail commitment. A number of people, having earned degrees in social work, moved into community organizing, choosing areas where they hoped to make a difference: inner city Philadelphia; "Over the Rhine" and the West End in inner city Cincinnati. Teachers made similar choices: Mary Anne Kimbell joined the staff of Seven Hills Neighborhood Houses to teach home economics to Appalachian and African-American women; Olive Wahl helped to staff a struggling Catholic elementary school in East Harlem; Beverley Scorrano worked in a community-controlled school in Brooklyn. Others, among them Peggy Linnehan and Carol Webb, developed expertise in teaching English as a second language to the Spanish speaking in San Jose, California. Sharon Joslyn, returned from serving with a Grail team in Brazil, began work as a nurse practitioner in rural Clermont County, Ohio, an area as lacking in medical services as any country in the "two-thirds world." Una Mae Hargrave helped to start the

Southern Consumers Cooperative with African-American sharecroppers in Louisiana. Dr. Mary Clifford and community organizer Lynn Malley, concerned to develop a model of comprehensive health care, joined the staff of a project of Tufts Medical School, a clinic to bring quality care to a neglected region of the Mississipppi Delta. These initiatives represented a new model for effective action "in the world." Alongside the familiar strategy of incarnating Grail values by building an integrated pattern of Christian living in a Grail Center, Grail work now expanded to include issue-oriented jobs in both secular and church structures.

Quite soon Grail members in these new situations, feeling the need for mutual support, formed a "Counter-Institution" group. They provided encouragement for the unconventional decisions of group members, for instance, nurse Doris Gibson's choice to study midwifery with the pioneering service in Kentucky, and the decision of Mary and Lynn to join the Tufts' Mississippi project. In the next decade, inspired by the same impulse, some of the same people formed "the Grail Professionals" as an official Grail group. From 1972 to 1985, they met three or four times a year, pooling their resources to cover the expenses of the meetings, and even managing to hold two international gatherings, one at Grailville and one in the Netherlands. They shared experiences, acted as a discernment group with individuals facing crucial decisions about life and career, and reflected together on how to express their values in their daily work. "We wanted to see our professions as our Grail work," Frances Martin and Ruth Gallant, founding members of the "Professionals" explained, "for ourselves and for others in the Grail. It is sometimes hard to maintain that perspective. People tend to see the Grail sponsored projects as the 'real' Grail work."[3] A professionals' newsletter stated "The Grail for us touches and involves our whole self; therefore, as professionals we want the Grail to give us also the possibility to discover the full meaning of our professional life and the 'how' of living it according to a communal Grail praxis coming forth from a communal Grail reflection."[4] At the 1974 international meeting, the group developed their purpose further in terms of its meaning for their own personal development, its effectiveness in furthering a transformation of society, its expression of Grail values. In the light of our new understanding of the relation of Church and world, the concept of social transformation was gradually replacing our earlier language of "lay apostolate."

This group is an example of autonomy in community. Although neither living together nor working in the same project, nevertheless they formed real and deep bonds with each other. They sustained each other in making the risky decisions that personal and career development demand; and they were ready with emotional and financial support in times of serious hardship—a crippling accident to one member, the lingering illness and death of another. The group certainly enabled its members "to keep the dream alive," as they strove to exercise a transforming influence on institutional structures.

One of the most significant new initiatives in the 1960s was in the field of education—the designing and launching of a new educational program for women, Semester at Grailville (SAG). SAG, and subsequent educational alternatives, are such important examples of the way in which Grail members were able to adapt their vision and values to a changing culture that they will be discussed in chapter 12.

Stresses and Strains

As the new ideas took hold among the first generation of American Grail nucleus members, we began to question some policies and practices, feeling slightly guilty as we discussed these matters with each other outside of formal meetings. In the classic spirituality we had been taught, the authority of the leader was bolstered by a strong condemnation of the sin of "murmuring." Once the leader had spoken, it was disloyalty, nay rebellion, to raise a question. *Roma locuta est; causa finita est.* (Rome has spoken; the matter is settled.) In the Grail this spiritual principle was translated into two strong norms: one did not discuss one's personal spiritual life and decisions with anyone but one's mentor; one did not join in criticism of decisions once made; rather, one supported the position the leader had taken. As we gained confidence in our own experience and insights, we began to question this Ignatian ideal of obedience, an obedience that demanded conformity to the decision of the leader not only in action, but also in thought and will. Thus, a certain unease had begun to permeate the group even before we felt the full effect of Vatican II. Grail expansion reached a peak in 1963, the year that the thirteenth Grail center in North America was established at Cornwall-on-Hudson, New York; a hundred young women had made a formal dedication in the nucleus of the Grail; more than a hundred Americans were serving in Grail teams overseas; five national councils were coordinating work in diverse fields. At this point, the stresses and strains involved in maintaining such a large movement became more evident and were more often the topic of discussion when we younger leaders met informally with each other.

There had always been difficulties in adapting the Grailville pattern of integrated Christian living to the circumstances in the cities, but in the mid-1960s problems multiplied and touched deeper levels. Practices that contributed to a satisfying pattern of life on Grailville's "cultural island" often proved difficult or impossible in the rush of city life. The Grail stressed living on principle, and the first principle of formation for the lay apostle was to take part in daily Mass. The Grailville schedule easily accommodated time for an unhurried recitation of lauds, a quarter of an hour of private meditation after Mass, a silent, meditative walk back from the parish church, and then a nourishing hot breakfast. However, for residents in the city centers, who had to leave for work or school at 8 A.M., the most that could be managed without sacrificing necessary sleep was a quick early Mass. Moreover, since the usual practice in city churches was to offer "black Masses" to commemorate the dead, this steady diet of requiems did not supply much inspiration for the day ahead. In the evening, it was difficult to gather the community for vespers and supper, since some residents arrived late from their jobs and some staff had to leave early to take charge of evening programs. Matins, which were a high point of Saturday night at Grailville, did not work at all with young people in the city for whom Saturday meant date night after a week on the job.

Having internalized Grailville's ways of concretizing spiritual values, we tended to absolutize both the principle and the applications we made to the daily life of the Christian. "When I found it impossible to have matins on Saturday night, or to buy unrefined sugar in the local market," Mary Buckley confessed to me, "I felt guilty. Was I losing the spirit? Had I compromised my principles?"[5]

Tensions inevitably developed between Grailville and the city centers, typical of the tensions between headquarters and branches in any organization. The centers were always in search of staff. Seeing Grailville with eighty or ninety people in residence, they found it hard to understand why no one could be spared to meet their urgent needs. On the other hand, when they were asked to take someone who was "difficult" or who was "not ready" for Grailville, they felt unduly burdened. The centers felt pressured to produce participants for the courses at Grailville. The Grailville staff felt pressured to produce resources and personnel for the cities. We did not have a theory of organizational behavior to help us understand these tensions in neutral terms. Rather conflicts and resentments were interpreted solely in spiritual terms, as personal failures—we were not being generous or charitable enough to each other, we were failing to recognize and embrace the cross as it presented itself to us in the daily work.

Attitudes toward community life and its rewards changed between the 1940s and the 1960s. In the 1940s and early 1950s living together in a house full of lively, friendly young women was an attractive option. There were both novelty and rewards in getting to know others in many dimensions of their lives—praying and studying, cleaning and cooking, working as teams and having fun together. In the 1960s, community living began to lose its attractiveness. As individuals matured and experienced new needs, they were less interested in community living. But even for young women, by the late 1950s attitudes toward community living appeared to change; individuals were much less willing to make the sacrifices of personal inclinations that are necessary to sustain common activities. The demands of the community became a source of tensions.

Another factor was simple overwork. The ideal of total dedication to God translated into total availability for the demands of the community, a norm that led to a very strong work ethic. "Give all that you have laughing," a line from Paul Claudel's play, *The Tidings Brought to Mary*, was a favorite motto. We had come together to accomplish something and we tended to work at it without a break. We talked about a change of activity as a form of recreation, and I certainly found that to go from writing reports to weeding the garden did renew my energies. But we seldom took time off to play a game or simply to relax. I remember that after the major effort of the Advent drama, ten weeks of ceaseless organizing and rehearsing, I did not even give my staff in the Brooklyn Center a single free day, but the very next morning proceeded with a new set of tasks. One of the Brooklyn priests tried, very gently, to suggest to me that the punishing pace at which the residents in the Center worked might discourage some girls from joining the group, but at the time I was quite impervious to his suggestion.

For those in charge of a project or a center, the burden was particularly heavy. When I was in Brooklyn, starting the Overseas Institute, I was overwhelmed by the multiple dimensions of my task. I was supposed to be "a spiritual mother" to twelve students and ten staff, fostering personal growth, taking the time to offer honest feedback on the individual's strengths and weaknesses, advising her on her choice of vocation, and in general keeping everyone happy and enthusiastic about her life and work. At the same time, I was responsible to make ends meet financially, to be a source of new ideas and creative approaches for programs, and to supervise all the varied activities of the house.

The strain of living up to the ideal and managing the workload proved too much for some individuals, who broke down under it. By the early 1960s many of us leaders were concerned with the problems of physical and psychological exhaustion that were surfacing in the group. We began to wonder whether the burden of coordinating the activities of hundreds of people in twelve houses from coast to coast had become too heavy to sustain. Even though we liked to repeat the dictum, "The Grail is not a frame into which you must fit; each one makes her own frame," there were always holes to be filled. While city center programs were quite flexible and could be developed around the specific abilities of the staff, there was also the demand for specific talents: someone who could work with teenagers or a person with a good business head who could take over the bookstore. I remember one year when as the "Round Table," my colleagues and I sat together for a full week trying to place a hundred individuals in the various centers and projects. We were torn between "filling the holes" and putting each individual in the situation most conducive to her own growth. This was not so difficult to do with young people for whom almost any experience could prove educational. But as people grew older, they wanted tasks commensurate with their experience and abilities. We were subject to conflicting pressures. On the one hand, there were never enough people to fill the holes. On the other hand, there were not enough good jobs for the mature. It was no longer challenging for a woman of thirty to be in charge of the laundry or to do the housekeeping for a city center. Individuals were less and less willing to be "jills-of-all-trades," always available for community needs.

By the late 1950s the Grail began to feel the effects of the increasing professionalization of women's lives in society at large. Women were moving into the labor force in larger and larger numbers; more women were going to college and embarking on professional careers. In the 1940s many young women responded to the Grail challenge to leave an academic program that held little personal meaning for them and to launch themselves into the risky adventure of the lay apostolate. In the 1960s, the college degree had become so important that the old challenge no longer worked. Grail members who had abandoned college (or in some cases the last year of high school) began to feel the need for academic credentials. They acknowledged that they had developed a host of leadership skills through their Grail training—they knew how to organize, publicize, speak up in public, take the lead in a group; still many felt that they needed the college degree in order to meet their peers on an equal footing. Some people went back to school part-time while continuing to work on city center staffs. A dozen others in the early 1960s took up residence in the annex of the Brooklyn Center which became a kind of "house of studies" for those pursuing either a BA or a graduate degree. It soon became clear that Grail training had provided a basic liberal education as well as leadership skills, for most of these students earned their degrees in record time, receiving academic credit for work done at Grailville.

In short, in the midst of the flourishing movement of the early 1960s, there was widespread restlessness and uneasiness among the younger Grail leaders. We were ripe for change, and major changes were soon to come in the form of a full-fledged Grail aggiornamento.

10

Aggiornamento in the Grail

Aggiornamento—the word chosen by Pope John XXIII as the purpose of Vatican II—literally means bringing up to date. Pope John sought to bring the Church into the modern world, not as a severe judge condemning errors, but as a loving mother, affirming goodness and truth wherever found. This positive and pastoral approach produced an enormous change of consciousness in a very short time.

In the spring of 1964, Dr. Magdalene Oberhoffer, the International President of the Grail, inaugurated a Grail Aggiornamento, a process of self-evaluation climaxing in an International General Assembly in the summer of 1965. For once, we fast women were not ahead of the Church but were following in the footsteps of Pope John XXIII, responding to the rapid change of consciousness which he had initiated. I was in Rome for the fourth and final session of the Vatican Council and was caught up in the new and sometimes confusing ideas. It was a tremendously exciting time to be in Rome. I loved attending the daily press briefings and the many lectures and discussions with leading theologians that went on along the fringes of the Council. I remember walking down Via della Conzilatione, the broad avenue leading to St. Peter's and meeting pacifist Dorothy Day, prominent journalist John Cogley, ecumenist Father John Oesterreicher, feminist nun Mary Luke Tobin, SL, and other leaders of the Catholic world.[1] I was working part-time in Cardinal Bea's office, the Pontifical Secretariat for Christian Unity, established in 1960 by Pope John XXIII. My job was to type the *modi* (amendments) for the document on religious liberty. The old Italian bishops in their "kitchen Latin" were against the document. They repeated the classic argument: error has no rights; the Protestant churches are in error; therefore, they have no right to conduct public worship. It was clear to me that these bishops had no experience of how the Church functioned in the United States under the Bill of Rights, and no conception of how much healthier Catholic life could be when the individual's adherence to the Church was freely chosen.

As I participated in all these activities, I came to understand that an intellectual revolution was taking place. The process that the Council began acted like an acid, dissolving a long-established worldview. The documents on the *Church in the Modern World* and on *Religious Liberty* did away with the notion of the Church as the perfect society, under siege in an evil world dominated by Satan. In its place, they set forth a vision of the People of God, witnessing to God's love, recognizing truth in other religious traditions, affirming freedom of conscience, affirming the goodness of creation and human inventions, and meeting God as much in the struggle for justice as in the withdrawal to the cloister and the silence of contemplation. While many of the Council documents were a pastiche of the old and the new, the main effect of the Council was to relativize the Church. It was no longer, *the* way, the only way, but *a* way. I remember how delighted I was to find an essay by one of the Council theologians—I think it was Bernard Haering—explaining the underlying paradigm shift. The philosophical perspective had moved away from the time-honored Aristotelian-Thomistic world of fixed, timeless essences to an existential view of concrete realities, historically and socially conditioned. The eternal, universal, abstract objectivity of the old philosophy gave way to the enlightened intersubjectivity of a new approach, which respected the diversity of multiple viewpoints. No longer could I conceive of the Church as a perfect society, instituted by Christ as an infallible guide for human life. Rather I saw an institution of fallible human beings, mixtures of holiness and sinfulness, terribly limited by their race, gender, ethnicity, class, education, social position, and historical epoch. The old absolutes were dissolving and it would take time to work out all the implications of that dissolution.

As in the Church at large, so in the Grail, aggiornamento was worked out on two levels: in immediate actions, both individual and collective; and in the slower work of theological analysis and structural changes, developing new guidelines and structures.

On the level of action, Dolores Brien, who was serving as one of the two International Vice-Presidents, and Jeanne Plante, who had been Director of Grailville for some years, announced their decision to leave the nucleus early in the spring of 1964. Their decisions sent shock waves through the movement, especially since in the United States very few up to this time had been released from the nucleus. The other International Vice-President, Benedicte Milcent, had also decided to leave, but agreed privately with the International President to stay on until the 1965 international meeting.[2] Following the customary top-down pattern of communication, the International President, Magdalene Oberhoffer, first called together an ad hoc International Advisory Council[3] made up of five senior leaders. This group decided to launch a systematic aggiornamento process. "First the other national leaders and then all the members of the nucleus were asked to give their 'spontaneous reactions' to this idea. . . . The responses were overwhelmingly favorable to the proposal,"[4] Magdalene wrote in a letter addressed to all aggiornamento participants.

The proposal called on the Grail, as an international community, to think through all aspects of its life, the vision and structures, the beliefs and practices. It outlined a three-year process of research, consultation, experimentation, and decision-making, which began immediately with the drafting of a comprehensive questionnaire sent out to all Grail centers, teams and participants. The responses were prompt and generous: thirty-two groups reported from fourteen countries; in addition, one-hundred-twenty-nine individuals (the majority from the Netherlands and the United States) sent personal replies. Ninety percent of the nucleus were represented by either individual or group replies, and four countries included movement members in the process. I was on the team, together with Maria de Lourdes Pintasilgo of Portugal and Eleanor Walker of the United States, who worked at the International Secretariat in Paris to collate the responses and feed them back to the participants in the form of a series of working papers. At the same time, an organized effort of research into the spiritual basis of the Grail, its relevance to the world, and the structures that could best serve the movement was carried on by various Grail members and theological consultants. All these materials formed part of the preparation for the International General Assembly held in The Netherlands in July, 1965, which drafted new guidelines and structures for the movement. These were adopted as a basis for operation and were evaluated and revised at a second International General Assembly in 1967.

New Guidelines

The new guidelines incorporated the insights of Vatican II. For the Grail, the Council in many respects represented not some new departure but rather a confirmation of insights and practices that were already alive in the movement. Thus, the document on the liturgy, which proved upsetting to many people in the pews and met with strong resistance in some quarters, simply put a Vatican seal of approval on things we had been doing and promoting for many years—for instance, as mentioned above, active participation by the congregation, greater use of the vernacular, sermons based on the Mass texts, the use of modern art. Similarly, the affirmation of the laity as *being* Church, called to the apostolate by virtue of their insertion into Christ's priesthood in baptism and confirmation, coresponsible with the bishops, priests and religious to bring the Gospel to the world, was familiar doctrine, in fact, the very basis of our existence as a movement. Again, the positive approach to non-Catholics and non-Christians was already part of our experience. As fast women we were ahead of the Church on all these points.

The first of the major changes brought about by the 1967 Grail guidelines and structures is assumed rather than explicitly stated: namely, the definition of the Grail as a movement of women of all vocations. The Women of Nazareth, the original group, founded by Jacques van Ginneken in 1921, was a group of unmarried laywomen in the world, pledged in virginity, poverty, and obedience to spread the Kingdom of God and to be totally available lifelong for the lay apostolate. "The Grail" originally was the name of the youth movement organized and directed by the WoN in Holland, England, and Germany in the 1930s. The two organizations were distinct, although the WoN held all the major functional roles in the Grail. In the United States, from the very beginning we had worked closely with married women and single professionals, but we did not formalize membership until the visit of Rachel Donders in 1951. As discusssed in chapter 6, she had formally established membership for the group who made a lifetime dedication in celibacy. At the same time, she had changed the terminology from WoN to "nucleus of the Grail," from "mother general" to "international president," thus moving the terminology at least in the direction of one all-embracing movement. It is not until 1958, in a working paper prepared by the theologians, that I find the Grail explicitly described as a movement of women of different vocations—virginity, marriage, widowhood, singleness, in professions. The 1967 Guidelines make no attempt to define the Grail as such, but simply affirm that "the different vocations within the Grail are different expressions of the same commitment to Christ, each one an answer to a personal call."[5] It remained for the structures to work out the implications of this affirmation, changing the organizational form from a patriarchal pyramid to a partnership of peers.

A second major change incorporated the conciliar perspective on the relation of Church and world. The guidelines called for awareness of the oneness of God's action in world and Church, hence the need for attentiveness to the "signs of the time," in an attitude of continual search and openness to the Spirit. As practical corollaries, the guidelines affirmed work in secular as well as Church structures, in collaborative projects with other groups as well as in Grail structures, in cooperation with all people of good will whatever their faith, in individual commitments to a work or profession as well as to corporate Grail efforts.

Third was the profound shift in the understanding of authority and obedience. The classic spirituality stressed the importance of obedience in overcoming self-will and identified the will of the superior or the spiritual director quite literally as the will of God. The Council spoke of collegiality and the bishops soon demonstrated their understanding of it by rejecting the agenda prepared by the Roman curia in favor of a positive and pastoral approach to the modern world, to the social sciences, to other religions. In society at large, the experience of totalitarianism and of brainwashing techniques had illuminated both the dangers of unquestioning obedience and the fundamental character of the human rights to freedom of thought, expression, and conscience.

In the Grail, the conciliar idea of collegiality was translated as "shared responsibility," that is, a greater sense of responsibility for the whole shared among all the members, with a corresponding change in the concept of the leader from charismatic, all-knowing director to catalyst. The responses to the aggiornamento questionnaire revealed a shift in lived experience from a more or less blind obedience (the leader knows best) to an obedience in dialogue. The model is neither the family, where the immature are subordinate to their elders, nor an aristocracy that by its superior gifts is called to direct the masses, but rather a sisterhood relating to each other in mutuality. The 1967 guidelines speak of a "fraternal [sic] dialogue," carried on in the context of the common mission, involving the individual, others in her group, and the designated authority, in which the final decision is made by the individual, not by the designated authority. Leadership is now understood not so much in terms of the traits of a more or less charismatic and powerful individual, but rather in terms of the actions needed to move a group toward its goals, actions that any member of the group can initiate. The designated leader is no longer the sole source of initiatives; rather she becomes a coordinator and facilitator of the contributions of group members.

Summing up the insights derived from the work on personalism, the guidelines speak of Christian life in terms of growth to maturity rather than in terms of an ideal of perfection one struggles to live up to. The focus shifts from external to internal, from self-abnegation to authenticity. The emphasis is on an experiential integration of human and spiritual realities. The guidelines call for a process of development in self-knowledge, in ability to relate to others, in internalizing ultimate values, in responding realistically to one's situation in the world. The emphasis is on respect for the gifts of each individual, the development of an adult conscience, the practice of an asceticism suited to the circumstances of daily life.

Finally, the guidelines affirm communion as a basic value in the Grail, to be realized in a variety of groupings, small and large, residential and nonresidential, national and international. What is new here is the stress on the small group as a way of helping each individual to discover and develop her unique gifts, and the call for improving communication at all levels, particularly the fostering of informal lateral relations. The old spirituality tended to distrust lateral relations and freely formed small groups as breeding grounds for opposition to authority; the new spirituality spoke of support groups as aids to personal spiritual growth. As a whole, the guidelines mark the vast change from "the quasi-religious nucleus of the lay apostolate" to a lay movement, from a patriarchal pyramid to a partnership of peers.

Structural Changes

Perhaps the most crucial work of the Grail aggiornamento was the design of new structures that would embody the new insights. The aggiornamento launched the Grail, particularly in the United States, into more than twenty years of struggle to create structures to free the spirit, to build participative forms of decision making that could also operate efficiently to get things done. I want to trace this process in some detail because I think it illustrates the difficulties of making a significant structural change in any organization. Those involved, viewing matters from the vantage point of their leadership positions, tend to think they are taking giant steps, when to an outside observer they seem to be barely moving.

The original structure of the WoN (and indeed of the Dutch Grail youth movement of the 1930s) had reproduced the hierarchical structure of the Church in a form closely resembling that of the Jesuits. This structure had remained largely unchanged in the 1940 version of the statutes that Lydwine van Kersbergen and Joan Overboss brought with them to the United States in the spring of 1940. The structure was a highly centralized pyramid with the International President at the top. She was the head of the chain of command and the guarantor of international unity. Her responsibilities included supervision of all the work, for example, setting up new foundations and training centers, appointing the national presidents, appointing members to go to the training, supervising the finances. She was also the spiritual leader, responsible for keeping the vision and spirit, visiting all the houses regularly to give spiritual instruction, counseling the members individually on their spiritual progress, giving the final approval to the acceptance of new members and having the final decision in case of a member who wished to be released from her commitment.

She and her two counselors and an admonisher were the only elected authorities. They were chosen by the votes of a restricted group—one delegate for every twenty fully fledged WoN in a given country. Moreover, the structures favored self-perpetuation of the ruling group, since the outgoing administration made up the slate of candidates from the list of nominees put forth by the delegates and the national presidents.

In this structure authority and communication flowed from the top down. There was a very limited provision for feedback: the counselors were instructed that they need not agree with the president but must say what they think best for the general welfare; and the admonisher was explicitly charged to meet once a month with the president, to point out her faults and mistakes and to report complaints from the members. Accountability was required only in an upward direction. The international president could terminate the national presidents at will. The same pyramid structure was repeated on the national level: the national presidents appointed the heads of centers, teams, and projects and could terminate them at will. The whole system functioned in terms of a spirituality based on the Ignatian ideal of obedience, that is, an obedience not only in action but in conformity of will and judgment to that of the leader. In fact, the ideal member was expected to try to anticipate the wishes of her leader, and, while she might privately express a difference of opinion to the leader, was always ready to accept her decision as the will of God. She would never criticize her leader's policies or actions publicly. In such an hierarchical system, information was carefully controlled by the leader; lateral communication was strongly discouraged. Decisions were taken in a restricted circle of leaders and were communicated at the discretion of the leader and in a more or less edited form. In short, the spiritual ideal held up to members and members-in-training of giving oneself totally to God was to be expressed concretely in obedience to the entire chain of command in small things as well as large, an obedience binding in conscience.

In a visionary movement of young people with strong charismatic leadership, those in command tended to see themselves as safeguarding the vision, preventing a watering down into mediocrity. This structure made it possible to marshall the energies of individuals effectively around a program or project—for instance, those mass dramas in Holland with thousands of young women. Also, under the impetus of assigned tasks, many individuals developed capacities and talents which otherwise might have remained dormant. I know that was true for me. And, in my experience of the early days of the Grail in the United States, the spirit was often so strong that we "played over our heads," as the baseball expression goes— we did things that would have been considered exceedingly unlikely if not impossible on purely rational grounds. But it is also true that in the hands of any but the wisest and most discerning of leaders, these structures could easily become totalitarian.

Father van Ginneken sought to balance the emphasis on obedience with stress on initiative and responsibility. He often made the point that almost all spiritual books had been written by men for men, were concentrated on the typical male vices, and did not apply to women. He mentions as typical faults of women vanity, passivity, fear of what others may think of them, shyness, avoidance of responsibility, oversensitiveness. Therefore, women should seek mortification in coming forward, speaking up, taking initiative, volunteering for responsible tasks. "With brute commanding and demanding that a woman should act but not think, you will achieve nothing," he declares. And he goes on to instruct the young Grail leaders: "Obedience will only become fully efficient when initiative is left to develop itself alongside it . . . see to it that you always give your orders in such a way that the subject may use her brains and her initiative and her resourcefulness by which to help you to achieve the *purpose for which you need her*"[6] (my italics). Blind obedience is necessary in the training house, to purge persons of whims and self-will, to develop humility and flexibility. "But in the active work it should be different. There they must leave you your own initiative alongside obedience." While he would like to see everyone in a group put forth ideas and plans, he also assumes that the leader "should keep the strings in her own hands." It apparently does not occur to him that women trained to undertake enormous tasks (the kind of responsibilities involved, for instance, in successfully bringing together ten thousand young women in the Olympic Stadium in Amsterdam for the 1932 Pentecost play) might eventually want to exercise their initiative and ideas in policymaking and goalsetting.

Two factors that served to modify the original structures somewhat were the trust in women's experience with the resultant sense of autonomy, and the concern from the beginning to adapt to the needs and circumstances of different times and different cultures. From my own exposure to the oral tradition in the Grail, my guess is that almost from day one any written document was modified by the experience of the group. I remember Lydwine van Kersbergen explaining to me in 1941 that the Ladies of the Grail did not have a rule, that they lived according to the Spirit. When I joined the training in 1942, the practice was for the group to meditate on the spirit of the feast or season and then decide on some group practices that would enable us to live out that spirit and to volunteer individually for special tasks of prayer or penance suited to our own needs. In planning programs, launching new projects, accepting individuals into the nucleus, there was always a good deal of consultation, sometimes with the whole group, sometimes only with the senior staff, and always at the initiative of the leader-in-charge. As the work in the United States expanded in the 1950s, there were efforts at a more formal delegation of responsibility. When Lydwine van Kersbergen was out of the country, in 1953, Rachel Donders delegated decision-making authority to a Round Table of the six leaders of the Grail Centers, with myself as *"primus inter pares"* (first among equals). A little later two vice-presidents, Barbara Wald and Eileen

Schaeffler, were appointed to assist Lydwine; these three together with Jeanne Plante, Dorothy Rasenberger, and Audrey Sorrento were constituted as a National Committee, sharing responsbility for Grail developments in the United States and aided by a National Advisory Committee of the city center leaders and the heads of the various councils for overseas service, international students, Christian culture, religious education, and service careers.

At the international level, Rachel Donders, who had been elected International President in 1949 and re-elected for a second term in 1955, found herself at the head of a rapidly growing movement with no constitution except the 1940 Statutes, which were clearly outdated and inadequate to the existing situation. At least three factors pointed to the need to find a new organizational form for the international government of the movement: (1) the expansion to many other countries besides Holland; (2) the existence in some countries of active members who were not part of the nucleus; and (3) the felt need to share responsibility more widely. Rachel brought together several working groups both to prepare for the 1961 international election and to revise the organizational structures. A group that began to draft new structures in a working paper dated November 19, 1960, set down the following underlying thoughts to guide the development of a structure better suited to the complex new reality of the movement:

- it is necessary to think of the Grail as a world movement, existing on all continents, embracing all kinds of members;
- responsibility for the direction of the Grail needs to be spread more widely;
- all members, nucleus and committed, should have some voice in the government;
- the worldwide unity of the Grail should be clearly apparent in the structure;
- the nucleus should be a clearly recognizable group in the whole movement; and
- in order to guarantee the continuity and stability of the whole movement, certain offices should be reserved for nucleus members.[7]

In the next several years immense amounts of work went into proposals for new structures—working groups, consultations with theologians, an East-West group, consultations with the national leaders, circulation of drafts to various members for comments. In some sense all these efforts were attempts to deal with the tensions in Jacques van Ginneken's original concept of "a quasi-religious nucleus of the lay apostolate, forming one big organization with the laypeople."[8] He insists emphatically that the relation of the Grail (he has in mind the Dutch youth movement of the 1930s) to the WoN is not like the relation of the Third Order to the Franciscans, that is, a mere appendage, a group of lay people organized and led by the friars. That pattern has long been established in the Catholic Church. The new thing is that the lay people, according to the papal directives on the lay apostolate, may now form a real hierarchy, like the army. He lists the ranks in the Grail at that time: Round Table, chief leader of a town, chief leader of a Grail Center, and so forth. His concept is of a highly organized body with a cadre of leaders who are totally available for this work, and who carry both the spirit and the functional roles. To secure the requisite intensity of spirit in the leadership, he turns to the only means he knows, namely the evangelical counsels of poverty, chastity, and obedience. To secure the lay character, he creates a legal device: the commitment to the counsels is not by vow, for then the WoN would be religious and would be bound by all the restrictions canon law places on religious; rather, the commitment is by oath and promise and therefore falls outside the province of canon law. But he also insists that the obligations are the same and the sacrifices should be at least as great as those of the most solemnly vowed religious.[9]

The concept has its difficulties. On the one hand, was it really possible to have one organization and at the same time have within it a core group with a lifetime commitment in celibacy who were totally available for the demands of the apostolate? Is the tension between nucleus and movement a source of dynamism or a real contradiction? Can a lay movement, attuned to the action of the Spirit in the world, base its spirituality on a monastic ideal founded on withdrawal from the world? Does the distinction between nucleus and movement create a barrier between them similar to the one Father van Ginneken explicitly tried to avoid, namely, that between the Franciscans and their Third Order? Will the initiatives of the nucleus weaken the sense of responsibility on the part of movement members? Will the weight of experience and life investment of the nucleus members make it impossible to frame a definition of membership that would put all on an equal footing in building and directing the movement? If all members are to have a voice in government, is it possible to reserve some leadership roles to the nucleus? On the other hand, is the nucleus necessary to preserve a unity of vision and continuity of work as well as an intensity of spirit? The English Grail had resolved this tension in favor of the nucleus— a clearly identifiable group, with its own community life and the status of a secular institute, undertaking various works. The Grail in the United States chose the other horn of the dilemma and moved in the direction of wider and more inclusive membership.[10]

The international elections were held in 1961, following for the most part the procedure outlined in the 1940 Rule, but with the change that two International Vice-Presidents rather than two counselors were chosen. The new team consisted of Dr. Magdalene Oberhoffer from Germany as President, Benedicte Milcent from France and Dolores Brien from the United States as Vice-Presidents.

By 1962 drafts of two documents had been elaborated out of the work groups and consultations: a set of *Statutes for the Grail Movement* and a *Charter for the Grail Nucleus*. These drafts spread responsibility to the extent of providing for two International Vice-Presidents and an International Board, all chosen by and from the nucleus. At the national level, there was a National Board made up of the National president, two Vice-Presidents, and several others, all nucleus members, whose selection must be approved by the International President and Vice-Presidents. A theologian consulted on these documents was of the opinion that the prominent part the nucleus played in the government of the whole Grail tended to set it apart as a secular institute, subject to the Vatican Congregation for Religious. In a confidential letter to the national presidents and leaders-in-charge, Magdalene Oberhoffer wrote:

> Recently, Benedicte, Rachel, Alberta and I had a study day with Professor Hirschmann.[11] His one strong warning is this: "The prominent part which the Nucleus plays in the government of the whole Grail tends to set the Nucleus apart as an institute and to regard the movement as a kind of 'third order,' directed by this institute! There is the danger that Rome will understand the Grail only from this angle, and will force the Nucleus to become a Secular Institute." (To make it clear, becoming a Secular Institute means that the Nucleus would no more be considered a lay group, but would fall, canonically, under the direction of the Congregation for the Religious—and this is exactly what Father van Ginneken has always warned us against.)
>
> Therefore, Professor Hirschmann advised us strongly:
>
> a. to open up in principle the possibility for participants in the movement to become members of a National Board and of the International Board;
>
> b. to bring a more democratic element in the way the members of the Board are chosen.
>
> The idea of "a genuine collaboration in the apostolate between women of all walks of life" will thus be safeguarded, also on the level of the policy-making and the executive functions. . . . In practice, we probably will not be so far yet, for some time, to have indeed "non-nucleus members" in the Boards.[12]

On September 8, 1962, the sixth and last version of the *Statutes and Charter* was sent to all nucleus members for their study and comments. In accord with Professor Hirschmann's advice, these documents provide a minimal opening of the government to "non-nucleus" members. The series of drafts reveal a struggle over the definition of membership. On the one hand, there is a desire for inclusivity, for providing a way that all those who are attracted by the Grail spirit can somehow be incorporated in the movement. On the other hand, there is the need for a clear definition of those who have voice and vote in a participative decision-making structure. The final draft defines the Grail as a movement of women of different vocations—married, single, in dedicated virginity—with two modes of participation: (1) lifetime commitment in the nucleus according to the Charter; and (2) a formal commitment for a definite period according to a "code" which spells out spiritual obligations and apostolic tasks in the person's own surroundings. Codes are to be formulated by the National Boards according to the circumstances of each country and culture and to be approved by the International Board. Major leadership roles are still reserved to the nucleus. However, one International Vice-President and members of the National Boards need not be nucleus members. While National Presidents are to be appointed by the International President, National Vice-Presidents and Board members are to be chosen from and by the Grail members in the country concerned. The structure is still hierarchical and the tone is cautious and hesitant about allowing "non-nucleus" members to participate in government at the national and international levels. The cover letter to all nucleus members which accompanied the drafts in September of 1962 explains:

> In actual fact, we are probably not yet far enough to have the proper persons from the movement for this task (i.e., first International Vice-President). But in principle, this possibility has to be there to guarantee a true sharing and genuine collaboration with "women of all walks of life." This participation of all members, also in the policy making and executive functions, is an essential element and characteristic for us as a lay movement.[13]

In spite of all the brave words about sharing responsibility and giving all members a voice in the government, the Charter and Statutes provide only the most minimal of openings for "non-nucleus" members. Why was it so difficult to open up the leadership positions to all members? I suspect that behind the reluctance to make significant structural changes was an assumption common to many organizations that "the leaders know best," in virtue of their broader overview, their experience, and their superior training.

Before these documents could be finally approved, the whole process was overtaken by Vatican II and the Grail's own aggiornamento process. In contrast to the careful selection of "consultors" to work on the statutes and charter that were eventually presented to all nucleus members, the aggiornamento process from the beginning invited reflections and suggestions from all nucleus members and from others as the national leadership thought appropriate. The delegates to the 1965 meeting included some non-nucleus members, both married and unmarried. The meeting was organized according to the newly acquired group dynamic skills of the American delegation, with many freely interacting small groups contributing their insights to the final documents. The 1965 and 1967 international meetings took decisive steps in opening up the structures and leadership roles to all members. As Magdalene Oberhoffer remarked, the Grail structure changed from a monarchy to a democracy. The International General Assembly was defined as the ultimate policy-making body. Leadership was shared through the mechanism of international and national boards to which any member could be elected who satisfied the following criteria:

- commitment to the vision and values of the Grail;
- at least five years of responsible association with the Grail;
- active carrying out of responsibilities;
- a financial commitment according to the circumstances of the person.[14]

The national and international presidencies were still restricted to nucleus members, but all members who satisfied the above criteria were qualified to vote in the elections. In 1979, the international presidency was changed to a three-person team, only one member of which must be a nucleus member who is responsible for nucleus matters.

Aggiornamento in the United States Grail

In the United States, the international guidelines were quickly put into action with an emphasis on democratization and decentralization. The members of the United States Grail were called on to evaluate their own qualifications for voting in national and international elections. Those who defined themselves as "responsible participants" then proceeded in 1967 to elect Dorothy Rasenberger as the new national president, chosen from the list of nucleus members.[15] In 1969 a national General Assembly set up new structures: a general asssembly every three years, a council made up of representatives of local groups and interest groups and meeting two or three times a year, and a small coordinating committee to handle finances, property, personnel, and administration. However, many in the United

States were unhappy with the requirement that the president be a nucleus member. In 1972, the office of president was eliminated altogether and her functions were divided between a continuity team, responsible for finances and personnel, and a movement development team for communication, programming, and orientation of new members.

In 1975, an eight-day General Assembly, attended by about half the membership, affirmed a proposal for "a completely decentralized structure," with emphasis on local and regional groups. This Assembly affirmed the three existing national task forces (religious search, women, liberation) and added two more teams: one for international concerns, and one on Grail participation for the orientation of new members. It also set up an annual meeting (which took the place of the Council) and a Lateral Sharing Group, made up of those handling any Grail property or finances, meeting annually to make financial decisions, with a small executive committee— the "Link Team"—functioning between the annual meetings. In the search for wider sharing of responsibility, regions were asked to volunteer to prepare the national meetings; and a few years later, responsibility for the national Grail newsletter was assumed by a regional group rather than by a central national office.

Continued evaluation of the structures—at national meetings (non-decision-making) and General Assemblies—identified many "holes" in the decentralized structures. Where does accountability lie? Who has a vision of the whole as each Grail entity pursues its own task? How to evaluate and set priorities for funding the various task forces and teams? In the 1980s, as these needs have made themselves felt, some centripetal forces have emerged. A discussion of "compelling works" paved the way for two centralizing developments: the expansion of the role of the Lateral Sharing Group to allow it to consider questions of policy and priorities as well as finance; and the addition of a Connections Team, as an arm of the LSG to coordinate movement activities.

At the present time, I think it is fair to say that the Grail in the United States has become a group of women of all vocations and orientations— married, single, celibate, heterosexual, lesbian, bisexual, widowed, divorced, separated—sharing equally in policy and decision making and eligible for any office or task. Structurally, then, the Grail in the United States has moved from a hierarchical organization inspired by norms of self-sacrifice and obedience to a feminist form of shared responsibility with emphasis on the empowerment of women and their bonding in the struggle for "a universal society of justice, peace and love."

The structures may seem complex for a group that counts two hundred and twenty-five members in the United States, but they are a direct response to the Grail commitment to participative decision making.

Hierarchical models are simple. Participative modes that take seriously the involvement and responsibility of all members inevitably become complex.

The work on the structures clearly moved the United States Grail in a feminist direction, but I do not think that we undertook it out of a feminist consciousness. In the background were elements of the original vision—the faith in women's potential to change and to create change, the trust in women's experience. But in the foreground, as I remember it, our discussions on the ideas underlying the structural changes centered on concepts of collegiality, shared responsibility, respect for the person and her growth toward maturity. We spoke of "structures to free the spirit"—the emphasis was on the authentic response of free persons and on trusting that the Spirit would be present in the community of those persons.

11

The Costs of Change

What has happened to the Grail in the wake of its aggiornamento? Some of the same dynamics that have played out in the Church as a whole played out in our small group, but we have not been polarized as the Church is today, perhaps because our personal bonds were strong, perhaps because our leadership was responsive to the diversity of voices that emerged among us. In the Church, from 1964 on, there was a massive exodus from the priesthood, from religious life, from the seminaries, all highly publicized in the media. In the Grail nucleus there was also a considerable exodus. People left for a multitude of reasons. As Eileen Schaeffler observed— she was National and then International President of the Grail and thus intimately involved in the release of nucleus members—some who had absolutized either the Church or celibacy or the Grail tended to leave when the new critiques revealed aspects that fell short of perfection. Like the rest of the Church, we struggled with the loss of the old certitudes and the emergence of wide diversities in belief and practice among us. As we worked to put the new guidelines and structures into practice, I found that, even though I knew that the old way was no longer viable, I missed many of its aspects: the clarity and serenity of following one inspiring leader; the vivid sense of a supernatural world with its orderly ranks of saints and angels; the assurance that we were fulfilling our task as women; the support of a strong, cohesive community, united in worship and work.

In the Grail as in the Church individuals did not wait for new guidelines or structures or theologies to reevaluate their commitments and take decisive action. In 1964, in the wake of the departure of Dolores Brien and Jeanne Plante, a few people acted immediately to request release from the nucleus; others took quite a bit longer. By 1972, out of the hundred and one North Americans who had made a nucleus commitment, forty-three people had been released and three had died. Between 1966 and 1975, six new members joined the nucleus. In the same period, one more member died and six more left, leaving fifty-four in the American nucleus. The new members used a significantly different form of commitment. Instead of swearing "the oath of absolute obedience to the International President of the Grail and to all her lawful successors," each one swore "to live out her commitment to the Lord in the international nucleus of the Grail, in communion with those who form this movement, accepting its designated authority now and in the years to come."

Under the old regime, people leaving the nucleus discussed their situation privately with the National and International Presidents and then quietly disappeared. Usually, nothing was said to explain their absence; the matter was simply not talked about in the total group, although individuals might have discussed it with one another. I had a sense that this practice had been taken over from religious communities and that the leadership did not want to make public mention of a departure lest others might think of following suit. Under the new regime, individuals made their decisions in consultation with the National and International Presidents, and then most wrote a letter to other nucleus members, explaining their decision.

I was in Paris from September of 1964 to September of 1967, working full-time on the aggiornamento process. Magdalene Oberhoffer, the International President, and Benedicte Milcent, the International Vice-President, had a holder for mail outside their office on which they had placed a line of musical notes for the melody of the Christmas carol, "Tidings of Comfort and Joy." I found it very painful to watch the mail come in every morning from different parts of the world, knowing that probably most of the letters contained requests for release from the nucleus commitment. It was even more painful to receive letters from my friends in the States, announcing they had left. It was a very hard time for me. While I enjoyed the cultural opportunities in Paris, basically I was deeply depressed by what I saw as the Grail simply falling apart. When we had been without a house in the early days in the States, I was buoyed up by the team spirit. We shared the burden together; we outdid each other in prayers and sacrifices, feeling sure that these spiritual means would be efficacious in bringing us to the perfect place. It was difficult to develop a team spirit in Paris. We were an international group: Dutch, German, French, Belgian, Portuguese, Scots, and American, with no common language. When we prayed together, whatever language we used, there was always at least one odd woman out. At a deeper level, Magdalene and Benedicte, as leaders, felt that they had to carry the weight of confidential information alone, so they shared very little of what was going on. We had few contacts with French people. Living in Paris with my beginning French was like being cast on a desert island with the in-house polyglot group. I worked very hard at organizing the international meetings, but I was lost in the details and it was not until several years later that I began to understand the broad significance of our work.

In the United States, to help people review their commitments, the National Committee arranged for three nucleus retreats in the fall of 1964 and the spring of 1965, centered on the meaning of commitment and the making of authentic choices. "The retreats were very free," Carolyn Gratton, one of the resource persons for the sessions, recalls. "We did not pressure people to stay. Much of the discussion dealt with the possibility of permanent commitment—is it really possible given that the person, the society and the Church are all in a process of change? Everyone was shaken to her roots by the severe questioning of commitment that was going on all around us."[1] Every week the press carried stories about people highly placed in Catholic institutions—a bishop, priest seminary professors, nun college presidents—who were seeking laicization. Florence Henderson, a Grail nucleus member, announced her marriage to former priest Charles Davis, one of the theological experts of the British bishops at Vatican II. The old theological framework that had given meaning to the counsels of poverty, chastity, and obedience had evaporated. Carolyn Gratton was one of the many who were searching for new meanings. "I remember that I used Gabriel Marcel, *Homo Viator*. I tried to give a new interpretation to the counsels: If your love is not chaste, you will step all over the privacy of the other; see obedience as a listening to the whole of reality, not just to one authority. During the retreats many realized that they had not made an authentic choice. I tried to help them see that they had made a human choice, and that human choices are never 100 percent pure but always involve some mixed motives."[2]

In a report to the International Nucleus Council written in July of 1969, Dorothy Rasenberger, then the National President, spoke of both development and diminishment. She saw as developments the recognition that the mission of the nucleus is the mission of the Grail, the maturing of individuals as they take responsibility for their own lifestyle, and the growing sense of lateral responsibility and caring for one another.[3] At the same time, there was a sense of diminishment, the demoralizing effect of people continuing to leave. I, for one, found it very hard to accept that so many of my friends and associates, women with whom I had lived and worked closely and shared both hardships and triumphs, were choosing to live and work in quite another way. I felt betrayed when several of my closest friends simply presented me with a *fait accompli* in a letter addressed to all nucleus members. At the time, I felt as though I had been divorced without my consent. I wanted desperately to be involved in the decision-making process, to make the argument for staying.

Jeanne Plante and Dolores Brien had made a point of coming to see me and explaining their decisions in a face-to-face conversation. Jeanne's main work in the Grail had been helping to recruit people and advising them while they were in training at Grailville. She was often worried about what seemed to be happening to people, feeling that undue pressure was being put on individuals to make commitments. I remember one time that Jeanne and I sat over the list of nucleus members and trainees, concerned about the number that were clearly either psychologically fragile or very unhappy in their current situation. We were working within a closed system in which the individual was largely cut off from family and friends, was surrounded by people who held firmly to the group norms, was striving to meet high expectations—those which she put on herself as well as those of the group—and was being counseled solely by a group leader. It was a situation that could create enormous pressures on the person. While we worried about it, we were not able at the time to analyze it. When Jeanne came to tell me of her decision, she said simply that celibacy was not for her, that she wanted to be married and "to have six children." She spent the next two years studying psychology at Duquesne University and then got married.

Dolores's difficulties were with the very structure of the Grail, and deeper still, with the Church. She too worried about the unhappiness of many of the nucleus people, but she was even more concerned with the concept of the nucleus and its relation to the movement. For a long time, since shortly after her election as International Vice-President, she had struggled with her doubts and questions, had taken times of retreat to try to sort out her thoughts and feelings. "We [in the Grail] are not exempt from the upheaval of values which characterizes our time . . . we can only try to be open, to suspend judgment, to be willing to undergo upheaval . . . I think this holds for the Church as well. . . . One deep-seated reason for our malaise is the insecurity about what we are . . . the very nature of our vocation. . . . She [the Church] who thought she had the truth . . . is beginning to discover she has no monopoly at all. . . . Perhaps the very idea of nucleus is one of these outworn modes which needs to be surpassed. . . . We seem to fall in between the classical form of religious life and the life of the Christian in the world for whom there is yet no absolute pattern and whose place in the Church is neither fully clear or accepted."[4] She was particularly troubled by the idea of the nucleus as a spiritual elite whose task was to guarantee the spiritual integrity of the movement. "If Baptism is a reality at all, then 'dedication' or 'commitment' to Christ is a reality for all Christians. . . . 'Dedication' is not the prerogative of any one group who can somehow or other be more 'dedicated' than other Christians. . . . We say we are a lay movement of women in which there can be an interaction of the different vocations, married, single and 'in dedicated virginity' . . . in the very nature of things it is not possible to achieve this kind of unity, interaction, mutuality or whatever else in this line we are looking for. It is simply unrealistic when the nucleus inevitably remains a group apart with all power—that is, of policy and decision-making, of finances, property and of 'availability' in their own hands. Even the idea that the nucleus is to be 'free for' the needs of the movement proves to be a greater weakness than strength though it sounds fine in the telling. What it means in reality is that the nucleus is free to run the show and to let 'the others' (always the separation) involve themselves as they will or can." She felt keenly her responsibility as part of the leadership. "What is more responsible," she wrote at the time, "to stick with something I no longer can give my assent to in order to provide security for others, to protect them from similar questions and doubts? Or to decide and act as I think I ought and to trust in the maturity, the intelligence and compassion of the others to react to it and to resolve it for themselves, according to their own insights?"[5] Her personal integrity led her to resign as International Vice-President and to leave the nucleus. She, too, entered graduate school, completing a doctorate in American Studies at Brown University and going on to a career as an administrator at Bryn Mawr College.

Why did other people leave? There were many reasons—and a complex of factors in each individual that were perhaps not fully understood even by the person herself. Certainly there were some young people who had been more or less pressured into an immature decision by a sheltered time of training, justified under the rubric of "protecting the vocation." Some decided that celibacy was not for them, that they really wanted marriage and children. For quite a few, the changed status of the nucleus, which Dorothy pointed to as a positive development, carried the corollary that if the mission of the nucleus was the same as that of the movement, the nucleus was unnecessary. If there is equality of commitment and equality of vocations, as the guidelines insist, then the nucleus loses any special mission or obligations and hence loses its raison d'être. Some people, on the basis of this insight, chose to continue to work in the Grail but no longer as nucleus members. Some simply wanted to be relieved of obligations that no longer had meaning for them. Others were more emphatic in their rejection of the nucleus as an outworn idea, uncomfortably elitist and moreover quite unworkable, since no one can really guarantee the spirit. The majority of those who left, although at the time they declared their intention to remain part of the movement, did lose contact, but a substantial minority remained actively involved after their change of status. The changing attitudes toward the world influenced some; the desire to be *in* the world, deeply involved, led some to leave the relative security of a Grail Center and test themselves "outside." Changing attitudes toward faith, Christ, celibacy—the dissolving of the absolutes—meant also the dissolution of their original commitment. Maria de Lourdes Pintasilgo, who did a study for the entire international Grail of those who left in the 1960s and early 1970s, found that most people chose to leave ten years after their dedication. She found also that during that same time period the majority of divorces took place ten years after the marriage. She concluded that something in the psychological development of the person might be a factor in these changes of life commitment.

Several people who had come into the Grail directly from high school, after ten or more years of an intense and all-encompassing community life, felt a need to find their own identity apart from the group. "I am afraid I took my identity entirely from the Grail," Mary Anne Holthaus told me. "I needed the freedom to fashion and take full responsibility for my own life."[6] And Mary Dolores Dorlac wrote me, "I had been swallowed up into a rich and overwhelming community life. I had wanted that. It was a security blanket."[7] After some years as a successful youth leader in the Grail, she knew she needed to attain an identity of her own, to become equipped to deal with the world and to support herself economically. She moved out of the Grail, put herself through college and graduate school, earned her living, and eventually married.

What of those who stayed? What motivated them? There was always the attraction of the mission of the Grail as a whole: women working together for the conversion of the world. The Grail aggiornamento reinterpreted "conversion of the world" in the light of Vatican II's affirmation of the oneness of God's action in the world and in the Church and the need for conversion in both Church and world. The guidelines speak of the Grail as a women's movement, "characterized by an attitude of continual search and of openness to the Spirit, attentive to the signs which the world gives." They speak of joining with all men [sic] in "shaping a world of truth, justice, love and freedom," and approve of Grail involvement in secular structures, in ecumenical work, in non-Western cultures, in professions, in family life, as well as in specific Grail projects.

This was an updated version of the mission that had originally attracted me—women working together to change the world. Even after I had abandoned the ideas of the Catholic revival and that vision of a new Christendom, the ideal of a world of justice and love still held me. I wanted to be part of something that was clearly worthwhile, not alienating as I had perceived the university structure to be, and as I thought the corporate world would be. After I took a part-time teaching position at the University of Dayton in 1972, I appreciated even more the freedom and support I enjoyed in the Grail for creating alternative education for women. I think many others of my generation who chose to stay in the Grail were moved by the holistic vision. Even in all the disarray of the 1960s, this vision came through. Dr. Mary Clifford, who came to Grailville in the fall of 1964 to rethink the direction of her life as a physician and professor, told me, "In the midst of the confusion of the sixties at Grailville, there was a strong social, ethical and religious search. It was life-giving to join people who shared values and search and were trying to be in touch with something meaningful."[8]

"I never considered leaving," Audrey Sorrento told me. "What attracted me was the total mission of the Grail. There was all this great work to be done, and I was disappointed and upset that they were not staying to help with it. I had joined the nucleus because at the time it was the way to express commitment. I wanted the freedom to work full time in the apostolate."[9] Many others echo the theme of attraction to the mission: "the breadth and spiritual dynamism of the vision . . . the possibility of a contemplative life in the world"[10] . . . "the connection to a wider picture, the challenge of bringing together Christianity with ecology, women, justice, making sense of it all"[11] . . . "the scope I could not find elsewhere"[12] . . . "collective effort to make religion relevant through cultural expression and lifestyle"[13] . . . "most of the great things in my life came via the Grail! I still haven't found anything better elsewhere."[14]

Many had a clear sense of vocation, a personal call from Christ with the Grail as the means for living out that call. However painful they found the departures, leaving was not an option for them. "I felt a real loss," Cay Charles told me, "especially when two of my best friends left, but leaving did not make personal sense to me. My commitment was and is still alive."[15]

The maturity of the individual at the time of her commitment was another important factor. "My decision had been made after much soul-searching and reality testing," Eileen Schaeffler wrote.[16] "From the first situation in which I met the Grail through to my international experience, I knew much of the behind the scenes elements which seem to have disillusioned many people later." Those of us who had to overcome formidable obstacles from family, friends, and pastors to come into the Grail had been obliged to make very deliberate, carefully considered choices. As Audrey Sorrento put it, "Every step I took into the Grail was so difficult. My mother was so against what I was doing that I had to make a really conscious choice each time."[17]

Those who were doing work that they enjoyed and that was making a clear contribution were strengthened in their decision to continue. In the late 1960s, many nucleus members returned to school and then undertook professional commitments, moves which the leadership encouraged as part of a policy of helping people to take responsibility for their own lives as mature adults. Frances Martin, who began the formal study of music at the suggestion of the National President, Eileen Schaeffler, commented, "Music saved my life in the Grail. I finished my MA and went to teach African-American children at Lincoln Heights (a suburb of Cincinnati). It was exciting. Whenever I could, I helped with music at Grailville—a contribution that was valued. If I had stayed at Grailville, I would not have been able to come into my own."[18]

Personal bonds no doubt played a role in some decisions. "I stayed because Margaret van Gilse asked me to," Mary Buckley told me.[19] The degree of distress and pain over the departures was certainly affected by one's personal bonds with those leaving. "I was shocked by Jeanne's decision," Ruth Chisholm confided. "Jeanne was the Grail for me."[20] However, the shock did not lead Ruth to question her own commitment. For people busy with work overseas, and even for those pursuing studies on their own in the United States, events in the U.S. Grail nucleus could seem rather remote. "I don't remember when I heard about Jeanne and Dolores," Anne Mercier remarked. "I was busy teaching at the school in Uganda, and the question of leaving the nucleus simply did not come up for me."[21] Nor did it arise for Debora Schak, concentrating on getting a degree in agricultural development at Ohio State University in 1965.[22] However upset or sad nucleus members were over the departures, they did not pass judgment on the leavers, but simply accepted that they were acting in accord with their own conscience.

As individuals became more autonomous—a necessary step in the process of growing to maturity—expressions of a common life receded into the background. Life in the nucleus had been intense and highly supportive with strong expectations but also strong recognition of individual contributions and a clear sense of accomplishing something important together. As more and more individuals moved into independent situations—in living arrangements, formal study, work in non-Grail structures—communication and vital, sustaining contact between nucleus members as such became difficult to achieve. As Mary Louise Tully, the first American nucleus member, commented, "The nucleus as an entity faded out. . . . I needed to develop ways of living according to my own insights, keeping Jesus central in changing circumstances. . . . I stay in the Grail so I will have a support group for the values I want to live."[23]

In the United States there have been no dedications in the nucleus since 1975. Concerned to build the movement, from 1969 until 1985 we did not meet together as nucleus. Rather nucleus members began to find support and renewal through groupings involving all Grail members—the small local groups meeting more or less regularly, the national meetings and seminars, the committees and task forces. The late 1960s and early 1970s were a difficult transition period, a kind of group identity crisis. While still deeply committed to certain values and struggling with the challenges of social transformation, we were not sufficiently sure of ourselves to talk about the Grail or to seek new members. As we moved from hierarchical into participative structures, there was a good deal of resistance to any authority as well as resentment against the nucleus as having too much power in the Grail. It has taken many years of living and working with the new structures to build trust and to satisfy the members that all the offices are really open to anyone who is willing to shoulder the responsibility and do the work.

Closing the City Centers

In this same period, the late 1960s, we began phasing out many of the Grail Centers across the country. Lack of personnel was certainly one obvious reason for closing down centers, but there were also other issues. Community living seemed to have lost its appeal for young women intent on college degrees and professional careers. Apostolic programs seemed to lose their urgency in the face of new insights into ecumenism and respect for the traditions of the other. Very few were willing to take on the heavy responsibilities of directing a city center. Moreover, with the new emphasis on collegiality, many were questioning the very idea of a director. Thus, the Toronto group by 1964 were asking themselves such questions as whether a center with a few people living together was the best way to draw together an open community and whether the presence of a full-time staff person tended to reduce the responsibility of the members. Feeling the tension between the demands of their professions, their Grail activities, and their need for more time for prayer and study, they decided to give up the apartment, to close the art and book shop, and to open a nonresidential center downtown near the university. They expanded their team to nineteen, divided all the tasks among these members, and no longer wanted a full-time coordinator.

A little later the Detroit staff began to raise questions about their own experience: how to keep the balance between maintaining the activities and reserving time for spiritual deepening, how to provide programs that would satisfy both beginners and the more advanced, how to build community in a staff with widely varying backgrounds and training, how to plan for the long-term development of the Grail movement, how to balance one's personal needs with the demands of "being in charge." An undated memo from Wynni Kelly notes that a large and competent staff and an obvious hierarchy—as in the highly successful triumvirate of Audrey

Sorrento, Cay Charles, and Wynni herself—was a mixed blessing. When the staff is so competent, the others do not feel needed and are not challenged to give of their best. Wynni was among those who reevaluated their commitment in celibacy, recognized their attraction to marriage, and obtained their release from the nucleus. By 1967 there was no Grail member willing to take on the leadership of the Detroit Center. A temporary arrangement was made to rent the house to a group of students from Monteith College of Wayne University, with a minimum of contact and coordination by two Grail members who were studying at Monteith. By 1968 the decision of the most responsible Grail people in Detroit—the members and the married couples who had helped to support the Center— was that it had served its purpose, that people had grown through it and moved on, that the time had come to sell the house and transfer the art and book shop to other ownership.

Similar steps were taken in other centers. In Cincinnati the Center occupied two large, gracious family residences next door to each other in the university neighborhood. Because recruitment for the family service program was always difficult, that program was gradually phased out, although urgent requests for this service continued for many years. The Center focused its programs around work with high schoolers, with families in municipal housing, and with international students. In 1969, when Grail members were no longer available as core staff, the building that belonged to the Grail was sold, and the other building was returned to its owners, the Berger family. They continued an international student residence there until 1973, under the direction of a Grail member, Roberta Trombly and her husband.

In Brooklyn, after the Overseas Institute was phased out, the main building was turned over to an African-American neighborhood group, who leased it for a modest rent with the hope to buy it. From 1970 to 1981, we were supportive of their struggles to maintain it as a child care center. However, they were unable to raise sufficient funds to buy the building or even to continue their child care program, and in 1981 the building was finally sold on the open market. The annex, a small house down the block, continued to be used as a residence for Grail members and others studying or working in the metropolitan area. Similarly, in Philadelphia, the large house was sold in 1966, the bookstore was transferred to the ownership of a young married couple, and the Grail purchased a small house which has continued in use as a residence and a meetingplace for Grail groups.

In New York, the international student center operated out of two large apartments on Riverside Drive. Other tenants in the building complained about the crowds that thronged the Grail apartments for meetings and for the popular Sunday morning breakfasts. "They are holding church in their apartment," indignant tenants protested. The search for a suitable and affordable house in Manhattan went on for years without success. In 1963, through the good offices of Msgr. Ligutti, the Grail received from Chauncey Stillman the gift of a fifty-acre property at Cornwall-on-Hudson, New York, just sixty miles north of the George Washington Bridge. Gradually, the residential programs were shifted to the Cornwall Center and in 1969 the International Student Center was phased out.

In 1963 there were thirteen Grail centers, from coast to coast, including the houses at Foster, Ohio, and Burlington, New Jersey, which were reserved for rest and prayer for Grail staff. By 1970, there were just three U.S. centers nationwide: San Jose, California; Cornwall-on-Hudson, New York; and Grailville. In 1965, the Grailville staff decided that the Year's School was no longer viable and began a process of study and research to design a new form of alternative education for women, Semester at Grailville, a major project and a creative new departure that will be discussed in the next chapter.

Part IV
Coming of Age:
Seeds of Hope,
1975–1995

12

From Alternative Education to
Feminist Pedagogy

As Grail, we have always been involved in education and had developed an effective educational model at Grailville which was then adapted to programs in the other Grail Centers. The sweeping changes in Church and society in the 1960s demanded a rethinking of our model. Therefore, in 1964 we discontinued the Year's School of Apostolate, which had flourished at Grailville since 1944, and took time out to study, to consult other educators, and to plan ways of incorporating the new insights and emphases into our program. In the spring of 1968, we began a new venture, Semester at Grailville (SAG), in cooperation with a number of Catholic colleges.[1] The new program embodied continuity and change, conserving some of the strengths of the Year's School and incorporating many new approaches.

My ideas about education had been formed in the Hutchins-Adler Great Books program, so I came into the Grail with a demanding set of standards. The leadership should be first-rate; after all, I was accustomed to discussions not only with Robert Hutchins, President of the University of Chicago, and Mortimer Adler, prominent philosopher, but also with Jacques Maritain, the major neo-Thomist philosopher; Mark van Doren, Columbia University's noted Shakespeare scholar; and Clifton Fadiman, host of the popular "Information, Please" program. One should always go to the primary sources, the first exposition of an idea, not the secondary works. Education is a vital process, like eating, requiring real assimilation by the learner. Therefore, it should change the way one sees the world, not simply fill the student's mind with, in Hutchins's phrase, "rapidly aging facts." Hence, it should be skill-oriented, developing ability in critical thinking, defining terms, putting together closely reasoned arguments and drawing compelling conclusions. It should be conceived as a life-long process—one could always go deeper into the great ideas, gain new insights, further develop one's powers of analysis and synthesis. And, in the Hutchins-Adler seminars, it was fiercely intellectual and highly adversarial. We tested every thesis by instant opposition. We "Great Bookies" tended to be intellectual snobs, reserving our respect for those who showed themselves to be brilliant thinkers and formidable opponents in an argument.

My first Grail course—Holy Week of 1941—both measured up to my standards and revealed to me new, richer dimensions of learning. In the first place, although twenty priests and seminarians came every day from nearby Mundelein Seminary to conduct the full solemn ceremonies for us, it was clear that at Doddridge Farm women were in charge and were directing the program. That was a change for a University of Chicago graduate who in five years at that eminent institution had never had a woman professor or read a book by a woman. The program satisfied me intellectually—the talks and explanations of the liturgy were first rate; the liturgies themselves returned to the sources, the full texts of the high holy days. But the Grail incorporated the intellectual elements in a context that was concrete, practical and communal, totally involving on every level of my being—body, mind, and spirit.

The ideas were not allowed to rest on an abstract plane; they were concretized in symbol and dramatization; they demanded our active participation both at the altar and in our everyday lives. The Great Books process had given me a coherent intellectual framework; the ideas we discussed had relevance to our contemporary world; we could and did use Aristotle's *Politics* to critique Hitler, but the Grail carried the living out of ideas and doctrines much further. I think the participation struck me first. There were no bystanders at a Grail course—we sang the Mass, we recited the psalms of *Tenebrae*[2]—this at a time when the congregation in my parish church were mute spectators. On Holy Thursday, we dramatized the Paschal Meal with the unleavened bread and bitter herbs. We worked in the vineyard, pruning the vines and meditating on Jesus' parable about the vine and the branches. On Good Friday, we erected a large wooden cross on a hill near the entrance to Doddridge Farm and gathered around it to pray, in our own words, "for the Jews and the pagans, for the Negroes and the workers, for the hierarchy and for our fellows in Catholic Action, for all young people, for the poor and oppressed everywhere."[3] And we pledged ourselves to take action against oppression wherever we found it.

The experience was both communal and individual in an intense way. We not only prayed set prayers together, we shared our own inner lives through spontaneous prayers. The quality of life was high and the contribution of each one—the cooks, the table decorators, the singers, the speakers—was gratefully acknowledged. Moreover, the community was quite diverse—teenagers and professional women, office workers and university graduates, young women from low-income families, and the daughter of a corporate executive. I was impressed with the bonding that occurred in spite of differences in education and family background. Perhaps most important of all was the communal and collaborative approach. Unlike the adversarial stance I was used to at the University, in the discussions at the Grail, the responses were affirmative, offering examples in support of an idea or elaborating on it. A vision of community opened before me, a sharing in both intellectual and spiritual life. One young woman remarked on Easter Sunday, "I wouldn't have believed that other people could be a help instead of a distraction during a retreat." For me that vision of supportive community translated into intellectual as well as spiritual life.

The Grailville Year's School

These aspects of Grail training—the leadership of women, the combining of the intellectual with the practical and concrete, the high quality of both the intellectual and the artistic elements, the supportive community fostering the development of the individual—formed the basis of the educational method of the Year's School at Grailville. We certainly offered role models of strong women running their own show. After the first few years, we took over the entire management of the 380-acre farm. The example was not lost on the participants. "When I saw Judy on the tractor," one newcomer remarked, "my world changed." And another participant in the Year's School commented, "I came here and I was assigned to hang the stations of the cross. I had never hung a picture in my life, but it was expected that I could do this. I had to figure it out. There were women doing everything—haying, plowing, planting. So I had this wonderful sense of the complete power of women, independence and competence, women completely fulfilled and total in and of themselves—a profound thing."[4]

While we drew on male scholars and teachers as resources, the control of the program was clearly in the hands of the Grail staff and much of the teaching was done by the Grail staff. We took great pains to search the history of the Church for women leaders, and to introduce participants to such courageous, outspoken women as Deborah and Judith in the Hebrew Bible, Lydia and Phoebe in the New Testament, Catherine of Siena, Anne Javouhey, Mary Ward in the history of the church. Our intellectual standards were high—participants in Grail courses were introduced to luminaries of the Catholic revival, among them Gerald Ellard, SJ, noted liturgist; Damasus Winzen, OSB, founder of Mt. Savior Abbey; Godfrey Diekmann, OSB, editor of *Orate Fratres*, a major liturgical publication; Luigi Ligutti, director of the National Catholic Rural Life Conference;

Dorothy Day, cofounder of The Catholic Worker; Frank Sheed, of Sheed and Ward publishers; Frank O'Malley, outstanding professor at Notre Dame University; and Christopher Dawson, British scholar and cultural critic. We read from Gilbert Chesterton, Hilaire Belloc, Vincent McNabb, E. I. Watkin, Leon Bloy, George Bernanos, and put on the plays of T. S. Eliot and Paul Claudel.

Practical responsibility for the daily life of the community was a key educational element. Everyone had a definite task—on the farm, in the housekeeping, in the music or art or writing centers. The proof of the pudding was quite literally in the eating: the meal for sixty people had to be well prepared and appear on the table on time; the milk house had to pass the county inspection; the reading or speech had to hold the audience; and the article had to make it to publication. With everyone striving to give generously of her particular talents and to do her work really well, the quality of the community life was extraordinarily high. We lived the simple life, with a minimum of material goods, but we had the luxury that only loving service can provide. We sang plain chant, the polyphony of Palestrina, and a variety of folk songs under choir directors who did not tolerate sour notes or draggy tempos. Our minds were filled with significant ideas. Our forms of worship were meaningful and enriched with original music and visual art. At the same time, we were concerned with the development of each individual. People were challenged to "double your talents" by trying new things and the community was supportive as individuals took the risk to lead a song or give a speech or milk a cow.

In the wake of the changes brought by the 1960s, we reevaluated and revised this educational model. The Year's School had operated within a Catholic framework of accepted Church teachings and with a traditional Catholic hierarchical structure of a leader-in-charge and a chain of command. The program was experiential in that, starting from the truths of faith, we endeavored to make these beliefs concrete. We lived the liturgy, taking inspiration from the feasts and seasons to shape the day, to influence the way we decorated the house, dressed, ate, chose themes for study.

Semester at Grailville

The new program, Semester at Grailville (SAG),[5] embodied major shifts: a new relation to the formal educational system[6]; a change in the integrating focus from a formation for the Catholic lay apostolate to personal growth without a specific religious context; and a new understanding of the teaching/ learning transaction as a mutual exchange rather than a hierarchical discipline. SAG represented the working out in education of the implications of the spiritual and structural changes achieved through the international Grail aggiornamento.

Our original stance had been forthrightly countercultural. When Joan and I toured the colleges in the 1940s, we often invited young women to quit their "stupid" courses and degree programs and come for a training that had real meaning for their lives. In preparing for SAG we sought the cooperation of the colleges. With the help of Patricia Jean Mannion, SL, then an intern in educational administration at Antioch College and later president of Loretto Heights College in Denver, we inaugurated a series of consultations with college faculty and administrators. The result was a program linked to the credit system, but preserving the maximum amount of freedom for students and staff to construct the program according to their felt needs. The colleges signed contracts with Grailville to grant approximately a semester's credit for the student's work at Grailville. We did not offer any catalog of courses; instead we promised "a post-audit of the educational experience," a wonderful phrase coined by Morris Keeton of Antioch College. The last few weeks of the semester, staff and students would put together their "book," an account of the learning teams, the topics studied, the resources used, the group process sessions that constructed and administered the program, the other learning experiences. This audit together with a transcript went back to the colleges and they granted the credits. We found, in writing the transcripts, that we had to disintegrate our living/learning experience in order to report it in transcript form. A long list of institutions, from small Catholic women's colleges to large state universities, participated in the program and granted the credits.[7]

In the Year's School, religion was the integrating factor. Participants came because they wanted to work in the apostolate. The goal of the program was to train women who could take leadership in a movement to Christianize society. That meant that they had to deepen in their own Christian life, a deepening that became the integrating center of the program. At the heart of the Year's School was the emphasis on the liturgy, personal meditation, and the ascetic disciplines of a spiritual life. The daily round of prayer, study, manual and intellectual work, and recreation was suffused with the spirit of the liturgical seasons, and thus seen as having a sacramental quality.

When we moved into a relation with the formal educational system, we informed the colleges that "Semester at Grailville is not a religious program, that is, neither religious practices nor religious studies are required as part of the program, although students may choose to pursue religious questions. Such studies could be credited under comparative religions or history of religions." We formulated the goal of the Semester as "exploring basic questions of meaning and value for the individual and for society,"[8] contributing to intellectual integration and personal maturing. We spoke the language of personal growth rather than growth in holiness; instead of training lay apostles we hoped to prepare change agents who would help to shape society toward a future of justice and love. Yet the underlying continuity was clear: Grailville has always been about empowering women as competent and compassionate leaders, able to make a difference in the world.

A major tool in the new approach was group dynamics. In the course of the Grail restructuring in the 1960s, several people had been introduced to this method in their university studies. Mary Brigid Niland had taken her MA in human relations at New York University. Mary Gindhart and I attended a two-week workshop of the National Training Laboratory on laboratory learning. We had extensive staff training at Grailville from Max Birnbaum of the Boston University Human Relations Institute and Rose McDermott of Management Design Consultants. In planning the semester program, we determined to use a group dynamics approach and to build on "laboratory learning." Laboratory learning took place in small groups; it was experiential, generalizations being based on direct experience of interactions within the group; it validated the expression of feeling as well as thought; it trained participants in observing group process as well as content; and it developed the communication skills of sending clear messages, listening actively, checking perceptions, resolving conflicts. In the first Semester at Grailville we launched what we called "clarification groups," adapted from T-groups: small groups of eight participants with a staff member as facilitator. A staff memo identifies the goals of these groups as

1. getting acquainted and identifying resources within the group;
2. building mutual trust and cohesion through understanding better where each person is "coming from," what group identifications have been most significant for her;
3. developing insight into self through examining one's own socialization process;
4. developing insight into socialization processes in general;
5. developing insight into intergroup relations and conflicts embodied in the lived experience of the persons present.[9]

Because these groups legitimated feeling, self-awareness and interpersonal relations as important elements of the learning process, in our all-women setting they served to bring women's experience into education as a central concern, the starting point for further reflection and analysis. Because of the communal context, the idiosyncratic experience of the individual was balanced by the group sharing, and analysis proceeded from both these sources. The other elements in the program—the group living, the community involvement with agencies in Cincinnati or in rural Clermont County, the group decision-making—all furnished further experiential data for the learning process. Without an explicit feminist consciousness, we nevertheless had created a womanspace in which women's experience could be voiced as central, not marginal. Explicit identification of this approach as feminist did not come until the 1972 Grailville program, "Women Exploring Theology," the forerunner of Seminary Quarter at Grailville.

A third innovation in SAG was a new understanding of the teaching/learning transaction. The Grail aggiornamento had transformed our structures from the hierarchical pyramid to a participative circle. It remained to work out the implications of this change in an educational program. The SAG prospectus spoke of the program as "an attempt to complement the large scale, highly structured, discipline-oriented and departmentalized academic program with another kind of learning experience—on a smaller and more personal scale; structured cooperatively by students and faculty in a flexible way; oriented around major issues rather than disciplines; striving for a close integration of learning and daily life." The first time we conducted the program, the staff had made up a packet of required books and had done some preplanning for five problem-centered seminars—The Arts, The Human Person, The God Question, Social Change, and Communication. Initially each seminar group generated a list of topics and questions in its own area and decided how to structure its sessions within the given topic. We had also set up a weekly "Group Forum," to which all participants—students and staff—could bring any concern about content or process of the program. I shall never forget the young woman from Wayne State who rose to her feet with the announcement, "Janet is *teaching* us." It was an accusation, and, for me, it was the beginning of a long process of reflection and experimentation around questions of "real learning" and how it takes place. The group rather quickly began to distinguish "real learning" from mere academic exercises. Real learning was emotionally involving, intimately related to the learner's personal goals, and therefore assimilated, long lasting, and available for use. Learning meant changing, taking something into oneself that nourished the person and enabled growth. I have often thought that learning is like eating, a vital process: if appetite is lacking, digestion will be poor. Only if the learner is hungry, driven by burning questions, will real assimilation take place and a new idea change the way one sees the world. Once a new idea has become part of one's mental landscape, it will be long-lasting; it will connect to other ideas; and it will be available for use. I remember my contempt for the mere "book learning" of an accounting student who could pass the course tests but was totally unable to set up the books for a campus organization.

Learning is the act of the learner. I had read Carl Rogers's *Freedom to Learn,* with his strong emphasis on self-direction. These insights inspired the SAG staff to ask ourselves often "How can one human being really help another to learn?" And we answered our own question: by providing stimulation, experiences that would give rise to real questions; by providing role models of people genuinely excited by learning, whose enthusiasm could be contagious; by providing an abundance of resources and materials; by giving support, interest, an attentive ear, and a warm response to the learner's discoveries; by raising questions; by direct sharing of knowledge and skills, on the model of the coach or the editor rather than the teacher passing judgment and assigning a grade.

The structure of the Year's School had been unambiguously hierarchical—there was a leader in charge of every activity, and the underlying assumption that the leader knew more and was qualified to guide the activity or project was seldom questioned. In the new culture, spawned by the civil rights movements and the student revolt, hierarchy was decidedly unpopular. After the first year of SAG, we carried the notion of self-direction throughout the program, limited only by the need to report back to the colleges and to fit our living arrangements into the larger context of the Grailville residential community. The orientation phase of the program was devoted to two emotionally involving experiences: small process groups and an urban-suburban plunge. Both of these elements were guaranteed to raise real questions in the minds of participants. The small groups, as described above, focused on personal identity and interactions. The emphasis was on legitimating the expression of feelings as well as thoughts, getting acquainted with each other and the resources each was bringing to the program, and building a level of mutual trust and open communication. The urban-suburban plunge brought participants into direct contact with the affluent suburbs, the Black ghetto, the poverty-stricken Appalachian communities in the city and the county, the underserviced rural areas, and the various social service agencies.

We then proceeded to honor our commitment to self-direction by constructing the program together. Each person—staff and students—first took time to reflect and write out her burning questions: what do I *really* want to learn. A small committee grouped the questions into interest areas. Interest groups formed, attempted to set priorities, subdivided, dissolved, reformed; individuals and groups negotiated with each other about what topics should be considered and in what way. Individuals began to discover possibilities for influencing a group decision. Groups became more sensi-

Figure 19. Women Breaking Boundaries, a mime choreographed by Claude Dupin and performed in the Grailville Oratory with participants in the Semester at Grailville, 1971.

tive to the needs of individuals. Everyone became more aware of the connections between questions and the need for a multidisciplinary approach in dealing with practical problems. At the end of the process, the group had

organized itself into a number of learning teams, each with a written proposal outlining what they wanted to do, why they thought their questions
were important, who was committed to the project, and what resources,
methods and time schedules they needed to carry it out. Since our numbers
were small—thirty-five or forty people—it was also possible for a schedul-
ing committee to work out a weekly calendar so that no one had a schedule
conflict.

We tried to carry through the principle of self-determination consistently in all phases of the program: in the living units, the residents made
their own house rules; in the Group Forum, the group made the agenda,
everyone being free to contribute items, and group members took turns
facilitating the meeting; in community involvement, after the initial orientation, each student chose a field, outlined the contribution she wanted to
make, and made her choice among the available placements. In each case—
living, learning, working—the individual faced a relatively unstructured
situation, one in which she could define her own goals, choose her own
commitment, and take the initiative to bring about the results she desired.
Participants could no longer complain about the administration because
they were part of it. The SAG educational model brought staff and students
directly in contact with basic questions of how human beings learn and
how they can help each other to learn, all in a context of relative freedom
from external restrictions.

It was not easy for the staff to adjust to our new role, to change from
"teachers" to "facilitators of learning." I was helped by Paulo Freire's
analysis in *Pedagogy of the Oppressed,* an analysis that he presented in a
weekend at Grailville in 1969. He spoke of the "banking concept of education" in which the teacher owns the knowledge and bestows some of his
wealth on the poor, ignorant student and then demands an accounting of
this deposit. This concept results in a form of education which domesticates the student rather than liberating her or him. But if we understand
that human beings are called to be subjects, aware of their own rooting in a
particular time and space, able to shape their own lives and to have an
impact on the world around them, then we see that the aim of education is
to enable the individual to realize fully his or her potential as a subject, to
be a maker of history, not merely an object swept along on the tides of the
time. Freire analyzes the process of education as empowerment in terms of
reflection, action, reflection, starting always from the concrete situation
and experience of the individual. In this model, the teacher/student relation
is not that of have to have-not, controller to controlled, judge dispensing
rewards and punishments to the judged. Rather in Freire's words, "Human
beings teach each other, mediated by the world." Or as Alfred North
Whitehead once observed, "the chief duty of the teacher is to exhibit him-

self [sic] in his true character, that of an ignorant man thinking." The individual, reflecting on the challenges presented by her world, and responding to them, is asserting herself as a subject, for this response demands critical thought, invention, choice, decision, organization and action, thus beginning not the vicious circle but the beneficent spiral. Action leads to further reflection that leads to further action. At each step the individual develops the inner self, gains insight, and has some impact on the environment.

Students responded enthusiastically. I quote from the SAG "books," the final reports prepared by student-staff teams and sent back to the colleges:

- Until I learned to listen to myself, I couldn't listen to anyone else . . . I'm not a new self. I'm only aware of the self I've always been. Only now that I'm comfortable with this self can I be honest and supportive with others. (1972)
- Learning didn't stop when we left our discussion groups. It went on. It followed us to the table, we'd talk it over doing the supper dishes, or maybe someone would knock on my door at night. (1972)
- The experience of SAG has been a gradual transfusion—a substitution of internal motivation for external motivation. (1972)
- Personal involvement—that is what I have become aware of at SAG. I am responsible for my education. I must be the one to decide I want to learn in order for the experience to be worthwhile. . . . Now that we are equally involved, teachers become facilitators and students become persons who have something to share. (1972)
- I never want to be in a group again where I let everyone else do the work for me. (1973)
- It has yet to be proved, obviously, but I have the feeling that I have retained a lot more of the content I was exposed to this semester than I have previously—it has to do with integration into my life. (1972)
- Probably the biggest thing that I'll carry with me is a belief that I can make a difference; that I have the strength and power to change myself and to change external structures in the places where I will be (work, school, etc.) to become more human and more equitable. (1973)
- I am really glad to have had this chance to not have guys around for a while. I feel much more united with other women, and I have found strength in the fact of having lived a productive semester without guys, which gives me hope for my courage to try and continue running my own life and holding

on to me, myself and my potential as something precious and necessary. (1972)

- I came from a predominantly all black environment to a predominantly white environment, which was quite a transition. I was forced to realize how little I actually knew about something that is such a big part of me, my own race. . . . I'm better able to define for myself what it means to be black, with hopes of doing something with this new identity in the future. (1972)

In 1973, we turned the direction of the program over to a team of three young women, just out of college themselves, with a few older and more highly degreed persons available as consultants. In each succeeding year, a new young team took charge. The team for spring of 1975—Rose Morin, Ann Heidkamp, Judy Semonoff, and Jackie Moren—expressed their vision as follows:

This book is about learning: that it cannot be fragmented into categories, rather it is fluid; that it originates in self-knowledge and overflows into action upon the world. . . . This book is about community as a viable alternative to the alienated society which surrounds us. This book is about women realizing their power and using it to direct their lives, free from roles created for them by a male-dominated society. (1975)

Much of the strength of SAG derived from the emphasis on experiential learning in a supportive communal setting. As the staff became more comfortable with our role as facilitators and resource persons, we focused our energies on two major tasks: providing challenging, stimulating experiences and resources, and fostering in-depth reflection on these experiences. We tried to make the living-learning community inclusive, the more diversity in race, social class, educational and cultural background the better. SAG was an ungraded college program, welcoming everyone from first-year students to seniors. We recruited from all kinds of schools—everything from small Catholic women's colleges to the large state universities. The diversity of campus cultures, from the elite liberal arts colleges to the big public institutions, provided valuable data for social analysis. We sought diversity in the community involvement placements where students spent one or two days a week: city, suburbs, and county; wealthy, middle class, and poor; Appalachian, African-American, Euro-American. We tried to find points of insertion into the local communities that would not exploit the community for the sake of student learning, or exploit the student with mere busy work. Sometimes students were able to do research that was useful to an agency or an activist group; more often they rendered direct service in child care agencies, as teachers' assistants in the public schools, as organizing transportation for the dental care program of head-start in rural Clermont County, as assistant to a local community organizer, as intern to a member of City Council.

All these experiences served as starting points for reflection that went on in personal journals, in community involvement debriefing sessions, in clarification groups, and in learning teams. Reflection had a twofold purpose: increased self-awareness, including insight into one's own socialization process and the limits it may have put on one's perceptions and values; and development of skills in social analysis. The diversity of campus cultures, for example, Wayne State in Detroit with tuition of $300 and Oberlin with tuition of $2,800, was a valuable entry point for social analysis, as were the students' direct observations during their community involvement days. Individual reflection was balanced by group sharing. We endeavored to bring together insights from all sources—direct observation, personal feelings and reflection, creative experiences in the arts, communal sharing, systematic research, reading and lectures—in forming and testing generalizations. The various learning teams approached the social justice questions from many different entry points, but for the most part came to some understanding of the interstructuring and mutually supportive character of the "isms," especially racism, classism, and sexism.

My hope was always that we would return to the campuses young women who were successfully maladjusted. Maladjusted, that is, more aware, more critical, less docile, less willing to fit in quietly to a system and accept things as they are; but successfully maladjusted, not against the establishment for the sake of being against, not eaten up by resentment or despair, but able, in Freud's definition of maturity, to love and to work, to give themselves to people and to tasks of their choosing.

Seminary Quarter at Grailville

With Seminary Quarter at Grailville (1974-1978), we applied the Grail educational model to theological education and took an explicitly feminist approach. In the late 1960s and early 1970s the women's liberation movement in the society at large began to impact women in the mainline U.S. churches. Already new waves of women had enrolled in law schools and medical schools. In the early 1970s a remarkable influx of women moved into the third traditional male preserve, the seminary. Between 1970 and 1973, enrollment of women in seminaries tripled. Moreover, they enrolled not in the religious education program, always considered suitable for women, but in the Master of Divinity program, the degree leading to ordination. These women found themselves in a more or less hostile environment, studying the work of male theologians under male professors with male colleagues who did not exactly welcome this addition to their ranks.

Seminary Quarter (SQAG) was a response to this new situation of women in the churches. Already in 1969, the Grail in Holland had sponsored a conference on "Cooperation of Men and Women in Church and Society," which had opened up an explicitly feminist approach for the Grail. In 1972, Audrey Sorrento of Grailville together with Claire Randall of Church Women United organized a weeklong workshop, "Women Exploring Theology," which was followed by a similar conference in the summer of 1973. The seminary women in these programs urged Grailville to offer a longer program, specifically for women in seminary. Thus, Seminary Quarter was born as a six-week residential program for women in seminary or graduate theological study.

The familiar elements of the Semester at Grailville model took on a new coloring in the theological realm. Like SAG, SQAG was lightly linked to the credit system, in this case through the good offices of United Theological Seminary in Dayton, which processed the transcripts with the approval of the Association of Theological Schools. Students could (and did) offer the six weeks at Grailville for credit toward the MDiv degree at major seminaries. Seminary Quarter proceeded from its inception with an explicitly feminist perspective. The program was presented as an opportunity to explore theology under the leadership of women in a context in which women's concerns were central. The 1975 Seminary Quarter group entitled their final report "Womanspace, Womantime, Womanspirit." Womanspace made two radical claims: First, that women's experience was a *locus theologicus*, a legitimate starting point for theological reflection; and second, that women were as capable as anyone else of "doing theology"; we took the radical step of claiming religious agency for women. As Elisabeth Schussler Fiorenza explains:

> Feminist theology is a plant (or some would say a weed) that has one of its major roots at Grailville in the 1972 conference on "Women Doing Theology." As a newcomer to the United States, I had the privilege to participate in it. I had a classical theological training behind me. "Women Doing Theology" (together with the Women's caucus in the A[merican]A[cademy of]R[eligion] and the S[ociety for]B[iblical]L[iterature]) was a decisive experience for me because here I learned to understand myself not as someone who is repeating, transmitting, teaching the theology of the great theological fathers, but as someone who is a theologian, who is *doing* theology."[10]

Because we had made a link with the credit system, we had to restrict SQAG to "women in seminary or graduate theological education." However, within this restriction we built an inclusive community, embodying as much diversity as possible in race, religious tradition (the program included Catholics, as well as women from many different Protestant traditions), age, career goals, lifestyles. An interracial staff and racially and religiously diverse resource people provided role models of different ways of doing feminist theologizing. They included leading scholars, authors of important books, seminary professors and administrators, pastors, campus ministers, activists in the struggles for social justice, national leaders in mainline churches. The categories overlap; most of those in the following list fall into more than one category. Among the resource persons were Rosemary Ruether, Yvonne Delk, Nell Morton, Karen LeBacqz, Letty M. Russell, Anne Wilson Schaef, Anne McGrew Bennett, Valerie Russell, Rena Karefa-Smart, Beatriz Melano Couch, Beverley Harrison, and Joan Forsberg.

Unlike SAG, the Seminary Quarter did not include a community involvement element, both because time was too short for taking on any responsible involvement and because most of the participants had already had experience in some form of fieldwork. But the experiential element was strong, in the arts, in planning and conducting worship, and in the group processes required by the self-directed learning model. The "Creativity and Renewal Work Group" in 1974 reported that they "never had a chance to spend much time doing art, particularly in seminary," an observation that participants in the other seminary quarters readily affirmed. But the desire was there, to explore and express one's creativity, and most of the women gave high priority to body movement and dance, music, and the opportunities Grailville offered for work in photography, printmaking, pottery, weaving, sewing, and macrame. The reports abound in original work—drawings, photos, poetry, and prose—testimony to the importance of creative experience in the process of claiming one's power as a woman.

Worship, in personal meditation and in community celebrations, provided another important set of experiences. Participants shared two assumptions: that worship was important, and that it was esssential to find nonsexist forms of language, content, and leadership to be true to our feminist perspective. These assumptions demanded that we experiment—we were already sensitized to the patriarchal character of existing forms, but very little in the way of feminist worship materials was in existence when Seminary Quarter began in 1974. Grailville did pioneer a program, *Image-Breaking/Image-Building*, in 1978 but the materials from that program were not published until 1981.[11] Seminary Quarter participants plunged enthusiastically into the task of devising nonsexist worship and quickly developed liturgies planned by a group, based on the experience of the living/learning community, utilizing songs and readings created for the occasion as well as searching the scriptures for images and texts that were affirming for women. One experiment which was particularly successful was inaugurated by Sheila Goldstein of the Living Judaism Institute at Grailville, who introduced the Jewish Sabbath ritual. As Christians, for whom Sunday, not Saturday, is the sacred day of the week, we began it at sunset on Saturday night and closed at sunset on Sunday. The simple, flexible form and the readily understandable symbols—candle lighting, washing of hands, sharing of bread and wine—lent themselves easily to a variety of Christian feminist contents. As Murphy Davis remarks in her essay on Seminary Quarter, the "worship life was qualitatively different from that which had been experienced by any of us before."[12] The experience soon resulted in insights with far-reaching implications. Jane Burr Stickney writes of a communion service, written by a SQAG group and with an ordained woman presiding:

> I remembered several different ministers who have been important to my life—ALL MEN, standing behind the communion table. It hadn't occurred to me that seeing a woman there would evoke any emotion, or a different emotion from a man in that place . . . BUT IT DID !!!
> Then I realized that I had stood in that place myself—how much I felt each word as I said it—but in all that feeling—it suddenly dawned on me—I had not felt myself a woman. From the beginning I have felt God's call to minister, but lacking all feminine models I have had to deny large parts of who I am in order to try to become what it seemed I needed to be. No wonder I have felt inadequate, insecure and confused. . . . My ambiguities about ordination have come from trying to force my very feminine/female personhood into a masculine/male image groove.[13]

Coming from an environment that was alien and often hostile, most participants needed a time of healing, of rebuilding a shattered self-esteem, of adjusting to recognizing and using their own powers. Here the group process model of SAG proved valuable—the small groups, the open communication, the building of mutual trust, the participative decision-making that shaped group living and learning. Participants expressed their sense of empowerment in different ways:

> The six weeks we spent together in the Seminary Quarter at Grailville was one of the most, if not the most, empowering times of my life. I had come with the expectation that life with thirty

other feminist seminarians would prove to me that it was all right to be a woman, and I left knowing that it was much more than all right: it is exciting and powerful and tremendously important for us to be full persons, human, females that we are. Many of the "I can'ts" in my life were turned into "I can" and "I will."
—Clare Guzzo, SQAG, 1974, p. 67

I feel that the educational process of the Seminary Quarter was as significant as the content of the work produced by the work groups. . . . How I felt about a particular person or experience became just as important in learning as doing research by reading books. . . . No longer were the academic and the personal split. . . . There was no rigid student-professor role. Each person shared her resources, the most important one being herself. Thus each woman was affirmed as a person. Our experiences and our feelings were seen as valid as they were. And we found that there was "knowledge" inside. This realization of internal knowledge and its relationship to our research and discussions provided a new-found freedom. Persons were emerging and we were not waiting for someone who "knew" more to enlighten us.
—Marilyn Cook, 1974, p. 68

I never looked on myself as an authority before, or realized that my questions are valuable and no less real questions because they come from me.
—Unidentified participant, SQAG, 1975, p.8

Six weeks was a short time in which to fully internalize these new learnings. Of course, there were exaggerations, conflicts, sometimes destructive dynamics of a sort that became all too familiar in feminist groups. On the one hand, there was what I came to call "falling into the pit of process." Luxuriating in the sense of being affirmed as a person and having her feelings taken seriously, an individual might bring a group discussion to a halt by declaring that she felt alienated by what the group was doing. Then the whole group would circle around the alienated one, trying to reassure her and bring her back into the circle, often to the detriment of the group task. Some individuals found it difficult to affirm excellence or leadership in another, somehow perceiving the other's strength as a put-down of themselves, a ploy which I called "Let's all be weak together." These attitudes could make group meetings long-drawn-out and exhausting affairs. We struggled to deal honestly with racism in a group made up almost entirely of white middle-class women. We found it difficult to deal with tensions around sexuality. Although we were willing in the abstract to affirm hetereosexuality, lesbianism, and celibacy as valid choices, we never managed to confront openly the sexual issues alive in the group.

Whatever its shortcomings, SQAG was a real success in that it broke new ground, provided a women-centered space in which to develop a feminist theology, offered a model of feminist pedagogy, sparked insights in many women who have gone on to distinguished work as feminist theologians, teachers, leaders in their communities and churches.

Ecofeminist Education at Grailville

In the 1990s a new emphasis has been added to the basic Grailville educational model, a deliberate and explicit emphasis on ecology integrated in an ecofeminist perspective.

Grailville has always been concerned with organic farming and from its beginnings has maintained a large organic garden. However, when it came to the field crops, we farmed in the conventional way until, in 1989, our growing awareness of the global dimensions of the ecological crisis led us to the decision to devote the entire farm to permaculture, that is, sustainable agriculture. The decision includes a commitment to eschew all chemical fertilizers and pesticides and to run the 300-plus acres of the farm on a totally organic basis. Our global ecological consciousness is reflected in ecofeminist programs at Grailville and other Grail centers. Seminars, including a four-month program, New Women, New Earth, have explored ecofeminism in a theological perspective, analyzing the relation between the patriarchal domination of women and the exploitation of nature. At a practical level, courses vary from a broad survey of permaculture to a detailed study of specific techniques for rotating garden crops or making maximum use of microclimates. Every summer a six-month program for interns at Grailville introduces young women to the basics of organic gardening. Grailville carries on a program of community supported agriculture in which local families buy shares in the garden at the beginning of the season and receive their share of produce each week. It also sponsors an agricultural exchange program with the Grail in East Africa. Tanzanians and Ugandans come to Grailville for training; Mary Lu Lageman, director of Grailville's Earth/Land program, visits East Africa to give permaculture courses.

What do these fifty years of Grail educational programs for women have in common? Education for transformation, transformation for the individual person as she develops her vision and skills, transformation for society, as she grows in desire and commitment to make a difference in the world. Out of the Grail experience of education, I can identify the following elements as contributing to a feminist pedagogy that empowers women: a living/learning community, residential if possible, rather than a series of classes; an inclusive community, as diverse as possible in race, age,

Figure 20. Garden interns Kirsten Heidel and Sarah Lynne Thorsen picking beans in the Grailville Organic Gardens, 1993.

religion, ethnicity, class; a women's space, organized and directed by women, with the presence of able women as role models; the honoring of each woman's experience as a starting point for learning; the enriching of each woman's experience through large and small group interactions and through exposure to the needs of the larger community; systematic reflection on that shared experience, both individually and in supportive groups; a nonhierarchical learning model, which honors student self-direction; the concretizing of ideas through all modes of perception and expression, making abundant use of all the arts—movement, music, visual arts, poetry, and drama; the concretizing of ideas through emphasis on their practical application.

These principles are exemplified in Grail programs wherever they may be held—not only at Grailville, but at Cornwall, San Jose, the South Bronx, Louisiana. There is a real continuity between the Grail's early years and the present; the goal is the same as it always was: women who are spiritually grounded, socially and ecologically aware, able to commit themselves in hope to the struggle for justice.

13

From Feminist Actions to Feminist Consciousness

The full development of women has been a Grail theme from our very first beginnings in Holland in 1921. In the United States at present we have the reputation of being a strongly feminist movement. How feminist in fact are we, given that our history now covers more than half a century and our membership ranges in age from the twenties to the eighties? How have we developed a feminist stance within a tradition as sexist, misogynist, and patriarchal as Catholicism? What role has the Grail Women Task Force played in this development?

Grail Women: Autonomous but Not Feminist

My thesis is that in the late 1960s the Grail in the United States of America began a profound shift in its self-understanding as a women's movement, an understanding that can perhaps best be described as a development of feminist consciousness. Gerda Lerner, in her book *The Creation of Feminist Consciousness*, defines feminist consciousness in terms of the following five characteristics:

1. awareness on the part of women that they belong to a subordinate group and are oppressed;
2. recognition that their subordination is not natural but has been sociallyconstructed;
3. the development of sisterhood, the joining together of women to work forchange;
4. the definition by women themselves of their own goals and strategies; and
5. the development of a vision of an alternative future.[1]

Applying Lerner's criteria to the first twenty-five years of Grail existence in North America, I think it is fair to say that we were prefeminist,
that is, we acted independently and safeguarded our autonomy even while
working within the patriarchal structures of the Roman Catholic Church
but did not consider ourselves oppressed and firmly refused to call ourselves feminists.

We certainly scored well on two of Gerda Lerner's five criteria: sisterhood and the defining of our own goals and strategies. We were a closely
knit group of women, our unity grounded in the conviction that we were
called to a great task, nothing less than "the conversion of the world," by
which we understood not so much the baptism of the unchurched but
rather the transformation of social institutions and individual lives by
Christian values. We were inspired by Father van Ginneken's vision of the
untapped potential of women, expressed in his survey of women's contributions through the ages. It was a heady affirmation of woman power,
though we did not use that language. We were absolutely convinced that
women together could make a difference, could turn the world in a
Godward direction.

Moreover, our vision included the affirmation of women as leaders,
who defined their own goals and directed their own work. "Women should
lead women"—this was a basic Grail principle, a very radical idea in the
1920s when the Grail began in Europe and still radical in the 1940s in the
United States. To call ourselves a Catholic organization, we had to have the
permission of a bishop, but we managed to preserve a sphere of relative
autonomy, even within the hierarchical structures of the Roman Catholic
Church. For one thing, we were laywomen—not clerics, not nuns—and
classified as a *pia unio* (a pius union, the lowest possible category for an
organization in canon law), so we did not fall under any of the rules and
regulations of the Sacred Congregation for Religious in Rome, with their
prescriptions about enclosure, special dress, community prayer, and so on.
Father van Ginneken advised taking a pragmatic approach to the bishop:
deal directly with him, ask him to be your spiritual director, he will be too
busy to give you much attention. At all costs, avoid getting a priest moderator. Do not have the same priest retreat master for two years in succession; better still, give your own retreats. These injunctions were very much
alive in the American Grail. We made our own plans, taking care to inform
the bishop and to ask his blessing but not his permission.

Our decision to leave Doddridge Farm, narrated in chapter 3, shows
how deeply committed we were to safeguarding our autonomy. We were
determined to define our own work. When Bishop Sheil required that we
run summer camps for boys as the condition for having the use of
Doddridge Farm, Lydwine politely but firmly refused, even though her

decision meant that we were immediately homeless. None of us regretted that decision—better homelessness than being diverted from our goal. I remember our ten months of homelessness as a wonderful time, full of spiritual intensity, a time of faith, hope, and unshakable trust in God's guidance.

In defining our own work, we blithely undertook all sorts of initiatives: we bought property (the 380 acres of Grailville and the houses for the city centers); we ran the farm; gave lecture tours; produced and distributed publications, contemporary works of art, recordings of liturgical and folk music; recruited and trained thousands of young women in programs which we designed and administered; promoted lay participation in the liturgy; wrote and produced original dramas based on liturgical themes; pioneered in ecumenism, modern catechetics, work with international students; trained and placed over a hundred young American women in overseas service in Latin America, Africa and Asia. We defined our own work, earned our own way, owned our own property, and exercised our resourcefulness to maintain ourselves as a lay group under lay—and female—leadership.

In short, in our first twenty-five years we moved consistently and intuitively in a direction that today would be called feminist. Clearly there were the seeds of feminism in the original Grail vision, but they were embedded in a psychology of complementarity and a distrust of the nineteenth-century movement for women's rights. On the one hand, Father van Ginneken had dismissed the movement for women's emancipation as being against the nature of woman, trying to make her into a man.[2] On the other hand, he rejoiced that technology had liberated women from the heavy burdens of housework, making it possible for them to earn a wage in the workplace and take a role in public life. He was in favor of the feminism that was mobilizing women for public life. "If only we could stop considering the man as the only force in public life," he told the young Dutch Grail members in 1932.[3] But he saw women's participation in terms of complementarity—head and heart, reason and intuition, theory and practice, abstract and concrete. "Alongside the powerful track of the man, the woman also wants to make her gentle imprint on the fate of humanity through the ages. The task for the Grail is to counterbalance all masculine hardness, all cruelty, all the results of alcoholism and prostitution and sin and capitalism, which are ultra masculine, and to Christianize that with a womanly charity."[4]

Even when we undertook actions that today seem clearly feminist—the emphasis on a holistic approach in our educational programs, the restructuring in 1965 to do away with hierarchy—we did so in a theological but not a feminist perspective. We spoke of integration of life in Christ, of collegiality, of shared responsibility in the Christian community, not of rejecting hierarchy and dualisms. This is why I call the early Grail proto-feminist, in that our actions were feminist but our consciousness was not.

My Personal Journey to a Feminist Consciousness

How did we come to develop a feminist consciousness in the U.S. Grail? The theologian, Romano Guardini, remarked "Ideas have their seasons." Many factors came together in the late 1960s to make a season favorable to the creation of a feminist religious consciousness. As a result of the social movements of the 60s—anticolonial, antiwar, pro-civil-rights—the ideas of self-determination and of questioning authority were in the air. The civil rights movement, in particular, stimulated the second wave of the women's movement. Freedom is catching—when one oppressed group rises up, it is not long before other oppressed groups make the analogy to their own situation. The young women who worked in the civil rights movement and Students for a Democratic Society [SDS] quickly discovered that radical men were as sexist as any others. When Stokely Carmichael, a leader of the Student Non-violent Coordinating Committee [SNCC], announced, "The place for women in SNCC is prone," he inspired a gener-ation of young radical women to leave SNCC and found their own autonomous women's movement. With amazing speed the second wave of the women's movement swept across the country.

New trends in religious circles also contributed to a new climate. Among Protestants and Catholics a host of new approaches developed— process, Black, political, liberation, and creation theologies. Among Catholic women's religious communities in the 1950s, some farsighted leaders began the Sister Formation Movement to give a first class education to candidates for the religious life. As a result, a generation of very well-educated nuns emerged on the American scene. As one priest commented later, "The mistake was teaching them to read."

Finally, the media, although for the most part hostile to the women's movement, played a significant part in its spread. Even a hostile press, ridi-culing "bra burners," got the message out. Time was ripe—all over the country small groups came together and began to share experiences in a process that soon came to be known as "consciousness-raising." The fer-ment in society at large had an immediate impact on women in the churches and synagogues. Let me trace my own coming to feminist con-sciousness as an illustration of this process. I did not come to feminism because I was suffering personally under male domination. I did not have an abusive father or husband or a domineering boss. My story is rather the account of an intellectual odyssey, a series of insights together with their logical consequences, which moved me gradually but surely to define myself as a feminist.

As a result of my Grail training, I had become a strong proponent of complementarity. In my college years at the University of Chicago (1930–1935), I certainly rejected the notion that women were intellectually inferior, yet I felt uncomfortable as an intellectual woman. Dorothy Parker's quip, "Boys don't make passes at girls who wear glasses," was current on the campus. I did not wear glasses, but I got straight A's and made Phi Beta Kappa in my junior year, factors which were not a help for my social life. I knew somehow, no one ever stated it explicitly, that I would have to be two or three times as good as my nearest competitor to make it in academe. There were no role models. In five years at the university, I never had a woman professor. The only faculty woman I remember even glimpsing was Sophonisba P. Breckenridge, who was pointed out to me as a professor emeritus [sic] when she scurried across the campus. There were no works by women on our list of the hundred Great Books. The women characters who occasionally appeared on the scene—Helen of Troy, Medea, Electra, Monica, Emma Bovary, Anna Karenina—did not satisfy my need for a role model. In the light of Plato's *Republic* and Aristotle's *Politics*, I sometimes argued with my male professors and friends over whether a woman could be a philosopher. I loved philosophy, but my personal aspirations did not rise beyond being a good student and a competent assistant. It did not occur to me to think of myself as creative, as actually becoming an independent thinker.

When I first met the Grail in the persons of Lydwine van Kersbergen and Joan Overboss at Doddridge Farm in November of 1940, I was enthralled. My first impression was one of vitality and self-confidence. Here were women who could tackle anything! The very first message I received from the Grail was that women *count*: together we can influence the course of history.

Moreover, Lydwine and Joan were intellectual women (Lydwine's PhD in philology was from the University of Nijmegen in the Netherlands). In their talks to our Catholic student group at the University, they combined a comprehensive analysis of secularism with a holistic educational approach that had a far deeper impact on students than anything I had experienced in my university years. I resonated to their presentation of a positive view of women in the context of an anthropology of complementarity. The notion that men and women are equal but different seemed to me to solve all my perplexities as an intellectual woman. In 1945 I wrote a pamphlet, "The Task of Woman in the Modern World" (with which I now heartily disagree), elaborating Father van Ginneken's ideas of complementarity as I had learned them from Lydwine and Joan with a little help from psychologist Gina Lombroso, writer G. K. Chesterton, and theologian Jacques Leclerq. Maker and lover, theory and practice, abstract and concrete, head and heart, initiative and response, instrumental and expressive, ruler and supporter, self-assertion and self-surrender—I made a case for all the stereotypes as rooted both in woman's essential nature and in her spiritual mission. The practical conclusion: I echoed Chesterton—if only men would be manly and women would be womanly, society would achieve a healthy, harmonious balance. "Woman's essential mission in the world," I wrote confidently, "is to be for mankind a living example of the spirit of total dedication to God." Women were to fulfill this mission either in religious life, in marriage, or in single life in the world. Whatever their specific destiny, they were meant to be spiritual mothers, redeeming the depersonalization and bureaucratic rigidity of the modern world by their loving nurturance and self-sacrifice. Bemoaning the loss of the concept of true womanhood, I condemned feminism as a fallacy. "Their whole struggle for women's rights has simply helped to destroy the difference between the sexes and has worked to make the woman a slavish imitation of the man."[5]

In the 1940s and 1950s I taught complementarity in Grail courses with great conviction, quoting happily from papal pronouncements and from priest writers like John Fitzsimons and Gerald Vann. "For human society the tension between the dominant male and the actively submissive female must be rediscovered and made operative."[6] I certainly was aware of the negative valuation of woman in Western civilization from Aristotle to Freud, but I credited Christianity with having brought about the true emancipation of woman. When I read Simone de Beauvoir, I thought that she failed to see the beauty of woman's capacity for loving self-surrender to the needs of husband and children. I dismissed Betty Friedan's *Feminine Mystique* as a shrill and self-pitying complaint. Nevertheless, my own observations in the 1960s of the marriages of women whom I knew well through their participation in the Year's School at Grailville did raise questions for me. In the approved Catholic style, they had large families—six, eight, ten, thirteen children. Some struggled to make ends meet on small incomes; some lost their health. After all, they were going through pregnancy and birth at a rate we considered unwise for our dairy cows. Moreover, I began to see that the doctrine of masculine and feminine "natures" often served to justify the faults of both sexes: husbands tended to become insensitive and domineering; wives either retreated into passivity and depression or became manipulative.

I was also aware of the great changes that the nineteenth and twentieth centuries had brought about in the position of American women: politically, the vote and the possibility of public office; educationally, the admission into the universities and the professions; technologically, the movement of most housekeeping tasks to the factory, leaving to the home-maker only the role of consumer; biologically, the improvement in life expectancy and the declining birth rate leading to a long period in most women's lives free from the tasks of motherhood. Vatican II had recognized these changes and called for an end to discrimination based on sex. It had also emphasized a more dynamic view of change, moving from an essentialist to an existential framework of thought. On my return from Paris in September 1967, I gave a talk to the Council of Catholic Women in which I developed the idea that masculine and feminine roles were largely, if not entirely, culturally conditioned and were in the process of change. Individuals come in all shapes and sizes, with all possible combinations of personal qualities and talents. To label either psychological qualities or particular occupations as masculine or feminine is crippling for the individual and impoverishes the society, I explained. Why should a male dancer be regarded as effeminate or a female scientist as masculine? Should we not be about educating both men and women for wholeness, for the human birthright of head and heart, competence and compassion? The elderly bishop who sat next to me at the luncheon was quite upset by my talk and kept muttering, "But there must be some abiding truths." Clearly I had grasped the second of Lerner's criteria, that sex roles are socially constructed, but I was not yet ready to call myself a feminist.

A key insight in my development came during a Grail course, "The Cooperation of Men and Women in Church and Society," held in 1969 at the international Grail Center near Amsterdam. Fifty men and fifty women had been invited to this ecumenical conference. When we actually gathered, we were thirty-five women and four men—the other men, for various reasons, had declined at the last minute. Everyone was eager to hear about the movement in the United States. I had brought with me a copy of *Newsweek* with "the Marlborough woman" on the cover, complete with tatoo and clenched fist. The high point for me was the presentation of an existentialist view of women as human subjects able to define themselves from within. "I am the subject of my existence, freely shaping my situation," declared philosopher Yvonne Pellé-Douël. "The subject can never be reduced to or identified with his [sic] vocations, roles or functions. . . . It is important not to freeze the woman in a feminine essence or vocation or role . . . the subject surpasses roles, functions, vocations, by taking on successive roles, by fulfilling many roles at the same time, by renouncing or changing roles."[7]

Pellé-Douël's philosophic analysis satisfied me. Now I had a philosophic basis for integrating my thinking. I had already been weaned away from essentialism by a study of existentialist philosopher Martin Heidegger and by the intellectual emphasis of Vatican II. A new idea, if one takes it seriously, requires a rethinking of one's entire mental landscape and that is a long, slow process. I began to work out the implications of this new insight, women as persons, self-defining subjects, actors in history. No more talk of woman's nature, destiny, or God-given vocation. No more talk of "woman," singular and abstract. What exists is women, concrete, individual women, with all the diversities of race, class, ethnicity, personal history. No more searching outside oneself for a task in life or attempting to conform to some external standard, predetermined destiny or idealized feminine role. The source of authority shifted for me from external to internal. I began to examine my own perceptions, feelings, and experiences and to believe that the Spirit could speak from within my own consciousness. In the summer of 1970, I finally began to call myself a feminist, even though I had butterflies in my stomach as I spoke the word.

Immediately on my return from Holland, Claire Randall, program director of Church Women United (CWU), invited me to join in a series of consultations on women's participation in the society of the future in preparation for the triennial assembly of Church Women United. CWU had involved in these discussions a number of outstanding feminist thinkers—among them theologian Nelle Morton of Drew University; radical feminist writer and editor, Charlotte Bunch of the Washington, D.C. Institute for Policy Studies; Sally Cuneen, an editor of Cross Currents, a scholarly Catholic quarterly; lawyer Pauli Murray, a leader in the civil rights struggle; philosopher Mary Daly who had just published *The Church and the Second Sex*, her first critique of the sexism of the Catholic Church; historian Elise Boulding, author of *The Underside of History*, her effort to trace women's history from prehistoric times to the present; and Viola Lindbeck, a prominent Protestant laywoman. One of these meetings was a consciousness-raising session, facilitated by Nelle Morton, which clarified for us how deeply we had internalized negative images of woman and how much we needed group support to change our own self-images and to tackle oppressive social structures.

In the early 1970s I did consciousness-raising work with women from the wealthiest suburbs of Cincinnati, women who apparently had everything promised by the American Dream—beautiful homes, exquisitely furnished; designer clothes, jewelry, and hair-dos; husbands who were rising executives in the corporate world; children in the best private schools and summer camps; Buicks and Cadillacs in the garage; treatment from the best therapists; and yet these women were often desperately unhappy. I was deeply moved by these sessions. Listening to the women's stories, I felt their pain, was often emotionally drained by it. I saw how devastating it was to be both economically and psychologically dependent on one's husband. Other Grail people, working on issues of poverty and racism in the inner cities, tended to dismiss these groups, but I knew that the pain was real, that many of these women suffered domination, that some were physically abused, that some were psychologically destroyed in their marriages. I immersed myself in the burgeoning feminist literature that led me to a searching critique of Western culture. I began to see how profoundly patriarchal was Western civilization, the civilization that traced its origins to the Greeks and the Jews. It valued males over females, regarded the male as the norm of the human, defined women as relative, dependent, and inferior. It was also sexist, embodying the preeminence of the male in an interlocking set of structures—legal, governmental, economic, educational, scientific, and religious. And it was deeply misogynist, permeated with an ancient mistrust of women and their bodily functions, leading to fear, hatred, and violence against women and to a mythic blaming of Pandora, Eve, and all their daughters for the evils of the world.

The final stage in my conversion to feminism came in applying this analysis to Christianity, to the Catholic Church. In 1972, the Grail and Church Women United cosponsored a week at Grailville, "Women Exploring Theology." Again, I can remember the shiver down my spine when I heard the title. Fr. van Ginneken had insisted that theology was for the men; its application in daily life was women's task. It was a fantastic week for the seventy-five of us—theologians, seminarians, professionals working in church structures, active laywomen. We told our stories in small groups, defined our issues, experimented with new language, imagery, and forms of worship, sparked moments of insight for each other which we labeled "Aha" and "Yeah, yeah" experiences. In this supportive environment, I found that my views on Scripture, God, sexuality, and church had undergone a radical change. No longer could I meditate on scripture as the word of God without examining what the patriarchs—writers, editors, translators of the Bible—and their assumptions had done with the message. I felt the affirming power of inclusive language. I experienced the difference it made to have a woman presiding at the altar. Our small group discussions revealed a complexity and variety of human sexual experience that made clear the inadequacy of the Church's teaching. I was launched into feminist theologizing, an activity that became central to my life from then on.

When I now look back on my thinking of the forties and fifties, I find it hard to understand how I could have remained oblivious for so long to the sexism in the Church, the misogyny in the Scriptures, and the oppressive character of patriarchal structures generally. In part, I suppose it was because the development of a full, coherent feminist consciousness is a slow process. In part, it was because I was living in a women's place, owned and run by women who made all the decisions and took the risks as we saw fit. Even in our worship, I did not feel a sense of oppression, perhaps because we created and led our own, often elaborate prayer hours, and when it came to the celebration of the Eucharist, as a staff member at Grailville, I shared in the planning. We worked with priests who were in sympathy with our approach, respected our ideas and followed our suggestions. In our lectures, readings, and meditations, we sought materials meaningful to women—the heroic women of the Bible, Mary as the strong woman "terrible as an army in battle array," the theology of the Holy Spirit as the feminine aspect of the Godhead.

Feminist Consciousness in the U.S. Grail

I have traced my personal journey. What about the Grail as a movement? To the end of the 1960s, in my opinion, the Grail remained prefeminist. In our courses, in the lectures and discussions at Grailville and in the city centers, we emphasized complementarity and womanly surrender, but in actual practice we challenged individuals by giving them real responsibilities and encouraging them to use their initiative and creativity to the utmost. Gertrude Morris, who was at Grailville in the 1950s, is representative of the way in which Grail training served to empower women:

> What I got out of Grailville was the conviction that you had to live up to your greatest potential. People really believed in you—it wasn't just a trick. . . . I got a chance to do all sorts of things, from cooking for a hundred people to directing the choir and receiving important visitors. I found I was capable of a lot more than I ever thought.[8]

Bruce Taylor, professor of history at the University of Dayton, after studying material in the Grail archives, wrote "Man as the head, leader, active, builder; woman as follower, passive, nurturer—these were the messages. . . . It would seem that Grail members did not realize that the rhetoric was in sharp contrast to the reality of their behavior during those years."[9]

By 1969 the Women's Liberation Movement was front page news. In the context of the Black and student movements, utilizing some of their tactics, helped by media attention to their guerrilla theater and other forms of protest demonstrations, a grassroots movement spread across the country with amazing rapidity, awakening women to the discriminations under which they were laboring. The Grail found itself in the midst of the second wave of American feminism, confronted by a host of difficult questions. In my files I find a memo dated November 1969, which I wrote to the Grail national coordinating committee about the response Church Women

United were making to the new movement. They were providing consciousness-raising groups, planning actions to challenge sexism in the churches, and developing support groups for women moving into action. My memo ends: "Where are we as Grail in all this? Do we want to develop a thrust in this area?" At this point, I was quite unware of the male image evoked by the word "thrust."

In 1974, a report to the Grail Council addressed the Grail role in women's liberation more sharply:

> What are the implications of being a fifty-year-old women's movement, maintaining a women's space, recognizing that being a woman is a political issue today? Do we see the Grail as part of the Women's Liberation Movement? as separate but sympathetic? as actively supportive on some issues and opposed on others? or as totally dissociated?

Grail members did not wait for formal approval to plunge into programming around the new ideas. Already Semester at Grailville begun in the spring of 1968, had brought to Grailville college women who were raising feminist questions. In 1970 SAG students wrote and presented a multimedia extravaganza entitled "XX—or Women in Man's America." To express their critique of sexism in history, the churches, law, education, marriage, work, and family, they combined skits, songs, and dance with huge visuals, projecting on the white walls of the Oratory images of women from current advertising. The summer of 1970 saw a weekend on "Women: New Lifestyles for the Seventies" with theologian Mary Austin Doherty of Alverno College and feminist activist Charlotte Bunch as speakers. In rapid succession there followed "Mobilizing Womanpower," with trainers from the Alinsky Institute in Chicago; "Women's Lifestyles across the Generations," with author Mary Daly; "Women Exploring Theology," and "Seminary Quarter," a six-week program for women in graduate theological study, offered every summer from 1974–1978.

As soon as the Grail Women Task Force was formally approved in 1974, it immediately set about educating Grail members on feminist issues: consciousness-raising sessions were held for the Grail Council in the spring of 1974; an urgent message went out for Grail members to take part in one of the six programs on women offered during the summer of 1974 (forty-four members did participate); and a questionnaire on the relation of the Grail to feminism was circulated as preparation for a weekend in May 1975, with psychotherapist and author Anne Wilson Schaef, which in turn was planned as part of the preparation for the General Assembly of August 1975.

Looking back at the mid-seventies, it is clear to me now that the task forces were ahead of the troops and, in fact, often appeared to be quite threatening to the troops. In the summer of 1974, the Liberation Task Force, after the international meeting in Toronto, proclaimed capitalism as the problem and socialism as the solution. At Grailville, the Women Task Force was announcing that patriarchy was the problem and feminism the key to a solution. The Religious Search Task Force was involved in a two-week international study meeting that raised questions about Jesus and the search for God. And the Cultural Exchange Meetings on Africa (CEMA) brought thirteen African women from five different countries to Grailville with their unique perspectives. It was quite a summer at Grailville. I can remember hearing puzzled Grail members asking, "Do I have to be a feminist and a socialist to belong to the Grail?" The Liberation Task Force dealt with the problem by its network, its publications, and its mobile team. The Women Task Force provided programs, questionnaires and feedback from the questionnaires.

The responses to the 1975 questionnaire reflect mixed reactions to this turbulent new movement with its impassioned rhetoric and sometimes threatening acronyms (e.g., WITCH, Women's International Terrorist Conspiracy from Hell and SCUM, Society for Cutting Up Men). Sent to some three-hundred Grail members and Grailville alumnae, the questionnaire drew forty-four responses, a third of which included pages of thoughtful qualifying statements in addition to the checklist answers. Sixty-two percent of the respondents voiced some criticism of Christianity as sexist, oppressive to women, needing to be reformed by feminism. Forty-six percent unhesitatingly identified the Grail as part of the women's liberation movement. The other 54 percent, however, saw the Grail as a separate entity, sympathetic on some issues, opposed on others. Two themes run through the lengthy responses: first, discomfort with the presentations of feminism as "too simplistic," "too angry and aggressive," "too absolute," in short, too ideological; and second, the conviction that in the Grail the religious commitment is primary, the deepest source of meaning and energy, the most inclusive and comprehensive basis for one's personal life, and that feminism is only one issue among many, "not a top priority."[10]

All the respondents were aware of some tension between Christianity and feminism. Further insight into this tension is to be found in the materials produced by a group of sixteen active Grail members who continued to deal with this question for two full days after the May weekend with Anne Schaef. We covered reams of newsprint with our personal perceptions: "We're divided on the most important things—God, religion, women . . . some call themselves feminists . . . several people are anxious to see the Grail moving on feminism . . . push to promote abortion and lesbianism . . . one, perhaps more, saying no to that." "Spectrum in Grail on Christianity, on feminism . . . a few cautious, most in middle, a few are convinced it is right." "Tension between traditional values under examination and new values and threats." "The Grail is a resource for strength, support, vision, permission for women . . . strongest feminist movement in this area. . . feminism does not equal lesbianism and abortion." "Grail hasn't taken a stand on abortion, lesbianism, birth control."[11]

For the Grail as a group committed to living out their Catholic faith as fully as possible, it was especially painful to discover how deeply we were divided on precisely those elements—faith and womanhood—that had previously been our most profound sources of unity. The pain of this discovery is expressed over and over again in the transcripts: "Religion painful yet need it for nourishment . . . pain in diversity, fear of dealing with it . . . refusal to deal with diversity on any real issues . . . most pain around whether religion is OK, whether feminism is OK. . . ."[11]

Moreover, the pain was intensified because of the general Grail commitment to openness and to personalism, that is, to sharing on more than a superficial level, and affirming the individual's freedom to make her own decisions. Individuals spoke of pluralism, of the need to respect each other's options, but it was difficult to realize this ideal in practice. As one participant said in 1975, "Some people in the Grail know my real thoughts, others do not." And another, "defensiveness around diversity . . . fear of the name feminism . . . fear of anger . . . fear of lesbianism . . . division on religious questions . . . division on socialism . . . support individuality, yet the person fears to speak her individuality . . . fear of women not like ourselves."[11]

At the end of two days of intense discussion, we named five points of tension between feminism and Catholicism. For me, and I think for the others as well, this was the first time we made explicit the difficulties inherent for the Grail in being a movement empowering women and also working in the context of Catholic values and structures. The report on the meeting summarized the conflicts:

1. trust in one's own experience versus obedience to "shoulds" set forth by the Church;
2. sexuality as it was being lived in our society versus the teachings of the Church on birth control, premarital sex, divorce, abortion, homosexuality;
3. individual versus community needs: the feminist insistence on taking responsibility to meet one's own needs versus the Christian demand to sacrifice oneself for the other and the community;

4. the feminist emphasis on the need to express anger and value it as a force for change versus the Christian view of anger as sinful and to be repressed;

5. the feminist affirmation of individuals as peers versus the Christian view of reality as a hierarchy with a male at the head. (The group did not explore whether hierarchy is of the essence of Christianity or whether it flows from the institutional structures of the Church.)[12]

In the next few years, various Grail entities contributed to the diffusion of feminist ideas throughout the movement. In 1975, the Religious Search Task Force prepared *The Grail Prayer Book* to meet the need for a non-sexist version of the psalms, and in 1978 organized the week-long program, "Image Breaking/Image Building," later published in book form. The program focused on encouraging women to plumb their own experiences of the sacred for new images and names for God and to create new forms of worship. While recognizing the reality of the contradictions between feminism and Christianity, the organizers, Eleanor Walker, Marian Ronan, and Linda Clark, insisted that these conflicts were not irreconcilable. That same conviction, that somehow we can be both Christian and feminist, inspired a 1977 weekend planned by the three Grail Task Forces on "Christianity, Feminism and Socialism." The same hope for an integration of feminism and Christianity was reflected in a second survey, conducted by the Grail Women Task Force in 1978. Most of the respondents recognized the sexism in the Church and experienced feminism as a source of energy and direction. A few confessed to being frightened by dogmatism, polarization, and antimale attitudes in feminism.

The three Grail centers—Grailville, Cornwall-on-Hudson, and San Jose—offered a variety of feminist programs. At Grailville, Semester at Grailville (1968–1975) and Seminary Quarter at Grailville (1974–1978) provided fairly long time blocks—sixteen weeks and six weeks respectively—for women-defined studies. From 1975–1978, the Grailville Women's Project (staffed by Meganne Root, Marian Ronan, and Cecile Christianaz from the French Grail) developed monthly weekend programs on women's empowerment. They also inaugurated a series of dinner and performance evenings, "Wine, Women and Song," which both showcased the talents of local women artists—singers, dancers, writers, painters—and demonstrated what a satisfying evening an all-women's group could provide. From 1980–1982 the New Directions for Women program, headed by Mary Gindhart and April McConeghey, and funded by the Women's Educational Equity Act, adapted feminist approaches to the needs of local rural women for personal growth and career development.

As a national Grail entity, the Grail Women Task Force betwen 1975 and 1995 offered fifty-five weekend programs and three one-week institutes on feminist approaches to theology, spirituality, ritual, ethics, personal growth, assertiveness, health, aging, child rearing, conflict resolution, nuclear power, economics, racism, power, and politics. We also organized twenty-six one-day events; nineteen Wine, Women and Song evenings; and eleven lectures for the general public, including a "Dialogue with the Men's Movement." Grail members were active in the Women-Church movement and the Women's Ordination Conference, serving on boards and committees and participating in considerable numbers at the Women-Church conferences in 1983, 1987 and 1993. Grail members Mary Bohlen and Elizabeth McGee participated in the focus groups that Mary Jo Weaver, Professor of Religious Studies at Indiana University, convened in preparation for her book, *New Catholic Women.* Grail members Mary Bohlen and Anne Heidkamp gave testimony to the bishops' committee that worked on the pastoral on "women's concerns," and also contributed to the critiques of that document, which fortunately was never passed.

Christianity, feminism, socialism—are they compatible? Can we integrate them in our life and work as Grail? Even as we proceeded with our outreach programs, we continued the dialogue among ourselves, inspired by the in-depth discussion under the guidance of Rosemary Ruether, Elisabeth Schüssler Fiorenza, and Dorothee Soelle at a weekend in March, 1977. The dialogue continued at the triennial General Assemblies, seeking to identify commonalities and differences. In 1981 the WTF presentation of the patriarchy, sexism, and misogyny of the Christian tradition met with lively responses from the other two groups: the Religious Search Task Force warned against absolutizing feminist insights; the Liberation Task Force insisted on the importance of class analysis for real improvement in the condition of women. The WTF countered with our conviction that all three roots of oppression—race, sex, and class—are crucial. We urged Grail members not to feel guilty about our middle-class privileges but to use them in the liberation struggle.

As an indication of the way feminist ideas have gradually permeated the whole Grail, I quote from the consensus reached by thirty members in study days before the 1984 General Assembly:

- There is a growing commitment to feminism and to feminist theology in the Grail.
- We are integrating into our worship elements from other traditions, for example, the use of elements from Wicca and from Native American traditions in our Holy Week celebrations.
- Work on issues of sexuality is slow and painful, but in eleven years we have moved from reactions of fear and shock to the

formal decision of the 1981 U.S. General Assembly that lesbianism should not be considered an obstacle to Grail membership.
- There is a growing understanding of the oppression of women
  as it is manifested in our lives, in our culture, and in other cultures.
- To be Catholic and feminist is conflictual but not impossible.

How feminist is the United States Grail today? We certainly have a
reputation as a feminist movement. Thus, Mary Jo Weaver writes in *New
Catholic Women:*

> In the sixty years of their existence, these two groups (the Grail
> and the National Council of Catholic Women) have developed
> along radically different lines, so that today the Grail is a strongly
> feminist group, whereas NCCW has taken positions against the
> Equal Rights Amendment and women's ordination. . . .
>
> Their [the Grail's] commitment to women has resulted in
> some stunning and influential programs. In 1972 and 1973 the
> Grail sponsored consciousness-raising workshops in conjunction
> with Church Women United. These Women Exploring Theology
> conferences brought women together from all over the country in
> order to discover and articulate the need for a more inclusive the-
> ology and liturgical language. The Seminary Quarter at Grailville
> program, which lasted from 1974 to 1977 [*sic*], involved women
> from twenty-eight seminaries and five universities in studying a
> theology "in which women's concerns are central rather than
> peripheral" in the task of church renewal. As such, the Seminary
> Quarter broke new ground for women and supported an emerg-
> ing feminist theology that begins not with God but with a theo-
> logical reflection on women's experience. The books that have
> been published as a result of these and other workshop experi-
> ences have interrogated traditional theological education and
> liturgical practice and the parameters of the quest for God. The
> Grail is small—claiming approximately two hundred members—
> and officially invisible, as contrasted with NCCW, but it is signif-
> icantly more influential as a forum for Catholic feminist thought
> and experience. It operates as a nonhierarchical collective com-
> mitted to structural change and so, unlike NCCW, is not part of
> the patriarchal structure of the church. Furthermore, it sets its
> own goals and reflects a more radical approach to women's issues
> than NCCW: the Grail is concerned with women's crisis prob-
> lems, whereas NCCW tends to focus on women's health and par-

enting skills; the Grail is committed to feminism, whereas NCCW has explicitly withheld support from two important feminist causes, ERA and ordination; and the Grail has taken on the issues of liberation, economic justice, and structural change, whereas the NCCW waits to see what the bishops will recommend. If NCCW has given women power in numbers, it has been at the price of autonomy and a denial of feminist perspectives. The Grail, on the other hand, has claimed its autonomy at the price of numbers but without relinquishing its influence.[13]

Ann Patrick Ware, SL, makes a similar judgment:

The Grail reminds me of the Quakers, that is, a small group with a great influence. Grailville and the Grail are known throughout the United States as a place and a group that has fostered the growth of feminism among religious women and indeed among all women.[14]

As noted in chapter 12, Elisabeth Schüssler Fiorenza regards feminist theology as having "one of its major roots" at Grailville.

When *Christianity and Crisis* ran a series on the future of feminist theology in the spring of 1985, both Rosemary Ruether and Diane Tennis (who had supported SQAG when she was an administrator in the Southern Presbyterian Church) referred to the importance of Grailville as an autonomous space for women. Ruether writes:

One needs to have . . . autonomous spaces, where feminist theology is normative rather than marginal, where the immediate struggle against patriarchy does not define the context of the discussion, where the agenda of feminist theology can be more fully and freely developed. Such autonomous spaces for feminist theology have already begun. The Grailville summer quarter in feminist theology was an important arena in the 1970s.[15]

To answer my own question: How feminist is the Grail today? As of December, 1995, it seems to me that we have made great progress both in dispelling fears and in dealing openly with diversity, but progress is slow and proceeds at different rates on different issues and with different people. I think of it as taking the form of a spiral—the issues remain pretty much the same but we are dealing with them at new vantage points. I see progress in the way we are dealing with the following major—and sensitive—issues.

Feminism as a True Liberation Issue

In my perception, Grail members initially responded more readily to racism and to Third World liberation struggles than to feminism and the pain of middle-class suburban women. As one Grail member remarked in 1975, "Being women is taken for granted by many. It's not as conscious a focus as religious search and social change." And another, "Catholic tradition . . . social justice for others, not for me." I remember my emphasis on feminism being met with the rejoinder, especially from Grail women recently returned from work in Africa, "Shouldn't we as Grail put the stress on human liberation rather than women's liberation?" I also remember, after working in the civil rights struggle, how good it felt to be working directly on my own issue, reflecting on oppression as I had experienced it myself and deciding what I wanted to do about it. It is quite a different experience from empathizing with and being supportive of another's struggle, however deeply convinced I might be of its justice.

As the Women Task Force and the Liberation Task Force developed their work during the 1970s, we were nourished by different experiences and elaborated different analyses. The LTF based its reflections on the involvement of Grail members in social action in inner-city Cincinnati and Harlem, in the farm worker struggles in California, in the effort of disenfranchised and unemployed African-Americans in Louisiana to improve their situation. They were influenced, too, by international experiences with the poor in Mexico, in Brazil, in Portugal. And they did extensive study of Marxist analysis in their search for more humane economic and political structures. Members of the WTF were involved in consciousness-raising groups among suburban women, among college students, among women in seminary; one helped to organize the first battered women's shelter; another developed a counseling program for victims of rape and incest. We studied the work of feminist theologians, philosophers, historians, anthropologists, and began to elaborate an analysis of sexism, misogyny, and patriarchy. Coming out of these different experiences, the LTF tended to regard class as the primary oppression, while the WTF pointed to patriarchy as fundamental.

In this area, I think the Grail has made great progress. I think the fears about socialism have pretty much disappeared. The energy the three task forces have expended in exploring the tensions between feminism, socialism, and Christianity has paid off in a widespread acknowledgment that sexism, racism, and classism are independent but intimately interlocked sources of oppression. This theme was effectively expressed in a four-day program, "Women Breaking Boundaries," which was held in a number of sites around the country—Grailville, New York, Louisiana, California—in the late 1980s and early 1990s.

Dealing with Anger, Confrontation and Conflict

As women's anger at victimization first erupted in the early days of the movement, there was a good deal of fear of this anger among Grail members. It was often labeled "unchristian." Some thought the women's movement was too aggressive, too selfish in fighting for women's rights. Here the Grail affirmation of the person helped us to come to clarity. The old ideal, "to give all that you have laughing" gave way to recognition of the legitimacy of personal needs. There has been a gradual recognition that giving is a choice, that it is right to recognize one's limits and to say "No" on occasion. To quote again from the May 1975 meeting, "We are getting out of always being a giver, there is support for this." The WTF has done a good deal of work on assertiveness training, both within and outside of the Grail. All the Grail entities have invested energy and time in group-process training. I think it is fair to say that while not everyone is comfortable with expressions of anger, we do recognize anger as a source of energy in the struggle for justice. While we still may evade conflict on live issues, the Grail as a whole has gained more skill at working through conflicts.

Sexuality

This remains a thorny issue. I think that most Grail members see clearly the inadequacies of traditional Catholic teaching and take direct responsibility for the decisions in their own lives. I would guess from the warm support I have seen Grail groups give members working through divorce that, while we value committed relationships, we also recognize that relationships can die, and that calling an end to them may be the only viable alternative. With respect to methods of birth control, I note that the daughters of the women who had eight or ten children in the 1940s settle for one or two and start their childbearing at a much later age. With regard to premarital sexual activity, difficulties first surfaced in Semester at Grailville. When the question arose as to where male friends of our students should stay on their weekend visits, at least one staff member wanted to exclude sexual activity on the Grailville property. The Jewish mother in me responded, "If they're going to sleep together, better here than in some sleazy motel!" In the end, we staff members arranged for visitor's quarters in a separate building, with no surveillance to determine where individuals were spending the night. The students, however, generally preferred to put up their visitors in their own quarters. A few years later, no eyebrows were lifted when a long-time, unmarried Grail member let it be known that she was going on a week-long vacation with a male friend.

Lesbianism surfaced both in the Grail and at Grailville at about the same time, the late 1960s. It was hard for a group, most of whom had a traditional Catholic upbringing, to deal with this issue, since most of us were brought up to regard homosexuality, if it was mentioned at all, as "a sin against nature." I had been introduced to an early lesbian novel, Radclyffe Hall's *Well of Loneliness* (in a plain brown paper wrapper), and Plato's *Symposium* in my first year at the University of Chicago. I was amazed to discover that for quite a few Catholic young women homosexuality was a new idea and they certainly were blind to signs of mutual attraction between women. The dilemma for the Grail was acute. On the one hand, respect for the person and her choices meant that those who "came out" were not rejected as Grail members. On the other hand, individual members were fearful about the presence of lesbians in the Grail: some were afraid of being approached personally; others worried that Grailville might become "a haven for lesbians." The policy question centered on the influence that lesbians in leadership roles might have on younger women, especially since there was a problem of a relationship between a young SAG staff member and a student. There was also concern as to whether women who had come out would be welcomed as Grail members. A series of processes—meetings, surveys, input from experts, study weekends, careful listening to each other in large and small groups—led to what one participant called "a civil rights for lesbians guide line for the Grail." In the 1981 General Assembly the following statement was approved: "We affirm that participation in the Grail is determined by an individual's commitment to accept and live out the Grail's vision. . . . Sexual preference and lifestyle choices are not determining factors in Grail participation."[16] In my opinion, there is still some discomfort around this issue—I suspect that some members do not feel safe in "coming out" to all their Grail sisters.

The homophobia in society at large and in the Catholic church in particular makes it hard for a group, some of whose members work in official church structures, to deal with certain specific questions, for example, a request by the Conference of Catholic Lesbians to use Grailville's facilities for a weekend. The consultation by mail which resolved the issue in favor of CCL was a model of a participative decision-making process, involving all two hundred Grail members and endeavoring to take into account all points of view and assessments of probable consequences. When the group arrived, they were delightful and very responsive to Grailville. After one day, their peaceful presence had completely converted the most recalcitrant member of the Grailville staff, an older Catholic woman employed in the dining room. Actual experience is a powerful means of destroying fantasies and fears of difference.

The abortion issue is also difficult. We have dealt directly with the substantive issue in the 1975 questionnaire and the 1985 weekend, "Toward a New Ethic of Reproduction." In both cases the Task Force approach tended to favor a pro choice position. In 1975 64 percent of the respondents agreed or strongly agreed that a woman has a right to choose an abortion; 20 percent disagreed or strongly disagreed. The remainder checked the "don't know" column, some adding comments on the complexity of the issue. One woman wrote: "In theory, I believe a woman does have these rights and I hope I would not judge anyone who took those options, but, for instance, there was such an aura of 'wrong' surrounding all my early perceptions of birth control, abortion, lesbianism and divorce that I know it would be very hard, if not impossible, for me to choose them or seek them as rights for myself." I suspect that there are others in the Grail who would echo this comment. In 1985, when the staff evaluated the weekend program, we felt that we had not done enough to develop a safe space for dialogue, with the result that we marginalized those who did not take a strong pro choice position. The program did good work in separating the moral from the legal issue, and made clear the need for a new ethic. As of 1995, I can only say that some feminists are devoting their energies to working toward that new ethic.

In the Grail, some of our disagreements have centered on the question of taking public stands on the abortion issue. Those of us who were working in coalitions with various advocacy groups were often asked to sign on to public statements in the name of the Grail. At the 1984 General Assembly, we came to consensus on taking political stands as the United States Grail on a list of liberation issues—for economic justice, arms control, the ERA, the Women's Educational Equity Act, against military spending and the U.S. interventions in El Salvador and Nicaragua—with the Liberation Task Force administering the guidelines. During the 1984 presidential election, twenty-four nuns and several Grail members were among the signers of a full-page ad in the *New York Times*, calling for dialogue on the present Catholic Church teaching on abortion. When the Women Task Force canvassed the membership on the question of public support as Grail for the nun signers who were under attack by the Vatican, 56 percent responded. Eighty percent of the responses agreed with the idea of public support; the other 20 percent objected to the process, insisting that the GA decision on public stands applied only to stands against the government and that we would need separate guidelines for taking stands vis-à-vis the Church. In the meantime, we sent a private letter of support to the sister signers and a considerable number of Grail members signed on as individuals to the follow-up ad in the *Times*, "Declaration of Solidarity with Catholics Whose Right to Free Speech Is Under Attack."

At the 1987 General Assembly, the Liberation Task Force was charged with developing norms and procedures for taking public stands in relation to the institutional Church. As of 1995, no such norms have been set forth and approved. I suspect that our reluctance to deal more decisively with this issue has several roots. There is discomfort on the part of those with a strong Catholic upbringing to stand in public opposition to Church authorities. Even more important, I think, is our commitment to respect for diversity and to consensus decision-making that makes it difficult to resolve the question of public stands. Even in the area of the liberation issues, where there is consensus and an established procedure, I find that to date we have not used the procedure.

Directly Religious Questions

For a group with a long history of creative, participative, unifying celebrations, the directly religious questions have been especially painful. How could the deepest sources of our unity turn so quickly into sources of serious difficulties? Some difficulties were solved rather easily. As we entered into the feminist critiques of Christianity, we experimented with inclusive language, new symbols and new sources, enriching our prayer life with materials from Native American, African, and Eastern spiritual traditions as well as with the works of contemporary women. We deleted the doxology when praying the psalms. We sought female images of the divine. However, the use of "Lord," for Jesus posed a problem. Could we continue with it or not? This is but one of the many questions of Christology that confront a group of women whose spiritual lives initially were centered in a personal relation to Christ. Those of us who focus on feminist theology wrestle with other questions. Can a male savior save women? Can Christology be liberated from the structures of patriarchy and really become an expression of the liberation of women? Can we approach Christology from below, that is, by beginning with the experience of women today? Can the historical Jesus be a role model for women, since liberation means freeing ourselves from all internalized male norms and models? Can we speak of the divinity as incarnated in a female body, as true God and true female? Can we understand Jesus as Sophia incarnate? Is there no other name in which we may be saved? What do we mean by salvation? Are Christ's suffering and death necessary to satisfy divine justice or is there another interpretation of the Atonement? Can suffering ever be redemptive? Are humans born fatally flawed or essentially good? Is Christianity irredeemably patriarchal or does it offer truly liberating elements to women? Hard questions all, with diverse answers among us.

One of the most difficult issues has to do with the sacramental life of the Church, particularly the Eucharist and the meaning of ordination. Must an ordained person be present to have "a real Eucharist"? If so, must that person be ordained within the Roman Catholic structure? Or, if the Spirit is present in the community, can a group of women celebrate " a real Eucharist"? Some of our Protestant members are ordained in the Methodist, Presbyterian, or United Church of Christ denominations.

Figure 21. A circle of celebration in the Grailville Oratory, 1995.

Initially, many of us experienced some discomfort at a Eucharist celebrated by a non-Catholic celebrant, although this soon dissipated for most, if not quite all, our members. Our next experiential discovery came in our programs at Grailville, where we found that it simply was disruptive to introduce a priest for Sunday Mass into a group that had formed into a cohesive community through an intense weekend experience. Then, some Grail members, rejecting the theology of the 1977 Vatican Declaration on the Question of the Admission of Women into the Ministerial Priesthood, found it too painful to attend Mass in the parish church. Others continued to find the parish Mass a central source of nourishment for their own spiritual journeys.

We have been struggling with the question of how to pray together since the 1969 General Assembly, when we first began spelling out what mutual respect demands in the face of diverse religious sensibilities. It seems to be necessary to process this question over and over again. In our national meetings, we usually provide both a Eucharist celebrated by a priest and a feminist ritual. In the 1994 General Assembly, the question was posed for discussion: Where in your life as an individual and in our collective life as Grail, do you find the struggle between self-definition and respect for the rights of others? My small group concretized the question in terms of the Mass, which had been celebrated the previous evening by a priest friend. One person insisted that whenever we come together as Grail we should have a Mass with a priest. Personally, I found it painful to bring a male priest into a community of women celebrating their own autonomy and strength. In the discussion, we made explicit once again what mutual respect for our diversities demands: do not insist that for unity all must attend a Mass with a priest or that all must attend a women-church Eucharist; approve each one attending the ritual she feels comfortable with; create new rituals that all can join. We two who disagreed with each other were able to process our differences to a point of mutual understanding.

To sum up: feminist consciousness has permeated the Grail in the United States—and internationally—slowly and unevenly, as might be expected in a movement that spans more than half a century and is involved in twenty different cultures around the world. In the United States, the feminists have worked hard at educating the movement; feminist education is welcomed and supported by the Grail nationally; feminist ideas are reflected in the themes of national meetings and General Assemblies. Particularly significant is the development of an ecofeminist approach, which stresses the way the various forms of domination—male/female, humans/nature, whites/colored, owners/workers—are interlocked and strengthen each other. As we face a global crisis of survival, ecofeminism offers a vision of wholeness and interdependence that gives hope for the future. Women are joining the Grail in order to find support for their feminism. Some members are active in such feminist religious organizations as Women's Ordination Conference, Catholics for a Free Choice, and Women-Church. Nine Grail members from seven countries—three from the United States—were present at the Beijing Forum in 1995. But as an organization the Grail has not taken public stands on feminist issues, particularly against the Church, but leaves such public political action to the initiative of its individual members.

To be Catholic and feminist, in the words of the 1984 Grail study days, is "conflictual but not impossible." The way of the religious feminists is not an easy one. Feminists are present today in many of the major religious traditions—Catholic, Protestant, Jewish, Moslem, Buddhist. We face similar problems: rejection from our secular sisters as too religious; suspicion from our coreligionists as too feminist; hard questions about doctrines and practices which we perceive as oppressive to women. We do not think we can deny the past yet we cannot create a new spirituality out of whole cloth. Therefore, we try to honor our rooting in our respective traditions. But we hold to the conviction that women are images of the divine and are determined to bring to the dialogue our experience, our analysis, our imaginations, and our voices.

14

From Secularism to Social Analysis

In the summer of 1974, when the recently formed Liberation Task Force announced, after participating in an international Grail meeting in Toronto on conscientization, that "capitalism is the root of the problems of our world, (and) therefore, we need a new socialist society," they sent shock waves through the rest of the Grail. But their statement could perhaps have been anticipated by someone familiar with Grail history, for it had its origins in a concern for social issues which had been part of the U.S. Grail from its beginnings. In the early 1940s, as Lydwine van Kersbergen and Joan Overboss went to meetings and conferences and met with Catholic leaders to familiarize themselves with the live currents in American Catholicism, they had recognized kindred spirits in the members of the Catholic Worker and Friendship House with their radical commitments. Clearly, poverty and racism were issues to be faced by all lay apostles. But as much as they admired the work of these two groups, they saw the Grail mission as distinct: a task specifically with young women, to draw them into a full Christian life and to help them find ways to bring a Christian influence to bear on their worlds.[1]

Social Concerns in the 1940s and 1950s

In the United States, with its lack of explicit class consciousness and its more fluid class structure, the Grail drew its membership largely from the middle class and from working-class families that were moving into the middle class. There were a few young women from well-to-do families, and many who were the first generation to go to college from families where the father was an electrician or a fireman or a street car conductor. In the 1940s and 1950s, our first concern was to find and train young women with a capacity for leadership. We expected to find them primarily in the colleges, but also in the high schools, the parishes, the Catholic Action groups. And in the training, we tried to awaken in these relatively privi-

243

leged young women a sense of responsibility and a desire to use their gifts "for the conversion of the world." Like the Catholic Worker, we brought them into contact with poverty; like Friendship House, we brought them into contact with African-Americans. The context was the spiritual and corporal "works of mercy." If you lived your faith, you would share your material goods and your knowledge and skills with the less fortunate.

Early on, the Grail leaders recognized the importance of the racial issue. I remember Lydwine talking to me in 1941 about the problem of race in the United States—the conversation was intended to give me a broad vision of the lay apostolate and the significant work that awaited me therein. Catherine de Hueck had already started Friendship House in New York's Harlem. I heard her speak at Doddridge Farm. For me the high point of her talk was her response to the often asked question about intermarriage, "Would you want *your* sister to marry a Negro?" Her reply: "What makes you think a Negro would *want* to marry your sister?" seemed brilliant to me. In Lydwine's considered opinion, which she shared with me that day, the long-term solution lay in intermarriage. In 1942, as soon as Mary Louise Tully could be spared from the work at Doddridge Farm, Lydwine sent her to Louisiana to make contact with young African-American women. In 1949, as soon as Joan Overboss could be spared from the work at Grailville, she chose to go to Detroit and to work in the factories, using the approach that had served so well in Holland. The factory workers were not responsive, but the university students were deeply interested. As soon as Joan had formed a small group who wanted to live together as a Christian community, they chose to move into a working-class, African-American neighborhood in the inner city.

In 1946 Grailville published an American edition of the simplified version of Pope Pius XI's encyclical *Quadragesimo Anno* under the title *This Is Social Justice* (the simplified text was originally produced by the English Grail). Courses on the papal social encyclicals were part of the program of the Grailville Year's School in the 1940s and 1950s. As the city centers were established in the 1950s, most developed outreach programs in inner-city neighborhoods. The Cincinnati Center ran play schools for children in the African-American community of the West End and home economics classes for the Appalachian women in the municipal housing projects. The Philadelphia Center worked with the Catholic Inter-racial Council and was involved in neighborhood development in a changing neighborhood. The Brooklyn Center worked with Puerto Ricans in the municipal housing projects. The Detroit Center worked with the pastor of St. Leo's to incorporate Negro spirituals and poetry into the liturgy. Like the Louisiana Center, they also developed a credit union and a food cooperative with their neighbors. The Louisiana team were very active in the war on poverty. The San

Jose Center settled in an Hispanic area and worked with the United Farm Workers. In each case, the Grail teams tried to bring together the relatively privileged young women from the schools and colleges with those suffering from poverty and racial discrimination.

Secularism and a New Christendom

In the 1940s, our analysis of the problems of poverty, racism, war, urban blight, and other social concerns was in terms of the categories of secularism and materialism. Eagerly I read the thinkers of the European Catholic Revival—Jacques Maritain, Hilaire Belloc, Gilbert Keith Chesterton, Eric Gill, and Christopher Dawson. I absorbed their arguments and used them in a talk I developed on secularism as the great underlying evil in the Western world. Christianity had shaped the culture of the West; we had broken away from our roots, deluded by the myths of scientific and industrial progress. We were living the split between private and public, Sundays and weekdays, the church and the world. The Christian values honored in personal and family life were irrelevant in industry, commerce, and government. The cure, and indeed the task of the lay apostolate, was to heal this split by bringing Christian values into all aspects of life, in short, by building a new Christendom.

In 1948 the Grail published the *Program of Action*, which I had written as an introduction to the lay apostolate for young women. It was designed for small groups, meeting weekly, and was intended to give an understanding of secularism and practical means to combat it in one's own life and surroundings. When I reread the *Program of Action* today, I am struck both by its insightfulness and by the great gaps in the analysis. Inspired by the vision of a new Christendom, I presented our critique of materialism and consumerism. I particularly enjoyed summarizing the role of advertising as creating in us consumers the desire for things we didn't need, didn't want, and couldn't afford.

Our long-term vision, following the English distributists and the Catholic Worker, was to promote decentralized intentional communities on a countercultural pattern with a self-subsistent homesteading basis. In the 1940s and 1950s at Grailville we modeled self-subsistence, working systematically to supply our own necessities. We not only raised much of our own food, we tried to farm with horses instead of tractors to be independent of fossil fuels; we bought a wood-burning stove for the small farm at Foster for the same reason; we equipped our cisterns with charcoal filters. And we encouraged young couples to settle on the land, at least enough land to raise their own food while they derived income from a city job. The book, *Five Acres and Independence* by M. G. Kains was much in vogue. A number of these intentional communities sprang up around the country, started by young Catholics who had been touched by the vision of the lay apostolate. Peter Maurin and Dorothy Day of the Catholic Worker, with the slogan of "Cult, Culture and Cultivation," promoted a back to the land movement, as did Msgr. Ligutti and the Catholic Rural Life Conference. Young women who had been trained at Grailville sometimes persuaded their future husbands to combine a homestead with a job as a sound basis for raising a family; young men who wanted this lifestyle often came to Grailville looking for a suitable spouse. Small groups of couples, seeking to meet their basic needs through a collaborative community based on a lived Christianity, settled around Grailville, around the Catholic Worker farm in Newburgh, New York; in Pearl River, New York; around Notre Dame University in South Bend, Indiana; around St. John's Abbey in Collegeville, Minnesota.

The Program of Action with its resource materials by Emerson Hynes of Collegeville, Professor Frank O'Malley of Notre Dame and Carl Bauer, founder of a center for laymen, remains on a rather abstract level. The tone is sober and sobering, looking at the ravages of World War II in Europe and the materialism, selfishness and boredom of young people in the United States, sated with the products of technology but lacking meaning for their lives. All three writers are convinced that modern civilization, the civilization born of the industrial revolution, capitalist economics, and the secular nation state, is in collapse and that a new world is struggling to be born. They predict that the new society arising from the debris of the old will be either a totalitarian tyranny or a Christian society, offering humankind freedom under God. The crisis is an opportunity for Christians to reform their own lives and to undertake the immense task of transforming the social order and all its institutions. Several of the writers quote approvingly Pope Pius XII's dictum: "It is no longer permitted to anyone to be mediocre."

When I look for specifics, I find sweeping references to the violence of war, the suffering of prisoners, the uprooting of peoples, the flight from the land and the crowding of people into the cities, the greed of capitalists, the breakdown of the family, the evils of production for profit instead of service, the misuse of the right of private property to justify corporate exploitation of individuals, the spiritual emptiness of modern people and the trivialization of human life. Only in the section intended to guide young women in assessing the effects of secularism in their own surroundings do I find a more concrete focus. They are asked to observe how young women spend their time, money, and energy, what determines their choice of a job. The text suggests that production for profit is destructive of health, creating undue stress for the worker and overprocessed food for the consumer. The young women are urged to examine one industry closely—cosmetics, clothing, or food production—for evidence of corruption of the product and exploitation of the consumer. They are told to pay special attention to advertising addressed to women: What ideals are held up for admiration? What emotions are appealed to? While there is clear recognition of the need for institutional change, the practical suggestions are focused on the individual, to increase her awareness of the evils of modern culture and to urge her to a more fervent spiritual life.

These ideas did move some young women to change jobs. For example, Mary Buckley gave up her job as a secretary at the American Tobacco Company to work in the greenhouse at Brooklyn Botanic Gardens because her Grail experience had convinced her that women should work with living things. On the same principle, some young women were attracted to the family service program at the Cincinnati Center by the importance of working with young children.

A New Approach: Toward a Marxist-Based Social Analysis

A number of factors came together in the early 1970s to shift the Grail approach from a general Christian concern for those suffering poverty, discrimination, and violence toward a radical social analysis: the experiences of Grail members in their concrete involvements; the influence of Latin American liberation theology; the work of Paulo Freire and his *Pedagogy of the Oppressed*; the challenges brought to the U.S. Grail by the international Grail, especially the teams from Mexico and Portugal.

As the city centers were phased out in the late 1960s, and Grail members embraced the new understanding of the Spirit at work in the struggles for justice, many individual members moved into professional work in line with their commitment to work for a transformed world. They were not looking for ways to build a "successful" career; rather they were asking themselves "where can I put my energies and skills so that I can make a difference in the world?" Among the health professionals, Sharon Jocelyn, a nurse, went to work in underserviced Clermont County, twenty miles from Cincinnati, but with fewer doctors per capita than Nigeria and most of those refusing to accept patients on welfare. Alice Drefchinski, another nurse, joined a group starting a clinic to serve poor and African-American people in rural Louisiana. Mary Clifford, MD, and Lynn Malley, social worker, joined the Tufts University medical project in Mound Bayou, Mississippi, an all-Black community dating back to the Civil War. After eighteen months of battling the racism of the environment and the narrow focus of the project, they left for Toledo to start a clinic in a Hispanic neighborhood.

Many of those trained as teachers chose to work with understaffed inner-city schools: Olive Wahl in East Harlem, N.Y.; Frances Martin in Lincoln Heights, an all-Black Cincinnati suburb; Beverly Scorrano in the Brownsville section of Brooklyn where she joined in the struggle of Puerto Rican parents for community control of the schools. Anne Mercier, after seven years with the Grail school in Uganda, went to work in the high school equivalency program in inner-city Cincinnati. Gabrielle Miner, after four years at Pius XII University in Lesotho, South Africa, brought her expertise in African studies first to Lincoln University in Pennsylvania, then to Central State University in Ohio. Staff members at the San Jose Center taught English as a second language to Spanish speakers. At the same time, they organized programs of summer fieldwork in Mexico for young Americans. The Louisiana Center organized similar programs of summer fieldwork within the United States, in the poor Black parishes of southwest Louisiana. The semester at Grailville program involved some students in health work in Appalachian Clermont County and all students in consciousness-raising around social issues. The key questions: What are the implications of my privileged lifestyle for poor people in this country? for people in the Third World?

Many Grail members were involved in the social movements of the 1960s and early 1970s: the peace movement, the civil rights movement, the war on poverty, the United Farm Workers, and the women's movements. A Grail team studied cooperatives and credit unions at St. Francis Xavier University in Antigonish and then sought to apply the Antigonish approach in community development work in Nova Scotia. The Cornwall Center worked with the Mid-Hudson Peace Network and the Newburgh Ministry. The SAG students joined protest demonstrations after the shootings at Kent State. The Grail in Louisiana helped to establish the Southern Consumers Cooperative and joined with them in the War on Poverty. Some long-term individual commitments resulted from these involvements. In 1972 Veronica Forbes left the Grailville staff to join the United Farm Workers, where she walked the picket lines and supervised the bookkeeping. Several of the San Jose staff, after the 1972 coup in Chile, joined Christians for Socialism. Jessica Stuber, after seven years with a Grail team in Uganda, moved into public housing in St. Paul, where she insisted that housing must include supportive social services and succeeded in empowering single-parent tenants to become housing managers. Monica Erler helped to establish Advocates House in St. Paul, one of the first U.S. shelters for battered women, and has influenced state policy on this issue. I started the Grail Women Task Force, which has educated the Grail and the general public on feminist issues.

These concrete involvements made people more open to social analysis. We began to study the Latin American liberation theologians—Leonardo Boff, Michael Bonino, Gustavo Guttierez, Juan Luis Segundo, and Jon Sobrino—and were introduced to the work of Brazilian educator, Paulo Freire, by Loretta Porto, who had returned to the United States after serving with a Grail team in Belo Horizonte, Brazil. Freire's method of conscientization had had such dynamic results among illiterate peasants in Brazil that the government had forced him into exile and in 1969 he was at Harvard in the role of visiting scholar. That fall, Freire gave a weekend workshop at Grailville. He explained his method of literacy training, which focuses on empowering the people, raising their consciousness of their own resources and their capacity to change the present oppressive situation. The first step is to listen to the local people in order to identify the words and images that represent their key problems; then to teach them to read and write those words, all the while raising questions about these problems, increasing awareness that the existing situations are not inevitable but can be changed. Later some Grail members undertook much more extensive studies with him. Sally Timmel and Anne Hope applied the Freire method in developing an extensive Catholic social movement in Kenya, East Africa. They documented their method in the three-volume *Training for Transformation*, which has been widely used in the two-thirds world. In the United States, Grail educational programs quickly made use of Freire's insights into the difference between an education that domesticates and one which liberates.

However, the strongest factor in radicalizing Grail members in the USA, moving us to a serious study of Marx and to a radical analysis of the American economic and political systems, has been the impact of the international Grail. The scores of Americans who served overseas—in Egypt, Uganda, Tanzania, Kenya, Nigeria, Ghana, Indonesia, Mexico, Brazil, and South Africa—returned home with quite a changed view of their country and its foreign policy. They no longer accepted the rhetoric of the United States as the generous defender of democracy because they had been exposed to repressive regimes that enjoyed American support and had seen firsthand the hardships suffered by the poor, especially women and children, in countries hard-pressed to pay the interest on their debts to Uncle Sam, that demanding creditor. Then, too, many of us had personal contact with individuals who were suffering oppression. A Brazilian woman who had been imprisoned visited U.S. Grail centers with her story. Anne Hope, a white South African who had spent several years at Grailville, had her passport confiscated by the South African government because of her work with the Christian Student Federation. There were many other personal stories, from Brazil, from Mexico, from South Africa that reinforced the general news reports with a sense of intimacy and urgency. We were challenged to ask ourselves whether our work was sustaining the status quo or attacking the structures that kept poverty in place.

In 1968 the Portuguese revolution dethroned Salazar. Shortly thereafter a Portuguese Grail team visited the United States, sharing their enthusiasm for the possibilities for radical social change that were opening before them. The Americans at work in Mexico City brought some of their Mexican colleagues to Grailville over Christmas 1972 to explain the dynamics of capitalism and their hopes for socialism. They critiqued the Grail clinic in Toledo as not going deeply enough into the contradictions of the society—"the work is reformist rather than being transforming . . . although the clinic was different for being situated and integrated into the base community of the Chicanos themselves, the Chicanos do not have a perspective of radical change and for this reason a work of deeper transformation was not possible."[2]

In an August workshop at Grailville in 1973, "Life through Liberation," a Dutch priest, Frank van der Hoff, made a thorough and dynamic presentation of the three levels of Marxist analysis: the economic, the juridical/political, and the cultural/ ideological and showed how these distinctions could be used to analyze specific situations. The workshop was international—seven countries were represented among the seventy participants. It was also enriched by the collective experience of four Grail teams—from South Africa, Canada, Mexico, and the United States who had been using the Freire method of conscientization. One of the participants, Carol Webb, writes:

> The summer of 1973 was a power packed time. I remember doing a weekend Alinsky training—good basic organizing skills; there was women's stuff with Dorothy Riddle—my first ever contact with "out" lesbians and the effort to more clearly link the personal and political; and there was the workshop with the folks from Mexico and the Dutch priest and the folks from Canada who were doing the news media analysis. Later that summer I went to Cornwall with the SAG staff to do a Freire training. Those workshops really have shaped the direction of my life in incredible ways. . . . Maybe the biggest learning for me was a clearer understanding of working class politics. I remember Frank and the Canadians talking about the importance of unions and working with the labor movement—that economic issues were the basis for how real change would happen. That was the summer when I learned to use the tool for analysis—the three tiers, economy at the

base, political in the center, social cultural at the top, a way to understand the world, particular institutions, etc.

The tools that I learned that summer and after, the process skills that I learned in the community—all these have served me well in my post-Grailville life. There was, just as we always claim in the Grail, a wholistic approach—the study of the economy, capitalism, multinationals, the struggles of peoples linked to the desire to be more human, more caring—the process matters in a way that is somehow as important as the outcome. Anyway I have centered my life in the labor movement because of contact that summer with all the programs I mentioned."[3]

The new ideas and new analytic tools percolated through the Grail, stirring both excitement and confusion. Over the Christmas holidays in 1973 two representatives of the United States Grail, Meg Root and Peg Linnehan, attended a series of meetings in Mexico City organized by the Mexican Grail team. Energized by this experience and excited by the possibilities of a liberation focus for the United States Grail, they sent out a letter to Grail members inviting them to join in implementing "Liberation" as a U.S. Grail priority. The letter explains that as people committed to opposing injustice in all its forms, we need "to examine globally what's been happening in the area of real social and political transformation." The Third World countries, because of their very powerlessness, have the best insight into oppressive economic and political forces and are organizing for fundamental change. What is needed is more analysis of the first world, especially North America: Who controls decision-making? Who benefits? Where are the real forces for change? Who are the oppressed? How can we be in solidarity with them? How can we be in solidarity with Grail people in the Third World? The invitation offered two options: (1) a Liberation Task Force, a core group of people involved in a concrete, local work for change and making a major commitment of time and energy to study, to develop materials about meaningful social/ political/ cultural action, to develop resources and skills for consultation with local teams; and (2) a Liberation Network of people interested in reflecting on their own work involvement and sharing their ideas and questions.[4] Eighty people immediately joined the network with twelve taking on the responsibilities of the Task Force.

The Liberation Task Force members were certainly women in a hurry, eager to share their new insights. They were exceedingly active, preparing for a study week in Toronto in August, 1974, and another at Grailville in January of 1975, a mobile team to carry the new message from coast to coast, a presentation on capitalism to educate Grail members at the General Assembly of August 1975, a study week at Cornwall, a newsletter to the new Liberation network, and a packet of materials for use by Grail members.

The Toronto issue meeting in August of 1974 was an international Grail gathering with an ambitious goal: nothing less than the development of an analysis of global socio/political realities to serve as a common basis for action for the Grail worldwide. First of all, the meeting sketched a vision of a new socialism, which remained the basis for Grail liberation work in subsequent years. The statement emphasized production for human needs rather than for profit in a collaborative society that embodied equality of sexes, races, and religions. The group insisted that "socialism and Christianity are not incompatible but are convergent," and noted the "need for new forms of the church that express a prophetic and fraternal community."[5]

The study days in January 1975, clarified terminology; explored models of socialism in China, Tanzania, and Chile; and drew up demanding criteria for Grail work in the building of a new socialism, refining the criteria put forth at the Toronto meeting. Individuals and teams were invited to ask themselves these questions:

- Is our work based on a Marxist analysis of the economic, political, and cultural aspects of society?
- Does it include an analysis of our own class backgrounds? How are we tied to capitalism? What moves us to revolt against it?
- Is our work in solidarity with those most exploited by capitalism?
- Are we working in a team that studies, plans, and takes action collectively?
- Does our work have a global perspective?
- Are we sharing our work with the Grail nationally and internationally in a way that helps the Movement to move more effectively toward new socialism?[6]

The Toronto meeting and the 1975 follow-up meeting dealt directly and openly with the threats posed both by the vocabulary and the analysis. The Toronto meeting noted the problem of "loaded language" with terms like revolution, socialism, communism, Marxism, class, collective, reformism, liberation, involving ambiguities and arousing fears. The meeting recommended that an international work group devise acceptable forms of communication for the countries that have a problem in speaking of Marxism and socialism. The international character of the group highlighted the complexities of finding a suitable vocabulary. For the Germans and the Dutch, the word "socialism" carried connotations of the imperialism of the Russians and the National Socialism of the Nazis. For the Latin Americans working with base communities, it had positive connotations.

The North Americans experienced some difficulties with publics that equated socialism with communism. When Grail members took part in demonstrations in Loveland on behalf of the United Farm Workers or against nuclear arms, they were often accused of being communists. A Loveland woman, who worked in the Grailville office and was fired for unsatisfactory work, retaliated by taking a copy of the Toronto report and circulating it to church authorities, hoping to discredit Grailville as a subversive organization. Fortunately for Grailville, the chancery office dismissed her as a crank.

A deeper issue had to do with identifying the prime forces for change in both the industrialized and the nonindustrialized nations. In theory, those most oppressed by the capitalist system should recognize oppression in their own direct experience and therefore be most motivated to create a new system. Hence, they should constitute the "base." In Latin America with societies of tiny elites and a small middle class, the base is large and readily identifiable. In industrialized societies, with a large class of comfortable middle-income people (who, because they do not own the means of production, in Marxist terms belong to the proletariat), it is more difficult. The group identified some progressive forces: radical unions; the unemployed or underemployed; oppressed cultural and racial groups. Insisting that there are no neutral positions in the liberation struggle, the Toronto meeting declared that "work with the middle class is valid only if it is done with and through the base."[7] Therefore, middle-class people— and most Grail work is with the middle class, students, women in the helping professions, religious groups—must make a clear option to struggle with those working for basic necessities, and must be in dialogue and alliance with the oppressed.

In mid-January of 1975 the mobile team—Alice Kraemer and Carol Webb—announced their availability to visit Grail centers and teams to share these new ideas and to find out what individuals and groups were doing at the local level. During the winter and spring they covered the country, from Boston to Louisiana and New York to San Jose, California, meeting not only with Grail members in each area but also with groups having similar interests, for example, Scientists for Social Reponsibility, Bread for the World, American Friends Service Committee, family groups, people doing antiracism work, people engaged in international solidarity efforts with the Third World. They conducted workshops on the new socialism and explained, to Grail and non-Grail, why the Grail nationally had made a commitment to the liberation issues. Carol Webb writes of the experience:

> We went on the road to move the whole movement to a new understanding of capitalism, to provide them with tools for analy-

sis of their communities, to find out what was happening in the country to bring about social justice and how Grail people were a part of that. . . . I had a deep feeling of being part of an extraordinary community—awesome.[8]

In a period of a few months, they held more than twenty meetings. While the participants in their evaluations noted that they needed more time for the sessions and better advance preparation, they also appreciated how well prepared the two team members were, how they could deal with socialism in a nonthreatening way and make the materials alive and useful.

After this impressive debut, the Liberation Task Force continued patient, consistent work, educating the rest of the Grail through presentations at General Assemblies, study days before national meetings, regular summer study weeks at the Cornwall Center, a newsletter, *Liberation News Notes*, resource materials in the form of bibliographies, audiotapes, and well-prepared study packets. Members of the Task Force were also available as consultants to advise local groups.

Characteristics of the Grail Approach

The Grail approach to the new socialism was characteristically holistic. It took into consideration everything from personal lifestyles to analysis of the world economy and the impact of the multinationals. First of all, it inspired an examination of conscience on personal lifestyles—were we really "walking our talk"? Grail training had always stressed simple living in the context of Catholic asceticism, a stripping away of attachment to material things in order to be free for God. In the light of the new socialism, the emphasis shifted to a global context of justice for all peoples and for the planet, a focus which makes equally strong demands on the individual. A program on "Simple Living—Global Justice," took as its theme Elizabeth Seton's phrase, "Live simply that others may simply live," highlighting the connection between first world consumption and Third World poverty. Participants were invited to adopt the Shakertown Pledge,[9] committing themselves to simple and ecological living, to sharing their wealth with the poor, to spiritual renewal, and to work for the reshaping of society's institutions.

Corporate Responsibility

Along with assessing our personal lifestyles, we assessed our corporate use of resources. Included in the assets of the national Grail is a portfolio of stocks and bonds set aside for the long-term needs of staff who have served many years on subsistence. A portfolio committee together with the Grail national treasurer evaluated these holdings for social responsibility in line with the guidelines of the Corporate Responsibility Group of the Inter-Church Center in New York. The Grail joined this group and took part in their actions at corporate board meetings. We decided that we did not want to hold stock in companies that were involved in the nuclear industry, in weapons manufacture, in polluting the environment, in damaging the health of the consumer or engaging in unfair labor practices. I remember a national financial meeting in which the portfolio committee asked for and was given approval of their recommendation to sell our Philip Morris stock, although it yielded good dividends, since their product was carcinogenic and there was no prospect of effective protest actions at a board meeting. We found that our criteria ruled out investment in most of the Fortune 500 companies. Our insistence on holding to these criteria served to educate the portfolio manager, a finance professional at a major Cincinnati brokerage firm. She eventually became the firm's authority on socially responsible investment.

From the beginning, with the Grail ideas about self-subsistence, we had seen Grailville with its farm as an ultimate protection in the case of social upheavals. The Cornwall study circle gave voice to a deeply held Grail value in a 1977 statement of purpose:

> our present dependence on a potentially explosive system for a livelihood indicates that we view Grailville and its land as being essential to possible freedom of being a movement in the future. We seek uses of this natural trust that are ecologically and corporately responsible.

In 1990 this value led us to the decision to stop using chemical fertilizers, herbicides, and pesticides and to commit Grailville's acres totally to permaculture, that is, organic, sustainable agriculture. And the international Grail, in the IGA of 1993, made "contributing to the survival of the planet" one of its three priorities.

Experiential Learning as a Holistic Approach

Another aspect of holism in the Grail is the stress on experiential learning, using methods that move ideas from the abstract to the concrete and involve participants imaginatively and emotionally as well as intellectually. For example, as holistic educators, in their study of the global economy the Liberation Task Force made good use of the "Global Dinner" in which participants drew lots according to countries and then were served meals representing the average caloric intake in that country. They were also given a fact sheet about their country, detailing the per capita income, the life expectancy, the infant mortality, the adequacy or inadequacy of the average diet. A mix of countries at each table ensured that the diner who was served a four-course steak dinner sat next to one who received a plate of beans or one who received only a glass of water. Readings and discussion followed the meal. The dinner served as a kind of Freire code, inspiring reflection at both a personal and a political level. The Task Force followed up with three pages of action suggestions, beginning with the individual's own consumption and ending with an analysis of U.S. policies related to food and hunger and recommended political actions.

Interstructuring of the Oppressions

Fueled by the energy and excitement of new insights, the three task forces tended to follow their own lines of development, each group pushing its own agenda with Grail members and with a wider public. However, at the same time, the Grail desire for holism inspired efforts to bring the three tracks together. In 1977, as mentioned in Chapter 13, a particularly noteworthy program, "Christianity, Feminism, Socialism," was organized by the three task forces with Elisabeth Schüssler Fiorenza, Rosemary Radford Ruether, and Dorothée Soelle as resource persons. In preparation for the weekend, each group formulated the issues as it perceived them in relation to the other two, preparing key questions and comments.

The Liberation Task Force insisted on class struggle as essential to social action, the women's movement, and the Church. It pointed to the lack of an economic analysis in the women's movement and to the way in which a priesthood tended to appropriate sacramental powers just as capitalists appropriate wealth. They asked, "What are the strains in the feminist movement we can identify with as socialists? "

The Women Task Force charged both socialism and Christianity with being patriarchal and paternalistic, seeing the other as a victim to be helped, whereas feminism raises consciousness of oppression as a step toward empowering the other for action. They asked, "Why are women's issues not regarded as social justice issues of equal importance with issues of class or race? Where in socialism is there room for contemplation, celebration, the aesthetic dimension of life, the sensual, the sexual, and the homosexual?" They critiqued the institutional forms of Christianity as male-identified, hierarchical, authoritarian, elitist and antisexual. They asked, "What are the consequences for Christianity of a more dynamic concept of human personality, for example, in the areas of sexuality, anger, relation of personal to group needs, concepts of power and powerlessness in relation to God?"

The Religious Search Task Force pointed to the importance of Christianity as affirming the value of each person, giving a vision of community that transcends time and space and enables a real solidarity with the dead, the absent, the imprisoned, those suffering hardship or injustice, holding up the value of love and caring, and nourishing hope. They asked "Is there anything intrinsically against socialism or feminism in a religious tradition of a male savior and a cultic priesthood? What are the limits on collectivity vis-à-vis personal freedom? What limits, if any, are there on the means of bringing about social revolution?"

Since all of us, resource persons as well as participants, were dealing with these same points of tension, there were no lectures. Rather, the weekend followed a feminist process model of free-flowing dialogue, focused on each area in turn. What emerged from the dialogue was a clearer insight into the interstructuring of the oppressions.[10] Subsequent theological work strengthened the conclusion that the oppressions were mutually supportive and added colonialism, militarism, heterosexism, ageism, and ableism to the list. Feminists were quick to point out that the interlocking of oppressive structures multiplies rather than simply adds to the oppression. Thus, to be poor and black and a woman is eight times as heavy a burden as simply being poor.

While some of the radical Catholics of the 1940s and 1950s subsequently identified with right-wing movements (Michael Novak and Carol Jackson, for instance), no right wing has developed within the Grail, perhaps because Grail members have been guided by values of social justice in their choice of careers. They have tended not to become involved in corporate structures. When Martha Heidkamp, with her newly minted MBA from the Wharton School, received a job offer from Standard Oil, both her Grail friends and her family, when consulted, advised her that she would not be happy putting her energies into increasing the bottom line. She chose to put her energies into work for nonprofit organizations and eventually set up her own business, a computerized billing service for doctors, in order to have more time to devote to her work as treasurer of the United States Grail.

Impact of Grail Social Justice Work

How does one evaluate the work of the Grail as a whole or of a subgroup like the Liberation Task Force on social justice issues? One measure of the effectiveness of the Task Force work in educating Grail members is the proposal on taking political stands as the US Grail, which it presented to the General Assembly of 1984. Initially, we had said that the Grail did not take political stands as a movement. However, as Grail groups worked with other social justice activists, the question of signing on in the name of the US Grail to various public statements arose repeatedly. For example, could we endorse Witness for Peace, the ERA, the protests against military aid to El Salvador? Thanks in large measure to the educational work of the Task Force, the consensus grew that we must undertake corporate work on social and political issues. Agreement on a host of specific issues developed, leading to a reconsideration of the old policy. In the 1984 Assembly, the Liberation Task Force offered a procedure and a list of issues—economic justice, military spending, disarmament, foreign policy, civil rights—on which members would be authorized to take public stands in the name of the United States Grail. The proposal passed unanimously. It had taken ten years of patient work to bring about this change of attitudes.

Having laboriously set this formal procedure in place, we have never actually used it. Rather the discussion served to give members affirmation in taking political stands in their local areas as they worked with other groups on issues of peace and poverty. We did commit to voter registration as Grail, as well as to the Family Medical Leave Act and to antinuclear protests, but not through this formal process.[11]

Individual Commitments

A second measure of the Task Force's effectiveness is the work that individual members have chosen to do, either in paid employment or as volunteers. On the one hand, certainly many women came to the Grail because of a prior commitment to social justice and a strong desire to find like-minded people with whom to work. On the other hand, some of us—and I am one—came in search of companions for the spiritual journey and with little interest in social issues. In my college days I devoted myself to questions of literature and philosophy, looking for universal truths and not at all interested in social action with all its ambiguities. It was in the Grail that I first learned about my Christian responsibility to reach out to the poor. I eagerly embraced the analysis of secularism and its implications for cultural and institutional change. I remember hearing Vincent McAloon, a lay leader speaking at Doddridge Farm, pose the question for the lay apostolate: If fish are dying in a pond, should you try to get them out with a hook and line or a net? The answer, which he gave triumphantly, was "Neither. You should change the water." Changing the water became the metaphor for the goal of the apostolate—to create a society in which it would be easier for people to be just and generous. I think it is fair to say that both groups—those who joined the Grail out of a prior commitment to social justice and those whose justice consciousness was raised in the Grail— deepened their commitment as a result of their Grail work. Certainly, a major work of the Liberation Task Force has been the education of Grail members on social issues. They raised awareness in the entire movement and provided tools around issues of race and poverty.

The impact can be seen in the work of individual members. Many moved into careers in which they could educate and influence a wider public. Here are a few examples. Sally Timmel, returning to the United States after her years of work in Kenya, became legislative coordinator for Church Women United, tracking pending legislation in Congress, issuing regular bulletins to guide the lobbying efforts of the far-flung membership of this national organization. Dorothy Rasenberger, after five years as Grail national president and seven years on the staff of the San Jose Center, became the director of the Religious Network for Equality for Women (RNEW). She helped to develop a six-session program in basic economic literacy for women entitled, *Learning Economics, Empowering Women for Action*, which became the basis for a nationwide series of leadership training workshops, preparing participants to use these materials for education and action in their own communities. Several Grail members have served as diocesan social justice or religious education directors for their respective dioceses. Mary Anne Heidkamp and her husband, James Lund, after working for the diocese of Rochester, New York, collaborated on a popular manual, *Moving Faith into Action*, which has been widely used in parishes seeking to develop effective social justice programs. Donna Ambrogi, after years of working as a generalist on issues of poverty and ecumenism, entered law school in midlife in order to be more effective as a social change agent. She has used her legal training on behalf of the elderly in California, founding the California Law Center on Long-Term Care and teaching health law and elder law in universities in the San Francisco area. On retirement, Donna and her husband, Tom, served from 1992–1994 as volunteers in South Africa, with church groups and human rights groups, assisting that troubled nation in its transition to a new democratic regime.[12]

Sharon Joslyn, after her experience as a nurse with Grail teams in Brazil, in Clermont County, Ohio, and with migrant workers in Saginaw, Michigan, was looking for work in the northeastern United States to be near her aging parents. "At that time, I couldn't accept this country," she said, "but then I recognized elements of Latin America in the South Bronx. I was looking for signs and I found them in simple things: there were fruit and vegetable stands in the streets; the Church gave communion under both species; the hospital had a plaque stating its commitment to the community; the People's Convention, a national event, was being planned for Charlotte Street where presidents had come and made 'broken promises.' It looked like a place where I could work."[13] She invited Mary Kay Louchart to join her. They use their work—Mary Kay as a religious educator for the parish, Sharon as staff in a small health clinic—as a base for community development, with a special focus on women and girls. They work with neighborhood improvement projects, serve on the parish council and on the board of Nehemiah Housing, an ecumenical project for affordable housing. They offer leadership training for women from teenagers to grandmothers and have sponsored exchange programs with the Mexican Grail team. The emphasis is on empowerment—the women become leaders in the parish and community, the teenagers organize programs for neighborhood girls. Living in the community, working for the parish, they have become an integral part of a multicultural community that is primarily Hispanic and African-American.

Trina Paulus, a gifted artist, author of the best seller, *Hope for the Flowers*, has in recent years become a strong advocate for environmental issues in New Jersey, where she is living. Founder of Cornucopeia, New Jersey, an environmental group, she does research on issues of solid waste disposal and water pollution, gives public presentations, organizes lobbying and has turned the small plot of land around her house into a demonstration of composting and organic gardening.

Personally, my educational work around social justice issues has led me to a concrete involvement in developing affordable housing for women and children. My friend, Maureen Wood, who had her own construction company, invited me to help her organize a housing conference, Sheltering Ourselves, Developing Housing for Women and Children, held at the University of Cincinnati in August, 1987. But we were not satisfied with education and advocacy—we wanted bricks and mortar, or rather, we wanted housing that embodied the concept of "complete shelter care," that is, well-designed physical space, ready access to employment and to services like transportation, shopping, health care, schools and churches, and management policies that foster a supportive community in the housing complex. In February 1988, we drew together a group of twenty-six Cincinnati women, attracted by the idea of doing housing in a feminist way, and began to learn about the development process. We struggled with organizing ourselves on a feminist model, we bought a six-unit building in the inner city and learned about renovating and about landlord-tenant relations, and as of September 1994 we completed a major project: the remodeling of an old school building into forth-seven units of affordable housing, designed especially with the needs of single parents and elderly in mind.[14]

These are just a few stories, chosen from among many others—almost as many stories as there are Grail members.

Outreach to Wider Publics

It is more difficult to evaluate the Grail impact on a wider public. In the first twenty years, the emphasis in Grail programming was strongly spiritual and cultural; social justice concerns were present but rather in the background. Starting in the 1960s, the concern for social and political issues emerged explicitly in program content, especially in the long-term residential programs. Thus, Semester at Grailville included a community involvement component that required participants to spend one or two days a week in a field placement in the city or county. Learning teams organized around such topics as social change, Black Studies, Appalachia, City Hall, Native Americans at Wounded Knee, Personal/Political, Political Economy, Third World, and Feminism. Similar themes were explored in Seminary Quarter, and more recently in New Women, New Earth. Global Village, an annual one-week summer program for teenagers, exposes young women to issues of poverty and racism. In the 1980s, programs like Women Breaking Boundaries, which was repeated in different parts of the country, involved participants deeply in economic and political analysis.

The Liberation Task Force greeted the bishops' pastoral on the economy with enthusiasm and immediately went to work on plans for its implementation. They prepared a study packet for use of Grail groups and others. The responses from the groups using these materials were summarized and sent to Archbishop Weakland as the Grail response to the first draft. The next year, 1986, the Liberation Task Force called together a consultation of fourteen grassroots groups and five educators working on economic issues in the northeastern United States. They produced a detailed critique of the second draft, praising its strengths and pointing to its weaknesses: "It appears to us that its power has been weakened by numerous changes in expression and deletion of some of the clearest statements and most telling examples, as well as by constant undermining of its own points through qualification." The paper calls for "a more forceful confrontation of the moral schizophrenia between private and social morality in Catholic life," for "recognition of the immoralities of upper middle class consumerism and complacency," and for "more systemic analysis . . . e.g., of the role of the transnational corporations, monopolies, profit, exploitation of labor." This document was also forwarded to Archbishop Weakland. A committee of the task force met with one of the bishops on the pastoral committee, Bishop Peter Rosazza of Hartford, pointing out contradictions in the system, urging that the bishops maintain their moral outrage and prophetic stance, and putting forth ideas for implementing the pastoral on the parish level.

The periodic examination of conscience as to how the Grail is using its financial resources has led the San Jose Center to launch an ambitious program of housing development on their two-and-a-quarter acres in Our Lady of Guadalupe Parish. As of December 1995, they have almost completed predevelopment work on a plan that calls for thirty-five three- and four-bedroom townhouses together with a child care center, a Grail Center, and a house for community functions. The architectural design has been worked out cooperatively with prospective home buyers, maximizes green space for gardens and playground, and incorporates ecological considerations. Subsidies from the City of San Jose, the Sisters of Loretto and the California Housing Finance Agency make it possible to keep the housing affordable for low-income families. Building community, sustainability, diversity, and empowerment of women are the guiding principles of the San Jose Grail Housing Community.

Another effort to organize around economic issues was the Women's Alternative Economic Summit (WAEN), a network of women economists in which the Grail participated from its inception at the Nairobi Conference in Nairobi, Kenya in 1985. WAEN attempted to bring together academics and grassroots community groups to analyze the impact of the economy on women, to articulate just and sustainable economic alternatives, to share skills and strategies, and to stand together in solidarity with women in particular struggles. The members came together out of the insight that women, who are often the most affected by economic policies, have the least voice in their formulation.[15]

International Outreach

On the international level, the Liberation Task Force has contributed to the articulation of the Grail vision at the international general assemblies. Thus in the 1979 General Assembly, they called on Grail members "to be ever more aware of the relations of domination and submission which are embedded in our social, political and economic institutions" and "to challenge particularly the system of production for the profit of the few which does not meet basic human needs." They helped to establish the international Grail network for joint action for liberation leading to a new world order.

The Liberation Task Force and the Grail International Team organized Grail members into an "Urgent Action Network" through a telephone tree that has proved effective in mustering support for individuals in other countries suffering unjust arrest and detention. For instance, when South African Grail member, Zodwa Mbaso and her husband Peter, were seized by the South African security forces and held incommunicado in solitary confinement, the Network quickly mobilized a flood of letters and telegrams to officials in South Africa and in the United States that were influential in securing their release. They were never charged but apparently their offense was that they were active in organizing marriage courses in their parish in Soweto. We were particularly outraged because they were seized in the middle of the night and forced to leave their young children at home alone.

The Task Force, together with the United States International Team and the Cornwall Grail Center, has carried on many programs of international exchange, for example, between the South Bronx and Mexico; has held study weeks and prepared study packets for North Americans on South Africa, Central America, and the Philippines, and has conducted workshops on liberation in Costa Rica and Nicaragua. A particularly important meeting, Women of the Americas, was held in Mexico City in July, 1992, for one hundred and twenty-five women from thirteen countries of North, South, and Central America. Convened by Ann Burke and Peg Linnehan of the Cornwall staff and planned by a Grail team from Brazil, Mexico, Canada, and the United States, the meeting took advantage of the teachable moment provided by the 500th anniversary of Columbus's arrival on our shores to reexamine our history in terms of its impact on women's lives. As women from Brazil, Canada, Mexico, Nicaragua, El Salvador, Cuba, and the United States told their stories, four themes emerged: health—for ourselves, our families, our communities; the global economy and its disproportionately negative effects on women; racism—the pernicious legacy of colonialism, dividing us from each other; and spirituality—a women's spirituality, as the base for economic, political, and social renewal. It was painful and difficult to try to weave together the different histories. Given the diversities—racial, ethnic, class—it did not seem possible to fit the separate agendas into one whole. Nevertheless, the meeting concluded with a commitment "to maintain this flow of living energy by means of mechanisms of contact, interchange, and action between the women of the Americas."[16]

Conclusion

The fifty-five years of the Grail in the United States have seen many changes in the relation of the movement to social justice issues. Initially, we were inspired by Fr. van Ginneken's vision of "the elbow of time," a critical moment when things were in flux and radical change would be possible. We dreamed of young women who by giving themselves totally to God would create a torrent of love and generosity that would change culture and society. The vision was quite abstract, couched in the traditional terms of a society of justice, love, and peace.

The 1960s brought a new historical moment. We felt called to immerse ourselves in the struggle for justice in the world, to join in the economic and political struggles. The strong challenges arising out of our international connections pushed us toward a radical economic and political analysis. Individuals made their personal decisions to work with the marginalized, eagerly utilizing the new social analysis as a support for the work they were doing. The analysis was a necessary tool, not the cause of their choices. Choices came from their Christian commitment. The next chapter looks at the ways in which the new ideas have found expression in Grail work in the two-thirds world. The final chapter examines how the Christian commitment has been maintained in the midst of the changes in our understanding of theology and spirituality.

15

From Lay Missions to Multicultural Exchanges

We began the overseas service program in the 1950s under the rubric of "lay missionaries." The phrase was a useful shorthand, easily understandable to the Catholic public on whom we depended for financial support and having the added attraction of something new and daring. Team members continued to use this language as a quick way to explain themselves to Catholics back home, but they saw themselves rather differently. From the beginning they had two other goals that influenced their self-understanding: they were committed to developing an indigenous women's movement that would be part of one worldwide Grail, and they sought to value and adapt to the local culture as part of that effort. As they gained experience and worked out the implications of their commitments, they moved more and more toward the ideal of multicultural exchanges.

By 1963, as mentioned above, there were a hundred Americans working on international Grail teams in Mexico and Brazil, in Indonesia, in Egypt, South Africa, Uganda, Tanzania, Kenya, and West Africa. Grail teams were deeply influenced by the work of Paulo Freire, author of *Pedagogy of the Oppressed*. "No education is neutral," he insisted. Either the educator is domesticating the students, training them to accept the status quo, or liberating them to take control of their lives. As Grail, we were definitely on the side of liberation.

As the teams studied and practiced the rapidly evolving ideas of community development, they found themselves pressured by conflicting forces. According to community development principles, the task of the foreign helper was not to impose her ideas but to empower the local people to define their own goals and devise the methods and structures for reaching them. Clearly this approach was essential for the Grail goal of developing an indigenous movement. However, in order to enter the scene at all, to gain a foothold, to get acquainted with the people and their culture, Grail teams had to start in the existing institutions, and the existing Catholic institutions—hospitals, schools, churches and parishes—were built on Western, mainly European, cultural patterns. Moreover, in Africa, we found that the people wanted the Western institutions. They wanted to belong to the modern world, wanted Western science and technology, Western certificates and university degrees, as evidence of that belonging.

Even when, as in Uganda, we were invited to start from scratch a Catholic secondary school for girls, we found that Archbishop Kiwanuka, the first African bishop of modern times, as well as the parents of our prospective students, wanted the girls to earn a certificate from the state system. That system had been established by the British colonial government and was connected to the British universities. The curriculum was thoroughly British, very good for its kind and holding the students to strict standards, prescribing the study of Shakespeare and other classics of English literature. The language of instruction was English, even at the village level, where teachers fluent in English were scarce. All the tests came from England. "I taught world geography and the history of East Africa, with emphasis on the British explorers," Anne Mercier told me. "One geography test seemed really unfair—students were required to identify the Brooklyn Bridge! I also worked in community development projects at the request of the local women. When we tried to set up crafts projects to preserve the local crafts, sometimes women would complain if they were not learning what they considered the modern thing. I remember one woman saying, 'You just don't want us to have sewing machines.' "[1] Mary Buckley had a similar experience at Pius XII University in Basutoland. She found that when she sought African crafts to decorate the dormitory, the students were not interested. They preferred plastic pitchers to the local ceramic pots and polyester dresses to the bark cloth garments of their mothers.

Some anthropologists trace certain stages in the meeting of a technically dominant culture with a traditional one. At first, the people of the host culture reject the new ways as irrelevant; then they see some aspects of modern medicine and technology as useful; then they tend to value all the modern ways and reject their own culture as old-fashioned. But eventually some of the intellectuals rediscover and appreciate aspects of their own culture and begin the difficult task of integrating old and new.[2]

In India, where Elizabeth Reid worked for a number of years, she found some highly educated young women who were beginning to voice a critique of Western cultural imperialism. She had trained a mobile team of young Indian women who took their van to the villages and to the city slums to give workshops and demonstrations. In 1975, she published the *Community Education Handbook* to make this work more widely available. The introduction, written by Indian Grail member Pearl Drego, analyzes the defects of the current development efforts. "The hand that

Figure 22. The student-teacher team of Mary Emma Kuhn and Mary Buckley with women students at Pius XII University in Roma, Basutoland, South Africa, 1953.

stretches to help also has a predatory claw and a paternal clutch. . . . The attitude of benevolent giving and philanthropic zeal is today quite suspect for it is often the handmaid of capitalism and economic domination. . . . All initiative is from the giver; the recipient is passive."[3] The new approach which she recommends works through a process of conscientization that enables people to discover the problems that are closest to them and to generate their own solutions. The people are free to take the initiative and make mistakes. The helpers share the life style of the local people as far as possible, aim at making themselves dispensable and enabling the people to become self-reliant.

The handbook contains materials and meeting outlines for a basic community education program: how to get started, tips on gardening, poultry keeping, nutrition, health, and child care. The educational approach repeats the saying:

> If I hear, I forget.
> If I see, I remember.
> If I do, I know.

However, the actual materials fall short of the excellent educational philosophy. Most of the material is just plain old-fashioned, teacher-centered lesson plans, relying on the expert speaking and perhaps using some visual aids.

Ten years later, in 1984, the Grail team of Anne Hope and Sally Timmel published *Training for Transformation*,[4] a handbook which grew out of the work they did in Kenya from 1973 to 1980. It represents a considerable advance over the earlier handbook. The three volumes combine Paulo Freire's method of conscientization, the principles of group dynamics and organizational development, a social analysis based on Marxist categories, and a Christian concept of transformation, and apply the resulting analysis to the concrete circumstances of each community. The book gives detailed methods for breaking the "culture of silence," for enabling the local people to take the initiative in uncovering their problems and originating solutions suited to their situation. The authors make clear the catalytic role of the outsider in raising questions and offering information while trusting the people to make the decisions. Their work attempts to exemplify Freire's comment on the real humanist:

> As they (members of the dominant class) move to the side of the exploited, they almost always bring with them the marks of their origins. Their prejudices include a lack of confidence in people's ability to think, to want, and to know. . . . They believe that they must be the executors of the transformation. . . . Trusting the people is the indispensable condition for revolutionary change. A real humanist can be identified more by his trust in the people which engages him in their struggle than by a thousand actions in their favor without that trust.[5]

Training for Transformation has been reprinted thirteen times since its first publication in 1984. It has been translated into Spanish, French, and partially into Arabic and Sesotho. Parts of the text have appeared in at least twenty other languages. A revised edition, published in 1995, expands the economic analysis, dealing with the globalization of the economy and its impact. Anne and Sally have completed an additional volume, dealing with ecology, environment, gender, racism, culture, and participatory governance, including policy-making on the micro- and macro-levels. It has been published by Intermediate Technology in London.

In Kenya, the government had made it illegal for more than five people to meet together without a permit unless they were doing religious education for the churches. Because the Grail team was working under the auspices of the Catholic bishops, they were able to build a large-scale social movement. Their program stressed the spiritual dimension as the source of hope and courage to persevere in the struggle for justice. They urged the users of the book to seek out the texts from their various religious traditions that reinforce the vision of transformation toward a just and peaceful society.

At the height of the movement in Kenya, over three million people—in a country of twenty million—were involved in programs for literacy, women, youth, cooperatives, economics. A national advisory committee of forty people, men and women, developed plans and projects at a national level. Sixty Kenyans worked full time in the different dioceses, and the budget ran to $3,000,000 a year. Funds came from many sources: Anne and Sally had more access to the European Catholic funders than the bishops did. However, while the bishops liked what the program accomplished in their own dioceses, they were uneasy about lay control of such large budgets. They were also uneasy at the level of critical thinking and initiative of the laity who had participated in the program. Anne and Sally turned the program over to the Kenyans in 1980. A few years later, the bishops disbanded the national team. However, most dioceses continue to have their own training program. Most of the forty people on the national and diocesan teams have continued to work in development education although many left the church agencies where their initiatives were not accepted and transferred to various nongovernmental organizations. As Clarissa Pinkola Estes remarks in her popular book, *Women Who Run with the Wolves*, "Asking the right questions is unlocking the psyche and you can't take that back."[6] Unlocking the blocked energies breaks the accustomed patterns of institutional behavior, a frightening prospect for the bureaucrats, who tend to respond with repression, but the questions, once raised, do not go away.

Another example that concretized the idea of multicultural exchanges was the Cultural Exchange Meetings on Africa, a project that took place in 1974. Audrey Sorrento together with Alice Dougan and Leni Schaareman, both of whom had extensive experience in East Africa, organized the five-month program that brought thirteen women from five African countries to the United States for a real learning exchange. The thirteen Africans shared their experience with Americans, touring the country from New York to San Francisco, giving a total of twenty-six workshops to diverse American groups. At the same time, they visited their counterparts in U.S. educational, medical, and social service agencies. They met with UN agencies, with Catholic and Protestant church groups, and with representatives of various movements—the YWCA, the United Farm Workers, the American Indian Movement, the American Federation of Teachers, the Gray Panthers, the League of Women Voters, and an African Students' Organization. Grail members and friends in the various places arranged the contacts and offered hospitality. In their summing up, they spoke of "a new awareness both of our own cultures and the cultures of other people, a realization of the need for critical self-evaluation of our attitudes and values."[7]

Approaches to the Question of Universal Values

Every culture has its own ways of dealing with food, clothing, and shelter, with organizing sexual relations and birthing and raising the next generation, with organizing economic and political life, with defining social relationships and giving expression to the spiritual dimensions of life. Acquaintance with other cultures helps to relativize Western ways of doing things, makes us aware of our own assumptions, and raises the question of whether there are any universal values. Certainly no culture is perfect. It is equally certain that criticism from an outsider is not likely to win acceptance from the insiders. As I look at how Grail teams in the field have dealt with this issue, I find several areas of concern where they as Westerners are deeply attached to certain values and practices. There is the general area of health—hygiene, sanitation, and modern medicine. The teams, doing their utmost to be sensitive and tactful, have educated local leaders on the reasons for such practices as building latrines, using boiled water for drinking and cooking where the local water supply is poor, washing fruits and vegetables before eating them, cutting the umbilical cord with a sharp, sterilized knife rather than a broken bottle. The local leaders in their turn find ways of disseminating the practices in their communities.

A second area has to do with approaches to decision-making. African cultures tend to be conservative and traditional, with great emphasis on respect for the elders and their authority. In the 1979 International General Assembly, we Westerners wanted to move from one international president to an international presidency team of three. The Tanzanians in particular objected—they were more comfortable with a hierarchical pyramid structure and wanted to be able to introduce *the* International President of the Grail to their bishop. We assured them that whichever one of the three came to visit could be introduced as *the* President, if they wished, and then proceeded to outvote them. However, I now think that we could perhaps have handled the question more sensitively, as April McConeghey told me her team had dealt with some decisions in Tanzania.

April had gone to Tanzania in 1974 at the invitation of Imelda Gaurwa, a leader of the Grail in Tanzania, who had asked the International Grail for help in staffing the school at Kisekibaha. Begun in 1971, with the encouragement of Eileen Schaeffler, the first American to serve as the Grail's International President, Kisekibaha was the first Grail Center in Africa to be started and staffed entirely by indigenous African leadership. April was attracted by the idea of working in an all-African setup, where she would be the only "European," despite warnings from experienced missionaries that "it never works to live where you are the only expatriate." But African students come to the United States and manage to survive in a strange culture as the only foreigner in an American group. "If they can do it, I can try it," April told me. "I went to help meet a need of the indigenous Grail members on their terms, as they saw it, in their way."

April described her approach to two questions: greater spontaneity in the liturgy, and wider sharing of leadership responsibility. Living in an hierarchical culture and an hierarchical church, the young women at the Grail Center were accustomed to praying in clearly structured ways. Thus, at Mass, when they offered specific intentions during the prayers of the faithful, individuals, who were officially appointed for this task, wrote their prayers down ahead of time and read them in a pre-assigned order. April suggested that if anyone at the moment wanted to add something, the group should let them do it. "Let's just try it," she said. Slowly, so slowly the group did not realize it was happening, more and more people spoke up at the moment, and the custom of writing prayers down gradually withered away. Similarly, with styles of leadership, the culture expects—and almost demands—a highly authoritative style. Imelda Gaurwa, as a founder of the Grail in Tanzania and one of the elders, was expected to tell the others what to do and they would do it. In the 1970s the Grail internationally was emphasizing shared responsibility and shared leadership. After Imelda gave reports on this policy from the International Council meetings she attended, the group grew accustomed to the idea and were able to accept the policy and elect a National Team. They soon recognized that alongside the finally responsible leader, they needed a wider group to consider policies and decisions for the whole Grail in Tanzania.

Still another question of how to handle a conflict in values arose for April. She made a point of sharing in whatever work had to be done, including the manual work. In the African culture, a sign of respect for an elder or a teacher is to do things for them—carry their books, do their dishes, wash the floor. April, influenced in childhood by Quaker ideas of doing your share and taking care of your own needs, felt very uncomfortable with these practices. "The things they did made me feel like they thought I was probably incompetent and they wished I really wasn't there." Even after she understood that they intended respect and accepted their help, the value of manual work was so basic for her that she could not change her feeling. After a time, she was able to tell them how she felt and they got used to her sharing in the hard work of clearing brush and carrying 2'x4's, rocks and buckets of water to the site for a new building. She observed that in the village where she was known as a teacher at the school, the families she visited always received her as an honored guest in the living room. In the place where she had helped to erect a building, even to the extent of carrying 2'x4's on her head in the local fashion, the families received her in the kitchen, as one of themselves, not an outsider. She entered into the culture to a remakable degree, quickly gaining fluency in the language and being able to think and dream in Swahili. In fact she had internalized Swahili thought patterns and speech patterns to such a degree that they influenced her English speaking style. When she first returned to the States, her speech reflected the measured rhythms of Swahili. She also internalized many of the cultural norms. "One day I heard myself saying 'What a beautiful girl! such a fine space between her front teeth!'"[8]

Impact of the Overseas Service Programs

As of 1995, out of the hundred Americans who have served overseas with the Grail, a dozen are still working outside the United States. How can one evaluate the impact of the half century of work by American Grail teams in the two-thirds world? It is no easy task, but I can point to certain indices.

The Americans had an impact within the Grail itself as members of international teams. They raised the consciousness of the Europeans about the culture-bound assumptions underlying a hundred and one details of daily life—menus, how to set the table, what clothing was appropriate. Two issues were particularly important: the relation of nucleus and non-nucleus and the style of leadership. Because we had started in the United States from the perspective of a broad-based movement, we were used to working in teams of nucleus and nonnucleus who were equally Grail. The Dutch made more of a distinction: the nucleus people were Grail; the women trained at Ubbergen[9] were not. "When there was a crisis—a bad accident with the car, for instance—then we all pulled together as Grail," one team member told me. "But once the crisis was over, we pulled apart again."[10] In the 1960s, this was a source of tension in Uganda, for example, but the American model has influenced the development of the Grail in East Africa. From the beginning, there have been married and single as well as celibate members in the African Grail. In the United States, we had been evolving toward shared leadership and participative decision-making for quite some time before the decisive structural changes of the International General Assemblies of 1965 and 1967. "In Uganda, having a voice in decision-making was new to the Africans and the Europeans," Alice Dougan told me. "We helped to move things along toward shared leadership instead of one anointed one."[11]

As to the impact of Grail teams on the countries where they worked, certainly they have passed on a variety of specific skills—medical, educational, religious—to the local women. As Jessica Stuber commented, reflecting on her seven years in Uganda, "One of the best things we did was to teach the women practical skills—how to mix powdered milk with the mashed bananas to wean the babies, how to identify diseases, how to wash

Figure 23. Jessica Stuber, about to plow a field at the Grail Center Mubende, Uganda, in 1962, in order to start a banana plantation. In Uganda, plowing is a man's work. Seeing Jessica on the tractor, the men addressed her with the forms of speech used for men.

fruits and vegetables before eating them, how to build latrines. We did good work helping the women to maintain the old crafts—basketry, bark cloth, drum-making—rather than bring in plastic. The spirituality was woven in with the practical."[12]

Gail Malley, who worked in Egypt from 1955 to 1978, helped to set up a project in Akhmim, Upper Egypt, to meet the needs of illiterate, housebound women. On getting acquainted with the women, Gail and her teammate learned that they were eager to get out of the house and earn money. The team developed a project in which the women used their skills in embroidery to reproduce old Coptic designs. Artist Trina Paulus was imported from Grailville to give design workshops and encourage the girls and women to undertake their own designs, inspired by the life around them. Each year, under the sponsorship of the Catholic Association of Schools in Upper Egypt, they put on an exhibit and sale in Cairo, which is well received. The women have a reason to leave their homes to go to the workshop; they earn money for the first time in their lives. Moreover, they have learned how to manage their enterprise as a cooperative. Many have gone back to school, many learned to read and do arithmetic—the project has opened doors for them.

Francine Wickes, a musician and liturgist, worked in Indonesia from 1954 to 1972. She learned the language, the dancing, how to play the gamelon. She was introduced to the rich cultural life, rooted in the ordinary people, whose singing, dancing, carving, painting—all their activities—are permeated with a vital spirituality that is imbued with Javanese mysticism. Her conclusion: "The Grail is primarily a Western movement. I question whether a culture rich in itself needs us." Nonetheless, as a teacher of liturgy, working in Catholic parishes, she was able to translate the liturgical songs into Indonesian. "They are still singing those songs," she told me. "It was a substantial contribution to the church."[13]

At another level, the mere fact of introducing independent women, who were not nuns, into other cultures has served as a catalyst, opening up new possibilities for indigenous women. Sometimes the presence of Western women has produced quite explosive effects. For instance, Anne Hope and Sally Timmel in 1970 were invited to take part in a program incorporating the Freire method at the University of Swaziland. There were eight women students at the University, for whom Anne and Sally offered a series on women. They also invited the faculty wives. The women did not want the men to attend the series. Immediately there was an uproar—the men were furious, declaring that they knew what was best for "their women." This incident played a part in the subsequent deportation of Anne and Sally as "prohibited immigrants." Sally returned to the States. Anne, who is South African by birth, returned to Johannesburg and her work with Steve Biko, the African leader who later died under mysterious circumstances while being held by the South African police. Anne worked intensively with Biko and his group of fifteen leaders on the Freire method combined with group dynamics. There were only two women in the group; when they raised the women's issue, they too caused an uproar. Radical men can be as sexist as other men, but as with colonialism, racism, and classism, once the questions are raised, they remain in consciousness and conscience.

In Uganda, the Grail training at the secondary school and at the Grail Center developed considerable self-esteem and self-confidence in the young women. Jessica Stuber noted that when she took a group of students from the Center to the dances at the nearby army base, "These young women, with at most a secondary education, were able to debate with the officers about the status of women—the bride price, the custom which required a woman to kneel when greeting a man, the status of a wife as a chattel valued only as child-bearer, housekeeper, and field worker."[14]

Perhaps the most lasting effect of the work of American and European Grail members in the two-thirds world is the building of an indigenous women's movement, for example, in East Africa. The fact that the Grail has focused on building one international movement has given a different starting point than that of many religious congregations who have trained the indigenous women to set up their own congregations. As Anne Hope observed, celibacy has an appeal for women in many of the African cultures. Many have blossomed in all-female religious communities.[15] The sense of belonging to a supportive community that is inclusive of different races and different vocations is a strong attraction for the Grail in East Africa. In spite of the difficullty of establishing the category of independent, single, laywomen in the African context, the Grail—as nucleus and movement—is growing in East Africa.

In 1995 Grail teams were at work in eighteen countries: Australia, Brazil, Canada, France, Germany, Italy, Kenya, Mexico, the Netherlands, Nigeria, Papua New Guinea, the Philippines, Portugal, Scotland, South Africa, Tanzania, Uganda, and the United States. Members of the American Grail have made a contribution in most of these countries. Some have entered so fully into their adopted country that they have chosen to stay permanently—like Mary Alice Duddy and Kay Kryvanek in Brazil, Carol White in the Netherlands, Marie Therese McDermit and Alice Kraemer (until her death) in Mexico. They become fluent in the language, form strong friendships, and feel fully accepted and at home in their new setting. Most return, after a shorter or longer time of work, enriched by their experience, with a deeper insight into their own culture, and a heightened awareness of the place of the United States on the international scene. They maintain friendships with their coworkers in other countries and are able to bring their international experience to bear on issues in the United States.

Always international exchanges go on as a normal part of Grail life— Frances Martin and Patricia Miller from Grailville spend five months in a Grail Center in Tanzania as visiting staff; Honorata Mvungi and Leocadia Malley, a Grail agricultural team from Tanzania, spend a year at Grailville, learning permaculture; Prisca Nakitto and Demmy Kangyenyenka return to Uganda after six months in the Grailville organic gardens; Catherine Leahy, longtime Grailville staffer, goes to the Philippines for a year to help set up an art and book store; Eva Fleischner spends the first four years after her retirement from a professorship at Montclair State University as volunteer staff at the Tiltenberg Grail Center in Holland; Jeanette Loanzan from the Philippines and Traude Rebmann from Germany serve on Grailville's program staff. And the worldwide network of women who want to transform the world grows wider and stronger.

16

From Religious Certainty
to Religious Search

The spirit is at the very heart of the Grail. We were founded for the spirit, not for any specific work, but to spread a spirit of fervent Catholicism in all spheres of life. Nowhere did the changes of the 1960s strike more deeply and painfully than in our religious life—our practices, our attitudes toward the Church, our self-understanding as women of faith. In this chapter I want to trace the evolution from our pre-Vatican II certainties to our present religious pluralism and religious search.

Pre-Vatican II

In the early 1940s, as mentioned above, we often spoke of the lay apostolate as "an all-saints movement." No real apostolate without holiness; no holiness without wholehearted giving of self to Christ; therefore, the necessity of a solid spiritual formation. To foster a fervent spirit, Grail training in the first twenty years of the movement in the United States stressed three aspects of Christian life: the liturgy, private prayer, and asceticism.

The liturgy was central to the formation program. It had an enormous impact on participants and visitors alike. As I interviewed dozens of women who had experienced Grailville in the 1940s and 1950s, the liturgy was almost invariably recalled as the heart of the program. "I loved the rhythm of life—the psalms, the prayer, daily Mass, singing the chant,"[1] one woman recalled. And another: "This is so beautiful—beautiful music, beautiful Mass, this is home."[2] We liked to quote Pope Pius X: "The primary and indispensable source of the true Christian spirit is the active participation of the faithful in the sacred mysteries and in the public and solemn prayer of the Church." Our goal was two-fold: to make the liturgy live for the participants and to live the liturgy, that is, to carry the spirit of the Mass throughout the day.

277

To make the liturgy live meant serious, sustained effort to enable the participants to experience the liturgy as the central, integrating force giving meaning to life. We were not satisfied with the theoretical understanding that the sacraments worked *ex opere operato* (by the work itself), that is, were certain to increase the divine life in any recipient who did not set up the obstacle of serious sin. We wanted a realization on the level of the concrete and personal; we wanted the individual to experience Mass, sacraments, and prayers of the Divine Office as invigorating sources of life. Therefore, we stressed the various practices described above: active participation through recited or sung Mass, offertory and communion processions, epistle and gospel read in English, a homily on the texts of the day. At a time when the ordinary parish offered a low Mass, hastily mumbled in Latin by a priest whose congregation was occupied with the rosary, Mass at the Grail was a new and energizing experience. Grailville quickly became a liturgical center, a magnet for clergy and laity who were seeking active participation around the altar.

Making the liturgy live also meant intelligent participation: we studied Benedictine Prosper Gueranger's classic fifteen volumes on the liturgical year, Father Pius Parsch's more pastoral works on the Mass, the breviary, and *The Church's Year of Grace* together with other commentaries and, of course, scripture. We invited the leaders of the liturgical movement, men like Reynold Hillenbrand, Gerald Ellard, H. A. Reinhold, Damasus Winzen, Benedict Ehmann, and Godfrey Diekmann,[3] to give courses at Grailville. It meant preparation: keeping the Great Silence to focus energies and come to the Mass in a recollected frame of mind; keeping Saturday as a day of special physical and spiritual preparations for the Sunday Mass as high point of the week. Saturday Mass preparations were a Grailville custom that translated readily to the cities. Most of the city centers organized Saturday evening Mass preparation groups, often with families meeting in one another's homes. At Grailville, on most Saturday nights, we would do our own version of matins, in English, a leisurely prayer hour, singing the antiphons and reading lessons chosen from contemporary sources.

Living the liturgy meant carrying the spirit of the Mass through the day with meal prayers, a breakfast reading and discussion, vespers before supper and compline before bed, and, most important, by endeavoring in our every action to remain true to the gift of self made at the altar. The sacraments worked automatically, as it were, but during the rest of the day, growth in grace depended on the disposition of the individual. One tried to be open and responsive to the inspirations that the Holy Spirit offered through every activity during the day.

As the Mass was the heart of each day and Sunday the summit of the week, the liturgical year was the unifying thread that set the mood and rhythm of the year. We were deeply imbued with a sacramental outlook, expressed, for example, in the notion of the three comings of Christ at Christmas: in history at Bethlehem, in mystery in the Mass and sacraments every day, in majesty at the end of time. The Mass and the feasts and fasts of the liturgical year were more than mere historical commemorations, as, say, February 22 commemorates the birth of George Washington. Our God had entered history, enabling us to live on a new plane, the level of the divine life. Through living the liturgical year, we relived the mysteries of Christ's life, death, and resurrection and his sending of the Spirit at Pentecost, and thus were growing in grace. This vision gave profound, satisfying meaning to the most ordinary activities of daily life. Washing the dishes, baking the bread, weeding the garden, greeting each other, receiving a guest—all could speak to us of the mystery of the divine life within us, all could be occasions to increase that life. Texts, in calligraphy on the walls of the work areas, served as reminder of the sacramentality of daily life: "He fed them with the fat of wheat," in the bakery; "Wash me, O Lord. Make me whiter than snow," in the laundry.

Liturgy and private prayer were seen as complementary, meant to nourish and enliven each other. Private prayer was fed by the liturgy—we usually remained in silent prayer for fifteen minutes after Mass—and by scripture study and other spiritual reading. For newcomers to the training program, the leader would choose from our fairly extensive library a book appropriate to her background and interests. Most days there was a group meditation, with the leader reading from a text of Abbot Marmion, Cardinal Newman, retreat leader Edward Leen, theologian Romano Guardini, Abbot Vonier, English writer Carol Houselander, or other spiritual writers, pausing often for discussion of examples and practical applications to daily life. The discussion was followed by at least half an hour of private prayer. We were very clear about the difference between reading and praying, encouraging the individual to put herself in the presence of God and speak from the heart to the Father, to Jesus, to the Spirit, or to Mary or the saints, and to pause often simply to be quiet and listen. Sometimes, especially in the fifteen minutes of silent prayer after Mass, the silence was intense—no one sneezed, or coughed or even moved a muscle. I felt I was in the presence of the Holy and I think others felt that too. At the same time, we were clear that one could not always expect to feel God's presence; that periods of dryness were to be expected; that one must stick to the scheduled times of prayer, even when, or rather, especially when they did not feel satisfying.

The arts—music, visuals, dance, drama, literature—played a significant part in nourishing prayer life. We were critical of the weak, sentimental, and garish images that abounded in American Catholic life. We searched art history and contemporary work for vigorous, well-designed religious images, and the artists in the group strove to produce both prints and sculpture to meet this need. Sometimes we acted out scripture passages or interpreted psalms or hymns in dance as ways of making a sacred text come alive for the participants. From time to time, we wrote and produced liturgical dramas for public presentation, combining music, dance, speaking chorus, and choir in *Desired of the Nations* on Advent themes or *The New Eve* on the task of woman. These dramas were prayerful on two levels: the performers meditated on the texts, endeavoring to unite their technical skills in music and movement with a prayerful spirit; and the performances themselves were intended to move the audience with a Christian message.

Perhaps most important of all in feeding private prayer was music. One of the regular work groups was the schola, the best singers, responsible to sing the more difficult chant and polyphony, to teach the rest of us, and to write new music, adapting the Gregorian melodies to English texts. We had a large repertoire of antiphons in English, published as *Feast Day Melodies*. We were steeped in the chant. I found that the melodies echoed in my consciousness, like a mantra, rising spontaneously in memory as I walked the paths or weeded the garden, contributing to a spirit of recollection throughout the day.

The third foundation stone for the Christian life was asceticism, based on accurate self-knowledge and on a self-discipline that aimed at doubling one's talents and halving one's faults. The training was based on the classic means—silence, fasting, watching (i.e., rising in the night for prayer), hard physical labor, willingness to accept criticism and admit faults. The emphasis was basically positive and apostolic. If we were to be real lay apostles, we needed to develop our talents and use them for the apostolate. Fr. van Ginneken thought that women did not suffer much from pride or gluttony, but rather from timidity and finickiness. Women, in his opinion, were often too passive and submissive and should learn to speak up and take responsibility. As mentioned earlier, the Grail motto, nothing *pro forma*, applied with full force to all our spiritual practices. Nothing should be done as a matter of routine. We were urged to use creativity and imagination in drawing up a personal program. For a fussy eater, there was no point in fasting; rather she needed to expand her taste to all kinds of food. A shy person should learn to speak out, to give talks in public. A person vain of her appearance should wear the same outfit every day for the four weeks of Advent. At the beginning of Advent and Lent, the group would meet and discuss what practices we would adopt in common, for example, fasting on the Ember Days in order to give to the poor, or the lovely custom of Kris Kringle by which we each drew a name from a hat, our Kris Kringle. Each day during Advent one tried to do something nice for her Kris Kringle without revealing her own identity. It certainly strengthened a caring spirit in the group. One year, during World War II, out of solidarity with all those without fuel in war-torn Europe, we did not start up the furnace until Thanksgiving. After the common program was set, each individual would discuss her personal program with her leader or mentor, adding to the general discipline some specifics tailored to her particular needs.

The Grail was a vanguard group in the emphasis on the liturgy, on the laity, on spiritual leadership by women for women, but our theology and spirituality had deep roots in Catholic tradition. We were doctrinally orthodox and followed a classic, quite monastic spirituality. In fact, Carol Jackson, co-editor of *Integrity* magazine, dubbed us "nuncs" (her word play combining nuns and monks, a coinage with disparaging overtones) for the rather Benedictine pattern of life followed at Grailville. We wanted "An All-Saints Movement," and we did not want to be condescended to, either as laity or as women. Struggling to develop a lay spirituality, we used the sources that were available; there was very little written for laypeople who wanted more than the rosary at Mass and an annual parish mission. The training was given a characteristic Grail flavor by its experiential and participatory character and by the emphasis on the arts and the development of a Christian culture. Grail spirituality in our first twenty years in the United States proceeded from a strong sense of certitude and an equally strong sense of community. We lived the theology of the Mystical Body of Christ: we understood that we shared the life of grace, that our individual actions either diminished or increased this common life. One of the aspects of Grail spirituality that was especially meaningful to me was the this understanding and experience of community. It made it possible for me to have real and deep relationships with people with whom I had little in common in terms of our educational, national, racial, and class backgrounds. We could take for granted when we met Grail people from other cities or other countries that we shared a common vision, a common faith, and many common practices.

The Winds of Change

But in the 1960s, both the certainty and the commonality were rudely shattered. The social movements of the 1960s—civil rights, antiwar, student protests, the women's movement—brought enormous changes. Vatican II wrought equally great changes in the Church: a new self-understanding as the people of God on pilgrimage, a positive appreciation of the world, an emphasis on collegiality, a call to renewal of religious life. The changes came with dizzying speed. At one moment, the Church defined itself as the city on the hill, holding up the light of truth to a society trapped in the evils of secularism. Then, quite suddenly, we began to see God at work everywhere in the world, in the growth of human knowledge and especially in the struggles for justice, and at the same time we saw sin at work in the Church, for example, in its failure to confront naziism and fascism. The atmosphere in both church and society became antiestablishment and antiauthoritarian. The controversies surrounding contraception contributed in no small measure to a new independence of mind among Catholics. After the publication of *Humanae Vitae* in 1964, church teaching on sexuality lost credibility with many thoughtful Catholics, who began to trust their own experience and judgment, and, at the same time, continued to consider themselves "good Catholics." Priests and nuns by the thousands reevaluated their commitment to celibacy and sought release from their vows.

In the midst of the tumult, the Grail, as a movement that helped to prepare the way for Vatican II, became an important gathering place for clergy, religious, and laity who were struggling with the profound changes that were shaking both church and society. A series of week-long summer seminars at Grailville, beginning with Charles Davis on "The Mission of the Church" in 1964 and ending with Eugene Fontinell on "Death" in 1972 dealt with a range of related issues: the autonomy of the secular in the light of Vatican II; how to build "The City of Man" [sic] in a truly human and humane way; the meaning of commitment in celibacy and in marriage; contemporary religious experience; the insights from other traditions— Protestant, Jewish, Buddhist; the meaning of radical social and political change for faith; where to find hope for the future. The 1972 program, the last in this series, dealt with death both on an individual level and on the level of the community, faced with letting go of old ways—it became a time of grieving for what was dying in Catholic culture. The diversity of human experience was breaking the boundaries of the old categories. The frameworks of orthodoxy and hierarchy could no longer contain all the new impulses. All these seminars were intense experiences of community, in the Grail educational mode. They were experiential and process-oriented, helping participants to leave behind old categories and to see reality not as a set of unchanging essences but as an ever-evolving process. The major contribution, in the view of Bill Birmingham, an editor of *Cross Currents*, who helped to plan several of these events, "was to affirm the questioning. People were learning that they were permitted to have thoughts and feelings without worrying about them. This revolutionized groups like the Grail and indeed the whole Church."[4]

The Primacy of Personal Conscience

Personalism and ecumenism were alive in the Grail before Vatican II. As a result of the Grail's ecumenical work, a number of Protestant women sought membership in the U.S. Grail, attracted by people and programs, delighted to find a community with whom they shared so many values. As Barbara Troxell, an ordained Methodist and one of the first Protestant Grail members, wrote: "It was the worship and the communal life of the Grail that drew us to participation—the centrality of the Eucharist, the best of Christian tradition and practice and the liberation of women and other marginalized persons in church and world."[5] Protestant participation raised a question of self-definition. We had started as a Catholic movement, with a big "C." But our own group ethos was existential and favored inclusivity, and this ethos won out. In 1969, the General Assembly of the United States Grail voted to admit women of other Christian traditions as full participants, recognizing that on both sides there would be some problems around common worship but also mutual enrichment in our understanding and living of Christian faith. In 1975, as a result of the Living Judaism Institute at Grailville and other contacts with Jewish women, the question of Jewish participation arose. Again the existential ethos won out; two Jewish women were welcomed as Grail members, and the question of what this might mean for Grail identity as a Christian movement was left for further reflection. In dealing with these and other issues, we used a process that would later be named as feminist, though I do not think we used that name at the time. First, trust the experience of individual women, then share the experience in a communal reflection, then do the analysis. Having developed relationships with Protestant and Jewish women, we tended to move intuitively and experientially to the practical decision, often able to decide by consensus, and trusting that in due course reflection and further experience would solve knotty questions of group identity.

The affirmation of Protestant membership was at the same time an affirmation of the primacy of individual conscience over common beliefs. We had already accepted the primacy of individual conscience in the matter of lifetime commitment. Those who reevaluated their choice of celibacy in the Grail nucleus and decided that their decision had been immature or for other reasons was now inauthentic were released from their nucleus commitment, choosing whether or not to remain in the movement. With Protestant membership, we had admitted a degree of religious pluralism. But by 1969, we found that the pluralism extended in quite another direction, to Catholics who had lost their faith. Some women deeply involved in the Grail were finding the institutional church more and more irrelevant to their lives and were disassociating themselves from it. As one Grail member wrote in a working paper on "Participation in the Grail of Concerned Persons without Religious Affiliation":

> We have people trying to maintain the old structures and categories without modification, and people who find that their human experience keeps overflowing those categories.

A striking feature of the Overflow People is their search for a basis for human values—Christians who have outgrown Papal Infallibility or Scriptural Fundamentalism and Humanists who have outgrown Scientific Determinism are all saying to themselves, "There's got to be more to it than this—but what?"[6]

The writer goes on to insist that truth, so far as it exists, is highly fragmented and therefore it behooves us to be open to truth wherever we find it. She calls on the Grail to be open to the full richness of human struggles and aspirations in all traditions. Another paper, written at the same time, asks, "Can we find a way to present the Grail as a movement with a Christian heritage that incorporates the possibility of a free religious search?" and answers its own question: "Through commitment to the task of the Grail in its fullness, we are called beyond ourselves in a way that is broader than any religious specification. . . . Previously the common vision could be assumed before you even knew the person; now we must discover it in interpersonal interaction . . . we need freedom to question, freedom to have certainties."[7]

Openness and Diversity

Grail members, individually and collectively, soon launched themselves into the free religious search. Some simply selected from the tradition the elements they found meaningful and let the rest go. A few found inspiration in the charismatic movement. Some found that they were unable to relate in any positive way to what they saw in their tradition. Many, whatever their basic stance, found insight and energy in the religious disciplines of other cultures, such as Native American, Asian, and African. In search of resourcement, others turned to new perceptions brought forward by the arts, science, psychology, and the contemporary feminist and liberation movements. Individuals turned to yoga and zen, to the intensive journal method of psychologist Ira Progoff, to psychosynthesis. Some saw themselves as taking part in a far-reaching Christian process of death and resurrection of Christian cultural forms that would eventually bring the tradition into a new relation with the aspirations of our world.[8]

It was exceedingly painful for a group that had always found its deepest unity in the Catholic Eucharist to realize that the Eucharist was now a source of disunity. We wanted to be able to celebrate together; we wanted to be able to affirm each individual in her religious options. As a group, we experimented with new prayer forms. We had always done some experimenting with contemporary materials, choosing lessons from current literature, composing our own English antiphons, voicing our own prayer intentions, and sharing our own spontaneous prayers, but remaining within the traditional forms of the Mass and the hours of the Divine Office. We had also devised some new rituals to meet contemporary needs, for example, the solemn engagement and the blessing of the bride on the night before the wedding.

In the 1970s, we became much more free in our experiments with worship, trying out new ways in both form and content as we attempted to meet the challenges posed by ecumenism, feminism, and the cosmological/ecological perspective of Thomas Berry and Brian Swimme.

Already in 1972, the Protestant women taking part in the week-long seminar, "Women Exploring Theology," had taken advantage of the freedom of the Grailville Oratory to devise a wide variety of feminist liturgies, a practice continued in Seminary Quarter, a six-week summer session for women in graduate theological study, offered from 1974 to 1978. Sheila Goldstein of the Living Judaism Institute introduced the first Seminary Quarter participants to the Jewish Sabbath ritual, which became a significant part of their Grailville experience. As Christians we celebrated on Saturday night, since our Sabbath is the Sunday, but we found the ritual form both flexible in allowing for Christian content and deeply satisfying in its symbolism. In 1976, the "Good Red Road," a one-week seminar at Grailville explored Native American spirituality and practice. This seminar later was documented in an issue of *Cross Currents*, a quarterly review devoted to exploring the significance of Christianity for our times.

When in 1973 the Grail Council decided to establish "Religious Search" as one of the three national task forces, Eleanor Walker, Marian Ronan, and Francine Wickes, who had been working on the religious issues, did not want to call their team a "Task Force." They thought that it was somehow on a different, more fundamental level than the other two, but nevertheless the name "Religious Search Task Force" stuck. Some years later the team (by this time composed of other people) took the name "Religious Undergirding of the Grail," giving the unfortunate acronym RUG. Still later, the name "Religious Dimension" was adopted.

One of the first activities of the Religious Search Task Force was to host a two-week meeting for Grail members from eight countries on the search for God, to study:

1. questions and affirmations relating to the person of Jesus Christ and to the Church;
2. insights that other religious traditions have to contribute to our own spiritual awareness;
3. the spiritual dimensions of our contemporary human/historical experience;
4. myth, symbol, ritual, and our contemporary culture.[9]

In 1975 to meet the growing need for nonsexist materials to inspire individual and corporate prayer, the Task Force produced the *Grail Prayer Book*, which was never formally published because of copyright problems but was distributed to Grail members only. The two hundred-twelve neatly mimeographed pages include prayers and readings from a wide range of sources: Native American, Jewish, African, Buddhist, Eskimo, Moslem, Hindu, contemporary secular poets, as well as Chritian writers, ancient and modern. The major section of the book consists of a nonsexist version of most of the psalms. In her thoughtful preface, Marian Ronan, the editor, writes, "The undertaking is not a simple one, with literary, aesthetic, historical, and theological as well as feminist considerations influencing the work." After a discussion of the ways in which she has tried to achieve a balance between male and female images of God, she raises a deeper theological question, what to do with the word "Lord," and its masculine connotations. She writes:

> In the New Testament, the proclamation "Jesus is Lord" seems to be really central. . . . One has to raise the question, at least, of whether the simple deletion of "Lord" does not tend in the direction of reducing Christianity to a contentlessness that is virtually worthless. On the other hand, a true adherence to the deepest symbols of the Christian message, to death and resurrection as our real call, may demand an end to some apparently essential kerygmatic language. . . . I certainly do not know the answer to this question. . . . I do know, however, that when we in the Grail speak of committing ourselves to living out the tension between feminism and Christianity, it is to hard questions like these that we are committing ourselves, and we do not have any idea, as yet, how deeply they are likely to touch the fabric of our lives.[10]

The section on "Canons, Liturgies and Series of Prayers" includes a number of versions of the canon of the Mass by contemporary writers, two attempts to modernize the renewal of baptismal vows (leaving out Satan and all his works and pomps), and various prayer services full of references to specific injustices in our present world. When we published *Promised in Christ* in 1955, we followed our usual practice of submitting the manuscript to the archdiocesan censor for an *imprimatur*, that is, the bishop's stamp of approval. We ran into difficulties with the juridical mind-set of the priests in the chancery office. Their first concern was that we make clear that the engagement, even if solemnized in church, was not legally binding, but might make the parties liable to a breach of promise suit. In the censor's official report to the bishop, he was especially concerned that we not give the impression that this procedure was part of the official liturgy of the

Church. To institute a ceremony or ritual was reserved to the Holy See, that is, the Pope; it was most certainly not within the scope of "girls at Grailville." By 1975 we were no longer concerned with imprimaturs, nor were the priests who had written several of the canons.

Throughout the 1970s the women's liberation movement with its consciousness-raising groups raised more and more penetrating challenges to all the institutions of society, including the churches and religious movements. The same process went on within the Grail, fueled in part by the general atmosphere of contemporary culture, in part by the many programs on feminist themes organized by the Grail Women Task Force. To deal with the resulting tensions between feminism and Christianity within the movement, we made a number of efforts specifically for Grail members: consciousness-raising sessions for the Grail Council in the spring of 1974, a sexuality workshop for Grail members in July 1974, two questionnaires on Christianity and feminism circulated by the WTF, intensive study days in May 1975, in preparation for the 1975 General Assembly, a program focused on Feminism and Christianity in fall 1975, a weekend on Feminism, Socialism and Christianity in March of 1977, sponsored by the three task forces.

Of particular importance in confronting the tension head-on was the week-long program in June of 1978, "Image-Breaking, Image-Building," organized by Eleanor Walker and Marian Ronan of the Grail and Linda Clark of Union Theological Seminary and funded by the Grail and the Committee on Women and the Church of the United Presbyterian Church. Their purpose was "to design an ecumenical seminar for women to explore the implications of feminism for styles and structures of Christian worship." Materials from the workshop were published in 1981 under the title, *Image-Breaking, Image-Building, A Handbook for Creative Worship with Women of Christian Tradition*. The accent is on creativity. In the introduction, the authors note,

> From the most primary level of conceptualization—that of the creation of mental images—the idea that God is male controls our religious lives. Furthermore, we are surrounded by male-dominated structures of authority in the church which subtly (and not so subtly) subvert the reality that God transcends the gender differentiation of human beings. We live out male-determined views of our own sexuality as well as God's. Finally, we participate in rituals that too often equate openness to God's grace with submission to (male) authority.[11]

They go on to point out the relation between language and patriarchy and to invite the women in the churches to find new ways to name their experience of God and to free their imaginations from the stranglehold of the traditional patriarchal images. They encourage women to claim themselves and their experience as authoritative. Most of the book consists of exercises designed to increase awareness of the individual's own religious depths as a source of new images of God together with a collection of the resources that emerged from these exercises. The resources include guidelines for the planning of rituals, a list of occasions for which rituals are needed, sample rituals for a meal, for celebrating the equinox, for ending a close relationship, for saying good-bye to the dying, and a variety of original prayers and poems. We found that changing traditional symbols could provoke some explosive reactions.. At one point in the week, in order to make the environment more suitable for a Native American ritual, the cross behind the altar in the Oratory was taken down. Two nuns in the group were so upset by what they saw as sacrilege that they immediately shook the dust of Grailville from their feet.

The book proceeds from a conviction that women's experience can be a *locus theologicus*, a source for knowledge of God, and that by reestablishing this truth we are righting a centuries-old wrong that associates women with the evil powers of darkness, sexuality, and earthiness and men with light, rationality, and transcendence. The authors insist that while the contradictions between feminism and Christianity are real, they are not irreconcilable, and suggest that "some may for a time have to bracket out reference to Jesus Christ in their definition of worship."[12] They see their work as a small step in ridding the biblical tradition of its sexism.

A third influence important to our worship experiments has been the scientific cosmology and ecological theology of Thomas Berry and Brian Swimme. Berry tells the New Story of the creation, incorporating the latest scientific thinking about the billions of years of evolution from the primordial particle that split into hydrogen and helium to the present complexity of the universe with all its galaxies, the solar system, the earth, its atmosphere, its living forms, and finally, the humans in whom the universe becomes conscious of itself. The old story, told in Genesis, of a transcendent creator establishing a static universe with man (male) as its crown and ruler, gave unity and meaning to Western civilization for centuries, but it has been discredited. Moreover, it is implicated in the present ecological crisis. Its emphasis on the immortal soul destined for eternal unity with the transcendent God has led humans to think of ourselves as separate from and above nature. Its emphasis on man as the ruler, "all things beneath his feet," has justified the exploitation of the natural world to the point where today as we pollute earth, air, and water with man-made toxins, we are on the verge of shutting down the major life systems of the planet. Berry turns to the New Story, the evolutionary story, as the context that will give meaning and value to human life, putting humans firmly within nature, creating an awareness of our dependence on the other members of the earth community, restoring a sense of reverence for the cosmic process and our role in it. We have tried to concretize this evolutionary vision through ritual, particularly during Holy Week, which from the earliest days of the US Grail has been a magnet drawing friends from near and far into a worshiping community of both sexes and all ages. In the vigil on Holy Saturday, we tell the New Story; we lift up the elements of earth, air, fire, and water through the arts—banners, music, dance, poetry. In place of the renewal of baptismal vows, the community makes a solemn earth commitment, spelling out what we must do "to ensure a future for life on planet earth." Audrey Schomer, who describes herself as "a cosmic troubador," has developed a prayer hour built on the notion of the evolutionary time line, laid out, somewhat in proportion, in a spiral on the Oratory floor, with markers indicating such crucial events as the formation of our solar system, the appearance of the chemical elements, the first life forms on earth, the beginning of photosynthesis, the first animals, and finally the first humans, appearing at the very end of the spiral, represented by the last tiny fraction of an inch. Individuals walk this time line in meditative silence and at the end introduce themselves in terms of their place in the cosmos and frame a wish or a prayer for the future.

Affirming Diversity in Community

As individuals pursued their diverse spiritual journeys, we found that it was much easier to affirm diverse journeys in the abstract than in the concrete. My first experiences with a Protestant Eucharist brought home this insight to me. One of our Protestant members, the Reverend Barbara Troxell, presided at a Eucharist in the Oratory, shortly after she was received into membership. I received communion from her, and found my Catholic sensibilities were quite disturbed. I understood that the Eucharist could be a means of unity, a sign of our desire to stand together even though we might not have exactly the same beliefs about the sacrament, but my feelings had been formed by the idea of the Eucharist as a sign of absolute unity. Catholic loyalty demanded one doctrine, transubstantiation, and one practice, a celebrant who put a paper-thin wafer on one's tongue. Also it felt strange, but exhilarating, to have a woman preside. My discomfort disappeared rather quickly, but I noticed that some other Grail members, particularly those who had been serving overseas and missed out on developments in this country, were sometimes uncomfortable when we had a woman celebrant and simply chose not to receive communion.

An insight that was helpful as we struggled to live with our religious diversities was theologian Paul Knitter's discussion of the difference between faith and belief in his book, No Other Name. Faith is like falling in love—the experience is intense but difficult to articulate. Belief is articulated and will be articulated differently in different traditions. Faith experience is prior to articulation of belief. Faith touches the Mystery which is in us and beyond us and which is ineffable, eluding our efforts to put it into words. When we speak of our experiences of the numinous, the Holy, the Sacred, we move into the realm of belief. We must perforce use the words and images that our particular subculture provides, with all their connotations and colorings of racism, sexism, classism, militarism, and other oppressions inherent in the culture. Moreover, when we speak of our faith experience, our personal idiosyncracies enter in—differences of temperament, personal history, education that make up each individual's unique standpoint. This insight helped us to accept different articulations of belief and to realize that all theology is contextual, based in the life situation of the individual or community doing the theologizing. We can try to honor the insights coming from each context and to keep the different theologies in dialogue with each other. Even before these distinctions were part of our vocabulary, we were careful, in the 1979 IGA statement of Grail identity to speak of "being rooted in Christian faith and challenged by the radical call of the Gospel," phrasings that do not imply a particular statement of belief.

The desire for a common celebration remained strong, no matter how diverse the paths of individual members became. The range of diversity posed knotty problems for those planning a General Assembly or a national meeting. On the one hand, we wanted to affirm those who were exploring new ways of worship; on the other hand, we did not want to pressure people into forms of participation that made them uneasy. Usually the planners solved the problem by planning two celebrations: a Mass offered by a Catholic priest in good standing and a Eucharistic celebration led by one of the ordained Grail members, ordained, that is, in one of the mainline Protestant churches. Often there would also be a third kind of celebration, noneucharistic, relating to the theme of the meeting. Carol White, one of the planners of the 1969 General Assembly, stated a policy based on our personalist orientation:

> Isn't our commitment . . . to search together as much as we can, and then to face and learn from our differences? And therefore, is it not appropriate that we *do* all come together in celebrations, but with each one participating in any particular celebration in the manner and degree her own convictions dictate. This implies an All Are Welcome policy—that everyone feels *invited* to participate as fully as she wishes. . . . But though everyone feels invited, no one

feels pressured. If you don't take communion from a Protestant celebrant, it doesn't mean you reject her or her church. It means that at this moment, you're *facing differences* in the celebration, while, by your very presence there and such participation as is true to you, you express unity and commitment to the others.[13]

Carol remarked that while she did not know how to put this idea across to the membership, at least it was communicable in English. Although her English was clear, the communication proved unexpectedly difficult, perhaps because the issue touched such deep levels in individual lives. The people who wanted the traditional Mass often felt threatened and put down by the experimenters. The experimenters, seeking a consistent feminist approach in liturgy as well as in social action, were puzzled and pained by those who were clinging to old forms. Experientially, we found that after a weekend or a week in a women's community analyzing sexism and affirming our own autonomy, it was jarring and painful, if not actually contradictory, to bring in a male priest for a closing celebration. We responded by devising our own closing rituals, drawing on the shared experiences of the particular group. We have made progress slowly, creating new rituals, employing texts and symbols from various traditions.

Nevertheless, twenty-five years later, in the General Assembly of 1994, we were processing the same basic issue we had faced in 1969, but this time in the context of its planetary implications. We understand ourselves as a microcosm, dealing in an intimate community with the diversities of class, race, and religion that are tearing today's world apart. After a presentation on "Women, Race and Planetary Survival," the presenters posed the question: "Where in your life, as an individual, and in our collective life as Grail, do you find the struggle between self-definition/self-determination and the respect for the rights of the other and of the earth?" The example we chose to illustrate the point was the Mass and the solution was the same in principle as the one Carol had proposed in 1969. Have a Mass with a priest; have a feminist Eucharist; create a new ritual in which all can join. No one should be made to feel as a despised minority. But this time, we were conscious of the worldwide implications of our principle: How apply it to the ethnic cleansing in Bosnia or Ruwanda? to the religious wars in Ireland? to the Arab/Israeli conflict? Can we affirm every option? Are not some options mutually contradictory? But how can there be peace unless there is some measure of mutual affirmation?

In the midst of our diversities, the search for God goes on with frequent opportunities, at Grailville and the other centers, for retreats in a variety of modes. We are eclectic: psychosynthesis, Dr. Ira Progoff's intensive journal, zen for beginners and for adepts, traditional Catholic methods adapted for modern women—all are available. We draw on a variety of resource people—female and male, ordained and lay, experienced in Eastern and Western traditions. Many of the programs at Grailville are led by Grail members: Carolyn Gratton, recently retired from the Institute of Formative Spirituality at Duquesne University in Pittsburgh, serves as resource for programs in developmental spirituality. Joyce Dietrick, a certified psychosynthesis trainer, offers workshops in this approach to spiritual deepening. Eva Fleischner, nationally known for her work on the Holocaust, offers biblically based times of meditation. Anne Marie Czyzewski, a longtime practitioner of Vipassana meditation, leads day-long introductions to zen. Sharon Thomson presents "The Poetry Path," a week-long workshop on poetry writing as a spiritual discipine. Reverend Barbara Troxell guides participants into "Sabbath Time," a time of contemplation, companionship and compassion. The number of people who choose the ten-day zen retreats testifies to the hunger for the contemplative dimension in the midst of our pressured modern lives. A silent week-long Grail retreat in 1994, attended by more than a third of the membership, drew from both Eastern and Western traditions. Carolyn Gratton presented the Catholic approach to centering prayer of Thomas Keating, OCSO, Cistercian monk and former abbot; Ann Marie Czyzewski and Victoria Jadez led the zen sitting and walking meditations. Each participant was free to follow her own path and in the shared silence and occasional bursts of song, we found each other and found we could affirm each other in our differences.

Difficult as it is to attain mutual respect and affirmation within the US Grail, the difficulties are multiplied many times over in an international movement with twenty branches in countries as different as Germany and Papua New Guinea, or the United States and Tanzania. Nevertheless in 1988 an International Grail Assembly was able to fashion a faith statement that all the membership around the world could affirm. It honors our rooting in Christianity and affirms the diversity of spiritual paths, the different wellsprings that nourish us. It is based on our understanding that God, the central Mystery of our lives, is beyond all our formulations and therefore it behooves us to be open to insights wherever we find them.

> We are a faith community of women.
> We are learning that we are nourished by different wellsprings.
> We share the hope that the Spirit will guide us step by step to
>   understand one another.
> We support one another's searching and discoveries.
> We bring our faith to a world which is becoming a global village.
> We want to use our collective talents and energies to transform the
>   whole global village into a place where each person and culture
>   will grow and enrich the others.

Our hope in the transformation of the global village and of the whole creation is strengthened by the conviction that terror, poverty, and oppression will not have the last word. We rely on God's promise: "Behold, I make all things new."[14]

In 1940 we were inspired by the vision of building a new Christendom in the midst of a secularized society. In 1995 we have accepted a large measure of religious pluralism in our own group, we are much more conscious of the precious pluralisms of human societies around the globe, and we are inspired by a pluralistic vision in which each person and each culture can grow and enrich the others.

Epilogue

People, Problems, and Promise

The drumbeat resounds as Imelda Gaurwa, Tanzanian member of the Grail International Presidency team, leads the procession of fourteen new members into the Grailville Oratory. The time is July 1, 1994; the occasion, the triennial General Assembly of the Grail in the United States. More than a hundred members have gathered to celebrate the official welcoming of the newcomers.

They are a diverse group, ranging in age from early twenties to late sixties; ethnically, two African-Americans, three Hispanics, a variety of Euro-Americans including one Latvian; in lifestyle, single, engaged, married, divorced, celibate, heterosexual, lesbian; five are mothers of grown children with families ranging in size from two to nine; educationally, the range is from high school diploma to PhD, with two theologians and a social scientist teaching in university. Two are resurfacing, that is, are now reactivating their membership after being out of touch for decades.

"I am joining the Grail because I am a feminist." Thus, Mary O'Brien, professor of gerontology at St. Vincent's University in Halifax, Nova Scotia, begins the ceremony, sharing her story and her concern for women rethinking the meaning of spirituality. Then, after voicing her commitment in the Grail, she moves to a central table and lights one of the candles that surround the alabaster Grail cup placed there. The rafters ring with a song of affirmation for her life:

> Proud Woman
> Brave woman
> Strong woman Mary
> The world is witness to your flame
> In solidarity we raise your name.[1]

Figure 24. *Imelda Gaurwa of the International Presidency Team and Cay Charles of the Cornwall Grail Center lead a procession of new members into the Oratory at the 1994 General Assembly.*

Next Patricia Miller, mother and grandmother, echoes Mary O'Brien: "I am joining the Grail because I am a feminist." She speaks of her commitment to feminist theologizing and her decision to work at Grailville as a community-based theologian. Rose Tau, Presbyterian pastor, recounts her steps on the journey that enabled her to find a spiritual home in the Grail and shares her desire to create feminist liturgies. Tamar Cedeno and Laura Pagoada, college students from the South Bronx, express their commitment in the song that Laura has composed for the occasion:

> Grita! Busca la fuerza en ti, mujer!
> Cry out! Look for the strength in you, woman!
> Woman, we shall be victorious!

The ceremony continues until each woman has spoken, and after each one the assembly responds with the song of solidarity. As I listen to each woman share her life journey and her deepest convictions, I marvel at the long road we have traveled on the question of lifestyles. I can remember a Grailville meeting in the 1960s when the issue was whether students in the Semester at Grailville could be allowed to wear slacks in the Oratory. I can remember the first time we encouraged a member to divorce an abusive husband. I remember the struggle in the 1970s to deal with lesbians in the Grail and to wrestle with our own homophobia. One speaker's story brought these lifestyle issues to my mind. She spoke of a happy marriage, of two sons and a daughter, who, when she and her husband grew apart, accepted the amicable ending of their marriage. Moreover, when she found a relationship with another woman, her children gladly affirmed her choice. Recently, her younger son, in his early twenties, confided in her: "You know, mom, we have more in common than you think—you're a lesbian and I'm gay." Her daughter is getting married shortly—lesbian mother and gay brother will toast the bride and groom at the wedding celebration. Love is taking new forms—forms I could not even have imagined thirty years ago—among persons who are trying to live with integrity and authenticity. The song that responded to this story was especially emphatic, "Brave woman, in solidarity we raise your name."

What is our future as Grail? Of course, I see—we all see—many problems. We are an aging group. Initially, a core group pledged to lifetime celibacy and living on subsistence provided continuity and direction, as well as abundant energies and very considerable resources for the movement. While a few individuals may be attracted to celibacy, it is unlikely in my opinion that such a celibate core group will continue in the future. It is not only unlikely, but perhaps not even desirable, as counter to the practice of shared responsibility that we have striven to cultivate since 1965. But

Figure 25. Grail members from eight countries participate in Dr. Carolyn Gratton's course on spiritual guidance at Grailville, summer 1997. Front row: Nadia Villefort, Brazil; Rebecca Nebrida, The Philippines; Anne Day, Australia; Lucy Kimaro, Tanzania; Regina Bashaasha, Uganda; Margaret Amol, Kenya. Back Row: Carolyn Gratton, Canada; Ann Burke, United States; Patricia Cummins, Australia; Simonetta Romano, Italy; Joyce Asfour, United States.

the question remains: Where will the energy come from to carry on and the creativity to take the risk of moving in new directions?

I am pleased by our diversity and take pride in being part of an open and inclusive community. But I wonder whether we can hold together the growing diversity of generations, race, class, lifestyles, educational attainments, ethnic and religious backgrounds, spiritual paths. Will we become so broad as to risk becoming empty of meaning, watered down to the lowest common denominator?

Moreover, we exist in a world scene of unparalleled violence, dominated by rapacious global free-market capitalism, a scene of massive injustice, rigid religious fundamentalism, bloody ethnic cleansing, and growing threats to the survival of all life on planet earth. We exist in a country with an increasing imbalance between rich and poor, where one child in five lives in poverty, where racial hatred and sexual violence are on the increase, where "liberal" and "feminist" have become dirty words. There is a mean spirit abroad in the land, a pervasive cynicism that sneers at any form of idealism.

In this dark picture, where can we find signs of hope? Where do we ground a hope for the future, not only of the Grail but of the world? At the

1994 General Assembly we dealt with these questions by placing ourselves squarely in a cosmic context as an evolving group in an evolving universe. The backdrop for the meeting was a mural of a swirling mass of fire ball, stars, and galaxies. We literally put ourselves in the picture, each one placing a polaroid photo of herself on the spot from which she drew her energies. We were explicitly aware of ourselves as a unique grouping, an energy event that would never again occur in exactly this configuration with precisely these individuals; and we were also aware of our capacity to generate energy and to draw strength from each other.

As I look around the world, I find the energy for change strongest among women's groups, feminist groups. Witness the 40,000 women at the 1995 Beijing conference, the largest meeting the UN has ever held. It is among feminists that the most trenchant criticisms of world conditions can be found. It is from feminists that I have learned to analyze the global economy, its escape from control by the nation states, its devastating impact on workers everywhere, its destruction of the environment on which all life depends.

As Gerda Lerner points out, women's spaces, spaces controlled by women, are crucial for the development of feminist consciousness. Women need places where they are free to be themselves, where they need not be on guard against attack or ridicule, where they can be encouraged to think for themselves, develop their own ideas, define their own ends, and organize to accomplish them. I think the Grail has always offered such women's spaces.

Lerner goes on to explain that feminist consciousness is a necessary prerequisite for conceptualizing a new order, "a society in which differences do not connote dominance." She grounds her hope for the new epoch of human history that we are now entering in the intellectual emancipation of women, which "has shattered the solid monopoly which men have held for so long over theory and definition. . . . the theoretical insights modern feminist scholarship has already achieved have the power to shatter the patriarchal paradigm."[2] I believe in that power. One of my hopes for the future is that in Grail spaces we can contribute, however modestly, to conceptualizing and realizing "a society where difference does not connote domination." I hope we can continue to draw together women who are determined to find a sane, healthy, peaceful, sustainable way for humans to live together on planet earth.

The power of women working together to make a difference in the world was part of the original vision of the Grail. There was an early Grail slogan in Holland—"Individually we may not be so much but together we are a genius!" That conviction is still strongly alive in the Grail today. In an interview with an American Grail member, Lydwine van Kersbergen, now in her nineties, expressed her faith in women's power: "I would say that history has hardly started because women have not had a chance, a real chance, to come forward. When that occurs, it will be a great happening for the transformation of the Church and the world."[3]

My experience of the evolution of the U.S. Grail in the past fifty-five years also gives me grounds for hope. It has been a phoenix-like experience, or perhaps a better image is the nurse tree in the forest. The nurse tree falls to the ground and decays but gives birth to many seedlings which in their turn constitute the forest. By all the theories of the life and death of organizations, we should have dissolved in the late 1960s or early 1970s. Almost every element that had made the Grail strong in its first quarter century was in question and either going out of existence or undergoing radical change: the utopian community at Grailville no longer existed; the city centers had been phased out; the systematic recruitment and training of laywomen for the apostolate at home and overseas had faded away. The centralized and hierarchical structure was replaced by cumbersome participative structures. Moreover, there was a strong reaction against the former spirituality of self-sacrifice and obedience that expressed itself in reluctance to grant authority to any structure. Vast amounts of energy were spent— some would say misspent—in revising and re-revising structures. There was a strong sense that the individual had too often been sacrificed to community needs and a consequent emphasis on the development of personal potential. Large numbers—almost 50 percent—of the nucleus members were released from their lifetime commitment.

Most serious was the questioning of the Catholic framework that had defined both the vision and the practice of the lay apostolate. The ideal of a new Christendom gave way to an affirmation of pluralism. We stopped talking about the lay apostolate and began to look for the signs of the times, to find the Spirit in the midst of the struggles for justice, in the civil rights movement, in the women's liberation movement. The spirituality of asceticism, obedience, and self-sacrifice that I had embraced as the sure way to holiness now seemed somehow irrelevant, replaced by a search for an authentic self. I enjoyed the new freedom but worried about the loss of community. For a long period, from 1965 to the mid-80s, while there was a burst of creativity in new projects and meaningful individual commitments, we were confused about our own identity and direction as Grail. We did not have sufficient clarity or agreement among ourselves to be able to recruit new members and membership slowly declined. In short, almost everything pointed to a group that was destined to dwindle away. In fact, one reviewer of Alden Brown's book, which took the United States Grail story from 1940 to 1975, entitled his piece "Volume Tells of a Short-lived Group."[4]

Why haven't we disappeared? In part, I think, because the personal bonds are strong, arising from a common history and a sharing of intense experiences. We are willing to share at a deep personal level, to take each other seriously, to process feelings until we come to understanding. There is an intensity of spirit when we come together that we do not easily find elsewhere. There is also a wholeness, an integration of multiple aspects of life—ecology and feminism, social justice and the arts, all related to religious search and an openness to diverse spiritual paths. We hold common values, even though we may not always be able to articulate them. I can meet Grail members whom I have not seen for years and pick up the conversation where we left off. The Grail is a context in which we can quickly come to a depth of mutual understanding that is otherwise rare in my experience. Even with all the diversity of spiritual paths, we are able to create forms of common worship that are nourishing and help to bind us together.

I take hope also from the signs of new life and new corporate commitments that are appearing in the 1990s. The old city centers are long gone, but a new Grail Center has emerged in the South Bronx, the fruit of a long, quiet, patient process initiated by Sharon Joslyn and Mary Kay Louchart. They had ten years of experience using a community development approach with migrants in Saginaw when lack of institutional support made them decide to leave in 1979. They were not sent to the Bronx in obedience to a directive from a Grail leader. "In 1980," Mary Kay explains, "we chose to work in the Bronx because we wanted to work in a low-income area which was ethnically diverse, where the churches and some of the other institutions were committed to the community, where we could be part of something alive."[5] They came without a program— simply to live and work in the area, make friends, listen, lend a helping hand. They work as parish staff, a role that the community understands and accepts. Mary Kay coordinates the religious education program; Sharon is coordinator of community outreach. They work as the only women on a pastoral team in a Catholic church where today the role of women is an issue, but they manage to center their work on empowerment, especially of the women and girls. They have introduced inclusive language in the liturgy, girl servers at the Mass, a new awareness of racism and sexism in the life of the community together with practical steps to change attitudes and structures. From the beginning they have identified themselves as Grail; the parish provides a large house (living quarters upstairs, meeting rooms downstairs) which the people have dubbed the Grail Center. It is a much less assertive approach than that of the old city centers, much slower, but proceeding from the same core values and exerting a strong influence in the community.

There are new initiatives at Grailville and Cornwall where both centers have committed their acreage to permaculture, sustainable agriculture
using organic methods. Grailville has embraced a whole series of new projects to build up the land: a large-scale composting project, taking all the
leaves from the city of Loveland every fall, thereby relieving the city's land-
fill and enriching the land; the reforestation of some areas, including planting hundreds of trees along the creek as part of a regional project to restore
water quality. The market garden, certified organic by the Ohio Food and
Farm Association, provides organic produce to some thirty area families
who are part of Community Supported Agriculture (CSA). They buy shares
in the garden at the beginning of the season and each week are entitled to a
share of whatever we have harvested—vegetables, fruit, flowers. Garden
interns come each spring and summer to share in the work and get training
in permaculture. There is also a three-year permaculture project with the
Grail in East Africa, whereby Grail women from Tanzania and Uganda
come to Grailville for training and Mary Lu Lageman, in charge of
Grailville's Earth/Land projects, spends time teaching in East Africa.

In San Jose, California, the team has undertaken a major project,
developing thirty-five affordable townhouses together with a Grail Center
and a child care center on the two and a quarter acres of Grail property.
This development has strong support from the local Hispanic community
and will enable some of the local families to become homeowners for the
first time.

After many years of a decentralized pattern of programming with each
task force, team, and center developing its own focus, in the 1990s efforts
were made to do joint programs. To strengthen these efforts at coordination, in 1994 the General Assembly approved a new initiative, a national
staff and budget for Unified Program Planning (UPP), charged with stimulating and supporting the work of Grail groups and individuals across the
country and assisting in outreach and movement development. With
Sharon Thomson as the on-the-road program consultant going from coast
to coast in her van to visit Grail members and Maureen Tate in
Philadelphia as resource coordinator, cataloging and supplying materials,
UPP is a catalyst for a new level of Grail activity. With their assistance, in
an eight-month period fifteen groups were able to offer introductory workshops on the Grail. Sharon also facilitates the production of her poetry ritual dramas, *The Circle and the Light* on the meaning of the Grail myth for
today, and *Ancient Healing* on the breast cancer epidemic.

The Grail vision, modified by the last fifty-five years of experience in
the United States, is drawing new members. As of 1995, there are twenty-
five women "in process," exploring the Grail with a view to becoming
members. The new members are coming from both ends of the age spec-

trum. Former members are resurfacing, catching up on the developments of decades and renewing commitments first made in the 1950s. Retired women are now joining the Grail and volunteering their energies, professional skills, and life experience—a far cry from the days when we thought a woman of twenty-five was too old! The Young Women's Network is drawing together women in their twenties who are attracted by core values of the original Grail vision: women, spirituality, world. "Strong is what we make each other," they say. "We provide space where young women . . . can come and deepen their commitment to social, racial and environmental justice, spirituality, the earth and women around the world."[6] I would not have used exactly these words in 1940, but they express much the same spirit that drew me when I first discovered the Grail.

Personally I ground my hope for the world and for the Grail chiefly in the strength of women, women who develop all their gifts and talents, women who act together generously and in hope to bring into reality their vision of a world where difference does not connote domination, a world where each person and culture will grow and enrich the others, a world where a hope-filled future awaits every child. We hold fast to our conviction that terror, poverty, and oppression will not have the last word. We rely on God's promise, "Behold, I make all things new."

Appendix

The United States Grail in Its International Context

The Grail in the United States is part of the International Grail. Structurally, an International General Assembly (IGA), held every five years, sets goals and policies for the Grail internationally. Delegates to the IGA are elected by the members in each country where the Grail is established. Implementation is coordinated by an International Presidency Team (IPT) of three persons, elected by the votes of individual Grail members around the world. Each country may nominate candidates for the IPT from within its own borders or from other countries. The IPT is assisted by an International Council, meeting every eighteen months and made up of one delegate from each member country. The United States and South Africa have each been allowed two delegates in order to better represent the racial and ethnic diversities in these countries. The bare bones of the structure do not do justice to the rich flow of communication and personal contacts between countries, by publications, mail, FAX, and e-mail, by exchange of staff and visits. The following chronology indicates some of the linkages.

November 1, 1921	The Women of Nazareth (WoN) founded in Holland by Jacques van Ginneken, SJ.
1921	Miriam Meertens, first superior, soon followed by Margaret van Gilse who served until 1949.
1928	WoN give up work in Java and begin Grail youth movement in Holland.
1932	The Grail begun in Germany by Mia van der Kallen and Joan Overboss and in England by Yvonne Bosch van Drakestein and Lydwine van Kersbergen.

1933	The Grail begun in Scotland by a team from England.
1936	The Grail begun in Australia by Lydwine van Kersbergen and a Dutch team.
1939	The Grail in Germany suppressed by Hitler.
April 1940	Lydwine van Kersbergen and Joan Overboss begin the Grail in the United States.
September 1940	They are joined at Doddridge Farm by Mary Louise Tully, the first American member.
October 4, 1942	The Grail in Holland dissolved by Hitler; all contact with U.S. Grail cut off.
May 1943–February 1944	Homeless period for U.S. Grail.
July 17, 1944	Official opening of Grailville on 186-acre farm outside Loveland, Ohio.
August 1945	Reunion of Grail leaders from Holland, England, Scotland, Australia, and the United States with Fr. van Ginneken and Margaret van Gilse held in England.
September 1945	Margaret van Gilse, Grail Mother General, begins a one-year visit to the United States. Two Dutch Grail members join the Grailville staff.
1946	Mary Louise Tully sent by Margaret van Gilse to Hong Kong to start the Grail in China.
1947	English Grail separates from the International Grail and becomes a secular institute.
1948	Grail teams from Holland begin work in Brazil, Surinam, Java. Teams in Brazil and Java are later joined by Americans.
1948	Mary Buckley volunteers to go to Brooklyn as staff for first U.S. Grail city center.
May 6, 1949	Rachel Donders elected as international leader of the WON to succeed Margaret van Gilse.
September, 1951	First visit of Rachel Donders to the United States. Twenty Americans formally dedicated as nucleus members
September 1952–February, 1953	Margaret van Gilse and Lydwine van Kersbergen tour Africa, seek places for Grail teams.
1953	U.S. Grail team of Marie Therese McDermit and Lorraine Machan sent to Uganda and team of Mary Buckley and Mary Emma Kuhn sent to Basutoland.

1952–1961	Grail city centers started in Cincinnati, Philadelphia, New York City, Queens, Detroit, Toronto, Lafayette, LA, and San Jose, CA.
1961	IGA in Holland elects Magdalene Oberhoffer (Germany) as International president, with Dolores Brien (United States) and Benedicte Milcent (France) as vice-presidents.
1962	Eileen Schaeffler appointed President of the U.S. Grail, to succeed Lydwine van Kersbergen.
1962–64	Grail begun in Nigeria, Japan, Italy. Evelyn Pugh (United States) serves in Nigeria.
1964–1967	Grail aggiornamento replaces hierarchical with democratic structures, writes new guidelines, creates new structures that open almost all offices to nonnucleus members.
1967	IGA, in Holland, ratifies new Guidelines and Structures, elects Eileen Schaeffler as president, Maria de Lourdes Pintasilgo (Portugal) as vice-president of the International Grail.
1967	U.S. Grail elects Dorothy Rasenberger as the first National President chosen by the members.
June 1, 1969	U.S. Grail General Assembly admits Protestant women to full participation in the Grail.
1971	International General Assembly (IGA) at Grailville with fifty participants from eighteen countries elects Simone Tagher of Egypt as International President.
1971	Grail begun in India by Elizabeth Reid (Australia), Deborah Schak (United States), and Pearl Drego and Marina D'Sa of India.
1972	U.S. Grail drops office of National President, establishes Continuity and Movement Teams.
1974	Mobile IGA organized around key issues:
•	7/74 Kisekibaha, Tanzania. Growing together a Grail; 25 Africans, 2 United States.
•	8/74 Tiltenberg, Holland. Work Involvement; 39 participants from 12 countries.
•	8/74 Toronto. Conscientization in light of Liberation Theology; 29 participants, 12 countries.
•	8/74 Grailville. Search for God; 16 participants from 9 countries.
December, 1974	First International Council meeting.

1975   U.S. G.A. adopts decentralized structure, approves Jewish participation, approves three Task Forces—religious search, liberation, women—and two teams: for Grail participation and international relationships.

1979   IGA, Portugal. 91 participants from 20 countries elect Ann Burke (USA), Gerda Kaufman (Germany), and Joan Dilworth (Scotland) as International Presidency Team and establishes four international networks: Living Faith; Women as Builders of New Societies; Action for Liberation; Grail participation.

1979   Grail in Kenya, prepared for by Anne Hope (S. Africa) and Sally Timmel (United States) since 1974, is officially recognized.

1988   IGA in Holland elects Rebecca Nebrida (Philippines), Marita Estor (Gemany), and Teresa Santa Clara Gomes (Portugal) as International Presidency Team; writes faith statement.

1990   USGA approves San Jose plan to develop affordable housing on the San Jose property; establishes and staffs United Program Planning to stimulate movement in Unites States.

1993   IGA at Grailville elects Marita Estor (Germany), Alison Healy (Australia), Imelda Gaurwa (Tanzania) as International Presidency Team.

1998   IGA: Grail women from around the world gather to pray, plan, and carry on the vision.

1998   Grail group from Sweden recognized as national Grail entity.

Notes

Personal Prologue

1. A gifted teacher of literature, Frank O'Malley introduced generations of Notre Dame students to authors of the twentieth-century Catholic revival in Europe—Paul Claudel, Leon Bloy, Hilaire Belloc, Gilbert Keith Chesteron, Etienne Gilson, Jacques Maritain, George Bernanos, among others.

2. Frank Sheed, an Australian lay theologian together with his wife, author Maisie Ward, founded Sheed and Ward, which became one of the most influential Catholic publishing houses in the English-speaking world. They played a crucial role in bringing the works of the European Catholic revival to America. Sheed was a witty and dynamic speaker. Baroness Catherine de Hueck Doherty was the founder of Friendship House, a pioneering interracial apostolate. Artist Ade Bethune at her studio in Rhode Island dealt with religious themes in a vigorous contemporary style and encouraged her young women interns to do likewise. All three speakers were household names in the Catholic world and stars of the first order in the lay apostolate in the 1940s and 1950s.

3. The priest was joined by Mary Widman, who devoted her life to continuing and expanding this project. Eventually the Center acquired a summer camp for the children, as well as offering an impressive program of legal and social services to residents of the neighborhood, and, of course, continuing recreation and education for the children.

4. At the time, the Church was so identified with the hierarchy that young laypeople were thrilled to be invited to join in the work of the bishops and priests. Both terms, "lay apostolate" and "Catholic Action," at first were used loosely for the various lay movements. Then in many European countries the movements using the Jocist method of "observe, judge, act" were mandated by the hierarchy as an official arm of the Church under the name of "Catholic Action." They tended to be under the

close supervision of their priest moderators. In the United States no movements were mandated at a national level. The specialized Catholic Action
movements—Young Christian Students (YCS), Young Christian Workers
(YCW), Christian Family Movement (CFM)—were begun under the leadership of priests from Chicago and Notre Dame. Of course, they had
approval of the local bishop—no organized Catholic activity could proceed without that—but not the official status implied by the mandate. As
Grail, we usually spoke of ourselves as engaged in the lay apostolate, pre-
ferring that term as broader, more inclusive, not restricted to a single
method. In the 1940s, tensions developed between the Grail and the
Catholic Action priests, particularly around issues of clerical control and
methods of training.

Introduction

1. The Oratory is the former beef barn, converted into a place of
prayer that has won architectural awards.

2. Report, IGA, 1993. GA.

3. Rule of the Society of the Women of Nazareth. Unpublished manuscript, English translation from the Dutch. GA, Box 2/5.

4. Gerda Lerner, "Placing Women in History: A 1975 Perspective,"
in *Liberating Women's History*, ed. by Bernice Carroll (Urbana: U. of
Illinois Press, 1976) p. 366.

5. The two book-length treatments of United States Grail history are
Alden Brown's *The Grail Movement and American Catholicism,
1940–1975* (*Notre Dame Studies in American Catholicism*, v. 9 [Notre
Dame, IN: U. of Notre Dame Press,1989]) and the *U.S. Catholic Historian*,
v.11, #4, fall 1993, neither of which attempts to trace the full story, nor
does Brown make use of a feminist perspective.

6. See Mary Field Belenky, Blythe McVicker Clinchy, Nancy Rule
Goldberger, Jill Mattuck Tarule, *Women's Ways of Knowing, The
Development of Self, Voice and Mind* (New York: Basic Books, 1986);
Sandra Harding, *Whose Science, Whose Knowledge* (Ithaca, New York:
Cornell University Press, 1991); Elizabeth Kamarck Minnich, *Trans-
forming Knowledge* (Philadelphia: Temple University Press, 1990); bell
hooks, ed.*Teaching to Transgress, Education as the Practice of Freedom*
(New York: Routledge, 1994).

7. bell hooks, *Talking Back, thinking feminist, thinking black*
(Boston: S. End, 1989) p. 28.

1. Grail Beginnings

1. Statutes of the Women of Nazareth (English), n.d. GA, Box 2/4.

2. The group van Ginneken founded in 1921 was called *Vrouwen van Nazareth*, Women of Nazareth (WoN). Members dedicated themselves to work for the conversion of the world as laywomen, committed in celibacy, poverty, and obedience, and totally available for their all-encompassing task. In 1928, the WoN founded and led a youth movement called "De Graal," which flourished among Dutch girls and young women in the 1930s. When the movement spread to Britain (in 1933) and to the United States (in 1940), *Vrouwen van Nazareth* was translated as "Ladies of the Grail." In the United States, this term was soon shortened simply to "The Grail," and individuals were referred to as "Grail workers" or "free workers." In 1951, when the first Americans made a formal commitment in celibacy, the name *"Vrouwen van Nazareth"* was replaced by the phrase, "nucleus of the Grail," and individuals were referred to as "nucleus members."

3. Conversation with Lydwine van Kersbergen, Amsterdam, 7/1/1991.

4. Conversation with Lydwine van Kersbergen, Amsterdam, 6/26/91.

5. Brom, *Grail Review* vii, #2, 1965, p. 47.

6. Jacques van Ginneken's writings that deal directly with the Grail consist of:

- *The Grail as a Young Woman's Movement: Its Aims, Methods, and Basic Ideals,* a course of thirty-two lectures delivered at the Tiltenberg in August, 1932, and referred to in these notes as JvG *Course.*
- A series of *Retreat Conferences,* also thirty-two in number, given at the Tiltenberg, August 10–19, 1932.
- The *Travel Letters,* sixteen letters written to the WON as van Ginneken toured Europe in 1931.
- Various speeches and lectures.

All of these materials—except the Travel Letters—were delivered in Dutch, taken down on a recording machine, and later transcribed, but were never edited by the speaker. The Dutch transcription was translated into English. All these materiels are available in the Grail Archives (GA) at Grailville in both the Dutch and the English versions. *The Grail as a Young Woman's Movement* is referred to in the notes below as J vG, *Course* GA Box 1. JvG, *Course* #24, p. 3.

7. op. cit., p.18.

8. JvG, *Course* #18, p. 3.

9. Ibid., p. 9.

10. Ibid., p. 12.

11. JvG, *Course* #24, p. 24.

12. JvG, *Course* #18, p. 11.

13. Ibid., p. 11.
14. JvG, *Course* #1, p. 1.
15. JvG, *Course* #19, p.8.
16. JvG, *Course* #20, p. 2, 3.
17. JvG, *Course* #22, p. 1.
18. JvG, *Course* # 20, p.3.
19. JvG, *Course*, #24.
20. JvG, *Course* # 22.
21. JvG, *Course*, #24, p. 27.
22. She took the name "Lydwine" in honor of Lydwina of Schiedam, patron saint of Holland, when she joined the WoN.
23. All these biographical details are based on conversations with LvK, Amsterdam, 6/26–7/6/91.
24. JvG, *Course* #12, p. 1.
25. Conversation with LvK, Amsterdam, 6/91.
26. Letter from LvK to Eileen Schaeffler, 7/21/95. JK files.
27. Letters from Brigid Huizinga to JK, 4/8/92; 4/29/92; 5/16/92.
28. Talk by Joan Overboss, Doddridge Farm, 1942. GA Box 83/47.
29. Conversation with LvK, Amsterdam, 6/91.
30. Ibid.
31. Taped interview with Sharon Thomson, Grail Oral History Project, 1979. GA.
32. Ibid.
33. Conversation with Catherine Leahy, 9/92.
34. *Time* Magazine, July 21, 1941.

2. Doddridge Farm

1. *Free workers*, a term Lydwine and Joan had coined to replace *Ladies of the Grail*, meant, as they used it, free from family and professional ties and therefore fully available to serve wherever the needs of the apostolate required.
2. Report to Bishop Sheil, GA, Box 40/9.
3. GA, Box 40/9.
4. Report to Bishop Sheil, GA, Box 40/9.
5. Report on Summer Camp, 1941, GA, Box 40/5.
6. *The Living Parish*, 4/43, pp.10–13.

3. Women in Search of Autonomy

1. Conversation with LvK, Amsterdam, 6/91.
2. Letter of Archbishop Stritch to LvK, 5/29/40. GA Box 40/4.

3. Conversation with LvK, Amsterdam, 6/91.
4. Memorandum by Joan Overboss, 9/41. GA Box 40/9.
5. Report, 5/15/43. GA Box 40, 9.
6. Letter of Archbishop Stritch to LvK, 5/24/43. GA Box 40/4.
7. Letter of Archbishop Stritch to LvK, 6/10/42. GA Box 40/4.
8. 1943 brochure. GA Box A1/27.
9. Ibid.
10. Grail National Legal File, Grailville Office.
11. Ibid.
12. Archbishop McNicholas in the Grail program brochure, 1946. GA Box A1.

4. Grailville—A Countercultural Oasis

1. Statement of Purpose, Land and Home Associates, JK personal files.
2. *Program of Action* (Loveland, Ohio, 1946) p. 18, 20. GA Box A8/38.
3. Ibid., p. 20.
4. School of Apostolate, pamphlet (Loveland, Ohio,1946). GA Box A2/1.
5. Conversation with LvK, Amsterdam, 6/91.
6. Letter of JvG to LvK, 10/14/44. GA Box 40/3.
7. Interview, 10/92.
8. Interview, 5/18/91.

5. Grailville—A Center of the Lay Apostolate

1. JvG *Course*, #23, pp. 2, 3. GA Box 1/12. He used the word *nucleus* in a general sense for any committed core group who, by their radiant spirit, would attract others to become nuclei in their turn. He spoke of the WoN as "the quasi-religious nucleus of the lay apostolate" and intended them to be the supreme example of a committed core group. In 1951 when Rachel Donders wanted to emphasize the unity of the WoN and the movement, she coined the phrase "nucleus of the Grail" to name the core group committed in celibacy.
2. This was long before concelebration was allowed.
3. Letter to JK, 2/10/94.
4. *Let Us Baptize Thanskgiving* (Loveland, OH, 1949) p. 2. GA Box A8/35. *Advent Ember Days*, Box A8/26.
5. A leading liturgical magazine, published by the Benedictines of St. John's Abbey, Collegeville, MN. In keeping with the emphasis on the

use of the vernacular in the liturgy, the name was later changed to *Worship.*

6. Apocalypse 3, 16.

7. Letter from Mary Mahoney to JK, 9/14/94.

8. Letter from Eileen Schenk to JK, 2/10/94.

9. Report of Meeting at St. Columban Church, 7/13/51. GA Box 102/1.

10. Letter of LvK to Archbishop Alter, 7/24/51. GA Box 102/2.

11. Report of Talk by Archbishop Alter at St. Columban Parish, 7/29/51. Archives, Archdiocese of Cincinnati, Alter Collection.

12. It is interesting to note that at much the same time some parishioners were objecting to Grailville's presence, we were gaining a national and international reputation from experts. Reverend H. A. Reinhold, a leader in the American liturgical movement, wrote in *Orate Fratres,* 11/6/49: "Without arguing, shouting and drum beating, these wholesome and realistic women have won a great victory . . . for parish participation." Evelyn Waugh, writing of Catholic life in the United States in *Life* magazine, 9/49, noted: "There is a fermentation everywhere . . . but something more must be said of Grailville. . . . Their life is in startling contrast to the ideals of the advertisement pages of the women's magazines . . . their number is minute, as was the number of the first companions of St. Ignatius who set out to reclaim Europe in the sixteenth century. It is seldom in gigantic rallies and conventions that great ends are achieved. There are the mustard seeds of the parable." And French theologian Jean Danielou, SJ, after visiting Grailville, wrote in *La Maison-Dieu, Premier Trimestre,* 1952: "This is what can really be called putting into practice the principles of the liturgical movement! It was a sung Mass, full of spirit, in which both the Grailville students and the parishioners participated. . . . It is a city which is being built here where souls wearied of jazz, television and restlessness come to seek an integral Christian atmosphere."

13. Letter to JK, 1/24/52.

14. Letter to JK, 2/13/94.

15. John Peter Sullivan, SJ: *Discovering the Grail, The Women's Role in the Lay Apostolate.* Pamphlet, Kingston, Jamaica, 1945. JK personal files.

16. Letter from assistant chancellor to Msgr. Stoll, 1/11/49. Archives of Archdiocese of Cincinnati.

17. Rev. Lawrence J. Mick to Msgr. Leibold, 4/28/57. Archives of Archdiocese of Cincinnati.

18. Letter of Archbishop Alter to Catherine Leahy, 7/8/67. GA.

19. Letter of Msgr. Paul Vogelpohl to Eleanor Walker, 9/9/59. GA.

20. Memo by Msgr. Stanley Bertke to chancellor, 8/3/54. Archives of Archdiocese of Cincinnati.

21. Letter of Msgr. Edward McCarthy to Catherine Leahy, 1/12/63. Archives of Archdiocese of Cincinnati.

22. Letter of Rev. Joseph Urbain to Archbishop Alter, 5/22/57. Archives of Archdiocese of Cincinnati.

23. JvG *Course*, #14, p. 5.

6. Deepening the Roots

1. R. Donders, *The History of the International Grail, 1921–1979* (Loveland, Ohio, 1983) p. 34.

2. Ibid., pp. 35, 36.

3. Conversation with Rachel Donders, Sintra, Portugal, 7/91.

4. By "virginal chastity," we understood that we were giving up marriage and committing ourselves to chaste control over sexual thoughts and feelings. In the 1950s and 1960s, we described this commitment as "dedicated virginity"; more recently, we speak of "celibacy." "Chaste" has two meanings that reflect the ambivalence toward sexuality in the Christian tradition: (1) abstaining from any use of one's sexual powers; (2) using these powers temperately, that is, without either self-indulgence or prudery. In the second meaning, both marriage and celibacy can be chaste. Some classical Catholic theologians thought that sexual intercourse was impossible without at least venial sin, even in marriage. In our Grail courses, we followed contemporary theologians who taught that the marriage act itself was a channel of grace for the couple rather than an occasion of sin.

5. GA Box 21/5.

6. Mary Helena Fong, Veronica Forbes, Helen Veronica Kelly, Lorraine Machan, Mary Brigid Niland, Martha Orso, Jeanne Plante, and Debora Schak.

7. "Get Six City Centers"

1. Conversation with Mary Buckley, 3/20/92.

2. Ibid.

3. Rachel Donders sent Eileen Schaeffler to assist in launching the Gateway.

4. *Gateway Brochure*. GA Box A3/9.

5. Joan Overboss, Account of Happenings at the Gateway. GA Box 41/7.

6. Report to Cardinal Mooney, 1955. GA Box 41/16.

7. Elsa Chaney, *This Is Gabriel House.* Leaflet, 1953. GA Box A3/20.

8. Conversation with Grace McGinnis, 8/25/92.

9. Ibid.

10. Conversation with Anne Harmon, 8/28/92.

11. Conversation with Mary Anne Kimbell, 8/23/92.

12. Conversation with Carolyn Gratton, 1/13/92.

13. Ibid.

14. Introduction to "The Flame of the Spirit," a Pentecost celebration. GA Box 45/1.

15. Report, 1969. GA Box 45/15.

16. Report, GA Box 45/2.

17. Ibid.

18. Report on Service Careers Program, 1959. Box 45/3.

19. Report to Bishop Schexnayder, 1963. Box 40/28.

20. Conversation with E. McGee, 9/94.

21. Letter of Rev. Elmo Romagosa to Archbishop Rummel, 4/2/55. GA Box 40/1.

22. Report of Barbara Wald to LvK, 2/5/59. GA Box 40/28.

23. Report on The Grail Movement in Louisiana, 1962. Box 40/28.

24. Eileen Schaeffler, Report, 5/10/62. GA Box 39/23.

25. Newsletter, San Jose Grail Housing Community, June, 1997, p. 2.

26. Letter of Veronica Forbes to LvK, 4/13/61, 5/1/61. GA Box 39/1.

27. Daily Program, 1962. GA Box 39/23.

8. Laywomen to the Missions, 1950–1964

1. Quoted in Elsa Chaney, "The Five Who Stayed Home," reprint from *Catholic World,* GA Box A11/13.

2. Unpub. mss., GA Box 8/2.

3. Sally Collett, "I Live in an 'International Family,' " in *St. Joseph's Lily,* 1953. GA Box A 11/16.

4. Lydwine van Kersbergen, *African Diary,* unpub. mss. GA Box 8/13.

5. UFER, Union Fraternelle Entre les Races et les Peuples (Fraternal Union of Races and Peoples) is an association of lay mission–sending societies with the status of a nongovernmental organization at the United Nations in New York and Paris.

6. Westminster, MD. 1962.

7. Interview, 5/29/96.

8. M. L. Tully, "I'm a Lay Missionary Overseas," *The Shield,* Jan. 1950. GA Box A11/13.

9. M. I. Buckley, "Leaders for the Continent of the Future," GV brochure. GA Box A 1/28.

10. A. McCarthy, "The Subsidiary Role of Foreign Lay People," pamphlet, *Overdruk uit Novella Ecclesiae Germina*, 1963. GA Box A8/16.

11. K. Walsh, unpub. report. GA Box A11/1.

12. 1979 IGA Final Report, p. 3. JK files.

13. Lay Helpers to the Missions, Grail Mission School, Ubbergen, Netherlands. GA Box A8/18.

14. LvK, *African Diary*, pp. 232–233. GA Box 8/13.

9. Tumultuous Changes and Creative Responses

1. They dressed in black and stood in silence at the opening session as a visible reminder of the small number of women among the delegates.

2. Reverend Jack Murphy, SJ, in a private conversation with Eva Fleischner.

3. Conversation, 7/94.

4. Newsletter, 11/20/73. GA Box 79/ 25.

5. Conversation, 8/22/92.

10. Aggiornamento in the Grail

1. All these were famous figures in Catholic circles in the 1960s. Dorothy Day, together with Peter Maurin, had founded the Catholic Worker movement, edited its challenging newspaper, written a number of important books, and lived her uncompromising pacifism, even when her antiwar protests resulted in jail terms. John Cogley, writer and journalist, was director of the Chicago Catholic Worker House until 1942, when he broke with the Worker over pacifism and enlisted in the armed forces in order to fight nazism. He was cofounder of *Today*, a national Catholic student publication; served as an editor of *Commonweal*, influential national Catholic weekly; was an adviser on religious issues to John F. Kennedy in the 1960 presidential campaign; and became Religion News Editor of the *New York Times*. Monsignor John M. Oesterreicher, himself a convert from Judaism, pioneered Jewish-Christian studies and founded the Institute of Judaeo-Christian Studies at Seton Hall University. Mary Luke Tobin, a Sister of Loretto, was superior of her religious congregation, president of the Leadership Conference of Women Religious, and one of the first Catholic women to be admitted as an auditor at Vatican II.

2. Interview with Maria de Lourdes Pintasilgo, 7/12/93.

3. The group consisted of Alberta Lucker, Germany; Elisabeth Caminada, Holland; Eileen Schaeffler, United States; Maria de Lourdes

Pintasilgo, Portugal; Magdalene Oberhoffer; and Benedicte Milcent. Interview with MdeL P, 7/12/93.

4. Letter of Magdalene Oberhoffer to Aggiornamento participants, 11/20/64. GA Box 4/4.

5. Guidelines of the Grail, Par. 39. GA Box 3/1.

6. JvG, *Course* #15, pp. 6–8. GA Box 1/12.

7. Preparative International Conference working group (PIC), *Proposal* 11/19/60. GA Box 2/7.

8. JvG, *Course* #20, p. 2.

9. JvG, *Course* #20, pp.1–7.

10. At the present time, the English Grail has three branches, the community of celibate members established as a secular institute, individual celibate members of the secular institute who do not live in community, and the Companions, married couples who must join as couples and who share in the spirit and works of the Grail. Conversation with Patricia Petrie, English Grail member, 7/93.

11. Professor Hirschmann, a theologian consulted during work on the Charter and Statutes.

12. Letter of Magadelne Oberhoffer to Eileen Schaeffler, 8/20/62. GA 5/4.

13. Letter of M. Oberhoffer, B. Milcent and D. Brien to nucleus members, 9/8/62. GA Box 5/4.

14. Official Version, Structures of the Grail, July–August 1967. GA Box 2/12.

15. Eileen Schaeffler, who was determined to be the last person to be appointed as National President in the United States, was pleased to see this election achieved.

11. The Costs of Change

1. Conversation with Carolyn Gratton, 1/12/93.

2. Conversation with Carolyn Gratton, 1/12/93.

3. Report by D. J. Rasenberger, 7/69. GA, Box 7, folder 7.

4. Letter of D. Brien to M. Oberhoffer and B. Milcent, 11/12/63. JK files.

5. Personal notes by D. Brien, 2/64. JK files.

6. Conversation with M. A. Holthaus, 12/28/92.

7. Letter, 1/9/93. JK files.

8. Interview, 1/17/93.

9. Interview, 7/13/96.

10. Letter, Victoria Jadez, 8/1/96. JK files.

11. Letter, Ruth Chisholm, 7/31/96. JK files.

12. Letter, Elise Gorges, 8/1/96. JK files.
13. Letter, Eileen Schaeffler, 7/29/97. JK files.
14. Letter, Eva Fleischner, 7/29/96. JK files.
15. Interview, 7/96, JK files.
16. Letter, 7/28/96, JK files.
17. Interview, 7/13/96, JK files.
18. Interview, 7/21/96, JK files.
19. Conversation, 7/21/96, JK files.
20. Letter, 7/28/96, JK files.
21. Interview, 7/96.
22. Interview, 7/96.
23 Letter, 8/23/96, JK files

12. From Alternative Education to Feminist Pedagogy

1. The initial planning was done with faculty and administrators from Catholic women's colleges, who saw in SAG an opportunity to offer an off-campus experience to their students. The program immediately attracted students from non-Catholic schools.

2. *Tenebrae* (Latin for darkness) is an ancient form of matins and lauds used only on the Wednesday, Thursday, and Friday of Holy Week. The service makes dramatic use of the symbols of light and darkness.

3. Letter from Janet Kalven, *Orate Fratres*, 1941.

4. Conversation with Carol Siemering, 7/2/94.

5. The acronym quickly took on positive meanings. Participants referred to themselves as "Saggers," and took as a motto, "SAG is a gas!"

6. In 1951 Grailville was affiliated with Catholic University as a community college. The affiliation program had been set up by the University to assist Catholic schools that were not yet able to meet all the requirements of the established accrediting agencies. This affiliation probably helped to reassure the registrars who gave credit for work done at Grailville.

7. Among the institutions that accepted the Grailville transcripts were Antioch, Alverno, Rosary, Rosemont, Clark, Case-Western, St. Catherine's in St. Paul, Xavier of New Orleans, Ohio Wesleyan, Oberlin, Brown, Temple, Wayne State, University of Vermont, University of Cincinnati, University of Dayton, University of Minnesota, and University of Michigan.

8. Semester at Grailville, prospectus, 12/67. GA, Box 67/ 20.

9. Memo, 1/4/72. JK personal files.

10. Talk by Elisabeth Schüssler Fiorenza at Grailville, 12/30/90 as reported in the Grail newsletter, *Desert Gumbo*, vol. xviii, #2, 2/91.

11. Linda Clark, Marian Ronan, and Eleanor Walker, eds.: *Image-Breaking/Image-Building: A Handbook for Creative Worship with Women of the Christian Tradition* (New York, Pilgrim Press, 1981).

12. Murphy Davis, "Seminary Quarter at Grailville: Toward a Feminist Approach to Theological Education," in *Theological Education* (Winter 1975).

13. Jane Burr Stickney, "Servanthood, Authority and Women in Ministry," in *Like a Woman River Flowing On* (Loveland, Ohio: Summer 1974), p. 13. Ga Box 68/33.

13. From Feminist Actions to Feminist Consciousness

1. Gerda Lerner, *The Creation of Feminist Consciousness*, p. 274.
2. JvG, *Course*, #18, p.10.
3. JvG, *Course* #24, p. 24.
4. JvG, *Course*, #18, p. 11.
5. *Task of Woman in the Modern World*, pamphlet (Des Moines, Iowa: NCRLC, 1946). Ga Box A9/15.
6. John Fitzsimons, *Woman Today* (N.Y.: Sheed and Ward, 1952).
7. Yvonne Pellé-Douël, *Etre Femme* (Paris: Editions du Seuil, 1967), pp. 13, 229.
8. Interview, 12/73.
9. Unpublished paper, delivered at Ohio Historical Society, 1980. JK files.
10. Transcript of newsprint from study days, May 1975. JK files.
11. Ibid.
12. Report of GWTF to General Assembly, 1975. GA, Box 16/45.
13. Mary Jo Weaver, *New Catholic Women*, pp. 119, 126–27.
14. Conversation, 4/30/83.
15. Rosemary Ruether, "Feminist Theology in the Academy," *Christianity and Crisis*, 3/4/85, p. 62; Diane Tennis, "Of Space and Power," *Christianity and Crisis*, April 29, 1985, p. 162.
16. Report of 1981 General Assembly.

14. From Secularism to Social Analysis

1. In Europe the Grail had worked to bring young women together across the barriers of class. In Holland, the first Grail leaders, well-educated young women from the middle class and the aristocracy, went into the factories as ordinary workers in order to draw together factory girls into "circles of action," which provided a serious formation for the lay apostolate. The mass dramas in England and Holland drew participants from all classes into a common project. In England, there were separate

centers for the upper class, the students, and the working girls, but they all took part in the Grail production of *The Hound of Heaven*. While the Grail made a deliberate effort to involve young women from all classes, the perspective was not one of class analysis but rather one of building unity in Christ, obeying the Gospel injunction to love one another.

2. Letter from Mexican Grail team, 9/2/73, "to those involved in the Mexican USA Exchange," August, 1973. JK files.

3. Letter of Carol Webb to JK, 8/3/94. JK personal files.

4. Letter from Meg Root to Grail members. GA, Box 18/2.

5. Report, Conscientization Issue Meeting, 7/27–8/4/74. GA, Box 18/8.

6. Report, Socialism and the U.S. Grail, 1/2–8/1975. GA, Box 18/7.

7. Newsletter, GA, Box 18/2.

8. Letter of Carol Webb to JK, 8/3/94. JK personal files.

9. The text of the Shakertown Pledge:

I commit myself to be a world citizen.

I commit myself to lead an ecologically sound life.

I commit myself to lead a life of creative simplicity and to share my personal wealth with the world's poor.

I commit myself to occupational accountability, and in so doing, I will seek to avoid the creation of products which cause harm to others.

I affirm the gift of my body and commit myself to its proper nourishment and physical well-being.

I commit myself to attempt to relate honestly, morally and lovingly to those around me.

I commit myself to personal renewal through prayer, meditation and study.

I commit myself to join with others in reshaping institutions in order to bring about a global society in which each person has full access to the needed resources for their physical, emotional, intellectual and spiritual growth.

10. Mary Buckley, who attended the 1975 meeting of the Theology of the Americas, reported that this insight had already been acted out by the caucuses that formed during that meeting and pointed to each other's weaknesses. It became evident that each group had its own blind spots: the feminists tended to be blind to racism and classism; the Latin American liberationists to racism and sexism; and the white male elite to classism, racism and sexism.

11. The Women Task Force attempted to use an analogous procedure to take a stand against Church authorities by giving public support to the nuns who signed the 1984 statement on pluralism and abortion. While the majority of those who responded were in favor of such an action, a strong

minority objected that we had only approved public stands against the government, not against the Church. Attempts to deal with the question of public stands vis-à-vis Church authorities foundered in committee, perhaps because some are not comfortable with making such a definitive break with the Church.

12. Interview, 12/3/95.

13. Interview, 7/95.

14. The building, Garfield Commons, as of January 1995, houses 53 adults and 47 children in attractive apartments, and includes offices, classrooms, and a community meeting room at a total cost of $4.7 million. I have contributed to the design of the organization and have served as a board member and as chair of the fund-raising committee.

15. The original dream was to stage a women's alternative economic summit at the time of the G-7 (the international meeting of the heads of state of the seven most powerful industrialized nations), but lack of resources made that dream unattainable. However, the group was able to meet with women workers in Appalachia, in California, and on the Texas-Mexican border before lack of funds led to its dissolution.

16. Report, *Women of the Americas*. Archives, Cornwall Grail Center.

15. From Lay Missions to Multicultural Exchanges

1. Interview, 3/19/97.

2. Letter of Joan Dilworth to JK, 11/29/96.

3. *Community Education Handbook*, GA, Box A7/16.

4. Anne Hope and Sally Timmel, *Training for Transformation, A Handbook for Community Workers*, rev. ed. (Gweru, Zimbabwe: Mambo Press, 1995).

5. Paulo Freire, *Pedagogy of the Oppressed*, tr. by Myra Bergman Ramos. (N.Y.: Continuum, 1993) p. 36, 41. Quoted in *Training for Transformation*, p. 18.

6. Clarissa Pinkola Estes, *Women Who Run with the Wolves, Myths and Stories of Wild Woman Archetype* (New York: Ballantine Books, 1992).

7. CEMA Report. GA Box 69/40.

8. A. McConeghey,*Tanzania, Development of the Indigenous Grail, 1975–79*, unpublished paper. JK files.

9. Ubbergen, the Grail Lay Mission School in the Netherlands.

10. Letter of Lenie Schaareman to JK, 12/96.

11. Interview, 7/29/91.

12. Interview, 4/91.

13. Interview, 12/91.
14. Interview, 4/25/91.
15. Interview, 7/94.

16. From Religious Certainty to Religious Search

1. Interview, Alice Gallagher, 9/14/91.
2. Interview, Carol Siemering, 6/22/93.
3. Msgr. Hillenbrand organized the liturgical summer schools for priests at Mundelein Seminary. Jesuit Gerald Ellard's works were a mainstay of the liturgical movement in the United States. Priest scholar H. A. Reinhold was a frequent contributor to *Commonweal* and *Orate Fratres* on liturgical topics. Damasus Winzen, OSB, founded Mt. Savior monastery, a center of full liturgical life. Father Benedict Ehmann was pastor of a parish noted for its liturgy. Godfrey Diekmann, OSB, was editor of *Orate Fratres*, the leading American liturgical journal.
4. Interview, 11/4/94.
5. Letter of Barbara Troxell to JK, 9/8/97.
6. Carol White, Working Paper. GA Box 16/3.
7. Anon. Unpublished paper. GA Box 16/3.
8. RSTF Working Paper for General Assembly, 8/1978. GA Box 18/31.
9. RSTF letter of invitation, 4/10/1974. Box 16/32.
10. *The Grail Prayer Book*. Loveland, Ohio, 1975, pp. 2–3.
11. Clark, Ronan, Walker. *Image-Breaking/Image-Building* (N.Y.: Pilgrim Press, 1981) pp. 2–3.
12. Ibid., p. 12.
13. Letter of Carol White to Committee for 1969 General Assembly. GA Box 16/3.
14. Faith Message of 1988 International General Assembly, reprinted in *U.S. Catholic Historian*, vol. 11, #4 (Fall 1993), p. 94.

Epilogue

1. *Song of Solidarity* by Carolyn McDade.
2. Gerda Lerner, *Creation of Feminist Consciousness, pp. 281–283.*
3. Interview with Mary O'Brien, Warmond, The Netherlands, 6/95.
4. Msgr. Charles Diviney, *Brooklyn Tablet*, 4/89.
5. Interview, 7/95.
6. Letter from Dierdre Cornell and Silvani Valentim of the Grail Young Women's Network,10/25/96.

Select Bibliography

Primary Sources

A. Archives

United States Grail Movement Archives, Grailville, Loveland, Ohio (GA).
International Grail Archives, The Tiltenberg, Vogelenzang, Holland.
Grail Liberation Task Force Archives, Grail Center, Cornwall-on-Hudson, New York.

B. Other

J. Kalven Personal Files: correspondence, memos, reports, and articles. Grailville, Loveland, Ohio.
Donders, Rachel. *History of the International Grail, 1921–1979.* Loveland, Ohio: Grailville, 1983.
——— with Mary Gindhart, Joan Dilworth, Ann Burke, Gerda Kaufman, and Mary Louise Tully.
Histories of the Grail in Individual Countries. Loveland, Ohio: Grailville, 1983.

C. Interviews

Author with
Ambrogi, Donna, 12/3/95
Birmingham, William, 11/4/94
Brien, Dolores, 12/30/92
Brooks, Jackie, 8/94
Bruck, Meganne Root, 8/9/94
Buckley, Mary, 3/20/1992; 8/22/92; 7/21/96

Burke, Ann, 9/16/91
Burns, Margery, 2/15/92
Charbonneau, Emilia, 5/21/96
Charles, Cathleen, 9/17/91; 11/3/94
Chisholm, Ruth, 9/17/91
Clifford, Mary, 6/14/91
Coyle, Marguerite Lunney, 7/15/91
Dietrick, Joyce, 9/5/92
Disalvo, Jacqueline, 12/91; 11/5/94 ; 6/24/96
Donders, Dirkje, 6/23/91
Donders, Rachel, 7/6-7/10/1991; 11/4/96
Dougan, Alice, 7/29/91
Erler, Monica, 7/24/92
Ferrari, Mary, 8/94
Figueroa, Cecilia, 6/27/92
Fleischner, Eva, 9/16/91
Flynn, Diane Watrous, 5/19/96
Gallagher, Alice, 9/16/91
Gallant, Ruth, 7/21/94
Gratton, Carolyn, 1/13/92; 1/22/93
Heidkamp, Martha, 7/17/92
Hill, Kate, 1/17/92
Holthaus, Mary Anne, 12/29/92
Hope, Anne, 7/11/94
Hunt, Mary E., 2/26/1992
Johns, Esther, 2/ 23/92
Joslyn, Sharon, 7/3/95
Kane, Daniel J., 10/27/94
Kane, Mary McGarry, 10/27/94
Kimbell, Mary Anne, 9/16/91
Kraemer, Alice, 6/21/95
Kryvanick, Kathleen Ann, 6/29/94.
Kuhn, Mary Emma, 7/91
Lageman, Mary Lu, 6/15/96
Ling, Lyllis, 7/29/91
Linnehan, Margaret, 9/17/91
Louchart, Mary Kay, 7/95
Malley, Lynn, 6/14/91.
Malley, Gail, 8/92
Markle, Judy Berning, 8/94
Martin, Frances, 7/21/94

McConeghey Goering, April, 11/1/91
McDermit, Marie Therese, 9/27/92
Mechana, Priscilla, 12/ 27/95
Mercier, Anne, 7/26/91; 3/97
Miller, Angela, 4/2/94
Miner, Gabrielle, 9/15/91
Morin, Rose, 4/26/92
Morris, Gertrude, 7/92
Mosher, Helen McDougall, 7/30/92
Mvungi, Honorata, 8/95
Nebrida, Rebecca, 7/15/91
Paulus, Trina, 11/91; 6/26/92
Pezullo, Caroline, 7/92
Pintasilgo, Maria de Lourdes, 7/9/91
Plante, Jeanne, 12/30/92
Price, Catherine, 9/15/91
Rasenberger, Dorothy, 9/14/91; 12/26/92; 9/22/92
Rodriguez, Flora, 6/94
Rodriguez, Maclovia, 2/28/92
Rogan, Grace, 7/92
Schaeffler, Eileen, 4/22/1992; 8/94; 9/14/91; 6/23/97
Schak, Deborah, 9/5/92
Schomer, Audrey, 9/17/91; 11/4/94
Scott, Frances, 6/26/91
Siemering, Carol, 8/2/92
Sisson, Bernice, 4/24/91
Sorrento, Audrey, 7/16/92
Stringer, Carol, 1/25/92
Stuber, Mary Jessica, 4/25/91
Timmel, Sally, 7/11/94
Troxell, Barbara, 1/25/92
van Kersbergen, Lydwine, 6/26–7/1/91
Wasmer, Beth, 12/8/92
White, Carol, 7/1/91
Wickes, Francine, 9/14/91
Wickes, Mariette, 4/21-23/97
Tully, Mary Louise, Audiotape, in *Grail Oral History Project*, recorded by
    Sharon Thomson, July, 1979. GA
Walker, Eleanor, Audiotape, in *Grail Oral History Project*, recorded by
    Sharon Thomson, June, 1979. GA

Secondary Sources

Books

Brown, Alden. *The Grail Movement and American Catholicism, 1940–1975.* Notre Dame Studies in American Catholicism #9. Notre Dame, Indiana: University of Notre Dame Press, 1989.

Buckley, Mary and Kalven, Janet, eds. *Women's Spirit Bonding.* New York: Pilgrim Press, 1984.

Clark, Linda, Ronan, Marian, and Walker, Eleanor. *Image-Breaking/ Image-Building: A Handbook for Creative Worship with Women of Christian Tradition.* New York: Pilgrim Press, 1981.

Cornwall Collective. *Your Daughters Shall Prophesy, Feminist Alternatives in Theological Education.* New York: Pilgrim Press, 1980.

Davis, Florence Henderson. *Rise and Decline of Catholic Lay Movements in New York City, 1933–1967.* PhD. Dissertation. Concordia University, Montreal, 1988.

DeFerrrari, Patricia. *Theologies of Women and Work: Catholic Social Teaching and the Grail Movement in the U.S.* PhD. Disssertation, Catholic University, Washington, D.C., 1998.

Dolan, Jay P. *The American Catholic Experience, A History from Colonial Times to the Present.* New York: Doubleday, 1985.

Hope, Anne and Timmel, Sally. *Training for Transformation, A Handbook for Community Workers,* 3 vol. rev. ed. Gweru, Zimbabwe, Mambo Press, 1995.

Kalven, Janet, with Patricia A. Johnson, co-editor and contributor. *With Both Eyes Open, Seeing Beyond Gender.* New York: Pilgrim Press, 1984.

Kaufmann, Christopher J., ed. "Labor and Lay Movements, Part II." in *U.S. Catholic Historian,* v. 9, #4 (Fall 1993).

Kenneally, James K. *The History of American Catholic Women.* New York: Crosssroads, 1990.

Kennedy, Sally. *Faith and Feminism, Catholic Women's Struggles for Self-Expression.* Studies in the Christian Movement #9. Manly, NSW, Australia: St. Patrick's College, 1985.

Marty, Martin E. *Modern American Religion, v. 3, Under God Indivisible 1941–1960.* Chicago: University of Chicago Press, 1996.

Miller, Patricia. *Constructing a Model for Theologizing as Developed by the Women of the United States Grail, 1940–1978.* PhD. Dissertation, St. Louis University, St. Louis, Missouri, 1994.

Sclafani, Robin A. *How the U.S. Grail Has Fought Racism, A Story of Women Discovering There Is No Formula.* MA Thesis, Antioch University, Brooklyn, NY, 1998.

Weaver, Mary Jo. *New Catholic Women.* San Francisco, Harper and
    Row, 1985.
————, with Debra Campbell, co-editors. "Grailville: Women in Com-
    munity, 1944–1994." *U.S. Catholic Historian,* v. 11, #4 (Fall
    1993).

Articles

Brien, Dolores E. "The Catholic Revival Revisited." *Commonweal,* Dec.
    21, 1979.
Davis, Florence H. "Lay Movements in New York City During the 30s and
    40s." *U.S. Catholic Historian,* vol. 9, # 4 (Fall, 1993).
DeFerrari, Patricia. "Theologies of Work in the U.S. Grail: The Founder's
    Vision." *Proceedings,* College Theological Society, 1996.
Kalven, Janet. "Women Breaking Boundaries: The Grail and Feminism."
    Journal of Feminist Studies in Religion, 5 (1989).
————. "Grailville, A Women's Place." *Women, A Journal of Liberation,*
    Winter, 1975.
————. "Women's Voices Begin to Challenge." *National Catholic
    Reporter,* April 13, 1984.
————. "Fifteen Years of Ferment." *Monthly Review,* July–August, 1984.
————. "Living the Liturgy: Keystone of the Grail Vision." *U.S. Catholic
    Historian,* v. 11, #4 (Fall 1993).
————. "Grailville in the Seventies and Eighties: Structural Change and
    Feminist Consciousness." *U.S. Catholic Historian,* v. 11, # 4 (Fall
    1993).
————. "History of the Grail in the United States 1940–1995." *The
    Encyclopedia of American Catholic History,* edited by M. Glazier
    and T. J. Shelley, pp. 598–599. Collegeville, MN: Liturgical Press,
    1997.
MacEoin, Gary. "Lay Movements in the U.S. before Vatican II." *America,*
    v. 165, #3, August 3–10, 1991.
Maun, Patricia Miller. "Women of the Grail, Tentative Research Results
    on a Model for Theologizing." Women in Evangelization:
    Proceedings of the Symposium, March 5–7, 1992, Barry Univers-
    ity, Miami Shores, Florida: Barry University Press, 1992, 71–81.
Miller, Patricia M. "An Introduction to the Grail Archives." *U.S. Catholic
    Historian* (Fall 1993): 59–67.
————. with Mary O'Brien. "A Woman of Vision: An Interview with the
    Founder of the Grail Movement in the United States." *U.S.
    Catholic Historian,* v. 15, #4 (Fall 1997).

———. "Leadership at Grailville." *Woman of Power, A Magazine of Feminism, Spirituality, and Politics.* 24, Fall 1995, pp. 76–79.

Weaver, Mary Jo and Campbell, Debra, eds. *U.S. Catholic Historian, Grailville, Women in Community, 1944–1994.* vol. 11, # 4 (Fall 1993).

Published Work by Grail Members

There is an extensive bibliography of Grail publications and works by individual Grail members in Alden Brown, *The Grail Movement and American Catholicism, 1940–1975.* The following bibliography brings his listing up to date.

Books

Adler, Mary Helen. *Inner and Outer Weather.* Bristol, IN: Bristol Banner Books, 1996.

Bechtel, Judith with Susan Hilgendorf, co-editors. *Mentors, Models and Mothers: A Community Writing Project.* Kearney, NE: Morris, 1997.

———, and Robert Coughlin. *Building the Beloved Community: Maurice McCrackin's Life for Peace and Civil Rights.* Philadelphia: Temple University Press, 1991.

Bedard, Marcia. *Breaking with Tradition: Diversity, Conflict and Change in Contemporary American Families.* New York: General Hall, 1992.

Cooney, Nancy Hennessey, and Nancy Cannon. *Come to the Table.* Kansas City: Sheed & Ward, 1997.

———, and Julie Sharpe, co-editors. *Together in Prayer: Mealtime Reflections from Grail Women Around the Globe.* Loveland, OH: Grail Publications, 1996.

Fleischner, Eva. Response in *The Sunflower—On the Possibilities and Limits of Forgiveness* by Simon Wiesenthal. New York: Shocken, 2nd ed. rev. and enl., 1976, 138–143.

———, and Michael Phayer. *Cries in the Night.* Kansas City, MO: Sheed and Ward, 1997.

———. "A Door that Opened and Did Not Close." In *From the Unimaginable to the Unthinkable,* edited by Rittner and Roth. Westport, CT: Greenwood Press, 1997.

Gratton, Carolyn. *Art of Spiritual Guidance.* New York: Crossroads, 1992.

————. Tapes, *A Way for Human Hearts*. Canfield, OH: Alba House, 1988.

Heiberg, Jeanne. *The Twelve Days of Christmas*. Collegeville, MN: 1955.

————. *The Good News in Pictures*. Collegeville, MN: 1962.

————. *Contemplation and the Art of Salad Making*. New York: Crossroads, 1982.

————. *Winning Your Inner Battle*. San Jose: Resource Publishing, 1989.

————. *Advent Arts and Christmas Crafts*. New York: Paulist Press, 1995.

————. *Arts and Crafts for Lent*. New York: Paulist Press, 1997.

————. *Clip Art for Seasons and Celebrations of the Church Year*. New York: Paulist Press, 1998.

Heidkamp, Mary, and James Lund. *Moving Faith Into Action: A Facilitator's Guide for Creating Parish Social Ministry Organizations*. Mahwah, NJ: Paulist Press, 1998.

Hope, Anne and Timmel, Sally. *Training for Transformation, A Handbook for Community Workers*, 3 vol. rev. ed. Gweru Zimbabwe, Mambo Press, 1995.

Kalven, Janet, et al. co-editors, and contributors. *Your Daughters Shall Prophesy: Feminist Alternatives in Theological Education*. New York: Pilgrim Press, 1980.

————, with Hall, Brian, L. Rosen, and B. Taylor. *Value Development: A Practical Guide*. New York: Paulist Press, 1982.

————, with L. Rosen and B. Taylor. *The Time Diary: A Work Book in Value Development*. New York: Paulist Press, 1982.

————, with Hall, Brian, L. Rosen and B. Taylor. *Readings in Value Development*. New York: Paulist Press, 1982.

————, with Patricia A. Johnson, co-editor and contributor. *With Both Eyes Open: Seeing Beyond Gender*. New York: Pilgrim Press, 1988.

Miller, Patricia. PhD Dissertation. *Constructing a Model for Theologizing as Developed by the Women of the United States Grail, 1940–1978*. St. Louis: St. Louis U., 1994.

Mohr, Marie. *Call of the Hibiscus—Indonesia's Message to the World*. Jakarta, Indonesia: P.T. Inti Idaye Press, 1984.

O'Brien, Mary. *Single Women*. Westport, CT: Greenwood, 1993.

Ronan, Marian with Linda Clark and Eleanor Walker. *Image–Breaking/Image–Building: A Handbook for Creative Worship with Women of Christian Tradition*. New York: Pilgrim Press. 1981.

Ronan, Marian, with Susan Cady and H. Taussig. *The Future of Feminist Spirituality*. San Francisco: Harper and Row, 1986.

———. *Wisdom's Feast: Sophia in Study and Celebration.* San Francisco: Harper and Row, 1989.

Articles

Thomson, Sharon. "Ritual Drama," in *Alternative Therapies: A Peer Reviewed Journal of Health and Medicine,* Sept. 1998.

Troxell, Barbara, co-editor, "Spirituality and Supervision," in *Journal of Pastoral Care,* v. 18 (1997).

———. "Spiritual Direction: An Interview with Barbara Troxell," in *Christian Century,* April 1998.

———, with Patricia Farris. "One Eye on the Past, One Eye on the Future: Women's Contribution to Renewal of the United Methodist Church," in *Quarterly Review,* Spring, 1998

Wilson, Teresa. "Crossing Borders," in *To Beijing and Beyond,* ed. by Janice Auth. Pittsburgh: University of Pittsburgh Press, 1998.

Index